Philadelphia

BOOKS BY
STRUTHERS BURT

Philadelphia

HOLY EXPERIMENT

By

STRUTHERS BURT

ILLUSTRATED WITH PHOTOGRAPHS

RICH & COWAN
LONDON
NEW YORK : MELBOURNE : SYDNEY

To
JOHN FREDERICK LEWIS, JR.
and his wife, ADA;
two Philadelphians who love their city
and really do something about it.

*"A great city is that which has the greatest
men and women."*—WALT WHITMAN.

THIS BOOK IS PRODUCED IN
COMPLETE CONFORMITY WITH THE
AUTHORIZED ECONOMY STANDARDS.

Made and Printed in Great Britain at GREYCAINES
(Taylor Garnett Evans & Co Ltd.), Watford, Herts.
for
RICH & COWAN
Eclipse Press Service Ltd.
London, W.C.2.

ACKNOWLEDGMENTS

MY DEEPEST GRATITUDE is due the following, who have been generous both with their time and knowledge.

Commander Marion V. Brewington, probably the greatest living authority on the Port of Philadelphia; Roger Butterfield, *Life*, who, although not born a Philadelphian, was a newspaperman for a while in that city and knows much more about it than the majority of Philadelphians; Harold West, librarian, the Mercantile Library; H. W. Wills, secretary, Philadelphia Chamber of Commerce; Lieut. Herbert E. Armstrong, Jr., 11th Airborne Division; Charles Lee and Thomas P. O'Neil, of the Philadelphia *Record*; Prof. Richard H. Shyrock of the University of Pennsylvania; Mrs. A. Nalle Corse; Oliver Swan, of Macrae-Smith Co.; W. D. Wilcox, of that most venerable and distinguished Philadelphia publishing house, Lea & Febriger; Horace G. White, of the equally distinguished and almost as venerable Blakiston Co.; Joseph Jackson, eminent Philadelphia historian and outstanding authority on Independence Hall; Carrol Frey, of the Penn Mutual.

These I thank more than I can say, and I must also pay my respects to two men, recently dead, who loved Philadelphia, although the second was a Baltimorean: D. Knickerbacker Boyd and Charles Abell Murphy.

Both these men had a vision of a Philadelphia beautiful and regenerate and, in some measure, living up to the vision of another Philadelphian, William Penn. They wished to recapture partially the city from the sad fate that has befallen it physically, as Napoleon III recaptured Paris, as New York is now recapturing New York, as any number of other cities are recapturing themselves: Chicago, St. Louis, even to some extent New Orleans. The dreams of these two men centred around Independence Hall, this country's greatest shrine; its proper protection and restoration, the encompassing of it with proper surroundings. Some day Philadelphia will awaken to what it has; meanwhile, sloth is one of the seven deadly sins.

And most especially I must thank two good and exceptionally generous friends: Austin K. Gray, Cambridge man, son of the master of Jesus College, Cambridge, former librarian of the Library Company of Philadelphia ("Mr. Franklin's Library"), and Julian P. Boyd, librarian of Princeton University, former director of the Historical Society of Pennsylvania, outstanding Jeffersonian and the leading authority on the early Indian treaties of this country. I must also thank Mrs. Austin K. Gray, born Christine Chambers, of Philadelphia, and great-niece of Mrs. Ann Carson, beautiful, lovelorn, and to say the least, determined, who startled the Philadelphia of the early 1800's. You will find the beauteous Mrs. Carson's story in the body of the book.

Mr. Gray, witty and scholarly biographer, is another one of those adopted Philadelphians—their name is legion—who know the city and its quirks and quiddities much better than most Philadelphians, and who love it in the wry sort of fashion one must love anything so individual, so obstinate, and so little to be moved. As I say later on, his much too short volume, *Benjamin Franklin's Library*, is the last word on that institution. As for Julian Boyd, "Promises may get friends, but it is performance that must nurse and keep them," and without his kindness, his patience, and his expert knowledge this book could not have been written. In the midst of the busiest and saddest winter he has ever known, having promised to read the manuscript of this book, he read it, and before then his encouragement and suggestions meant much. He, too, is not a Philadelphian but a North Carolinian. For some strange reason, it seems to take, on the whole, non-Philadelphians to make real ones.

This series wisely, and especially now, considering the paper shortage, does not carry bibliographies; bibliographies for the most part being lists of books one intended to read but didn't. Lists are handed down from historian to historian like the ceremonial beads of Indians. Nevertheless, I think I have read almost everything so far written about Philadelphia, and I have examined numerous documents; at all events, I have done enough of this so that frequently the only relief was aspirin. But bibliographies or not, I must mention three books all those interested in Philadelphia should read; they are not very long, they are extremely interesting and informative. These books are—*Philadelphia: the Place and the People*, by that wise and witty and distinguished Philadelphia essayist, Agnes Repplier; *Rebels and Gentlemen*, by Lieut. Carl Bridenbaugh and his wife, the late Jessica Bridenbaugh; and *The Delaware*, in the Rivers of America Series, by my friend Harry Emerson Wildes, connoisseur on Pennsylvania and its folk ways and folk stories.

Philadelphia is a fascinating place and one of the hardest subjects imaginable to write about. The trees are so thick, the little wandering forest byways and paths so numerous and so interesting, that it is almost impossible at times to see the forest.

S. B.

CONTENTS

ILLUSTRATIONS

End Papers by Courtesy of the Historical Society of Pennsylvania.

ÆTIS.22.
1666.
OCTOBER 14

PAX QVÆRITVR
BELLO

WILLIAM PENN IN ARMOUR

TREATY TREE, SHACKAMAXON (Birch)

CHAPTER I

Horn of Plenty

"At break of day when dreams, they say, are true."
                                                    DRYDEN.

IN APRIL 1681, a month after the signing of the patent for his new and lovely land, his "Holy Experiment," William Penn published, through Benjamin Clark, bookseller, of George Yard, Lombard Street, London, a prospectus for the use of possible settlers. Being a good business man as well as a man of scrupulous integrity and taste, he studiously avoids any trace of exaggeration. His understatements, coupled with his announcements of what actually was to be found, form a model that could be followed profitably by modern advertisers.

"I shall say little in its praise," he writes, meaning his "Holy Experiment," his province of Pennsylvania, "to excite desires in any, whatever I could truly write as to the soil, air and water; this shall satisfy me, that by the blessing of God and the honesty and industry of man it may be a good and fruitful land"; and later on he warns prospective immigrants that "they must be willing to be two or three years without some of the conveniences they enjoy at home," but having done with this, he enumerates some of the advantages.

"The place lies six hundred miles nearer the sun than England," he states, "further south, that is, no mean lure to northern Europeans who, not having much of the sun, cherish it more than most." And then he goes on to dwell upon the opportunities for navigation and commerce afforded by the magnificent bay of the Delaware and the broad and placid river of the same name; the variety and plenitude of timber; the food for the asking, or, at the most, a little effort—fish, wild fowl, game; while, when it comes to business, commerce, manufacture, farming, the outlook is unlimited. To the south is the province of Virginia, eager to trade; to the east, across the ocean recently travelled, is the mother country equally in the mood; and the list of commodities or products native to the "Holy Experiment," or which could be introduced, is endless.

"Silk," says Penn, "flax, hemp, wine, sider, wood, madder, liqourish, tobacco, pot-ashes, iron." These are only a few of the possible exports, and to them can be added: "Hides, tallow, pipe-staves, beef, pork, sheep, wool, corn or wheat, barley, rye, and also furs, as your peltrie, mincks, raccoons, martins, and such like stores of furs which is to be found among Indians." All this, and much more, and heaven too, as it were, for finally Penn comes to the most important inducement of all, to the gist of the matter where free-minded men and women of the struggling and troubled seventeenth century were concerned. The sixteenth century, having fought for religious freedom, willed to its successor that firstfruit of freedom, the tyranny of those who have just achieved freedom themselves. There is no man so dogmatic as the man who, having recently shaken himself loose from the dogma of others, suddenly finds himself at liberty to tell others what to do. It is almost impossible for the modern mind to conceive of the impediments and hazards, legal, political, economic, social, and religious, large and small, and reaching into the innermost recesses of life, which confronted the intelligent and upstanding man and woman in Penn's time, even in England, where the leaven of individual dignity has always been at work.

To think for yourself in the seventeenth century was the surest possible way, sooner or later, to get into trouble, just as Penn himself had got into trouble in his tumultuous youth.

To such men and women, Penn in his prospectus—"Some account of the Province of Pennsylvania in America, lately granted under the Great Seal of England [etc.]"—gives solemn assurance of all possible freedom and tolerance and non-interference under the law, and he promises that they shall make their own laws to suit changing conditions and a new environment, so long as such laws do not conflict with the sovereign authority of England, and as confirmation of this he states that he will speedily draw up a suitable and detailed constitution.

"Colonies," he says—this at the very start of his prospectus—"are the seeds of nations, begun and nourished by the care of wise and populous countries, as conceiving them best for the increase of human stock and beneficial for commerce."

With which, as is so often the case with Penn, arise ghosts to mock the efforts of later, and supposedly more civilized, generations; in this case, the smoky and bloody and unhappy ghost of nineteenth-century colonization and imperialism, cruel-eyed and crooked-fingered.

But Penn, as usual, is not content until he describes those best suited for "holy experiments" and settlements in general. He is indeed the perfect Quaker, after which, one has reason to believe, the mould was broken or at least badly cracked. Penn is the epitome of that mysticism plus practical common sense, that large vision plus infinite care for details, that tolerance and unquestioning fairness, that quiet dignity expected for oneself and taken as granted for others, that head in the skies but two feet on the ground and both hands constructively engaged, which was the original design of the most protestant of sects. For a while there was something in the world that might have combined the transcendentalism of the Orient, making it sensible, with the sense of the Occident, making it alive and beatific with the imagination. But this is a difficult ideal to live up to, as was borne in upon Penn himself, much to the wounding of his spirit, before he died.

"When I came into the silent assemblies of God's people," writes Robert Barclay in his *Apology*, "I felt a secret power among them, which touched my heart, and as I gave way to it, I found the evil weakening in me and the good raised up."

Penn proceeds to say in his prospectus:

Providence seems to have most fitted for plantations, 1st, industrious husbandmen and day laborers that are hardly able (with extreme labor) to maintain their families and portion their children; 2nd, laborious handicrafts, especially carpenters,

masons, smiths, weavers, taylors, tanners, shoemakers, shipwrights, etc., where
they may be spared or low in the world, so their labor is worth more than here,
and there, provisions cheaper; 3rd, ingenious spirits. . . .

to wit, younger sons and younger brothers, and all those of energy and
ambition who, without inheritance or very little, wish to better their lot,
many of whom, as Penn admits, have large families. And fourth, and
lastly—and here is Penn at his best, and here also is Penn the expert user
of fine prose—there should be, and most especially, "men of universal spirits."
    What a lovely phrase and what a high and accurate seventeenth-century
use of the adjective, since when proper respect for adjectives has declined.
And what unerring instinct for what the world has always needed most and
has never had in any quantity! Writes Penn:

There are another sort of persons, not only fit for but necessary in plantations,
and that is men of universal spirits, that have an eye to the good of prosperity,
and that both understand and delight to promote good discipline and just govern-
ment among plain and well-intending people; such persons may find room in colonies
for their good council and contrivance, who are shut out from being of much use
or service to great nations under settled customs; these men deserve much esteem
and would be hearkened too.

As for the cost of passage to this paradise, it was moderate: six pounds
per head for masters and mistresses; five for servants; children under seven,
fifty shillings, "except they suck." For these, the cost was nothing. Moreover, arriving in September or October, as he was likely to do, considering
the summer sailings of those days and the length of the voyage, the new-
comer, if he were a farmer or of the ordinary sort, could begin at once to lay
the foundations of prosperity.

Two men may clear as much ground by spring (when they set the corn for
that country) as will bring in that time, twelve months, forty barrels which makes
twenty-five quarters of corn. So that the first year they must buy corn, which is
usually very plentiful. They must, so soon as they come, buy cows, more or less,
as they want or are able, which are to be had at easy rates. For swine, they are
plentiful and cheap, these will quickly increase to a stock. So that after the
first year, what with the poorer sort sometimes laboring to others, and the more
able fishing, fowling, and sometimes buying, they may do very well till their own
stocks are sufficient to supply them and their families, which will quickly be, and
to spare, if they follow the English husbandry as they do in New England and
New York, and get winter fodder for their stock.

William Penn knew that he had been granted by Charles II a valuable
land, a land veritably flowing with milk and honey, a Land of Canaan;
sweet-smelling, fertile beyond measure, teeming with fish and birds and
game, rich and shadowy with forests through which ran great rivers and
small clear streams. America was not the *terra incognita* of a hundred years
before. New England was some sixty years old; Virginia almost eighty;
Maryland had been founded in 1634; New York was a respectable village

of at least two generations, as generations are counted, fo
and New Jersey, or *Nova Cæsarea*, as it had first been callec
settled.   In 1638 thirty Swedish colonists had landed on tl
of the Delaware at what is now Wilmington and had built
and since that year the Swedes, the Dutch, and even, on a cou
the English from the colony of Connecticut had been qu
much energy and singularly little loss of life, over the low
reaches of that stream.   In 1677, five years before Penn's arrival and iou
years before any formal landing at what was to be the city of Philadelphia,
the ship *Trent*, bearing a Quaker colony, had stood up the river, passing the
site of Philadelphia, and had finally come to anchor at Burlington.   And a
year later, the ship *Shield* had arrived, bringing further settlers.   For this
colony Penn, one of its proprietors, had done most of the work in the planning
and the drawing up of its proposed government, contained in a charter, the
sub-title of which was "The Concessions and Agreements of the Proprietors,
Freeholders and Inhabitants of West Jersey in America": a charter which
incorporated most of the liberal and far-visioned provisions later to be found
in the Frame of Government Penn wrote for his own "Holy Experiment."
So Penn knew about all there was to know at the time of his province of
Pennsylvania.   He had collated and sifted reports, he had interviewed
numerous eye-witnesses.   But he had no idea, nor had anyone else, that
by the turn of the wheel of fortune, among all the colonists of the New Land,
it was he who had become Lord Proprietor and owner of what was to be
the wealthiest and most varied and most productive section of the most varied,
most productive, and wealthiest continent in the world; a continent so kind
to men that for almost two hundred and fifty years only the fool, the wastrel,
or the saint could prevent himself from becoming rich.

Nor had he any idea that the tiny town he founded was an inevitable city:
a city that had to happen.

Some cities arise at the express will of man; they are the result of "main
strength and awkwardness," of a *tour de force*.   As a rule these are inland
places made by railways which have been surveyed in that direction, or
because in early days some trader has built a general store at a cross-roads
or along a trail.   Or they are sometimes the result of pure speculation.   Or
they are capitals of states, for the most part arbitrarily designated, or county
seats, or, in some instances, like Washington, even the seats of national
government.   These are synthetic cities and remain such, beautiful as many
of them are, and about them always, never to be overcome, lingers a slight
atmosphere of fictitiousness.   Other cities—the vast majority—come into
being for intrinsic reasons and cannot help growing.   They stand where men
naturally converge; where geography and what is below the surface of the
earth and what is upon it come together and call men in from the four directions
of the wind to trade and distribute, to buy, to make, and to reship.   These
arise where two rivers meet, or at the head of navigation, or along its course
where raw materials, lumber and coal and metals, or beef and grain come
down from the mountains to find quieter waters and processing and land
transportation, or from across the plains and deserts for the same reason.
Or along the coasts of every country, these cities sit where harbours are.

These are the ancient cities of the caravans, of the camel train and the sumpter mule, or the modern cities of steam and electricity, or they are, the latter, ports of entry or exit, and they are all inevitable cities, and their shape is usually that of a peninsula, a point of land, or the crescent of a bay, or the irregular course of some river. But they are essentially market-places, and no matter how large and rich they grow, they never altogether lose that character. A metropolis is something else. A metropolis is an inevitable city where all the factors mentioned, and many others, are raised to a supreme degree. It is a concatenation of circumstances, material, spiritual, and intellectual, and such cities from the moment they are founded are destined to greatness no matter what their inhabitants, or time, or history can do to them.

London is such a city, and New York, and Paris, and San Francisco, and New Orleans, and Chicago. They draw men to them for all the reasons that impel men, and not for business or commercial reasons alone. They are centrifugal as well as centripetal. Like great spider webs they spread out in concentric circles, busily woven; like man-made lakes they gradually absorb all the surrounding neighbourhoods for miles, the smaller towns, the villages, the countryside, their inhabitants, and coerce them towards a centre.

Such cities are destined.

And despite its crotchettess, its determined provincialism, its sloth and complacency, Philadelphia is a metropolis, a sort of willy-nilly metropolis, and has always been; to begin with potentially, for most of its history, actually. It is not just another big American city; nor is it merely the third largest city in the United States. Philadelphia is one of the great cities of the world; greatness under this definition being a matter of character, bad or good, of intellectual, social, and commercial achievements, of history and traditions, of point of view, however neglected, thwarted, or perverted, but principally of atmosphere. It is never merely a question of size.

But the "Holy Experiment," like most holy experiments, bears little resemblance to the original plan.

William Penn envisioned a place where in the already proven fruitful-ness and opportunities of a new continent many "plain and well intending people," and a few not so plain and of greater intentions, could live in sober but solid prosperity. Some would get rich, and the majority, provided they were hard-working and far-sighted and well behaved, could sit secure under their own vines and fig trees; but Penn had no more notion of the Golconda he was touching upon than had the original settlers of California that they were treading upon earth underlined with gold. Had Penn known this, he would have had considerable doubts about the outcome of his dream. Wealth—and no one knew this better than Penn—does not necessarily make for holiness.

Penn, with one fine, open, straightforward eye cocked toward business and possible profits, as behoves any good Quaker, profits which he never got, incidentally, was nonetheless primarily interested in a social and religious and political venture. His colony, unlike all others—even the equally liberal one of Lord Baltimore to the south—was designed first and foremost as a sanctuary, a place of refuge, not for one's own particular church as in the

paradise

case of New England, but for all God-fearing men and women everywhere, no matter what they thought and how they worshipped; and in this sanctuary these men and women were to attain their full stature and come into their full fruitfulness, released from a Europe recently devastated by sectarian wars and still bewilderingly hampered. Penn had suffered for his faith and his honesty; he wished mightily to help other honest and faithful men. Of all the various settlements in America his was the only one that bore any resemblance to what we now call "the American Idea"; the American vision, which at the time hardly existed at all, not even, except for Penn, in the minds of the best and most prophetic of men, and which in any definite shape was not to emerge for almost a century later and then, save for a few seers like Thomas Jefferson and Thomas Paine, still unformed.

In this sense, Penn was indeed the "first American".

On the banks of the Delaware, no matter how little aware the inhabitants of the "Holy Experiment" have always been of their crucial importance in this respect, and how much in many cases they have been antagonistic to the theory, were planted the seeds of the spiritual side of the War of Independence, and the spiritual side of every war save one this country has fought. And by the same token were planted the seeds of this country's entire political and social evolution.

Strong seeds, however, strongly planted, flourish whether cared for or not, and always a certain number of discoverers find them and savour their worth, and the news spreads abroad.

But there would have been a Philadelphia had William Penn never existed. Sooner or later someone would have recognized the potentialities of the alluvial peninsula, toward its southern end a swamp, situated between the broad and once shining Delaware and the narrow and once shining Schuylkill, for in all the world there is no fitter place for a great city.

It has everything.

*   *   *   *   *   *

To begin with, it had a long and safe and land-locked bay; that is, when eventually a breakwater was built: ending in one of the best harbours on the Atlantic; that is, when it was properly dredged and several small interfering islands were removed. To end with, it sits at the gate of the richest farming and mineral land in the United States. Just west of it are York and Lancaster and Lebanon counties, and half a dozen more, with their magnificent fields and huge stone barns, the finest in America; just north of it are Lackawanna and Schuylkill, and Carbon, and Luzerne, and Northumberland, where millions of years ago great forests were turned into coal, and not only coal, but hard coal—anthracite—at that. Outside of two small areas in New Mexico and Colorado, Pennsylvania has the only anthracite deposits in the country. And it has bituminous coal as well, of the thickest veins and highest quality. And the famous Connellsville coal for coking purposes. And iron ore almost everywhere. And limestone for building purposes and the making of cement. And glass-sand. And feldspar. And innumerable other products. And in the north and west of the state are magnificent forests. There are mountains scattered about, real ones; and plains; and wide shining valleys. And wherever you go are creeks or broad, full rivers. Indeed, Penn's province, his commonwealth, has almost all that man needs, and if it hasn't gold and silver and precious stones, the inheritors of the "Holy Experiment" have for many generations been in a position to buy and store, or wear, these luxuries. Not long ago the mine products alone of the "Holy Experiment" amounted to some $2,000,000,000 annually, or a little more than one-sixth of the mine products of the entire United States, and nearly twice that of any other state.

All this runs downhill to the alluvial peninsula between the Delaware and the Schuylkill, the meaning of whose Dutch name will always remain a mystery, and the alluvial peninsula is the catch-all, the terminus, the basin. Wealth rolls into it by the law of gravity, if nothing else. And just to pile blessings on top of others, the alluvial peninsula has a climate peculiarly suited to the manufacturing of textiles where dampness and mildness meet in the exact proper proportions. So you have not only a great port, with its concomitant, ship-building, but in addition a great factory town, and a great market, all this situated on a peninsula which is the terminus for the entire province until you cross the Appalachians far to the west and slide down into Pittsburgh and another country. Without exaggeration this is Manchester and London and the metropolitan market town of Paris rolled into one; or rather, and once more, it is there potentially, for you can give men everything, but what they do with it depends upon themselves.

The two rivers stretch out like veins from a heart. The Delaware heads far north in the state of New York but leaves that territory, like all good Pennsylvanians, as speedily as possible after a wild brief period. The Schuylkill is indigenous; it angles off to the north-west into the mountains of the coal district. The alluvial peninsula itself is the shape, not of a point or an arrow-head, but of an hour-glass; slim-waisted in the middle—where Penn first put his town –and where the richer and more fashionable folk have always chosen to live and still live intermittently; broad toward the swampy southern end, where the Schuylkill runs into the Delaware; still broader to the north, and without any ending, where the city merges into Germantown and Chestnut Hill and, off to the north-east along the Delaware, the great manufacturing districts of Kensington and Frankford and Tacony.

Roundabout cluster the home counties with their lovely English names of Delaware and Chester and Montgomery and Bucks, the last abbreviated from Buckinghamshire. And here, too, is a land which, if not so opulent as the great farming counties of Lancaster and York, is nonetheless admirably suited for small diversified agriculture, and dairy herds, and market gardens, and flowers, and above all for green and hedged and tree-shaded suburbs. It is a land of small rolling hills and little streams running beneath maples and elms and oaks and huge tulip poplars, and—until the blight—tall and spreading chestnuts; a land of woods and meadows, green and cool with the extravagant richness of the flora of eastern Pennsylvania: a flora so rich and varied that, without being told, one knows that he has come to a place of almost perfect adjustment, to a delicate balance of latitude and thermal belts, between the too-cold of the North and the too-hot of the South.

Moreover, these home counties are amazingly easy to reach. The city is not a formidable island, as is New York. The only hampering river, the Schuylkill, is a narrow stream, easily bridged. A man can leave his office and in half an hour or so be in the country—an advantage in some ways, a great disadvantage in others, as we shall see later on. But it has always given, this home-county life, a country air to Philadelphia and to Philadelphians, one reason why the latter are so long-lived and healthy and pink-cheeked despite what their city government has done to them.

The motto of the state of Pennsylvania, of the commonwealth, of the "Holy Experiment" is "Virtue, Liberty and Independence." Had the first noun in a moment of candour been omitted, there would not have been so much opportunity for sardonic reflection.

One is tempted to swell upon the odd twist of fate, the paradox which presented William Penn, of all people, Penn the visionary, Penn the prophet, Penn the believer in "plain and well-intending people", the simple and direct man despite his love of good clothes and a feather in his hat and good wine and stately living, with this Aladdin's Lamp, this cornucopia.

CHAPTER II

The Seeds are Planted

"One of the finest, and best, and pleasantest rivers in the world."
HENRY HUDSON'S DESCRIPTION OF THE DELAWARE.

THE PLANTING OF a wilderness is a difficult and dangerous business. In the beginning the wilderness rejects cultivation, resists settlement. The first sparse crops must be planted again and again before they take hold. It is as if the wilderness resented the intention to change the slow, forested rhythm of its ways, the accustomed pace of its long and aboriginal centuries. And this is no pantheism, although, on the other hand, maybe it is. At all events, men, confronted by the wilderness, become different.

To begin with, most of them are restless or adventurous men, and the wilderness plays into the hands of these traits. On a frontier men both diminish and increase; they become more egotistical, more sensitive and less co-operative, more difficult to argue or reason with, and, on the other hand, they become more self-reliant, more persistent, more observant, more patient with Nature and life if not with their fellow-men. Reading history and chronicles, one wonders how any country was ever settled. The preparations as a rule are so ignorant, the expectations so exaggerated, the early colonists so little prepared, and once arrived, with few exceptions, they behave in such a reckless and often fatal manner. As a rule, the first thing they do is to begin to quarrel amongst themselves.

This wonder rises to a climax when one considers the seventeenth century and the beginnings along the Atlantic seaboard of what some hundred and fifty years later was to become the United States of America. United was the last adjective anyone would have thought of at the time. Chaotic would have been nearer to it, for added to the vicissitudes of Nature, the resistance of the wilderness and of the frequently resentful tribes which inhabited it, were the conflicting visions and commercial enterprises of various breeds of Europeans, magnified and rendered even more antagonistic and complex by the regal generosity of their rulers, kings, or States General. French, Spanish, Dutch, Swedish, and English, with a flourish of their pens they gave their friends and adherents, usually in the form of a chartesed company, everything in sight and a great deal that wasn't, and the English kings, the Jameses and the Charleses, the most generous and the vaguest of them all, not only gave away everything in sight and all that wasn't, but did this in such an overlapping fashion that it is a tribute to the ingenuity and good sense of man that the counter-claims were ever disentangled.

Virginia extended about as far north and south as possible, two hundred miles north and two hundred miles south of the mouth of the Chesapeake, and as far west and north-west as "the South Sea," or in other words, the Pacific, about the eastern shores of which at the time no one knew anything. But then practically all the royal deeds and grants either included or took that minor matter for granted. And Maryland was equally encompassing. While later on, Pennsylvania, more modest, merely laid claim, under the first article of its charter, to—

ull that part ot America, islands included, which is bounded on the east by the Delaware River from a point on a circle twelve miles northward of New Castle Towne to the 43rd degree north latitude, if the Delaware extends that far; if not, as far as it does extend, and thence to the 43rd degree by a meridian line. From that point westward five degrees of longitude on the 43rd degree parallel; the western boundary to the 40th parallel and thence by a straight line to the place of beginning.

That takes in the northern part of Delaware, quite a lot of New York, and part of what is now Ohio.

As a result of this generosity, the English settlers not only had to keep their eyes and ears open for the Dutch, the French, and, toward the south, the Spanish—all these and the Indians, and, along the Delaware, the Swedes —but for each other as well. Even Connecticut, regarded nowadays as one of the more demure, if one of the most crowded, of states, also cherished at one time designs upon the Delaware and part of New York, an ambition which eventually led to a real, if fortunately not very bloody, war with Penn's province in what is now Luzerne County, but which Connecticut called Westmoreland. Nor were Connecticut's claims without reason. They were based on a good and prior charter. Early in its history Pennsylvania was involved in serious boundary disputes with Maryland, Virginia, the same Connecticut, New York, and Delaware—the first three disputes leading to bloodshed.

Interesting, isn't it, that hardly less than one hundred and fifty years

B*

ago—for the Connecticut-Pennsylvania dispute wasn't settled until 1803—
we were all stalking each other so enthusiastically? Makes one feel better
about the present.

Unlike the Gilbert and Sullivan hero who might have been a "Proosian"
or might have been a "Roosian" but who deliberately chose to be an Englishman, one marvels that there ever became such a thing as an American.
One marvels even more that the North American continent did not settle
down into being merely another Europe, the home of a hundred warring
tongues and warring beliefs. The American can be excused for having felt,
almost as soon as he became an American, that there was some sort of destiny
about him. The pity is that so far this has been taken out more in talk than
in action. But it is true that against the pages of history the American fool
and marplot, the small, the selfish, the mean-minded American, does stand
out in blacker and bolder type than anywhere else. There seems less excuse
for him or her. America has always been a promise and a vision.

And now, in all candour, and lest there be a misunderstanding, I think
I had best say that this is not a history.

By no means a history—and no more of it than necessary. To begin
with, I would not dare to write a history; I am no historian. To end with,
I would not want to write a history even if I dared. History is not my trade,
nor my interest, nor my training. Nor is it the purpose of this book. There
have been a score of histories, massive or brief, written about Philadelphia,
and some are interesting and some are not. But all are worthy. To add
to them would be merely adding plethora to plethora. Nor need any casual
reader be alarmed by the sub-title, "Seaport Series". I take that to be
merely a delimiting phrase, the purpose of which is to still any possible protests
from such great inland towns as Denver, Omaha, and St. Louis. Otherwise,
one would never get through; the series would never end. So this is no
formal history of Philadelphia, nor is it a history of maritime Philadelphia,
of "the Port of Philadelphia," although since Philadelphia is a great seaport,
and being a seaport alters a city's personality, it will be necessary at times
to refer to that fact. But outside of this, since I seek to avoid writing any
sort of formal history, I most certainly would seek to avoid writing anything
as technical as the history of a city's port.

It seems necessary to say this, although I sigh, for unfortunately the
moment a man touches upon facts (of course, there are no such things, except
for a few dates and documents), the wolves gather. They are welcome to
any bone they can find so long as they don't bring it back to my doorstep.
They will probably find a lot.

This book, to the contrary, is a sort of civic biography, one of those
novelistic biographies where you treat the hero as a human being and try
to find out what he is and how he got that way. There will even be occasional
psychoanalysis, for cities are individuals, and like individuals have their
conscious and unconscious beings, their open and suppressed desires, their
frustrations and satisfactions, their complexes, mother and father and family,
and the rest of them; ancestor worship, or what is equally bad, entire lack
of it; and of course, their own peculiar brand of love life. Since cities are
peculiarly things of man, built by men and inhabited by them, each is the

sum total of the men who built it, and who have inhabited it, and who now live in it. Their characters do not change very much. No more than does the essential character of the various generations of a family. It is astonishing how little, essentially, they do change; astonishing how different their characters are. But men and cities are conditioned by what has gone before, by ancestry, by traditions, by the physical characteristics they have inherited, by climate, by a world of other circumstances, and so that is where history comes in.

You can't get away from it, any more than you can get away from the moment, and both make the future, and perhaps the main failing of the American is his disregard for history in his excellent, but too fervid, interest in the present. A grave fault, since the principal purpose of history is to teach one to improve upon his ancestors, worthy as they may have been. That, and to avoid repeating their mistakes.

The sons of drunkards and pirates seldom have to be told this.

As to my qualifications as a biographer . . . there, at least, I have one definite claim. I am a Philadelphian, bone of the bone, and so I cherish a passion, often against my better judgment, for the city I am going to berate, compliment, despise, and hold up to admiration.

It is one of the queerest, and most interesting, and most nostalgic cities you ever saw, and let who will, who doesn't really know the city, laugh, which includes many of its citizens. At all events the ancient saying, "Once a Philadelphian, always a Philadelphian," holds good. You can meet them everywhere—Philadelphians—for it is also true that no city sends out more of its sons and daughters, frequently discontented, to the four quarters of the globe, but they seldom change much, and they are always a little homesick, to the great annoyance of their children who know only the outlandish places where they themselves are born.

And so having cleared, I hope, my skirts, I can proceed to the primary statement, which is that the name originally, believe it or not, was Coaquannock—or Kúequenáku, as I understand it was actually spelled.

That was the name the Indians called the point of land, the hour-glass of forest and swamp, between the Delaware and the Schuylkill, and it means "grove of tall pines". And so at once you have a picture of it, as you should have of Tacony, "an uninhabited place, or wood"; of Tioga, "a place at the forks"; of Tulpehocken, "the place of turtles"; and so on for any number of aboriginal names scattered about the city. But the grove of tall pines was more than that, or there was also a wealth of hardwood trees, black oak and white oak, and maples of all kinds, and sycamores or buttonwoods, and birches, sweet or black, and ash and beech and gum, and the flowering dogwood, and the locust, and the wild plum, and scores of others, for this was a place of great strength and fecundity, and in the spring it must have been a very sweet-smelling place, and colourful, and in the summers it was heavy and fruitful.

Underneath was a tangle of wild grape, and too much here and there, as nowadays, poison ivy and poison sumach. And the forest was haunted with birds. The insect life, too, was incredible, for we have the testimony

of the early settlers; the butterflies and, unfortunately, the midges and mosquitoes.   Here was a virgin land much more difficult to attack than the unknown
prairies far to the west, or the tall, clean-timbered country of the Rockies,
or even the endless woods beyond the Appalachians.   Often a man had to
hack his way through, foot by foot, once he left the Indian trails, as if he
were in a jungle.   As you approach Philadelphia from the north you feel
more and more the faint far edge of the tropics where they fade into the
north and add their luxuriance to the north's hardy persistence.

And here on the hour-glass, and all about, lived the Lenni-Lenape, later
called the Delaware by the English, divided into three main tribes—the
Unalachtigo, the Unami, and the Munsee.   And an excellent people they
were, and still are, what is left of them in Oklahoma and Wisconsin and
Ontario.   A hundred and sixty years or so later, west of the Mississippi,
they were to be very useful as scattered individuals to the fur traders and the
wagon trains.   On the Delaware they were a river folk, living in villages of
birch wigwams, and agricultural in a primitive way as all American Indians,
lacking draught animals, had to be.   An Algonkian people, they belonged to
the great Algonkian linguistic stock, and so were related to many distant
and warlike nations such as the Cheyennes and Blackfeet and Ojibwas, or
Chippewas, who were to appear eventually, and often disastrously, in American
history.   According to the Lenni-Lenape traditions they, too, had been a
western nation, always a comparatively small one, which had drifted east.
At the moment they were principally concerned with keeping out of the way,
and on good terms, with their fierce neighbours and uncertain allies and
war lords to the north, the Iroquois, whose runners and occasional war parties
came down the thousand-mile trails from the edge of Canada to the far south.
Trails, like the game trails, later turned into highways by the white man.

There is disagreement about the language of the Lenni-Lenape, many
scholars saying it was one of the most musical of the American Indian languages,
and William Penn thought the same.   And there is a fine Lenni-Lenape
tribal poem, the "Walum-Olum," first translated by Rafinesque, and later
by D. G. Brinton; but Delaware place-names were not too beautiful, if one
is to judge by the numerous remnants scattered about Penn's city and its
environs.   Remainders, also reminders, with which Philadelphia is more
liberally endowed than most.   Passyunk is not a pretty name, and Manayunk,
"the place where we drink" (I'd like to see anyone try it nowadays), is no better,
and Wissahickon, "the catfish stream," or perhaps, "the hidden stream,"
or "the yellow stream," can only be assimilated and forgiven because of the
beauty of this small creek's gorge and its parked, ascending woods.   Up in
the north-eastern section of the city, flowing into the Delaware, is a creek
now known as the Wissinoming, but which once had the alternate name of
Sissiniockisink, or "the place where we were scared," and no wonder.

Philadelphians are used to such names, they are born to them and hear
them constantly, and they take them for granted as much as they do such lovely
Welsh names as Merion and Narbeth and Bryn Mawr and Rydal and St.
David's and Bala, or such fine English names as Overbrook or Chestnut
Hill or West Chester; but a stranger to the city, especially one just learning
the idiom, standing in a suburban station and hearing a train dispatcher

calling out, "Express for Wissahickon, Manayunk, and Conshohocken," should be forgiven for thinking English, or at least the American version of it, a queer language.

To the west and south of the Lenni-Lenape when the white man first arrived were the Susquehannocks, or "Black Minquas" as they were known to the Swedes, hence the name of the great river that cuts Pennsylvania in half from north to south and flows past Harrisburg, the capital of the state —a Maryland tribe that had moved north. And also for a while a small branch of the Shawnees, likewise moving north, were located on the flats south of the mouth of the Schuylkill, but the Susquehannocks, a fierce tribe and not so tactful as the Lenni-Lenape, were in the habit of waging bitter war with the Iroquois and so were eventually driven west into the forests of the mountains, while the Shawnees also migrated toward the west and the centre of the province, leaving Penn and the Quakers to deal only with the Lenni-Lenape.

That Penn dealt surprisingly and exceptionally with them, and never conceived of doing anything else, we all know, although it must be remembered that as a seventeenth-century Englishman it never occurred to him that the land was not his after a few inexpensive formalities. As a result of his courtesy and fairness and understanding, however, everything went beautifully, where the Indians were concerned, until John Penn, "The American", so called because he was the only one of Penn's children born in this country, and his brother Thomas thought up the "Walking Purchase" of 1737, and until, several decades before, the arrival of the Scottish-Irish a hardy and magnificent but cantankerous breed who for the most part by-passed Philadelphia to seek the frontier which they adore and where invariably they make trouble. Necessary trouble perhaps—that is, if you're a white man, but nonetheless trouble.

Being also a grimly religious clan, the Scottish-Irish have never lacked, in their trouble-making, aid from an equally fractious and business-like deity. In 1730, seizing without anybody's permission, Indian or Quaker, Conestogoe Manor, fifteen thousand acres of the best land in the province, they proclaimed that " it was against the laws of God and Nature, that so much land should be idle while so many Christians wanted it to labour on and to raise their bread." The Provincial Assembly, acting with unaccustomed vigour, sent a sheriff and his posse to dispossess them, and he did so, burning their cabins to the number of thirty, a deed the Scottish-Irish never forgot. But it is only fair to add that if it had not been for the Scottish-Irish, with their habit, among other things, of taking scalps in return when they felt it necessary, the settlement, for bad or good, of Pennsylvania and the rest of the United States would have been considerably delayed.

Neither the Puritans to the north, nor the Catholics nor the Church of England men to the south, nor the Quakers could have done so well—once more from the point of view of the white man. The religion and ideas of life of these other settlers did not present the proper admixture of piety, plus percentage, plus pillage. What was needed was Presbyterians looking for land. As for John Penn, at an early date the "Holy Experiment" began to be vitiated by real-estate schemes which have been a large part of its history.

In a letter written in 1683, a year after his arrival in Philadelphia, to his more or less affiliated company, the Free Society of Traders in London, Penn describes his new friends charmingly:

For their persons, they are generally tall, straight, well built, and of singular Proportion. They tread strong and clever and mostly walk with a lofty Chin. Of complexion Black, but of design as the Gipsies in England. They grease themselves with Bear's fat clarified; and usually no defence against the sun or weather, their skins must needs be swathy. Their eye is little and black, not unlike a straight-look't Jew. The thick Lip and flat Nose, so frequent with the East Indians and Blacks, are not common with them; for I have seen as comely European-like faces among them of both sexes, as on your side of the Sea. And truly an Italian Complexion hath not much more of the White; and the Noses of several of them have as much of the Roman. Their language is lofty but narrow; but like the Hebrew in signification, full. Like shorthand in writing, one word serveth in the place of three and the rest are supplied by the Understanding of the Hearer; Imperfect in their tenses, wanting in their Moods, Participles, Adverbs, Conjunction and Interjections. I have made it a business to understand it that I might not want an Interpreter on any occasion, and I must say that I know not of a language spoken in Europe that hath words of more sweetness or greatness. For instance, Octokekon, Rancocas, Oricton, Shak, Marian, Poquesian, all of which are names of places and have grandeur in them—Sepassen, Passijon, the names of places; Tamane, Secane, Menanse and Secatareus, are the names of persons.

If an European comes to see them, or calls for Lodgings at their House or Wigwam, they give him the best place, and first cut. If they come to visit us they salute us with an Itah! which is as much as to say, "Good be to you!" and set them down, which is mostly on the ground, close to their heels, their legs upright; it may be they speak not a word, but observe all passages. If you give them anything to eat or drink, be it little or much, if it is given with kindness they are well pleased; else they will go away sullen, but say nothing.

In sickness, impatient to be cured; and for it give anything, especially for their children to whom they are extremely natural. They drink at these times a Tisan, or Decoction of some Roots in Spring Water; and if they eat any flesh it must be of the Female of any Creature. If they dye they bury them with their Apparel, be they Men or Women, and the nearest of Kin fling in something precious with them as a token of Love. Their Mourning is blacking of their faces, which they continue for a year. Some of the young women are said to take undue liberty before Marriage for a portion; but when married, chaste.

Their Government is by Kings, which they call Sachama, and those by succession, but always by the Mother's side. For instance, children of him who is now King will not succeed, but his Brother by his Mother, or the Children of his Sister, whose Sons (and after them the children of her Daughters) will reign; for Woman inherits. The Reason they render for this way of Descent is, that their issue may not be spurious. The Justice they have is Pecuniary. In case of any Wrong or evil Fact be it Murther itself, they atone by Feasts and Presents of Wampun, which is proportioned to the quality of the Offence, or Person injured or of the Sex they are of.

For their Original, I am ready to believe them of the Jewish Races.

So these were the initial Philadelphians, unless we choose to go back to prehistory, and vaguely the memory of them haunts the narrow streets of Philadelphia, just as does the memory of the tall pines, and the oaks, and the maples and the gums; and the memory of the small clear streams, forest reflections in them.   Especially on hot nights, and on misty quiet afternoons in Indian summer, is this memory strong.

The small clear streams are still there, but they are no longer clear, and for generations they have been hidden, first under cobblestones, then Belgian bricks, now asphalt.   The sun no longer reaches them even through leaves, for they are part of the city's sewer system.   A sad fate for a forest stream.

CHAPTER III

Dutch, Swedes, Finns, and the English

"This would be an excellent place for a towne."

SUPPOSED TO HAVE BEEN SAID BY A MEMBER OF THE CREW OF THE SHIP "SHIELD," AS SHE PASSED THE SITE OF PHILADELPHIA ON HER WAY UP THE DELAWARE IN 1678 TO THE QUAKER COLONY OF BURLINGTON.

POSSIBLY GIOVANNI VERRAZANO saw the bay in 1524; and Vasquez d'Ayllon in 1525; and Estavan Gomez, the Portuguese in the service of the Emperor Charles V; and at various times other early pathfinders.   But so far as anyone knows, Henry Hudson, the Englishman, that extraordinarily lucky—until the end—and congenital explorer, was the first white man to enter the mouth of the Delaware.   A week later he found the Hudson.   This was in the summer of 1609.

It was by the merest chance he saw either; for to begin with, three months earlier, on board his tiny ship the *Halve Maen*, or *Half Moon*, eighty tons, eighteen men in his crew, some English some Dutch, he had been headed in the opposite direction, trying to find, by means of the east Arctic Ocean and Nova Zembla, a way to the Indies and China, and he had already doubled the North Cape when overtaken by late-spring fogs and cold.   His crew, a fractious one, the same crew which in big Zeeland breeches is supposed to play at bowls every time there is a thunderstorm in the Catskills, and whom Rip Van Winkle met, was close to mutiny; so Hudson, more reasonable than most explorers, after consultation, turned about and stood south-west across the Atlantic to find if possible in warmer climates the Westward Passage instead of the Eastern.

Hudson had been subsidized by the Dutch East India Company for the sum, small even at the time, of sixty-four pounds, plus sixteen more to be paid to his wife if he failed to return. But on this new course he was not entirely without directions, for he was a good friend of Captain John Smith, and Captain Smith had told him about Virginia. Late in August the *Half Moon* was off the Virginia Capes and, heading north, on the 28th Hudson saw the grey bay that led to Penn's province, seventy-three years before Penn did. Hudson stayed only a day and then proceeded up the Jersey coast to the river that was to bear his name. But he loved the Delaware and left a glowing description of it.

A fascinated visitor he would be to modern New York and Philadelphia, this strange, perpetually interested Englishman! The memory of the *Half Moon* hangs in the sky above the Delaware Capes and Sandy Hook.

The next transient was another Englishman, Captain, or Sir, Samuel Argall, who a year later, July 1610, coming back to Virginia from Bermuda, where he had gone for supplies, dropped in upon the wide bay that led to the wide river—Hudson's sweet-smelling and "pleasant" river—and gave the bay its present name. He called the bay and the cape he sighted Delaware, in honour of the governor of Virginia, Sir Thomas West, Twelfth Baron de la Warr, who had arrived post-haste at Jamestown only a month earlier to prevent the dissolution of the starving colony to the south.

Once more chance, this time influenced by flattery, as it so often is, made history.

For some reason Delaware is a singularly beautiful and appropriate name for a great river and a great bay, but Argall wasn't thinking of beauty. He was a man obsequious to his superiors and bitterly tyrannical to his inferiors. Eight years later, in 1618, Lord de la Warr had to start again for Virginia to try to piece together the wreckage left by Argall's rule as deputy, but he never reached Virginia; he died at sea. Meanwhile, in 1613, Argall, exercising his authority, had sailed into the North River and had informed the astonished Hendrik Christiaenzen, superintendent of the small Dutch trading-post recently established on the island of Manhattan, that under the great charter granted the London Company by James I in 1606, the Hudson, the Delaware, and everything else, belonged to Virginia, and that if the Dutchmen wanted to stay they would have to pay tribute.

The cat was out of the bag; the jinn of exploration and settlement had escaped from his bottle, never to be put back again.

For fifty-four years, from 1613 to 1667 and the Treaty of Breda, when the English gained final possession of all the lands contained in the states of New York, New Jersey, Pennsylvania, and Delaware, save for a brief period in 1673-74 when the Dutch were in control again, for two generations that is, the Dutch, the Swedes, and the English wrangled, and sometimes fought, and claimed and counter-claimed, and settled tentatively or otherwise along the Delaware. During that period the Swedes were the most tenacious and intelligent of the new-comers, and had they been better supported at home, would have accomplished more.

To Sir Samuel Argall and Virginia the Dutch States-General made quick reply. Virginia or no Virginia, and the same to James I, in 1614 the Dutch States-General passed an ordinance claiming exclusive trade privileges to all of America, and seven years later, in 1621, amplified this by chartering the

Dutch West India Company with rights as wide as any king of England could imagine. Not only was the new company granted exclusive trade with the Americas from the Straits of Magellan to Newfoundland, and exclusive trade along the coast of Africa from the Tropic of Cancer to the Cape of Good Hope, but exclusive colonization rights as well. No one could have asked for more. The only problem was how to get it and keep it, especially with such people as the English abroad in the world.

When it comes to restraints of trade, modern man, compared to the seventeenth-century variety, for all his cartels, is a child.

The first result of the comparatively mild Dutch ordinance of 1614, so far as Pennsylvania was concerned, was the further naming of Delaware Bay.

In that year the United New Netherland Company, dispatched from Manhattan Captain Cornelis Jacobsen Mey, of Hoorn, Holland, with his ship *Fortune*, and Captain Cornelis Hendricksen with his cockleshell of sixteen tons, the sloop *Onrust*, or *Restless*, to explore more thoroughly what the Dutch called the Zueydt, or South River, to distinguish it from the North, or Hudson, which flowed past their new fur settlement. Captain Mey, with a weather-eye out for future fame, no sooner saw the Delaware Capes than he named both after himself; the north one Mey, the south one Cornelis. Unfortunately he mistook a long sand-bar for another cape and named this Hindlopen, and in time the false cape submerged with its name the real cape, and—the name Hindlopen corrupted—the real cape became known as Henlopen. Cape Mey also became Cape May, a spelling that the majority of Philadelphians take for granted because it is in that month that the thoughts of many of them turn vaguely towards the peculiarly Philadelphian summer resort which in the 'eighties and 'nineties of the last century first began to look down its nose at the more cosmopolitan, and therefore more vulgar, Atlantic City to the north.

Captain Mey in his bid for fame failed utterly to reckon with the obstinacy of the English, especially where their language is concerned.

All through history, English mouths, unashamed, have changed foreign syllables to their liking. On the Delaware were two examples of this so dramatic as to bear repeating. Captain Mey named a small creek Hoornkill after his native town in Holland; this became Horekill, and so to the English, Whorekill, a corruption which led to the assumption of complacency on the part of Indian maidens, exciting but unfounded on facts. In the same way Morderskill, or Mother's Creek, named later on by the Swedes, became Murderkill.

Before long, Captain Mey sailed back to Europe, leaving the expedition in charge of his associate, Captain Hendricksen, who, from his reports to Holland, seems to have ascended the Delaware as far as Coaquannock, the future site of Philadelphia, although this is by no means certain. At all events Captain Hendricksen said that he found three rivers, which were probably the Delaware, the Christina, and the Schuylkill. Also, he explored the banks of the Delaware, trading with the Indians. As interesting a feature of this expedition as any was the fact that his cockleshell, the *Restless*, was the first American-built ship. The year before, its keel had been laid near Manhattan by Captain Hendricksen's friend, Captain Adriaen Block, discoverer of Long Island, whose name is perpetuated off the north-east tip of that lobster-shaped principality.

Above all, somewhere near present-day Wilmington, Captain Hendricksen came upon three lost and hardy Dutchmen, captives of the Minquas, who almost a year before had left Manhattan and, ascending the Hudson, in a big circle had made their way south across mountains and through forests to where Hendricksen found them. They told him what they had seen. Says Hendricksen in his report to Holland, speaking in the respectful third person:

First he hath discovered for his aforesaid Masters and Directors, certain lands, a bay and three rivers situate between 38 and 40 degrees.

And did there trade with the Inhabitants; said trade consisting of Sables, Furs, Robes and other skins.

He hath found said country full of trees, to wit, Oaks, hickory and pines; which trees were, in some places, covered with vines.

He hath seen, in said country, Bucks and does, turkeys and partridges.

He hath found the climate of the said country very temperate, judging it to be as temperate as that of this country Holland.

No wonder the Dutch thought they had prior rights, and in 1623, two years after the all-embracing charter granted the West India Company, they set out to prove their belief. In that year Captain Cornelis Mey, returning to the new country as director of the trading-post at Manhattan, encouraged by the report of Captain Hendricksen, shortly after his arrival sent a handful of Walloon colonists and a handful of troops to settle on the Delaware.

This proved to be a half-hearted, unsuccessful expedition. The Dutch were preoccupied with their post to the north and had neither men nor money to spare. The meagre attempts at colonization on the part of the Walloons near the mouth of Delaware Bay petered out, but the few troops with them did achieve a further historic advance.

Leaving the Walloon families to the care of themselves, the soldiers went up the river as far as the site of Philadelphia, and on the New Jersey side, directly opposite League Island, built of logs the first permanent settlement in that part of America. This was Fort Nassau, part military post, part fur post, and with Fort Nassau it might be said the port of Philadelphia was officially opened, although it was another fifty-nine years before anything much happened. Nor was Fort Nassau ever more than an in-and-out permanent settlement, the Dutch alternately occupying it and abandoning it, and occupying and abandoning it, until in 1651 they abandoned it completely and removed its guns to Fort Casimir at New Castle.

Meanwhile the English had not been idle. They never were during the sixteenth, seventeenth, and eighteenth centuries. In 1634 two Englishmen, Robert Evelyn and Thomas Young, had sailed as far up the Delaware as Coaquannock and had started to build a trading-post at the mouth of the Schuylkill, but they stayed less than a week. The next year an expedition under Captain George Holmes, more determined, and under orders of the governor of Virginia, attempted to capture Fort Nassau, with the result that Captain Holmes was captured himself and sent to New Amsterdam in chains. Not content with this, six years later, in 1641, Connecticut, acting under the delusions of grandeur already noted, sent a group of sixty Puritans, disgusted with the New England weather and conditions there, from New Haven to build a blockhouse, also at the mouth of the Schuylkill, and form a colony. The Puritans had no better luck than the Virginians. The Dutch of Fort Nassau burned their blockhouse and sent them, too, to New Amsterdam. But in 1649 the persistent New Englanders tried again. On their way south, however, stopping off at the Hudson with extraordinary self-confidence to say the least, they ran into Director-General Peter Stuyvesant who had arrived two years before, and that man of vigour told them in no uncertain terms to mind their own business and go back where they came from unless they wanted to get shot.

At the time the Delaware was under the control of the Swedes, and it wasn't that Stuyvesant loved the Swedes, but that he liked the English less and recognized that they were much more dangerous rivals.

Poor Peter Stuyvesant! For the seventeen years of his directorship he lived like a thin-skinned nut between the jaws of a nut-cracker, and shortly before the taking over of New Amsterdam by the English in 1664, he wrote a letter to the Dutch West India Company containing this despairing sentence:

"Alas, the English are ten to one in number to us, and are able to deprive us of the country when they please."

By 1664, the year in which Colonel Richard Nicolls appeared before New Amsterdam with his calm demand for surrender, there were at least, to the south, fifty thousand English in Maryland and Virginia and, to the north-east and east, an equal number in New England, while at no time were there more than ten thousand Dutch around New Amsterdam. As for the Swedes on the Delaware, they were an absurd handful; at the most, and this not until later, a thousand or so soldiers and settlers with their women and children. Peter Stuyvesant, also the Swedes, were between what we now call "a pincer movement."

And now here is a strange thing.

For some reason not explained, some mysterious coming together of circumstances, the Delaware all during the latter two-thirds of the seventeenth century was the Samarcand, the Carcassone, the focal point of "holy experiments"; more or less holy, that is. At least they had more of the spiritual in them than the majority of colonization schemes. William Penn's "Holy Experiment" was merely the last.

The great Swede, Gustavus Adolphus, weary as all wise men must have been of the endless wars of Europe, also dreamed a dream of a Rasselas Valley, a place of goodness and simple toil where men "fleeing from bloody battlefields, and homes made desolate by the fire and sword of the persecutor", as set forth to him by Willem Usselinx, of Amsterdam, could find security and content. There was to be absolute freedom of conscience (so long, that is, as one was a Protestant), there was to be no slavery of any kind, there was to be equal opportunity for all. Gustavus Adolphus dreamed this dream in 1624, but before he could do anything about it, the Thirty Years' War swept over Europe, and eight years later Gustavus Adolphus died on the field of Lützen, November 6, 1632.

And a grim death it was.

Badly wounded and lost from his men, he lay in the mist and the dusk while his enemies, a couple of Wallenstein's horsemen, worked an hour or so to find their way inside his flawless armour. Finally they stabbed him in the eye through his open visor.

Also about this time occurred the most tragic, and also serio-comic, "holy experiment" on the Delaware, and certainly in many ways the most romantic: "holy experiment" distinguished by a wistful sort of madness in the person and plans of Sir Edmund Plowden, an Irish knight, who never having been in America, but saturated with the Irish legend of St. Brendan and his miraculous voyage, and obviously wearied of a nagging wife and eighteen children, finally badgered Charles I into granting him a huge tract of land comprising practically all of what is now Maryland, Delaware, New Jersey, and Pennsylvania. St. Brendan, you remember, was the Irish saint who, setting sail across the Atlantic in the sixth century with some followers, found "The Promised Land of the Saints" or "The Isles of St. Brendan". This story, like the story of Atlantis, in one form or another is found in practically all European mythology, and so there may be more to it than formal historians allow; in any case, it is indicative of the urge toward the western sun that since time immemorial has haunted Europe, and which has had so much to do with the development of America.

Like the lemmings, they have come, not always knowing why.

Sir Edmund Plowden, like St. Brendan, thought of America as a land "where angels in the guise of birds sang matins, prime, and evensong, and all such service as Christian men delight to hear," and where the sweet breezes were never too hot nor too cold—an exaggerated picture to say the least of the American climate. However, he was a persistent man as well as a poet, and a true fanatic, not to mention a real-estate promoter, for it is clear that it was with a gesture of royal weariness that Charles I deeded him land his father, James I, had already in great part deeded, Maryland and the Calverts; also he made Sir Edmund an Earl Palatine; a large title, since it implies practically a sub-kingdom. Sir Edmund's intention was to found a principality called New Albion and establish a new nobility, at the core of which was to be an order called the Knights of New Albion. His oldest daughter, Barbara, for example, was to be Baroness of Richneck with an estate in southern New Jersey "of twenty-four miles compasse".

Sir Edmund got out a prospectus and started to sell stock and grant lands and titles of nobility; but, meanwhile, his less lyric wife sued him for divorce because he beat her, and in this was assisted by the local parson's wife, who sued Sir Edmund for assault and battery. Sir Edmund was living on his estate at Wanstead, England, at the time. Also Cecil Calvert, second Lord Baltimore, objected strongly to the proposed intrusion. When ten years later Sir Edmund, Earl Palatine, finally did get to the Delaware by way of Virginia and Maryland, he met with a completely cold reception on the part of the settlers already there, and eventually his mutinous crew marooned him half naked on an island, from which he was rescued in the nick of time.

He went back to England, and the province of New Albion went with him.

One hates to leave Sir Edmund. The Sir Edmunds of the world are engaging characters so long as one does not have to see too much of them or buy any of their stocks. Nor is the breed extinct; it is perennial. Almost everyone has a Sir Edmund or two in his life. Whatever success they have, outside of their hypnotic personalities, is based on man's conviction that no matter how much of a hell he makes of his own particular environment, somewhere, if only he has the price of the voyage, paradise awaits him.

As for the Swedish holy experiment, not until 1636, five years after Gustavus Adolphus' death, and in the reign of his daughter, Christina, then a child of eleven, did the first Swedish expedition leave Europe, arriving on the Delaware the following spring, and by that time the Swedish holy experiment had become more commonplace and commercial. The Swedes landed far down near Cape Hindlopen, but did not stay long, and making their way upstream, finally settled on the site of what is now Wilmington, where twenty-three years earlier Captain Hendricksen had come upon his three lost Dutchmen. Here where the Brandywine—that lovely and rural stream which Philadelphians think belongs exclusively to them and to their rolling, fox-hunting country to the west—joins a sluggish creek, the Swedes began to build. And in this fashion began Pennsylvania's proud and tiny neighbour to the south, Delaware; a state, except in its northern reaches, where it is practically the same, as different from Pennsylvania as is imaginable.

The Swedes called the sluggish creek and its quick-running confluent the Brandywine, the Christina, after their child queen, and so small is Delaware that its inhabitants still think Christina Creek a river.

Along with the Swedes came some Finns, Finland at that time belonging to Sweden. "Forest-destroying Finns," they were called in a royal Swedish mandate of the period, who "against our edict and proclamation, destroy the forests by setting tracts of wood on fire, in order to sow in the ashes, and who maliciously fell trees". But the Finns, whatever they were in Sweden, made a contribution to American living and history far in excess of their numbers; they gave this country its symbolic dwelling. Forest people, timber men, they found the magnificent new forests exactly to their liking and built the first American log-cabins.

CHAPTER IV

Printz, the Tub

Joram Bagman, and Lasse Cock, and Göstaf Göstafsson, and Paul Mink, and Peter
Stalag, and old Uncle Olle Stobey, and all.

NAMES TAKEN FROM LIST OF SWEDISH SETTLERS.

ODDLY ENOUGH, THIS first Swedish expedition was led by a Dutchman, Peter
Minuit, or rather, a French Huguenot who had become a Dutchman, and
had been proposed originally by another Dutchman, or, once more, a Dutch
citizen, Willem Usselinx, a Belgian who had settled as a merchant in Amsterdam, and who was the first to interest Gustavus Adolphus in America.   Moreover, after the death of both Usselinx and Gustavus Adolphus, the plan for
a New Sweden had been carried to completion by Samuel Blommaert, Peter
Silfverkrona, and other Dutchmen, disgusted, like Usselinx, by the arrogance
and indifference to the Delaware country of the Dutch West India Company.
So, paradoxically enough, New Sweden was largely a Dutch idea.   Minuit
himself had been director of New Amsterdam for six years, and was the man
who had completed the famous purchase of that island at a price New Yorkers
should remember when swollen with pride:

Beads, other trinkets, and a few pieces of bright cloth to the value of
sixty guilders.   Something less than twenty-four dollars.

The Swedes were excellent colonizers.   For twenty years they dwelt in
peace with the Indians, and Christina grew to be a comely village, and
Swedish outposts and farms, especially in the time of Governor Printz, spread
out thinly along the Delaware north of Christina and a little way up the
Schuylkill.   On the site of Philadelphia itself were a couple of Swedish
blockhouses.   All this to begin with was done with about ninety men, settlers
and soldiers.   It was in 1643 that the huge and famous Printz arrived—
and stayed ten years; and for those ten years there was much colour in New
Sweden, and swearing and roaring and drilling and discipline and progress,
but in 1653 Printz, worn out by lack of support, returned to Europe, leaving
his son-in-law, Johan Papegoja, and his daughter, Papegoja's wife, Armegot
Printz, in charge.   Armegot Printz was as colourful as her father, a blonde,
handsome giantess of a woman, who continued her father's viceregal court
at Printz Hall on the Tinicum: a sort of backwoods palace Printz had built,
with "orchards, pleasure house" and so on, "all very handsome".[1]

---

[1]Armegot Printz was one of the most fascinating personalities who ever haunted what were
to be the suburbs of Philadelphia.   Large like her father, beautiful in her own way, wilful
and domineering, she became a tradition that persisted for over a hundred years along the
Delaware.   The lady deserves at least one novel and at least one biography, for she is as rich
a subject as "The Tub" and as delightful to read about, although, so far as one can make out,
equally objectionable to live with.   Johan Papegoja, her husband, a mild fellow, apparently
found her so, for just as soon as possible after the departure of his father-in-law with all the
Printz family except Armegot, a wife and four other daughters, that is, John sailed for Sweden

Printz, "The Tub," Lieut.-Colonel Johan Printz of the Swedish Cavalry, was a huge and extraordinary man, and despite his swearing and drinking an energetic and capable administrator, although his record in the Swedish Army had not been very good and he had been court-martialled for his behaviour at the Battle of Chemnitz and had been sent out as governor of New Sweden more or less as a punishment. David Pietersen de Vries, the Dutchman, describes him as weighing "four hundred pounds" and taking "three drinks" with every meal. It was fortunate, considering his irascibility and obstinacy, that he had sailed for home before Peter Stuyvesant, up in New Amsterdam, really got going, Peter Stuyvesant would have broken Printz's heart. For peg-legged Peter Stuyvesant, West Indian hero, was a man of equal irascibility and much more sense and decision; also there were more Dutchmen in America than Swedes. Stuyvesant, arriving as director of New Amsterdam in May of 1647, eight years later, everything ready, sent seven ships and seven hundred men to the Delaware to take over New Sweden. No nonsense this time. The armada, huge for the time and place, anchored off the Swedish forts and demanded their surrender. Johan Printz was gone; the Swedes had neither enough men nor enough ammunition —two rounds only for their handful of troops. For nine years the Dutch remained in undisputed possession, and then, September 8, 1664, Peter Stuyvesant had to surrender New Amsterdam to Colonel Nicolls and the English under circumstances as humiliating as those attending the Swedes-surrender of Christina to him.

In the spring of 1664 Charles II of England had presented to his brother —James, Duke of York, later to be James II—all the land between the Con-

---

too, leaving Armegot in sole possession of Tinicum Island and Printz Hall, or Printsdorp Manor. Armegot, assured in her holdings by Peter Stuyvesant, whom she had petitioned to this effect, settled down to almost a quarter of a century—twenty-three years—of irascibility, lawsuits, quarrels with neighbours, and, wherever possible, tyranny.

A hundred years later, the Rev. Israel Acrelius, Swedish visitor and chronicler of the Swedish settlements along the Delaware, writes: "They still tell of the lady of Tenacong, how haughty she was, and how she oppressed the poor when in prosperity."

Armegot finally sold Tinicum to a Frenchman named De la Grange for six thousand guilders and sailed off to Sweden in 1662, but De la Grange dying during her absence before final payment was made, Armegot came back and sued his widow for the balance, or else restoration of the estate. At this juncture, another Frenchman appeared, suitor for Madame de la Grange's hand, a M. la Motte; but Armegot, suspecting his ability to pay, continued her suit and won it in the New York Court of Assizes. For a while she lived on Tinicum entirely alone save for one manservant because, as it is recorded, no one had the least "inclination to live with her." While living in this solitary fashion, most of her income was derived from a still with which she made "corn liquor" under a licence from the new English governor, Sir Francis Lovelace, who, apparently having heard all about her, added the proviso that the making of this corn liquor "be done with such moderation that no just complaint do arise thereby."

In 1676, Armegot, having sold Tinicum again to one Otto Cock for the considerably smaller sum of three hundred guilders, sailed back to Sweden for the last time and died there in 1695.

Armegot cannot exactly be claimed as "a Philadelphia girl", for she lived down the river near what is now Upland, and besides, she departed from this country six years before Philadelphia was founded; but nonetheless she was more or less the mould of a certain type of Philadelphia beauty, tall, well boned, blue-eyed, free-striding, proud and self-sufficient. Like all cities, counties, or countries, Philadelphia has produced several distinct breeds of women, conditioned by climate, environment, and inherited ideas. Women, although even nowadays more hampered than men, perhaps for that very reason are more individual than men; within the circle allotted to them, more distinct. Armegot might be described as having "the blonde Philadelphia female characteristics" as exhibited by outdoor maidens and especially, perhaps, widows left to administer their husbands' estates.

necticut River and Maryland. This *tour de force* was confirmed three year later by the Treaty of Breda, but without waiting for the Treaty of Breda, immediately following Stuyvesant's surrender, Sir Robert Carr was sent by Colonel Nicolls from New York to rule the Delaware, and English-speaking the Delaware has remained ever since except for a year, 1673-74, when it went back to the Dutch, only to be returned to the English by the Treaty of Westminster.

Unlike the Swedes, the Dutch were not especially good colonizers; they were better traders and sailors. For one thing, and extremely important at the time, they were suspicious of the Indians and harsh to them on the slightest provocation. They were neither as easy-going and as opportunistic as the English, nor as just and considerate as the Swedes. As early as 1631, and their first serious attempt at colonization along the Delaware, Zwaanendael, Swan River, where Lewes, Delaware, now stands, the Dutch had begun to have trouble with the Indians, with the result that Zwaanendael was wiped out, burned to the ground, and its handful of colonists massacred to the last man. But the Swedes were as determinedly peaceable as the Quakers, save for the reign of Johan Printz, and, once incorporated into the life of Penn's province, added much to the vigour and intelligence of its south-eastern tip with their learning, their tolerance, and their good taste. On the other hand, unlike New York and its state, where everywhere their influence remains, the Dutch made hardly any impression upon the Delaware at all. The Pennsylvania "Dutchmen", who were to come later and spread all through Bucks and Berks and Lehigh and Lebanon and York and Lancaster counties, and who represent one of the four main streams of eastern Pennsylvania culture, were not Dutchmen at all, except for some of the earlier Mennonities, but Germans—Palatinate Germans.

Even the Swedish architecture slipped gracefully into the spiritual mood of Quaker architecture, and in that country of easy quarries and beautiful rock, if it did not influence, at least blended perfectly with the Pennsylvania stone house which, farmhouse or country house, is the most quiet, the most four-square, the coolest, the warmest, and the most dignified house in America. If you don't believe this, go into one on a hot August afternoon when its shadows are as blue and deep as water, and the air smells of wheat and leaves and gilliflowers and hollyhock and geraniums, and the China matting that once, and so sensibly, was popular.

As you pass through Wilmington on your way to Baltimore and Washington, you can see Old Swedes Church—now Holy Trinity—built in 1698; and in Philadelphia, on the banks of the Delaware, is Gloria Dei, built in 1700, on the site of a Swedish blockhouse dedicated as a church twenty-five years earlier, also called Old Swedes. These are among the two loveliest small churches a man can find, but to find Gloria Dei you have to pass through some of the most dejected slums in the world until there it sits, church and close and graveyard, like a jewel in a toad's head. Almost any city but Philadelphia would have done something about those slums. But perhaps the contrast is salutary.

The dead, and a place like Gloria Dei, cause energetic men to take up arms against the stupid and bitter selfishness of man.

*   *   *   *   *   *

It has been necessary to condense a long and colourful period, seventy-two years of it, almost three-quarters of a century, into a few pages. The condensation was obligatory, but even more so the history, if for no other purpose than to impress on Philadelphians the fact that their city did not spring full-armed from the brow of William Penn as Minerva sprang full-armed from the brow of her father Jove. Nothing human springs that way, and to think so limits the areas of proper pride and one loses the necessary sense of the pageant of his past.

Philadelphia did not start with a stout gentleman in a broad-brimmed Quaker hat and a shad-belly coat making a treaty with the Indians as the heroic painting of Benjamin West, the Philadelphia painter, a painter greatly reproduced and distributed, has led all but more scholarly Philadelphians to believe. To begin with, William Penn at the time was not elderly, he was only thirty-nine and was an exceedingly handsome man, in the full tide of his career. To end with, the Quakers had not as yet adopted any definite form of plain clothes, and if they had it is doubtful if William Penn would have worn them. He liked gallant and dashing clothes; inherently he was a gallant and dashing man. But that is not the principal point.

The principal point is that Philadelphia, so far as the white man is concerned, did not begin with William Penn at all, nor with the few Swedes, sixty or so, settled there when he arrived. Actually Philadelphia is three hundred and thirty years old, not two hundred and sixty-two years old as the more conservative historians would have you believe. Just as San Francisco began when Don Gaspar de Portola, governor of Lower California, sailed through the Golden Gate in 1769, so Philadelphia actually began when Captain Hendricksen, from the deck of the *Restless*, if it was Captain Hendrick-sen, or if not, then the first white man to do so, saw the junction of the Delaware and the Schuylkill.

Cities are like people. The site of a city, and what took place on or near it, are as much a part of the city as are the slow months in the mother's womb a part of a man or woman; as are the long and misty generations that have culminated in that womb.

Henry Hudson and the *Half Moon*, Captains Mey and Hendricksen, Sir Samuel Argall, Gilles Hossett and the butchered colony of Zwaanendael, David Pietersen de Vries, Sir Edmund Plowden, Willem Usselinx, Peter Minuit, the huge tub Johan Printz, Peter Stuyvesant; scores of others, Dutchmen, Swedes, Finns, and English; some who actually saw the tall pines of Coaquannock, some who did not; and all the hundreds of settlers whose names are now forgotten, are part of Philadelphia.

And so, too, is Gustavus Adolphus of Sweden, dead on the battlefield of Lützen, and every other man, or woman, proud or simple, rich or poor, who dreamed of something fine along the Delaware.

CHAPTER V

Green Countrie Towne

"I have led the greatest colony into America that ever man did upon a private credit. I will show a province in seven years equal to her neighbours of forty years planting."

WILLIAM PENN.

IT WAS THEREFORE no new land, no unknown frontier, to which William Penn came in October of 1682. The Dutch, the Swedes, and other Englishmen had done the spadework. Philadelphia slipped into the world quietly and pleasantly and almost at once began to be prosperous, in exact reverse to the little girl of the fairy story who, given her choice, preferred to be lucky after she had grown up, instead of before. In the background of Penn's province was no memory of the harsh toils and dangers of the earlier colonies. Eleven years after the Lord Proprietor's first visit, a Swede in Delaware could write back to Sweden this pastoral letter, reminiscent of Gray's *Elegy*:

As to what concerns our situation in this country we are for the most part husbandmen. We plough and sow and till the soil; and as to our meat and drink we live according to the Swedish custom. This country is very rich and fruitful and here grow all sorts of grain in great plenty. . . . We have here also all sorts of beasts, fowls, and fishes. Our wives and daughters employ themselves in spinning wool and flax and many of them in weaving. . . . We also live in peace and friendship with one another, and the Indians have not molested us for many years. . . . Further, since this country has ceased to be under the government of Sweden we are bound to acknowledge and declare for the sake of truth that we have been well and kindly treated as well by the Dutch as by his Majesty the King of England, our gracious sovereign.

While a Swedish missionary, writing in the same year, 1693, mentions the excellence of the judges and other officers, the smallness of the taxes, and once again, the abundance of food and drink.

Perhaps Sir Edmund Plowden wasn't so wrong after all. Not for a while, anyway, except for the angels who sang like birds and the climate.

Nor was Philadelphia solely that bodiless dream, a spiritual and legal and social experiment; it was also that much rarer thing, a planned city physically.

There was nothing haphazard about it; at least, in the design. It did not just take place, as do most cities. If Penn was too wise to think that man could live by bread alone, he also knew he could not live by the spirit alone, and every detail of his "Holy Experiment" had been considered for many months and years: envisioned, amended, and finally fixed upon. For example, he rewrote and revised his constitution, his Frame of Government— not finished until the spring of 1682—twenty times before he was satisfied, consulting with numerous experts, including his friend Algernon Sidney, the great English Liberal, who was to lose his head the year after Penn's departure, for his part in the Rye House Plot preceding the Monmouth Rebellion, and even more with the philosopher, John Locke.

No commissioners and deputies ever arrived anywhere with more instructions in their pockets than did the men sent out to found the "City of Brotherly Love". Penn wrote under date of October 10, 1681:

Let the rivers and creeks be sounded in order to settle a great towne. Be sure to make your choice where it is most navigable, high, dry and healthy. Let every house be pitched in the middle of its plot so that there may be ground on each side for gardens or orchards or fields, that it may be a green countrie towne that will never be burnt and always be wholesome.

Like every Englishman of his generation, Penn had a vivid recollection of the Great Plague of 1665 and the Fire of London a year later. He had just reached his majority when these had happened. And so he wished no holocaust for his city, nor black nor ulcerous death in any form, and as much as anything he wished to make certain of a comely and a gracious town. There was no need to tell a man of his nationality and training what trees and greenness and a homestead meant to other men in the way of contentment and good citizenship. He intended city parks, and open spaces, and a wide promenade along the Delaware where at the time the land rose in a forest-covered bluff twenty-five feet high. His city was to extend clear through to the Schuylkill, which it eventually did, a distance of almost two miles, and was to run north and south a mile between what are now Vine and South streets, and it was to be laid off in the parallelograms that Penn loved, in this case the narrow streets running at right angles to each other that still distinguish it. But, as has been said, each man's house was to sit back beneath its trees on its own plot.

There is not much left of that original plan; the "green countrie towne," what there was of it, has vanished, except for the narrow, right-angled streets, which Penn thought at the time were wide streets and intended to be such, and except for a few tree-shaded squares—Washington Square, Independence Square, Franklin Square, Rittenhouse Square, and so on—but a year after his arrival, and the formal founding of his city, Penn, in the first flush of his enthusiasm, was able to write in a letter to London:

This I will say for the good Providence of God, that of all the many places I have seen in the world, I remember not one better seated, so that it seems to me to have been appointed for a towne, whether we regard the rivers or the conveniency of the coves, docks, springs, the loftness and soundness of the land and the air held by the people of these parts to be very good. It has advanced within less than a year to about fourscore houses and cottages, such as they are, where merchants and handicrafts are following their vocations as fast as they can, while the countrymen are close at their farms.

And again, upon leaving his "Holy Experiment" at the end of his first visit of two years, he exclaims:

And thou, Philadelphia, the virgin settlement, named before thou wert born, what love, what care, what service and travail has there been to bring thee forth and to preserve thee from such as would abuse and defile thee!

During those first two years this note of exultation was unchanged. Trumpets and wood winds! *Fortissimo*, if Penn hadn't been a Quaker. Later on, in another letter to London, this time with more of the mixture of sentiment and the material man which distinguished both the author and the hearty age in which he lived, he writes:

The soil is good, air serene and sweet from the cedar, pine and sassafras, with wild myrtle of great fragrance. I have had better venison, bigger, more tender, as fat as in England. Turkeys of the wood I had of forty and fifty pounds weight. Fish in abundance, especially shad and rock. Oysters are monstrous for bigness. In the woods are divers fruits, wild, and flowers that for colour, largeness, and beauty excel . . .

and much more, and in detail, of the numerous gifts of Nature.

One hates to leave these early statements of Penn; like the country and the small growing town, they are so fresh and virginal and so illuminative of the scene and a certain side of Penn's character—the most delightful side. "Oh! how sweet," he says, "is the quiet of these parts, freed from the anxious and troublesome solicitations, hurries and perplexities of woeful Europe." What happened to this vision makes to a large extent the plot of this story, as it must make, alas, the plot of most men's dreams through the ages. Within a few years Penn's letters were filled with disillusion and bitterness.

Good moves forward slowly, if it moves at all, and with plenty of backward steps; and in the case of Penn there were too many handicaps, most of them pleasant. For one man ruined by hardship, five have been ruined by good fortune.

The principal liability of Penn's great city on the Delaware has always been that its feet have been set in paths too comfortable and that everything has been too easy. From the very beginning, Philadelphia has been the spoiled child of American cities, although it was also, and still is, the most symbolic; first, gathering to itself the aspirations of that extraordinary century, the seventeenth, and then, carrying these forward into the expanding search for enlightenment and political liberty and urbanity of that equally extraordinary century, the eighteenth.

After that, something happened.

And it is these two voices talking side by side, the strong and directional one and the fat and indifferent one, sometimes the former in the ascendancy, but usually the latter, that makes the history of the place peculiarly interesting.

"We promise according to our hopes," says La Rouchefoucauld, "and perform according to our fears," and Penn's town is a yardstick both local and national.

After his second visit to his province in 1699, Penn, back in England, in debt, assailed by calumny, hurt by the reception he had had and the attitude of his Provincial Assembly, in a letter to his faithful friend and former secretary and American adjutant, James Logan, apostrophizes his "virgin settlement" in very different terms from the ones he had originally used:

O Pennsylvania, what hast thou not cost me! Above thirty thousand pounds more than I ever got from it, two hazardous and most fatiguing voyages, my straits and slavery here, and my son's soul almost!

Penn's vision was no sudden illumination, no blinding flash of light like the knowledge that came to Paul of Tarsus on the road to Damascus. Penn had cherished his plans for a long time. He claimed that even in boyhood he had been haunted by dreams of the kind, although then they could have had nothing to do with Quakerism and persecution. Undoubtedly, however, he had heard much of Jamaica, from his father, the admiral who had served in those waters. But it was not until 1675, when he was thirty-one, that Penn had his first opportunity. In that year he acquired a large proprietary interest in New Jersey which, eleven years before, following the surrender of New Amsterdam by Peter Stuyvesant, had been granted by James, Duke of York, to Lord John Berkeley, Baron of Stratton, and Sir George Carteret, and had been named New Jersey, or *Nova Cæsarea*, after Jersey, the channel isle, of which Carteret between 1643 and 1651 had been governor.

For a while this grant was in considerable dispute, what with New York to the north and the interregnum of 1673 when, for a short time, the Dutch came back, but in 1674 the English were again in possession under the Treaty of Westminster, and Charles II confirmed his brother's grant by making Carteret sole proprietor of the eastern part of the new province, while Lord Berkeley, not so confirmed, sold his by now vague interest in the western part to Major John Fenwicke. Fenwicke, a former Parliamentarian soldier, who later became a Quaker, had as his partner Edward Byllynge, an English Quaker merchant, who before long, on the edge of bankruptcy, disposed of his share to three members of his church, Nicholas Lucas, Gawen Lawrie, and William Penn, and these three as promptly as possible bought out Major Fenwicke also. Fenwicke was glad to sell; a bad-tempered man, he had had a hard time of it trying to enforce his misty claims, with the result that he had spent a good many days and nights in local jails, put there by annoyed local magistrates. In full possession, the three partners petitioned for a formal division of the province, and on July 1, 1676, under what was called the "quintipartite deed" (and so modern man need not think himself entirely responsible for such dreadful terms as "unilateral" and the like) New Jersey was divided by a diagonal line running north-west from Little Egg Harbour to a point somewhere near the present Easton.

All east of this line belonged to Carteret; all west of it, or about five-eighths, to Penn and his associates.

Penn immediately began to put into effect his political and administrative talents and to express his longings for toleration. He drew up a Frame of Government for the new possession, as has been noted, which was adopted in March 1677, and in August of that year the ship *Kent* arrived in the Delaware with two hundred and thirty Quakers from London and Yorkshire; and

Burlington, or as it was first called New Beverly, and then Bridlington, after the Yorkshire home of some of the first settlers, hence Burlington, was founded. A year later the *Shield* arrived with further colonists, and there was considerable Quaker settlement up and down the river. Burlington is, therefore, the dignified foster-parent of Philadelphia, and the West Jersey Frame of Government was the model for Penn's more famous Frame of Government of five years later, although the second Frame was not quite so liberal as the first. Penn evidently had come to the conclusion that one could be too tolerant.

In any case, the germ of the "Holy Experiment" had evolved, and the Quakers, described by that ordinarily kindly English diarist, John Evelyn, as "a fanatic sect of dangerous principles, who show no respect to any man, magistrate or other, and seem a melancholy, proud sort of people, and exceedingly ignorant," now had their chance to settle down and show that talent for toleration and solid acquisition in the name of the Lord which has so distinguished them. Toward this increase in esteem and respectability Penn had been a powerful aid, with his name, his father an admiral, his wealth, his charm, his eloquence, and his refusal, at least in his youth and contrary to the teachings of the great George Fox, to turn more than one cheek at a time. Any Oxford undergraduate who publicly describes the vice-chancellor of that ancient institution as "a poor mushroom," as Penn did while up at his college, Christ Church, or as it is called, "The House", is not a complete pacifist.

Three years after Burlington came the great year of 1680; great for Penn, that is, and great for Philadelphia.

In that year Penn was ready to ask the Crown, Charles II, for another tract of land in America; a tract "north of Maryland, bounded on the east by the Delaware, on the west limited as Maryland, northward as far as plantable," but this time in payment of a debt and not merely the confirmation of something for which Penn himself had paid. And the Crown was in no position to refuse; the Crown, in modern slang, was on the spot.

The Crown had borrowed £15,000 from Penn's father, Sir William, and the admiral, dying in 1670 at the comparatively early age of forty-nine, had left his son this claim in addition to the then handsome income of £1,500 a year. Nor had the Crown any more ready cash than usual. Its private overhead was large. In Charles's daybook is this note: "Mar. 28th. Paid to Duchess of Portsmouth £13,341.10s. 4 1/2D." Certainly an exact accounting, but also certainly a large sum of money—sixty-six thousand dollars at the least, which can be tripled to bring it up to date. One wonders what the four and a half pence was for. At all events, it was easier to give away the future Pennsylvania than to dig down in one's pockets, and within a year, after some bickering with New York and Maryland, on March 14, 1681, the royal deed was signed. It was more than signed; the name Pennsylvania, first spelled "Pensilvania," or Penn's Woods, was also designated in memory of Penn's father, despite his son's immediate and vigorous objections to such an honour. The Quaker in him protested against such worldly pomp, and would have protested even more strongly had he foreseen that of the forty-eight great states to come, his alone would bear the name of its original proprietor.

"Lest it be looked on as a vanity in me," Penn wrote, and offered the scrivener who drew up the charter twenty pounds to delete the name, which was not done.

History is persistently paradoxical, also persistently amusing in its own way. Pennsylvania cost exactly one thousand, six hundred and fifty-eight pounds, nine shillings, seven and ha'pence more than the Duchess of Portsmouth was costing at the moment, and if that lady had not been so expensive —she and others—the "Holy Experiment" might never have taken the shape it did. Philadelphians can be thankful to the Duchess of Portsmouth.

Fate moves in mysterious ways its wonders to perform. Sometimes its methods are bawdy.

As for the name of the future town, unlike the name of the province, that was never in question.

Penn knew exactly what he wanted to call it. It was to be known as Philadelphia, after the ancient city of Lydia, and it meant just what it said —the green country town was to be a place where everyone loved each other, and behaved better than anyone had ever behaved before, and in the Frame of Government was a special clause against backbiters, scandalmongers, defamers, and spreaders of false news. Something to be remembered.

The province and its great city-to-be got off to a fine classical start with the name of the former Latin and of the latter, Greek. Rabbath-Ammon had been the title of the Palestine original, but in the second century B.C. this had been changed to Philadelphia in honour of the Egyptian of Greek descent, Ptolemy Philadelphus, and to the pious the name meant even more than "brotherly love", for later on the Palestine city had become the seat of one of the Seven Early Christian churches.

By 1681 Penn, working hard on his Frame of Government, was ready to send out the first of his deputies, his cousin Captain William Markham of the British navy. Markham's initial job (he is supposed to have landed at Boston and at all events was in New York by June) was to iron out as much as possible boundary difficulties with Maryland and New York, read the King's proclamation, establish courts, and so on. All this he did well except for the boundary disputes, plenty of which were left to plague the new province for a long while to come. In the same year, late in the autumn, the ship *John and Sarah*, Captain Smith, arrived at Coaquannock, bearing the very first Philadelphians, and they stepped ashore into the great pines and tall hard-woods; into the cool, damp, sweet-smelling Pennsylvania autumn. The forest was not entirely deserted, however; here and there smoke rose from some small Swedish clearing, and there were Swedish farms across the Schuylkill and north along it beyond the Wissahickon and Manayunk. Up around Tacony was a Swedish settlement of some sixty-nine men with their wives and children, and several of these Swedish names are still prominent in present-day Philadelphia, while down in what is now known as the Southwark section of the city, where Gloria Dei stands, but which then was called Wicaco, was a Swedish blockhouse and another settlement.

They are a tenacious folk, the Swedes, fecund also. Three generations later the Swedish minister, Israel Acrelius, memorialized Joseph Cobson—

there must have been some English blood there, or else the corruption of a name—"who had the blessing to have his wife have twins, his cow two calves, and his ewe two lambs, all in one night in the month of March", and the services at Gloria Dei were conducted in Swedish until toward the middle of the eighteenth century.

But the grave and sober adventurers of the *John and Sarah* spoke the coming language of the province, the proud and stately language of the King James Version that was to conquer all the hinterland, and they also had the distinction of being the only English Philadelphians who ever had to undergo the rigours of real pioneering, at least on their home grounds. No preparations had been made for their coming, and winter was at hand, and so a number of them had to live for a while in caves along the bluff facing the Delaware; no great hardship according to Pastorius, the famous German immigrant, who, arriving in June of 1683 with the nucleus—nine people—of his colony of Germantown, said of the caves, "Herein we lived more contentedly than many nowadays in their painted and wainscoted palaces".

Some of the caves the passengers of the *John and Sarah* found already dug by the Indians or the Swedes, some they had to dig themselves, and in one of them, later an underground tavern known as the Penny Pot, was born the first Philadelphian, John Key. All his life he was known as "the first-born" and took much pleasure in this honour, as the "first-born" everywhere have done in their somewhat adventitious fame. "The first-born" lived to be a very old man—eighty-five; dying, that is, only nine years before the Declaration of Independence. By this time the caves had turned into a bustling, and fair, and brick-built, and most important city.

When "the first-born" was thirty-one, in 1713, William Penn, in recognition, not of any deed of his, but the deed of his mother and father, presented him with a lot between Fourth and Fifth streets. Two years later, "the first-born" sold this for twelve pounds, or sixty dollars.[1]

Two other ships had left England with the *John and Sarah*, but one had been blown south to the West Indies and the other had been icebound at Chester and did not reach Philadelphia until the following spring. In April of that year, 1682, Penn dispatched his surveyor-general, Captain Thomas Holme, from London on the ship *Amity*, and Holme, reaching his destination

[1] As is always the case with "the first-born" anywhere, John Key's title is in dispute. There are two schools of thought. Actually the first white child born on that site of Philadelphia was Edward Drinker, who opened his eyes on what was to be that large city in a log-cabin located on the main, or north-western, branch of Dock Creek, near the present junction of Walnut and Second streets. His father, a Quaker, had settled on Coaquannock several years before the coming of Penn, and Edward was born two years before that date. All, therefore, are entitled to make a choice as to who, actually, was Philadelphia's first-born.

Edward Drinker, like John Key, lived to be a very old man, not dying until after the Revolution, and one wonders whether the two old gentlemen saw much of each other and whether they quarrelled as old men are likely to do over the disputed title. The Drinker family is still prominent in Philadelphia and is one of those Quaker families distinguished generation after generation by intellect and talent. The late Henry S. Drinker was president of Lehigh University, and his son, another Henry, is a distinguished amateur musician, while one of his daughters is Catherine Drinker, the well-known biographer. Another daughter, Ernesta, was the first wife of William Bullitt, Philadelphia diplomat and recently unsuccessful candidate for mayor.

Edward Drinker's granddaughter was Elizabeth Drinker, who kept one of Philadelphia's famous diaries.

The Everly Residence (Kennedy)

THE EVERLY RESIDENCE (Kennedy)

RESIDENCE OF THOMAS SCULLY (Kennedy)

in June, immediately began to lay out the city. The following October, far along in the month—the 24th—the Lord Proprietor himself, having finished his Frame of Government, arrived on the ship *Welcome* (Captain Robert Greenway in command) at the mouth of the Delaware, from where the *Welcome* stood up-river to New Castle, at which town Penn first landed.

At New Castle, Penn showed the deeds which gave him possession of his province and received the submission of the settlers, and then proceeded to Upland, now called Chester, where he issued a call for the election of an Assembly and a Council. From Upland he went still farther up-river to Philadelphia, landing at Dock Creek, where there was already a wharf and a tavern, Philadelphia's first but not last, the Blue Anchor. Roundabout, new, and rough were the beginnings of the town.

Penn must have been heartily glad to be ashore. No wonder he spoke of his voyages as fatiguing. He used a mild word. The *Welcome*, only three hundred tons, had left Deal, England, eight weeks before and had battled gales all the way across the Atlantic. In addition to that, the plague had broken out, and of the one hundred passengers on board—Quakers bound for the new colony—thirty had died and had been buried at sea.

The name of one of the surviving passengers is so beautiful it bears repeating: John Songhurst, Quaker preacher, a member of the first Assembly and a great friend of Penn's.

On his first visit Penn stayed two years, returning to England against his will in 1684. Fate, until his sad declining years, never allowed Penn to settle down anywhere for any length of time. He was the stormy petrel of a church devoted to placidity.

During his first visit Penn, so a well-established tradition said, used for his winter quarters the jewel-like little Letitia House, which, again the tradition says, had been built for him in Letitia Court down near the Delaware, a property Penn named for his daughter and later gave her. The Letitia House, which was also for a long while supposed to have been the first brick house in Philadelphia, now stands in Fairmount Park, to which it was carefully transferred at the time of Philadelphia's Bicentennial Celebration. But modern research has decided that the Letitia House was not built until somewhere between 1703 and 1715, and that Penn never saw it. Wherever he lived during that first visit, one thing is certain: Penn presided like a handsome deity over his growing colony, which for a little while was the elysium he thought it. He was immensely pleased with everything. One of the features of primitive settlements is that for a few years everyone is too busy and too afraid of the surrounding wilderness to misbehave.

This is frequently mistaken, as it was by Jean Jacques Rousseau, for the "natural man".

Penn's most dramatic and historic behaviour during this period was with the Indians, of course. He set a standard to which white men have thrilled ever since and honoured almost exclusively in its breach. Whether the great treaty of Schackamaxon with its Treaty Elm ever took place as described is not known, as there are no records of it; but something of the kind happened, and the Historical Society of Pennsylvania has a wampum belt presented

c

to Penn by the Indians, while the Schackamaxon tradition, at all events, is
a magnificent one which for decades shook the liberal world. Voltaire called
the supposed treaty the only one ever made between Christians and savages
"that had not been ratified by an oath, and that was never broken," and
in 1777, when the English occupied Philadelphia, they placed a guard around
the Treaty Elm so that no harm would come to it.

Penn's attitude toward the Indians was his attitude toward all men,
until one or the other of them betrayed him, and perhaps it is the most
successful of attitudes, for although a man is likely to be betrayed eighty
times out of a hundred, it is the twenty times he isn't which sends the world
forward. And Penn, although he died in poverty and great distress, has
lived. And his name is great. And what it stood for has affected greatly
American thinking. No name more. The Indians adored him and called
him "the white truth-teller". They trusted him completely and made him
a chief, with the name of Onas, and he moved among them freely, sitting
cross-legged at their councils and pretending to smoke their peace pipes—
although he didn't smoke—and occasionally joining in their games, and
learning to some extent their language. He had, to be sure, an easier task
than most.

The Lenni-Lenape—the Delawares—had known the white man for two
generations and had been well treated by the Swedes; moreover, like many
other Indian nations in the future, the white man appeared as a bulwark
against the dangers of their own race; in this case the fierce Five Nations,
or if you count the Tuscaroras, the Six Nations, of New York. The Delawares
were allied to the Five Nations, but were looked upon by the Iroquois with
not too much respect. The Iroquois called the Delawares "women", because
they were weak and not as warlike, but also they called them "the grandfathers", because the Delaware nation was an old one. Penn, however,
would have got along well with almost any primitive man; he had neither
fear nor reservations. "Affable and friendly with the humblest," so he is
described. "The handsomest, best-looking, and liveliest of gentlemen." At
the time, as has been said, he was in his late thirties; tall, broad-shouldered,
with magnificent eyes, arched eyebrows, and very particular about his wigs
and clothes.

He liked to wear a broad silk sash of light blue and was fond of sports,
especially riding, boating, and jumping.

Penn did not behave as he did because of Quakerism, but became a
Quaker because Quakers were supposed to behave as he thought men should.
"I have great love and regard toward you," he said in a message to the
Indians, "and desire to win and gain your love and friendship by a kind,
just and peaceable life."

Compare this with the statements and behaviour of some of the other
colonists, of which the following letter written in 1628 from Manhattan
by the Rev. Jonas Jansen Michielse to the Rev. Adriaen Smout of Amsterdam
is typical:

*As to the natives of this country, I find them entirely savage and wild, strangers
to all decency, yea, uncivil and stupid as garden poles, proficient in all wickedness*

and godlessness; devilish men, who serve nobody but the Devil, that is, the spirit which in their language they call Menetto; under which title they comprehend everything that is subtle and crafty and beyond human skill and power. They have so much witchcraft, divination, sorcery and wicked arts that they can hardly be held in by bands and locks. They are as thievish and treacherous as they are tall; and in cruelty they are altogether inhuman, more barbarous, far exceeding the Africans.

One hears the distant war-whoops and the dancing drums of Sitting Bull and Red Cloud, and sees two centuries and more of massacre and pillage and the taking of scalps in the Rev. Jonas Michielse's "Christian" statement.

Fate shapes itself early in the affairs of men and follows a pattern. New York has always bullied Philadelphia, most of the time unconsciously. The Iroquois bullied the Lenni-Lenape and stole from them, and called them "women" and "grandfathers". With the building of the Erie Canal in 1825, New York, a minor town, began to surpass its greater but duller rival to the south, and since then has repeatedly stolen both its "thunder" and its wealth. The seeds of the first theft were planted in 1683, the year of the supposed Treaty of Schackamaxon. At that time the leading sachem of the Delawares was Tamend, or Tammany, a great friend of Penn's and described as an extremely noble and wise man. Years later, with the growth of separatist feelings in the colonies, the more radical, the democrats, organized themselves into bands known as the Sons of Liberty, or, in derision of the societies of St. George, St. Andrew, and St. David, more loyalist in tone, called themselves the Sons of St. Tammany.[1] After the Revolution, on May 12, 1789, William Mooney, an upholsterer of New York, organized formally the Society of St. Tammany, or the Columbian Order, for a long while an extremely discreet and upright body to which automatically all democratic-thinking New Yorkers belonged. What it eventually became, however, is hardly fair to an Indian chief who was spoken of as having been blessed in the highest degree with "wisdom, virtue, prudence, charity, meekness, hospitality; in short, with every good and noble qualification that a human being may possess".

And the name doesn't belong to New York, anyway. Tammany is buried outside of Doylestown, near Philadelphia.

Philadelphia, at all events, is the only city in the United States which has an Indian camping-ground in its very midst, and in perpetuity. That it has never been used for this purpose is something else, although it has long been a matter of debate, among Philadelphians who know of it, what the police would do if some itinerant brave and his family decided to put up wigwams and light a cooking fire. An enticing legal question. Meanwhile, the Indians would be very uncomfortable unless they were used to roughing it, for the plot is paved with cinders and surrounded by tall buildings. It is in what is now the business centre of the city, at Broad and Walnut

---

[1] This is not to imply that there were not numerous excellent patriots among the sons of St. George, St. Andrew, and St. David. There were, on the whole, probably as many as there were among the sons of St. Tammany; but naturally, during the Revolution and the War of 1812, the British saints were open to malicious gossip. They still are.

streets, directly behind the Ritz-Carlton Hotel. John Penn, grandson of William Penn, himself a Lord Proprietor, although by that time the title meant little politically if a great deal financially, owing to the increase of values of the great estate in the new province, presented this plot to the Indians in 1755. In 1922 five Seneca chiefs from New York came down for a ceremony presided over by John Penn-Gaskill Hall, a direct descendant of William Penn, 2nd, Penn's only surviving son by his first marriage.[1]

The Lord Proprietor when he left his province in 1684 intended to return shortly; he stayed in England for almost fifteen years, and when he did return in 1699 his visit in many ways was not a happy one. The auspices from the beginning were bad: the ship on which he sailed, the *Canterbury*, did not leave the Isle of Wight until September 9, and so Penn and his new wife, Hannah Callowhill, daughter of a Bristol linen merchant, and the two surviving children of his first marriage, his daughter Letitia and his son William, did not arrive until winter had gripped the town and bay, and in the town, the "green" and "wholesome" town, and along the bay was a grim, ochre visitor, the yellow fever. The visitor was to come again through the decades, and more terribly; this was its first visit. "Great was the fear that fell on all flesh," wrote Thomas Story. "I saw no lofty or airy countenance —nor heard any vain jesting—but every face gathered paleness, and many hearts were humbled." But at least this was fortunate, Penn had brought with him a great American and Philadelphian in the person of his secretary and confidential agent, young James Logan, like Hannah Penn also from Bristol, and this was unusual and a piece of good luck, for one of Penn's weaknesses was the picking, for the most part, of incapable or even dishonest deputies.

Logan was the first of that group of men which, during the eighteenth century, made Philadelphia one of the outstanding cities of the English-speaking world.

Otherwise, it was a grey and cold arrival. Only the Indians and the older and more thoughtful Friends were unfeignedly glad to see Penn, although he was welcomed with proper formality and the symptoms of enthusiasm.

Just to make the portents worse, at Chester, where Penn arrived December 1 and spent the night, when a salute of cannons was fired, a young man had his arm blown off.

---

[1] In 1805, a mysterious "William Penn" created a furore by demanding that the rector of Christ Church marry him, although the lady in question was of such a character that she was led into the rector's home by the back door. There is a book on this subject in the library of the Pennsylvania Historical Society.

CHAPTER VI

Sea of Troubles

"... *the undeserved opposition I meet from thence sinks me in sorrow, and I cannot but think it hard measure, that while that proved a land of freedom and flourishing to them, it should become to me, by whose means it was made a country, the cause of trouble and poverty.*"

WILLIAM PENN TO JAMES LOGAN, 1710.

AND THE LORD PROPRIETOR had changed, too; he was fifty-five and no longer the eager, charming, gracious founder he had been. Already he was beginning to take on the corpulency which plagued his latter years, and the imperiousness which had always been latent in his character was now under less control; the imperiousness which years before, upon his return as a young man from the court of Louis XIV, whither his father, the admiral, had sent him, hoping to rid him of his Quakerism, had caused the acid Mr. Pepys to write: "Comes Mr. Penn to visit me. I perceive something of learning he has got; but a great deal if not too much, of the vanity of the French garb, and affected manner of speech and gait."

Nor had the fifteen years in Europe been such as to improve a man's temper or outlook on life.

To begin with, his lovely Gulielma, born Gulielma Marie Springett, daughter of Sir William Springett, a Quaker gentleman of Brayle Place, Ringmere, Sussex, and the mother of Letitia and William 2nd, had died in 1694, and two years later, his younger son, Springett. And it was to Gulielma that Penn had written his lovely letter upon his first departure to his province, and also, not to be forgotten, since they are equally typical, his extremely irritating injunctions advising punctuality, treatment of servants, and care in the selection of any companions that might be made during his absence. But both the farewell letter and the injunctions, taken together, are evidences of a deep passion. As a rule men do not bother women unless they themselves are bothered by adoration. Hannah Callowhill was a fine and handsome person, and she made Penn a good wife, but she wasn't Gulielma, and pretty soon it turned out that she didn't like the new world any better than her stepdaughter Letitia, or her stepson, William 2nd, although the latter was to see a good deal of it and make a nuisance of himself.

Hannah and Letitia were afraid of Indians and spoke more delightfully than they knew of "insolent bears".

Personal sorrows and cares, however, were only a part of it. As was inevitable with a man of Penn's personality and temperament, he had become a leading figure in the life of England; unofficial head of his church, and a propagandist and missionary for it—in 1682 he made his third missionary journey to Holland and Germany. He had become a political figure as well. Charles II had died in 1685, five months after Penn's return to England, and with the accession of Penn's intimate friend, James II, Penn found himself in high favour at court and went to live at Holland House in London to be near his sovereign. Quaker and papist—this at once got Penn into trouble, both with his own church and with all of James's numerous enemies, but Penn used his influence well and constantly in the direction of tolerance, one result of which was the Declaration of Indulgence of 1687; and few people have stopped to consider the fact that it was entirely in keeping with Penn's record to like well a man if he liked him, and to take it for granted that anybody, even a king, had a right to his own religion. One of the surest proofs that James II was a better man than prejudiced sectarian history would have us believe is that Penn liked him. This intimacy, however, did Penn no good when James lost his throne and William and Mary took his place.

Penn for a while was in grave disfavour and came near going to gaol again as he had done in his youth, but this time for political, not religious, reasons, and he was saved only by powerful friends at the new court. Accused of treasonable correspondence with James, he was told by these friends— Somers, Buckingham, Rochester and so on—that the case would be dropped, but he insisted upon a public trial, and, heard in full council before the King, was honourably acquitted. Meanwhile, this enforced retirement had been fortunate along certain lines, for Penn the author emerged again. *The Fruits of Solitude* was the result of this comparative leisure; and *The Fruits of Solitude* is a seventeenth-century classic, far finer than the tracts of Penn's impetuous youth, despite their engaging titles: *No Cross, No Crown; Innocency with Her Open Face; The Sandy Foundation Shaken* and so on. In addition to his other worries, Penn's finances were on the edge of the deterioration that eventually became complete, and during his absence his province, his "Holy Experiment", was beginning to go its own way and to forget him, except when it remembered him with annoyance.

Fifteen years is a long while for a parent not to see his child, especially in the child's formative years. And fifteen years is a long while for a man to stay away from his property. Penn was to learn the evils and penalties of absentee landlordism, and this, too, is symbolic, for absentee landlordism, both actual and spiritual, has been one of the grave liabilities of his town, and Penn, the founder, began it.

But despite the yellow fever, and despite the grey winter, Penn's heart must have been large with pride when he saw his city again. The little frontier settlement he had left in 1684, the tiny place of three hundred or so houses, brick or lumber, on the bluff facing the Delaware, its back to the great forest, had become a bustling and prosperous community of at least five thousand inhabitants, its buildings and its population more than doubled and constantly growing. Already in the town, a sure sign of growth, were a hundred or so wheeled vehicles of various kinds, and in the air was the feeling of vigour and the future.

A demure, neat town, this town at the time, despite its unpaved streets; beginning to be a bright red town from new brick. It was not yet the notoriously dirty town it was soon to become. The narrow criss-cross streets were pushing steadily north and south, and up and down the Delaware, and west into the trees toward the Schuylkill. And up the Schuylkill, and across it,

in Montgomery and Delaware and Chester counties, were numerous farm and
many of the great "manors" Penn had originally planned for the richer
Friends and other settlers. But the surest sign of growth was along and on
the Delaware, still a shining river. Here were numerous docks and ships,
and four shipyards; and on the water-front, where Penn's proposed promenade
had never been built, strolled sailors of many nationalities, adding a new
outlandish note. There were plenty of taverns for these sailors too, and for
the other visitors or residents.

When Penn had left in 1684, his town had been laid out, his government
well established, and he had sold 600,000 acres for a hundred thousand dollars.
Also his province was assuming shape with six counties, divided into twenty-
two townships. But in all the province there were only about seven thousand
souls, twenty-five hundred of them in Philadelphia. Now the population
had grown to twenty thousand, with one-fourth of it in Philadelphia proper
or its Northern and Western Liberties, the latter a term for what we would
now call self-contained suburbs with their own jurisdictions and especial
rights. Even more important, however, than material growth, which was
bound to come to this advantageously placed peninsula, the city had begun to
assume a personality of its own: the individuality which for good, and also
evil, and no matter what future changes or vast expansion were to happen,
would always remain.

The city was in its teens. Seventeen years old. A strong and muscular
adolescent. Quaker by profession, but with hot and alien blood in its veins.

Cities are like people; they grow, they mature, they age, they learn, or they
don't, they experience and make use of experience, or forget it easily, their
manners improve or deteriorate, they sin and repent, or fail to do so, but
underneath there is always the same person. This is an interesting thing
to observe, although the signs and differences are subtle. You can see them,
however, in the houses of a city, and the look of its streets and its shops, and
the appearance and dress of its inhabitants, and the furniture they use, and
the way they decorate their rooms, and the food they eat, and their accent,
and in countless other ways. No one is more stupid than the man who thinks
all cities are alike; he is the same man who talks of women as a sex, and of
men as "men," and who finds humanity level and painfully similar. Boston,
for example, is more Irish-American now than Puritan, but it is still fundamentally the Puritan city of its birth, and all one has to do is to enter a Boston
house and smell it and look about. And New York, great and bewildering
metropolis, is still the Dutch trading-post and the Dutch and English and
Huguenot town of the Revolution.

Altogether justly Philadelphia is still spoken of as the "Quaker City,"
although there are few professing Quakers left within the city limits—most
of the old Quaker families long ago turned Episcopalian, with a distinct
tendency toward ritual—and you seldom see "plain clothes", and not much
then, except at the time of the annual meeting when the country Quakers
come in. "Plain talk", too, wherever it persists, is confined largely to the
family. Even by the time of Penn's second visit, Quaker influence was
on the decline and on the defensive. Nonetheless, the seal had been set, and
the Church of England men, and the German Mennonites and Lutherans,

and the Scottish-Irish Presbyterians, and the Welsh Baptists, and the Catholics, and all the others beginning to filter in could wriggle and twist and do whatever they would and yet not escape it, any more than they can to-day.

But by the time of Penn's second arrival these various elements were at work.

In the first place, underlying everything was the Quaker belief in non-resistance and the growing Quaker desire for peace at all costs, not to mention ease and increasing estates. This placed them, except for some spirited Quakers like Logan, largely at the mercy of everyone else politically and hampered the necessary protection of the province. At the moment there were pirates operating off the mouth of the Delaware; indeed, it was rumoured that some of the wealthier merchants were in league with them, and it was even said that two who had been arrested had been secretly released and had been seen walking the streets of the city. It was hard to get the Quakers aroused to the danger. Later on they were equally unable to handle with proper firmness the inflammatory Scottish-Irish to the west. In the French-Indian War the city could not function with decision, and in the War of the Revolution and the parlous years leading up to it this strain of weakness showed again, despite the Free Quakers, the "Fighting Quakers". And even in the Civil War, although Philadelphia was a fiery northern and Republican city, and acted on the whole with great gallantry, the spirit of non-resistance, this time not in any physical sense, but an unconscious ally of the Irish immigration of the 'thirties and 'forties, produced anti-draft riots almost as sinister as those in New York. There is no doubt that the same spirit has had much to do with the supineness of Philadelphia politics.

It had not been there to begin with, however, not in the form it was now taking. Revolt begins with courage and ends with the timorousness of property. Quakerism preached physical non-resistance, but not spiritual non-resistance. A sea change had taken place. The early followers of George Fox had preached and proselytized, and had been whipped to the glory of God at cart-tails and had gone to prison. Nor was this extra caution present in the young Penn, nor ever very much in the older one. At the age of eleven he had seen "an external glory in the room", and despite the stern opposition of his otherwise devoted father, and numerous beatings, and despite many fluctuations in his youth when he went from the extremes of fashion to devoutness and back again, and even to fighting as a volunteer against an Irish rebellion which broke out in 1666 while he was managing his father's estates in Cork, he kept pretty much to his purpose as if he had a lode-star. He was as thoroughly a devotee as Joan of Arc, although, being a Quaker, a quieter one.

Not so quiet at that. In his youth he went twice to prison; once for the unlicensed publication of *Sandy Foundations Shaken;* once for "speaking in Gracechurch Street," to which he added the offence of refusing to remove his hat in court.

Not to begin with, and not much ever, although as he grew older Penn, too, became slightly more non-resistant, retaining, however, a pretty and flaying tonge when attacked. There is a story told about his second voyage over on the *Canterbury* when a vessel, thought to be a pirate, was sighted while Penn was walking the deck with his young secretary, James Logan. Penn went below to pray. Returning to the deck, the danger over, Penn found his secretary among those who had prepared to defend the ship, and upbraided him for his bloodthirstiness. Logan, always a man of great courage, retorted: "If thee didn't want me to fight, why didn't thee order me below?"

But one feels that the episode, if true, was the result of a deliberate effort of the will on Penn's part. He was living up to a theory not altogether sympathetic to his nature. At all events, he was on his way to a situation demanding firmness.

Already, by the time of his second visit, there was a Church of England party in Philadelphia, and Lutheran and Mennonite elements, and the emergence of various other sects to start the bitter quarrelling that lasted for many years. The war of the Philadelphia churches is something yet to be written, especially as it took place on a virgin field dedicated to tolerance. And this, of course, entered deeply into politics. The war of the churches did not come out into the open until around 1701, when Penn had left again for England, but it was clearly visible during his second visit as well as many other growing seams in the structure.

The Church of England men, soon to be known as the "Hot Church Party", under the leadership of Judge Robert Quarry of the Admiralty Court, bitterly resented almost from the start, the Quakers: their manners, their pacifism, their ascendancy, and their quiet, not un-smug, theory of tolerance. One of the rewards of Episcopalianism is to be able to look down your nose in a Christian fashion at your neighbours. And if you are officially discouraged from doing this, it is annoying.

The Church of England men began to move toward depriving Penn of his province and turning it directly over to the Crown, as had happened for two years between 1692 and 1694, when Penn had been in temporary disfavour at court, and as had happened to New Jersey in 1688. Nor had the Quakers met the Church of England men with their customary tact; for the moment they had forgotten their live-and-let-live beliefs. Petitioning for a parish, the petition of the Church of England men had been denied, and some of the Church of England men had been gaoled for a while. Penn was furious about this, and the petition was shortly granted; but the damage had been done.

Nor were the Church of England men to be trifled with. As usual they were wealthy, well educated, and aggressive, and as a result exercised power out of proportion to their numbers. In 1695 they built the first Christ Church, thirty-five or so years later to be replaced by the present lovely structure, now almost lost among the warehouses of Second Street, and their numbers were constantly growing. Within a year after the first rector, Mr. Clayton, came out from England, his congragation increased from fifty to seven hundred members.

Meanwhile the Lutherans and Mennonites, centring mostly in Germantown, sided with the Quakers or Church of England men as best suited them, and in the outlying districts were enough Scottish-Irish to send, increasingly, anti-Quaker members to the Assembly. The Welsh Baptists and the few Welsh Church of England men, up along the Schuylkill and west of it, were too clannish as a whole, and too occupied with local affairs, to make much

C*

trouble. But Penn's control, and that of his followers, was slipping away, although the Lord Proprietorship continued as a form without much real power long after Penn's death; and during the time of Thomas Penn, the most capable of Penn's descendants, recaptured for a while its power and popularity. On their part, the Quakers managed to retain a tenuous authority in the Assembly for almost a hundred years, or up until the Revolution, by means of granting or withholding appropriations, and by the even simpler method of unbalanced representation. Bucks and the other eastern counties, although they had a minority of the population, nonetheless elected a great majority of the representatives.

Divergence and centrifugal forces were inherent in Penn's plan.

The picture presented is a somewhat depressing commentary on any attempt at complete tolerance. Like philosophic anarchy or Jefferson's dream of "the less government the better", complete tolerance is an ideal to which the human race must work, but until all men are fairly good, tolerance must be mitigated. By circumstances. By common sense. By intelligent opportunism. So long as a single bad man, or woman, remains in the world, or even a completely selfish one, governments must bear down at moments to retain any sort of order. Individuals, however Christian, must at times fight for their lives. Fortunately, the preponderance of tradition in America has been English, and not German or Latin. Logic has never bothered the Anglo-Saxon.

Penn, Pandora-like, by his proclamation of tolerance, and his missionary work in England and on the continent of Europe, and his beguiling prospectuses, half saint-like, half Chamber of Commerce, had opened the way to every form of disagreement, and it is a compliment to the early citizens of Philadelphia that the city was as peaceable as it was and that all these differences were finally adjusted. But a certain cynicism was achieved, nonetheless, a *laissez-faire* attitude about that mysterious and inner enthusiasm, the Holy Ghost, which persists to to-day.

Philadelphia has yet to produce a Roger Williams or a Nathan Hale.

Driven inwards, man's natural intolerance produced, as well, a quiet and hardy snobbishness: social, religious, and political.

At once from all over northern Europe and the British Isles men seeking tolerance, also, a good many of them, increasing land values, had begun to pour into the "Holy Experiment". Scores of ships began to arrive annually, each shipload with its carefully done-up, watertight bales of convictions and prejudices; each individual, in that century of religious controversy, determined to maintain his point of view. And from the other colonies, from New York and New England, and even tolerant Maryland, free-thinking and energetic men began to immigrate to the lands of the Delaware. And this had its advantages as well as its disadvantages, as both the future and the immediate present proved.

In no time at all, Philadelphia began to grow. To become a city. In population. In wealth. In breadth and diversity of point of view, and the last resulted in a really "Golden Period" from about 1720 to 1800. Men of talent were attracted from everywhere, including many, like Benjamin Franklin, from other American towns, and men of talent were born and encouraged to expand. The diversity of national strains was also a good thing; although oddly enough, heterogeneity turned rapidly into homogeneity, and remained such, to make Philadelphia one of the most homogeneous of American cities, and one of the most American.

Despite its beginnings and the huge immigration—Irish in the earlier decades of the nineteenth century; German a little later on; Jewish, Italian, South European more recently—that has poured into Philadelphia, the city has kept its integrity to a marked degree, and its national character. There is a far-spread Italian quarter, a city in itself, and many scattered smaller ones; a large German quarter, and many smaller German districts; Philadelphia has foreign quarters of every kind, and foreign-language newspapers are published in a score of different tongues: Spanish, Armenian, Hungarian, Russian, Lithuanian, Ukrainian, Yiddish, the list is endless. And yet no city more quickly puts its stamp upon new-comers. Despite all their variety, before long they begin to look like Philadelphians, dress like Philadelphians, think like Philadelphians, and talk like Philadelphians; the last, in its better brackets, a pleasant, quiet, rather precise tongue; in its lower brackets, a careless and slovenly speech, but in either case stemming from the same roots and unmistakable anywhere.

The original strains, the principal ones, were three: English—the majority of the Quakers were English, although a great many of them were Welsh—German and Welsh.

The Germans came almost at once. Penn had preached among them on his mission trips to the continent of Europe, and they knew all about him. Some of the Germans were Quakers; the ideals of the others, the Mennonites especially, were similar to those of the Quakers. At the same time Welsh settlers began to pour in by the hundreds. In 1683 over fifty ships arrived crowded with new Americans. The majority of these original Welsh settlers were Quakers; the Baptists came later, although a few, as has been said, were Church of England men. For the most part the Welsh did not settle in the city itself, but on the Schuylkill and west of it in townships that began to blossom with such names as Merion, Haverford, and Radnor. The Welsh were the original "main-liners", an esoteric term which means a great deal to Philadelphians and which, for the benefit of those who are not Philadelphians, will be explained later.

Philadelphia and its suburbs are thick with Welsh names, especially among the more prominent, and hardly a Philadelphia family of long standing but has Welsh blood in its veins; an inheritance that makes at least for energy, shrewdness, and imagination, if not always for candour.

The high cheek-bones of the Welsh, the sandy, or straight black hair, the narrow faces and small-boned, wiry figures, are still common in Philadelphia streets.

The Welsh purchased from Penn, to begin with, 5,000 acres of unsurveyed land, part of a larger tract he had set aside for their exclusive use. Later on, they obtained a tract of 40,000 known as the Welsh Barony.

The first German of prominence to arrive was Francis Daniel Pastorius, founder of Germantown, who reached Philadelphia, as has been noted, in the autumn of 1683 on the ship *America* out of Deal, England.   With Pastorius were nine other German settlers, forerunners of the large immigration immediately to follow.   Six weeks after Pastorius, came what were called the Mennonite Weavers, and from that time on German immigration was an established thing; but then, history immediately becomes contradictory the moment you speak of national strains.   The Welsh were pretty pure in their Celtic inheritance, but just as the "Pennsylvania Dutch"—the majority of the German Mennonites who came later—were not Dutch, but German Palatinates, so most of Pastorius' early followers, the first Mennonites, were not Germans but the descendants of Swiss and Dutch Protestant families who had moved into Germany.   The Mennonite Church was founded in Zurich in 1523.

To the west then, out through the lovely valleys of Chester County, were the Welsh, and up along the Schuylkill on the far side of the Wissahickon, in Roxborough and toward Norristown, were the Welsh, too; and to the right of the Welsh, a wedge spreading out fanwise from their settlement in Germantown into Montgomery and Bucks counties, were the Mennonites with their various growing sects, conservative and liberal; Old Order, or Amish, who wear beards and are opposed to everything modern, and who sing hymns of the Ausbund of 1571 to tunes never printed, and Dunkers, or Brethren in Christ, similar to the Amish, and who forbid buttons on clothes.   In the more cosmopolitan precincts of Germantown was the mother church of the General Conference.

Richard Frame, Philadelphia's first poet, and not a very good one, wrote in 1692 these lines about Germantown:

> *The German Town of which I spoke before,*
> *Which is at least in length one mile and more,*
> *Where lives High German People and Low Dutch,*
> *Whose trade in weaving Linnen Cloth is much.*

Side by side the Welsh names and the Mennonite names persist in the little towns and villages and the farms immediately adjacent to Philadelphia, and a number of the old customs persist too among the Mennonites.

These "Germans" added another strong thread to the texture of Philadelphia, and, in a sober way, a colourful one.   They were dogged, earnest, home-loving and, save for the small, more fanatical sects, devoted to books and paintings and music.   They were good farmers and good manufacturers; inspired craftsmen.   Much of Philadelphia's love of painting and its one-time pre-eminence in that art, and much of Philadelphia's real and indigenous and pervading love of music, not superimposed like the music of some other cities, are due to these Mennonites.   Also to these Mennonites, together with the Moravians who came around the middle of the eighteenth century under Count Zinzendorff, but who settled for the most part far from the city at Bethlehem and in other sections of the Lehigh Valley and west of it, are due Philadelphia's good printing and a great deal of its fine and peculiarly Philadelphian cooking.

The Mennonites laid out Germantown and incorporated it as a borough in 1689, and pre-empted the waters of the Wissahickon for mills of various kinds. The first paper-mill in the province was built somewhere around 1693 on Paper Mill Run, a small creek emptying into the Wissahickon, by David Rittenhausen, whose ancestors before they emigrated from Holland into Germany had been papermakers for many generations. This David, the name was anglicized to Rittenhouse, was the father of the more famous David, mathematician, philosopher, and revolutionary, who was one of the group of brilliant men who adorned the Philadelphia of the eighteenth century, and the name Rittenhouse has attached itself to Philadelphia almost as much as the name of Penn or Franklin, although most of the people who use it for their laundries and bakeries and other businesses do not know its origin.

If they knew that it meant "to live or be apparelled as a knight", they would be pleased.

Germantown retains many of its original features; a long wide street with a number of fine old houses still left on it, wide tree-shaded side streets, with houses set back on their lawns, many churches, and an air of deceptive demureness and quiet. Beyond it are the reaches of Chestnut Hill. It is the most interesting of the Philadelphia suburbs, and from the beginning has had a character and will of its own. It is, as a matter of face, Penn's "green countrie towne", substituting for the original, and to begin with was an extremely selective community, unless you were a Mennonite; Philadelphia's first "restricted real-estate development". You weren't allowed to settle there unless you were properly accredited, and there was a curfew law prohibiting inns from taking in a traveller after nine o'clock at night unless he was equally well introduced.

One has a vision of weary men and women walking the streets of Germantown until dawn. No one is more exclusive than a refugee.

But politically the men of Germantown were more liberal than they were socially. In 1688 they issued the first American protest against slavery. So Germantown can be called truthfully the birthplace of Abolition, not Boston, although it was not until a hundred and thirty years later that the term meant much.

Pastorius—his real name was Francis Daniel Scepers—was a remarkable man, a spiritual descendant of Erasmus. Born in 1651, three years after the close of the Thirty Years' War at Sommerhausen on the Main, Franconia, he attended four universities and spent many years travelling and studying from one end of Europe to the other in intimate friendship with the intellectuals of his time. He became a famous scholar himself and a leader of the Frankfurt Pietists. When he first arrived in Philadelphia he lived in one of the caves facing the Delaware, and then, before establishing Germantown, for a while in a little house he had built himself, thirty feet long, fifteen wide, the windows of which were oiled paper because of the scarcity of glass. Over the door in Latin was this welcome, and also this bit of Teutonic assumption and exclusiveness:

"A little house, but a friend of the good; remain at a distance, ye profane."

Welsh to the west and north, Germans to the north, Swedes to the south, and at the centre, on the hour-glass between the Delaware and the Schuylkill,

English Quakers and English churchmen, and more and more immigrants from all over the world as the nucleus of a cosmopolitan city. On the ship *America* which had brought over Pastorius were eighty passengers, and among them had been Roman Catholics, Anabaptists, Lutherans, Calvinists, and Episcopalians.

Penn had other problems besides the ones mentioned. The three counties to the south where the Swedes lived wanted nothing to do with Penn's Woods. Penn settled this with his usual common sense. He let them depart in peace to help found the state of Delaware, although until 1776 the governor of Pennsylvania was still their chief executive. Penn also took effective measures against the pirates, doing a little under-cover detective work. He could not settle the perpetual boundary disputes with Maryland, although he did the best he could; nor the church quarrels; nor the resentment against his Lord Proprietorship, and, as a side issue of this, resentment against his great private holdings. There were two sides to this resentment; the Church Party wanted greater nearness to the Crown, but there was a growing sentiment as well toward greater independence for the province. In the latter were the seeds of the American Revolution.

And above all, Penn could not check the increase in wealth and fashion. In worldliness.

The devil when he attacks the godly between their shoulders and their knees is a very handsome and beguiling fellow.

CHAPTER VII

Growth of a City

"You shall be governed by laws of your own making and live a free, and if you will, a sober and industrious people."

WILLIAM PENN.

PEOPLE WERE GROWING rich, including a good many Quakers. Fine houses were being put up, and out in the country fine baronial estates, with fine baronial houses on them, were shaping themselves. In his original plan for his provinces, Penn, a country gentleman himself, had intended just such estates and landowning upper-class, but had changed his mind in favour of "plain and well-intending people". Now Fate had taken this out of his hands. Almost at once, increase in real-estate values had destroyed his conception of a "green countrie towne". The rich could have their trees and lawns and space, as they always have had; as for the middle class, the small merchants and mechanics, they began to live in crowded if respectable quarters; as for the poor, they, as always, began to live in hovels and slums.

The pressure of demand had been too much for Deputy Governor Markham. He began to divide and subdivide, and where he didn't, many of the original owners did. That peculiar and malodorous feature of Philadelphia, the alley, began to appear, where you take a city block and cut a narrow street directly through it and build on it a row of tiny and sunless houses so that crime and disease and vice of all kinds can flourish conveniently near to the well-to-do and supposedly clean.

Penn's spacious town, its population intelligently controlled, 10,000 acres for its site, was gone for good, although it must have been still a delightful place compared to seventeenth-century London. And it had become much more urbane and well dressed and luxurious than when Penn had last seen it.

In addition to those who were becoming rich, a certain number of the original settlers had been wealthy, both Quakers and churchmen.

Until recently, for thirty years or so the most popular school of American history, fictional or actual, has taught that America was settled by the rejected of Europe. A romantic thought, ministering to individual prejudices and complexes; but not so. As with most other places in the country, the immigration to Philadelphia was normal: a certain number of leaders of wealth and education, a large stratum of plainer farmers and artisans, a percentage of rogues and adventurers. The only difference, still existing, was that these classes were much more fluid in the New World; you could rise to one, or descend from one, much more readily. The modern American cannot excuse any of his faults by blaming them on his ancestors—the majority were good people. Dukes did not emigrate, but then, neither did the lazy or poor-spirited; they stayed at home. Nor were all the Quakers by any means "plain folk" any more than was William Penn; any more than were all the Welsh Baptists; any more than were men like Daniel Pastorius. In those days the Baptist Church was steadily gaining power in Wales. During the seventeenth century many cultured English families, a number of them connected with the English aristocracy, became Quakers. Under the sober surface gravity of their church, they still cherished a deep love of comfort and restrained luxury: good food, good wine, and good clothes. Many of them arrived in Philadelphia with numerous servants; some even with packs of foxhounds.

Fox-hunting, such as it then was, flourished from an early date in the country adjoining Philadelphia. Penn himself on his second visit imported Tamerlane, a thoroughbred stallion out of Godolphin Arabian, the famous barb. He was a fearless rider and proud of his stables at Pennsbury. The tradition of horsemanship among the wealthier Quakers and in Philadelphia as a whole is almost as old as the city.

Nor did Penn in other ways do anything to rebuke the growing luxury, nor is there any hint that it bothered him. He, too, loved stately living and good food and the best of wine. A fine house, the Slate Roof House, on Second Street, had been built for him, and he lived there the first winter and used it throughout as his city residence; but in the spring he moved up to Pennsbury on the Delaware, where a really magnificent country place had been made ready: a brick house with its outbuildings, two and a half stories high and sixty feet long by thirty, surrounded by lawns and formal gardens, and the vistas beloved by the period. Penn had spent five thousand pounds on this house. Trees had been transplanted from Maryland, wild flowers had been domesticated to grow beside imported varieties, the lawns had been seeded with English grass. Gardeners had been sent over from England. There was a carefully selected wine cellar. Twenty or more servants and farm-hands, most of them black, some of them slaves, looked after the place. There were five gardeners and four carpenters, and Penn gave fine dinners, and came down to Philadelphia in a twelve-oared barge, or on the rutted muddy road in a four-horse coach or, occasionally, a calash.

He was very active, spending much time in Philadelphia on matters of state or business, and driving or riding about his province. And he visited his Indian friends a great deal, accompanied by his wife Hannah and his daughter Letitia, and took much delight in these visits and conferences and feasts. When he went back to England, part of his luggage was a pair of buckskin breeches and a dozen bottles of Madeira, and at Pennsbury there were always Indian wigwams on the lawns of "English grass", set up by chiefs who had come for council.

But you can see how all this offended the simpler Quakers and annoyed the churchmen, and how with justice the Assembly regarded Penn as an interloper and an absentee landlord and a meddler in affairs not his. After all, they had come to this country, and settled here, and made the town, and burned their bridges. Who was Penn to come over whenever he felt like it and tell them what to do? He was still an Englishman. One Bugg, and a good name for him, an apostate Quaker turned Church of England, had this to say, and much more, in a tract called *News from Pennsylvania*, published in London in 1703. A nasty fellow, Francis Bugg:

Our present Governor, William Penn, wants the sacred unction, tho' he seems not to want majesty, for the grandeur and magnificence of his mien (tho' his clothes be sordid in respect to his mind, being not arrayed in royal robes) is equivalent to that of the Grand Mogul, and his word in many cases as absolute and binding. The gate of his house (or palace) is always guarded by a janissary armed with a varnished club of nearly ten feet long, crowned with a large silver head, embossed and chased as an hieroglyphic of its master's pride. There are certain days a week appointed for an audience, as for the rest you must keep your distance. His corps du gard generally consists of seven or eight of his chief magistrates, both ecclesiastical and civil, which always attend him, and sometimes there are more. When he perambulates the city, one, bareheaded, with a long white wand on his shoulder, in imitation of the Lord Marshall of England, marches grandly before him and his train, and sometimes proclamation is made to clear the way. At their meeting-houses, first William leads the van like a mighty champion of war, rattling as fast as the wheels of his leathern conveniency (i.e. the state coach referred to). After him follow the mighty Dons according to their several movings, and then for the chorus the Feminine Prophets tune their Quail pipes for the space of three or four hours, and having ended as they began with howlings and yawlings, hems and haws, gripings and gaspings, they spend the remainder of the day in feasting each other, and tomorrow they go into the country, and so on from meeting-

house to meeting-house, till, like the Eastern armies in former times, they have devoured all the provisions both for men and beasts about the country, and then the spirit ceasing, they return to their own outward homes.

At the Slate Roof House on January 29, 1700, was born John Penn, "The American", Hannah Callowhill's first child. ". . . a comely lovely babe", Isaac Norris called him, sending the news to London, "and has much of his father's grace and air, and hope he will not want a good portion of his mother's sweetness . . ." Which John Penn most certainly did.

But John Penn has at least this undeserved credit: "The American" was born at the very beginning of the first great century of America.

Meanwhile, neither the Slate Roof House nor the arrival of a son and half brother, nor Pennsbury, for all its stateliness and luxury and formal gardens, made Hannah Penn and Letitia any the more content. The formal gardens of Pennsbury were too near the forests and the "insolent bears". Penn, writing to James Logan in September of 1701, complains: "I cannot prevail upon my wife to stay and still less with Tish. I know not what to do."

He wished to leave them in America, expected to be back soon. Instead, he left with all of them, and only his son William returned.

Gabriel Thomas, a lyric Friend, who, coming over on the ship *John and Sarah* in 1681, resided in Philadelphia for fifteen years, has left a detailed description of the early city in his *A Historical Description of Philadelphia*, published in London in 1698.

Gabriel Thomas saw everything through rose-coloured spectacles, and his pamphlet set a standard for real-estate promotions which has never been bettered—all he lacked were some bathing girls. But there must have been a good deal of truth in what he said.

After describing the Indians and suggesting, as Penn did, that they might be the ten lost tribes of Israel, a belief very popular at the time and which persisted for a long while, and after a paragraph devoted to the Dutch and what he calls the "Sweeds", he finally comes to the city.

Like everyone else he finds its sudden growth a miracle:

Since that time the industrious inhabitants have built a noble and beautiful city and called it Philadelphia, or Brotherly-love (for so much the Greek word Philadelphia imports) which contains a number of houses all inhabited; and most of them stately, and of brick, generally three stories high, after the mode of London, and as many as several families in each. There are very many lanes and alleys, as first, Huttons-lane, Morris-lane, Jones'-lane, wherein are very good buildings; Shorters-alley, Yowers-alley, Wallers-alley, Turners-lane, Sikes-alley, and Flowers-alley. All these alleys and lanes extend from the Front-street to the Second-street. . . . There are also, besides these alleys and lanes, several fine squares and courts within this magnificent city; as for the particular names of the several streets contained therein, the principal are as follows, viz.: Walnut-street, Vine-street, Mulberry-street, Chestnut-street, Sassafras-street, taking their names from the abundance of those trees that formerly grew there; High-street, Broad-

street, Delaware-street, Front-street, with several of less note, too tedious to insert here.

It hath in it three fairs every year, and two markets every week. . . . More-over, in this province are four great market-towns, viz. Chester, the German-town, New-castle, and Lewis-town, which are mightily enlarged in this latter improve-ment. Between these towns the water-men constantly ply their wherries; likewise all those towns have fairs kept in them; besides, there are several countrey villages, viz., Dublin, Harford, Merioneth, and Radnor in Cumbry; all of which towns, villages and rivers took their names from the several countries from whence the present inhabitants came.

Gabriel Thomas then goes on to describe the harvests and the fertility of the land: *"twenty to thirty bushels of wheat for every one they sow. . . . Poor people, both men and women, will get near three times more wages for their labour in this countrey, than they can earn either in England or Wales."* For ten or fifteen pounds you could buy one hundred acres, but land within the city that could have been bought for fifteen or eighteen shillings a lot had, in twelve years, risen to "fourscore pounds in ready silver", and some larger lots, purchased for three pounds, within two years had been sold for a hundred pounds apiece. Stone of all kinds, building and otherwise, was plentiful, such as "tile-stone" with which "governour Penn covered his great and stately pile, which he called Pennsbury-house". There is also, let it be noted for the future, "iron-stone or oar (lately found) which far exceeds that in England, being richer and less drossy". Already preparations were being made to work this ore; and coal, too, had been discovered, and on the Delaware front were large wharves, and ships of two and three hundred tons' burden could come up to the city. As for the fruits, the nuts, the melons, the grapes, the wildfowl, the fish, the healthful herbs—everything a man could want—there was, and this was of course true, a prodigious plenty, and although wine was not as yet made commercially, ale and small beer were being made, and wine in various households, and, unlike Europe, adulteration of these products would probably never happen "through a natural probity so fixed and implanted in the inhabitants, and (I hope) like to continue".

It is a busy scene Gabriel Thomas paints: tradesmen with every kind of shop, mechanics and artisans of all descriptions; silversmiths, goldsmiths, "wheel- and mill-wrights, joiners, braziers, pewterers, dyers, fullers, comb-makers, wyer-drawers, cage-makers, watch-makers, clock-makers, sadlers, collar-makers, barbers, printers, book-binders"; and scores of others. But so good and God-fearing and robust were the inhabitants that two large classes of men, found almost everywhere else, were noticeably absent: "Of lawyers and physicians I shall say nothing", writes Gabriel Thomas, "because this countrey is very peaceable and healthy. Long may it so continue, and never have occasion for the tongue of the one, nor the pen of the other, both equally destructive to men's estates and lives."

Could Gabriel Thomas have looked into the future he would have seen that within a hundred years Philadelphia was to become the great medical centre of the country, a position it maintained for a long while, and a great legal centre as well. And he would also have seen recurrent visits of the yellow ghost which had greeted Penn on his return, and quite a lot of the smallpox. During most of the nineteenth century he would also have seen typhoid, as endemic as malaria in the rice-fields of Charleston. He would have heard, had his ears been tuned to air waves not yet on the ether, the phrase, "Philadelphia lawyer". But he did divine the employment problem which is present in any country where there is free or cheap land and much opportunity. Maidservants were paid the huge wage of from six to ten pounds a year—thirty to fifty dollars, "with very good accommodation". Even at that, a lot of them married menservants, or other young men, and went out on to the land.

Women were scarce, a pretty maidservant didn't have to remain a cook for long: she became a wife. Most young women of all classes were married before they were twenty, and immediately, if they had any money, increased the competition.

". . . Once in that noose," says Gabriel Thomas, with unusual acerbity, "[they] are for the most part a little uneasie, and make their husbands so too, till they procure them a maid servant to bear the burden of the work, as also in some measure to wait upon them too."

But outside of this inconvenience there was not another fly in the ointment.

Philadelphia already far exceeded its namesake in Lydia; "a noble town-house or guild hall" had been put up, a handsome market house, and—sinister note in this paradise—"a convenient prison". How necessary that already was, we shall see. There were numerous fine places, especially that of Edward Shippey (sic! Shippen is the name), who had an orchard and gardens "adjoyning to his great house that equalizes any I have ever seen, having a very famous and pleasant summer-house erected in the middle of his garden, abounding with tulips, pinks, carnations, roses (of several sorts), lilies, not to mention those that grow wild in the fields". But this was only one of the "many curious and spacious buildings" which the gentry had erected for "their countrey houses" and for their city houses as well.

As for the dispositions and appearance of the inhabitants, these matched the physical surroundings.

"Jealousie" among men was very rare; an old maid was hardly to be met with; and "the Christian children" born in Philadelphia were "generally well favoured". Gabriel Thomas had never seen a single one with "the least blemish". And then, lest anyone think that perhaps he had some ulterior motive in this enthusiasm, he prefaces his final praise with this disarming statement:

Reader, what I have here written, is not a fiction, flam, whim, or any sinister design, either to impose upon the ignorant, or credulous, or to curry favour with the rich and mighty; but in mere pity and pure compassion to the numbers of poor labouring men, women and children in England, that are wandering up and down looking for employment, who need not here lie idle a moment, much less vagabond or drone it about. Here are no beggars to be seen, nor indeed have any here the least temptation to take up that scandalous lazy life.

Gabriel Thomas did not notice the slightest cracks in the new edifice; no schisms. It stood as four-square and true as Penn had intended it. The lion lay down with the lamb, and he specifically mentions the tolerance the Church of England men and the Quakers showed toward each other.

At an early date Philadelphians acquired the habit of seeing only what they wanted to see. For the first decade of its existence Philadelphia in reality was a small frontier settlement, comfortable but rough. Then it began to take on more luxury.

But we have more objective testimony to prove that the infant city speedily became, at least for most of its inhabitants, a pleasant place in which to live.

Twelve years after the publication of Gabriel Thomas's description, an English gentleman, Mr. Richard Castleman, shipwrecked in 1710 on a voyage from Bermuda, came to Philadelphia to recuperate, and stayed for many months and was loath to leave. He too found "a noble, large and populous city" with houses that cost six thousand pounds to build: a place where all religions were tolerated, which, Mr. Castleman shrewdly observes, is one way to increase a city's wealth; and a place where any honest man could make an excellent living and "even the meanest single woman marry well". And he, too, thought the city—it was still a town and a small one—exceptionally healthy. Even the Philadelphia horses were healthier than horses elsewhere. Like Gabriel Thomas, Mr. Castleman saw little occasion for physicians. The climate was so good that the people could cure—by means of simples —the minor diseases likely to afflict them. Mr. Castleman praises the climate in so many words, although Penn himself had been forced to admit that it was "inconstant," and even the most loyal Philadelphian is more likely to agree with William Penn than with Richard Castleman.

As a matter of fact, save for Washington and Baltimore, and save for the spring, when it is lovely, and October, when it is equally lovely, Philadelphia has probably the worst weather in the United States. Unlike Englishmen, who find the weather an interesting topic of conversation, Philadelphians have long ago adopted a conspiracy of silence, as if it were better taste not to mention the weather at all, although they do not have to travel very far to know what it is in all its vagaries.

In summer Philadelphia is as hot and humid as Bengal; in winter it may be April one day and February the next. As a result, the city is the mecca of nose-and-throat specialists, and no Philadelphian can pronounce his R's, owing to early catarrhal difficulties; a disability which should cause barbarians to sympathize, not laugh. The sum total, however, adds to the hardiness of the citizens.

Mr. Castleman loved to walk about the streets and on warm days, with some of his new friends, to stroll out to the Schuylkill, to "Faire Mount . . . a charming spot, shaded with trees". And he found, as have so many people —once they understand them—Philadelphians the most warmly hospitable of people. He writes:

The generosity of the Philadelphians is rooted in their natures, for it is the greatest crime among them not to show the utmost civility to strangers; and if I were obliged to live out of my native country, I should not long be puzzled in finding a place of retirement, which should be Philadelphia. There the oppressed in fortune and principles may find a happy Asylum, and drop quietly to their graves without fear or want.

The city was only twenty-eight years old, and yet see how quickly a city begins to take on the many-sided character it never loses.

Thirty-four years later, another Englishman, but a younger one, Mr. William Black, coming up from Virginia in 1744 as secretary of the commission appointed by Governor Gooch of that state to confer with Pennsylvania and Maryland about a proposed treaty[1] with the Iroquois concerning certain disputed lands in Maryland and Virginia, left a diary in which he also refers to the hospitality—and in detail—of Philadelphia and, an equally favourite theme, the beauty of its women. Bad weather makes for good complexions so long as it is moist, just as it does in England. Mr. Black had a wonderful time. We shall come back to him again; but, meanwhile, here is his description of a visit to Christ Church on a Sunday, after what, to judge from his diary, was probably a hard Saturday night:

A very stately building but not yet finished. The Painting of the Alter Piece will when done, be very Grand; two Rows of Corinthian Pillars and Arches turned from the one to the other Supports the Roof and the Galleries; the Peughs and Boxes were not all done, so that everything seem'd half finished. I was not a little surpris'd to see such a number of Fine Women in one Church, as I had never heard Philadelphia noted extraordinary in that way; but I must say, since I have been in America, I have not seen so fine a collection at one time and place.

Mr Black knew. He was a man of expedition in this respect. He made desperate love to Miss Molly Stamper, afterwards Mrs. William Bingham, mother-in-law of the famous Mrs. William Bingham.

Miss Stamper was at the time fifteen, and Mr. Black, having what psychologists call "distributive attention", also fell in love, but not so desperately, with a beautiful young Jewish friend of Miss Stamper's, having met both at a party where he had heard "good singing by ladies".

That is one side of the picture, here is the other.

Men and women, high or low, have a disheartening way of being reckless, disorderly, dishonest, and, above all, persistently bifurcated.

[1] This treaty of 1744, signed at Lancaster, Pennsylvania, and presided over by Governor Thomas on the eve of one of the French wars, was probably the most important of all the early Indian treaties, and it is interesting to note that the Philadelphia government—to wit, the Pennsylvania government—was the only colonial government powerful enough, and sufficiently trusted by both the other colonies and the Iroquois, to be able to act as arbiter in the dispute, this due, among other things, to Governor Thomas' and Thomas Penn's excellent reputation with the Indians, and also, of course, to some extent to the tradition left by William Penn.

Incidentally, while we are on the subject of Indian treaties, it is the fashion among Pennsylvania historians as a whole to favour in all matters Philadelphia's especial Indians, the Lenni-Lenape, or Delaware. This is loyal, but not always accurate. The Iroquois, or Six Nations, had won their right to overlordship by performance, and the Lenni-Lenape frankly acknowledged this overlordship except on those occasions when, it not suiting them, they thought the white man would back them up. The Iroquois were a highly developed and intelligent people; a real nation. In both their war-making and their treaty-making they were like the Sioux who, generations later, were to dominate the plains of the North-west as the Iroquois had dominated the forests of the East.

CHAPTER VIII

Crime and Punishment

"There were no poor in his dominions, no thief or robber, no flatterer or miser, no dissensions, no lies, no vices."

PRESTER JOHN.

IT WAS MAX BEERBOHM, I think, who said that the past is always a little funny; and so it is, unescapably, but one often wonders why. And this tendency toward gentle amusement, or outright derision, has its categories. For example, the way our fathers and mothers dressed in their youth, or even ourselves, if we have lived long enough, is terribly funny—just as funny as our present way of dressing will seem to our sons when they are well along, and to our grandsons. On the other hand, the way our great-great-grand-fathers dressed seems to us now dignified and becoming, despite wasp-waisted satin coats and lacy stocks, or if they were not so well placed, smocks and jerkins.

A time element enters in apparently, ranging from underclothes to outer garments. Nothing is so sure of loud guffaws, in a play or motion picture, as a young lady of the 1890's removing one by one the voluminous skirts then worn and what, until recently, were called her "more intimate garments". This is so innocent and absurd that even the Watch and Ward Society of Boston can find no harm in it, and yet if we have any historical perspective we will realize that the young lady would have had a very different effect on an audience, single or multiple, of her own generation.

There is not the slightest doubt that the budding knights of the time of Maximilian I of Austria, wearing their new Spanish helmets, found the less ornamented headpieces of their immediate ancestors most amusing.

But again one often wonders why.

And one wonders especially when it comes to ancient crimes and mis-demeanours, for no matter how blithely the living may choose to regard them, and how much they may smilingly patronize them, they couldn't have been particularly blithe to the principals. A good many of them were bloody and horrible both in their commission and the retribution. And yet, in this especial field of retro-active amusement, some reason does appear, for outside of the fact that it is natural for the living to find delight in proving that the dead were no better than they, the living, are, in the vast flow of the centuries nothing seems less important than personal sorrow for the criminal, unless both had to begin with some point.

To have permanent meaning, sorrow or sin must have had contemporary meaning, grave, or gallant, or terrible. Joy needs no excuse and is universal; sorrow and crime are particular unless they have some rationale. Otherwise they are flotsam.

The "convenient" prison at Third and High, now Market, streets was not finished until 1723. Meanwhile, to meet growing demands, a cage seven feet long, seven feet high, and seven feet wide was constructed, and the "hired house of Patrick Robinson" was used as well for more important prisoners. But even the new "convenient" prison was not sufficient for long, and in 1774 the Walnut Street Prison was built just in time to receive American prisoners during the British occupation; and from then on Philadelphia prisons have kept up manfully with Philadelphia crime, culminating in what were until recently, at least, two of the grimmest schools of misbehaviour in the country: Moyamensing, the country prison—the name Moyamensing in Indian means "place of filth—dung-heap" and is appropriate—and the Eastern Penitentiary, which bears the sardonically pretty familiar name of "Cherry Hill".

Penn would have been startled by both, but although the more serious criminal code designed by him was the most tolerant in the colonies—only murder merited a death sentence—the list of minor delinquencies, confirmed by the first Assembly which met in 1682, was long. The seventeenth century never even contemplated the ordinary civil liberties which we now think inherent to the state of being a man. In the "Holy Experiment" you could think as you wanted, but outwardly you had to mind your p's and q's, and there were so many things you couldn't do that Queen Anne over in England protested and then shrugged her shoulders.

"Evil sports and games," for instance, were forbidden. The drinking of healths, "stage plays", "masks and revels", card playing, "profane swearing". Horse-racing also, despite the Quaker love of horses and William Penn's stable and blooded stallion. And intemperance, of course. But then that falls into another and a legitimate field. If you smoked in the streets you were fined twelve shillings, if you worked on the Sabbath, twenty; if you tippled on the same day, ten; a strange adjudication, as apparently it cost less to get drunk on Sunday than to do some necessary job. Even the ancient English celebration of May Day was prohibited, although those who lived close to that festivity did not find it as "innocent" as do modern commentators who are unable to speak of it without using the adjective. May Day has always been about as "innocent", no more, no less, than an evangelical camp meeting. Exultation seldom promotes virginity.

And since we are on the subject, women who had illegitimate children were publicly whipped, which is indeed adding insult to injury.

Queen Anne exclaimed that much of this, if not the last, deprived her subjects of their wholesome pleasures. The subjects themselves, as always, took the matter into their own hands. They began to break these minor laws right and left, with the exception of the Quakers, who avoided everything but possible intemperance. When they did drink, and everybody did, they held their liquor well, a quality bequeathed to their descendants. As early as 1684, "12 of 4 mo.," in the minutes of the Council is found this note: "*Evidence of the abusive epithets of Col. Talbot on the border lines, and of driving off land holders saying, 'Off you brazen nosed dog—or I'll ride you down, &c.'*"; and in 1702 George Robinson, butcher, was hailed into court "*for swearing three oaths in the market-place, and also for uttering two very bad curses.*" It is only fair to add, however, that George Robinson was also a person of "evell fame", a common swearer and a common drinker.

In the "3 Mo.," 1685, more serious matters were to the fore. On the 15th, before the Council, Thomas Lloyd, president, presiding, three pages of charges were read against Chief Justice Nicholas More, accusing him of high crimes and misdemeanours, the first impeachment proceedings in America. Nicholas More, an exceedingly arrogant and arbitrary man and an outstanding example of Penn's weakness in selecting deputies, had been sent out by Penn to act as his representative before the Assembly and had been made chief justice. The Assembly lost its case, but only because the Lord Proprietor, then in England, loyally supported his subordinate.

Colonel Talbot and the chief justice were no more than pioneers. Since then the police blotter of Philadelphia has never been empty.

In 1682 John Skeetch, also a pioneer—this time in the field of bigamy —was arrested for having two wives in Bristol, England, and for having "now taken Mrs. Smith here to wife"; and some years later, John Joyce, Jr., was presented for the same offence, although he had only two wives, not three. Even two, however, was obviously against "ye law of God and Man". In 1683 Philip England, who seems to have been a courteous citizen, complained against James Kilner for kicking a serving-maid who had spilled a slop-jar on the deck of Kilner's vessel anchored in the river; Kilner having succumbed too easily to what we all at times have wished to do.

And so the list goes—and grows.

"Joseph Knight for suffering drunkeness and evil orders in his cave"; "Two Swedish women for being drunk". Reinert Peters fined twenty shillings "for calling the sheriff a liar and rascal in open street"; Peter Shoe-maker, Jr., accusing the horses of John van der Willderness of being "unlawful because they do go over the fence where it had its full height".

Horses, too, were beginning to act like horses.

Peter Shoemaker, Jr., lost his case because, after due consideration, his fence was deemed not up to regulation.

And then there was George Muller, who not only had got drunk but had laid a wager "to smoke above one hundred pipes in one day". He was told to pay the constable two shillings for serving the warrant. And here, also, are two men of strong tempers and strong tongues: Herman Dors, who called Trinke op den Graeff a vile name, his children thieves, and his own sister a witch—plus another vile name; and Daniel Falkner, who summoned to court, behaved "like one who was last night drunk, and not yet having recovered his wits", and who shouted at the court, saying, "Ye are all fools!"

In 1685 occurred a very curious case involving one Peter Cock of Kipbah and his young neighbour, John Rambo. Peter Cock accused John Rambo of having had criminal intercourse with Bridget, Peter's daughter, and there didn't seem to be any doubt about it, although the charitably inclined might well call the incident no more than a somewhat forceful proposal of marriage.

John Rambo, it seems, shortly before Christmas of 1684, climbed upon the roof of Peter Cock's house and, prying up some boards, dropped into the room where Bridget, the heroine, was sleeping with two younger sisters, aged sixteen and nineteen. John then got into bed with Bridget, proclaiming loudly that he was resolved to be her husband, just as his brother was the husband of Bridget's older sister. With this the two younger girls, apparently very obliging, had arisen and left the room. The court decided to aid John in his bold enterprise; it fined both him and Bridget ten pounds each on condition that John would marry Bridget at once, but ardour seems to have cooled, for subsequently John was fined another one hundred and fifty pounds for non-compliance.

A reckless young man, for Bridget's brother Lasse Cock was a prominent citizen and a justice of the peace.

And now more and more cases of this kind appeared, if not so dramatic, and in 1705 the City Fathers resorted to that last exasperation of the outraged moralist and passed an act outlawing fornication and adultery. Both continued to increase, and have ever since maintained a fairly high level both among the rich and the poor. For the first, or simple, fracture, the offenders were to be fined ten pounds or could take the choice of twenty-one lashes. For the latter, or compound, fracture, the punishment was the same amount of lashes and imprisonment at hard labour for a year, or—and this has all the appearance of class legislation favouring the lecherous rich—the account could be settled for fifty pounds, if you had it, except that the innocent spouses of the guilty parties had the right to sue for divorce. But even the rich had need to exercise care, for the second offence meant seven years in jail, and no alternative.

Meanwhile numerous couples had seized time by the forelock, including John Moon and his serving-wench, Martha Williams—a mere matter of twenty and ten pounds respectively—and Elizabeth Glann and Peter Packonet; in the latter case, Elizabeth Glann being fined ten pounds and Peter Packonet nothing.

The last two indictments are mentioned, not because the offence involved is an especially original one, but because of the charming names of the male participants. What honest woman could resist a man named John Moon or one named Peter Packonet? And from the evidence it is obvious that Elizabeth Glann was frail.

More serious crimes also occurred, and in 1691 there is record of the first officially recognized murder prepense in the vicinity of Philadelphia. William Bradford, who was operating the initial printing press of the town and had not yet gone to New York, issued a pamphlet entitled, *Blood will out, or an Example of Justice in the Tryal, Confession and Execution of Thomas Lutherland, who murthered John Clark of Philadelphia, Trader—Tried and Executed at Salem, W.J. the 23 Feb.*

Those who complain of the present sordid interest in crime overlook the broadsides and pamphlets of the sixteenth and seventeenth centuries, also the fact that the one thing that can never be improved upon is vulgarity.

Thomas Lutherland had gone to the cabin of the little boat where John Clark lived, and picking up a rope had put it around John Clark's neck. He had then said, "Give me your money and I will not kill you." And, John Clark having given him the money, Thomas Lutherland had completed the strangling. The extraordinary thing about so many murders is their apparent placidity.

In 1702, the human mind being fertile, what at first glance seems a night of transvestitism disturbed the quiet of Front Street, although it was probably no more than a spontaneous forbidden "mask and revel"— a private one.

The "Holy Experiment" had now reached its majority—in 1701 it was incorporated as a city—and so there had been plenty of time, especially in those days of early marriage, for the emergence of its first "younger generation"—one of those depressing and alarming "younger generations" who, all through our history, have gone their "soft" and decadent ways, only to fight magnificently our wars when called upon.   John Simes, owner of an ordinary, was arrested for keeping "a nursery to Debotch ye inhabitants and youth of this city . . . to ye Greef of and disturbance of peaceable minds and propigating ye Throne of wickedness among us", and together with this Fagin of immorality were arrested four of his patrons, who had behaved as follows:

John Smith, who against the laws of God and those of the province of Pennsylvania "to the staining of holy profession—whatever that may mean—"and Incoridging of wickedness", the night after Christmas had dressed as a woman and had left John Simes's nursery of vice and had walked the streets openly, going from house to house.   And Edward James, his friend, who had done likewise, both at "an unreasonable time of night".   To these were added two feminine sprites who had reversed the process: Dorothy, wife of Richard Canterill, and Sarah, wife of John Stiner.   Dorothy, dressed as a man, had contented herself by "walking and dancing" in John Simes's house until the dreadful hour of ten o'clock, but the more brazen Sarah, also dressed as a man, had paraded the streets, like John Smith and Edward James, "contrary to ye nature of her sects", and to "ye grate Disturbance of well minded persons".

About the same time three barbers were fined for shaving customers on the "First Day"; and the grand jury petitioned for a ducking-stool and a house of correction in order that there might be just punishment for "scolding Drunken women, as well as Divers other profligate and Unruly persons in this place, who have become a Publick Nuisance and disturbance to the Town in Generall."

The grand jury, quaintly enough, described the ducking-stool and the house of correction as "public conveniences".   It would have been better if the grand jury had petitioned for actual "public conveniences", and then Philadelphia would have set a fashion among American cities which would have caused future generations to rise up and call her blessed.

We and the English are the only nations in the world who walk miles to "wash our hands".

Even the duel, that bane of the eighteenth and early nineteenth centuries, began to raise its murderous head, and in 1715 Peter Evans, gentleman, challenged the Rev. Francis Phillips, Church of England clergyman, in no uncertain terms:

Sir,

   You have basely slandered a Gentlewoman that I have a profound respect for, and for my part shall give you a fair opportunity to defend yourself to-morrow morning, on the west side of Jos. Carpenter's Garden, betwixt seven and 8, where I shall expect to meet you, Gladio cinctus, in failure whereof depend upon the usage you deserve from yr, etc.

I am at ye Pewter Platter.   Peter Evans

The Pewter Platter was a famous inn on Pewter Platter Alley.

The Rev. Francis Phillips seems to have been both a coward and a philanderer. He evaded the duel but made a great complaint, and Peter Evans, who to his profession of "gentleman" added the post of sheriff, arrested him. A fight in the congregation broke out, as is usual under the circumstances, and Governor Charles Gookin, who had succeeded John Evans as governor in 1709, sided with Phillips and released him. Subsequently the Rev. Francis Phillips was dismissed from his parish when word reached the Bishop of London that the clerical Don Juan had been boasting of his conquests among the ladies of his congregation.

From then on duels flourished, but in an intermittent fashion, and nothing like the way they did in the South.

The *Pennsylvania Gazette* of February 10, 1730, has this social note: "Two young gentlemen of Hibernian extraction met on Society Hill and fought a gallant duel before a number of spectators—not very usual on such occasions." As no attempt was made by either to do any damage, it was suspected that the whole thing was Irish "theater". But in 1721 Selom Fry, mariner, wounded Francis Jones and was wounded in return, and in 1750 the same thing happened to Thomas Crosse, gentleman, and Hugh Davy. During the Revolution tempers were short, and so General Conway was wounded by Colonel Cadwalader—and a good thing too. And Jonathan Dickinson Sergeant, Esq., was challenged by Gunning Bedford, Esq., both members of Congress —perhaps duels weren't so bad after all—but was rebuked by Congress. And somewhere around 1778 or '79, Henry Laurens, president of Congress, the friend of Thomas Paine, and John Penn, member of North Carolina and no relation to William Penn, were getting ready to fight a duel when, walking silently together along the street, they came to a muddy crossing. Penn, being the younger man, offered to assist Mr. Laurens, and they both laughed and suggested that the folly be called off.

John Penn of North Carolina seems to have had considerably more sense than John Penn of Pennsylvania and England.

Finally there was a mysterious duel between a Doctor W. and an even more anonymous gentleman over "a young Quaker lady" who, considering her "sect" and religion, must have been immensely pleased. The doctor, a brave man, discharged his pistol into the air and no one was hurt.

The vague beginnings of the Naval Academy in Philadelphia after the War of the Revolution—Philadelphia was the parent of Annapolis—also added its quota to Philadelphia's record in this respect. Duelling was common among the midshipmen.

By 1824 close to a hundred Americans had been killed in formal duels— no one knows how many were killed in informal ones—and of these, sixty were officers of the army or navy, including so necessary an officer as Stephen Decatur, who was only forty-one when he fell before the pistol of Captain

James Barron in 1820 at Bladensburg, Maryland. Meanwhile, a former
Vive-President, Aaron Burr, had killed on the heights of Weehawken a former
Secretary of the Treasury, Alexander Hamilton, both of whom had lived in
Philadelphia and had helped to make of it the brilliant city it was during its
years as the capital of the United States. This had happened in 1804.

As to the feeling against "masks and revels", that continued to be very
strong among the Quakers, just as their feeling against the theatre, card-
playing, dancing, and formal musical instruments such as the piano—informal
musical instruments too, such as women whistling—and these prejudices
lasted until the end of the last century. As late as 1814 a French dancing-
master announced a public masquerade ball at his house, only to be stopped
by a special Act of the legislature, and the Mummer's Parade, Philadelphia's
only public carnival, and surely one of the most outwardly sober and con-
ventionalized, if not to say dull, of performances, had a hard time of it and was
not officially recognized by the police until 1901.

Philadelphians have never believed in expressing their joy too openly,
and even nowadays the Devil, when he wishes really to relax, buys a return
ticket to New York.

The Church of England people, of course, did not feel this way about
"masks and revels", and at an early date began to indulge in dances, soirées,
and, as the town grew older, balls and various other routs, which reached a
climax in the famous *Meschianza* given by the British officers in 1778 to
Lord Howe upon his departure from the city. And some of the wealthier
and more fashionable Quaker families also speedily became more lenient.
If the fathers and mothers clung to the older ways, the male children, when
they reached their majority, had an easy out—they became Episcopalians.
As for plain talk and "profane swearing", it is a privilege occasionally to
hear some such remark as, "And I said to him, damn thee to hell."

Major Patrick Gordon, of the British army, who succeeded Sir William
Keith as governor in 1726, and who held office until his death ten years
later, was supposed to have given the first dancing assembly in Philadelphia
at the Governor's Mansion, or "Great House", on Second Street above
Spruce; tall candles in front of mirrors, gentlemen—the older ones—in full-
bottomed wigs, the younger ones in the new tiewigs, ladies in flowered brocades
and stomachers, their hair done in the fashionable "French curls" of the
period, or else the equally fashionable unpowdered curls caught together at
the nape of the neck. Fiddles squeaking, as they squeaked in the eighteenth
century. High red heels clicking.

Two hundred and more years after the unappreciated Dorothy, wife of
Richard Canterill, and Sarah, wife of John Stiner, and their male companions
had behaved contrary to the nature of their "sect", there was in Philadelphia
for a couple of decades a famous Mardi Gras ball known as the "Bal Masque",
which in every way lived up to anyone's ideas on the subject. New Orleans
has never done better. The mention of it still brings a reminiscent and
wistful look to the eyes of those old enough to have been present. On the
list of the directors, among the descendants of the Church of England men,

were numerous Quaker names, Christian and last, identical with those of some of the grave Friends who came over with William Penn. And the only moral of the story is that times do change, and that young people haven't the slightest idea how much, and in what ways, their parents enjoyed themselves.

Pretty soon the variety and solidity of crimes in and around Philadelphia increased, and the Assembly widened the possibilities of capital punishment. In 1720 John and Martha Hunt were hanged for making counterfeit coin, and other felonies such as highway robbery were named as being equally heinous. No Johnathan Wild or Dick Turpin, however, appeared, and although there was some footpadding, the roads leading to the city were fairly safe. Three pirates, it is true—Joseph Baker, or Boulanger, Joseph Berrouse, and Peter Peterson, alias La Croix—were hanged on Windmill Island in 1799; Windmill Island being in the Delaware, just off Market Street Pier, until it and other small islands were removed when the immediate harbour of the city, comparatively recently, was properly dredged.

But these pirates were an amateurish and sorry lot, although the story of their attempted ship seizure is one of the grimmest and bloodiest in American merchant marine annals, and, where the captain of the ship is concerned, one of the most courageous. It is a pity that it cannot be told in full. It is enough to say that the schooner *Eliza*, Captain William Wheland in command, sailed out of Philadelphia in the year mentioned, bound for St. Thomas in the Virgin Islands, with this crew on board: the three pirates-to-be—foreigners who could hardly speak English—Captain Wheland, Mate Richard Croft, Supercargo Charles Rey, and an American seaman named Jacob Suster of Germantown. Two weeks out, the amateur pirates killed with an axe the mate, the supercargo, and seaman Suster, and threw them overboard, and badly wounded Captain Wheland who was asleep in his cabin; and then, realizing that they knew nothing about navigation, dressed the captain's wounds and promised they would set him ashore in safety at the first island they sighted if he would steer the ship.

For nine days the captain did this, and then on the 21st of September, seeing his chance, knocked Berrouse out with a billet of wood and imprisoned the other two in the galley. In this he was assisted by the dead mate's bulldog. Afterwards, for another thirteen days, the captain unaided sailed south, afraid to sleep even for a moment. On the deck, just below him, lay Berrouse, whom he had chained to a bolt. Presently up over the horizon came the island of St. Bartholomew, and in the harbour lay an American man-of-war.

The pirates were returned to Philadelphia and tried, and as they were ascending the scaffold they shook hands with Captain Wheland; a strange southern-French idea of courtesy. In 1812 an account of this crime was published under the title, *The Criminal Recorder, or an Awful Beacon to the Rising Generation of Both Sexes*, although why the author should have thought that the youth of Philadelphia would go in for anything so exotic when there were so many cosier opportunities close at hand, it is a little difficult to see. The moral, moreover, proves nothing except that if you want to be a pirate, you should first learn navigation.

Despite all this, however, Philadelphia has never been a very turbulent or disorderly city as so many other American cities have been. Even during Prohibition, bootlegging was conducted in a comparatively gentle and mannerly fashion, and Philadelphia's "gangsters", good-looking men for the most part, well mannered and well dressed, have always been popular, not to mention intimate, with numerous leading citizens. At its worst, the city's crime has had a nice comfortable neighbourly atmosphere, with little hard feeling on either side. One has always felt that if any rough stuff started, the nearest "gangster" would take the right side and protect the weak as inevitably as a Richard Harding Davis hero. They are much better-mannered, as a matter of fact, than the Philadelphia police, who are notoriously uncivil, except for the excellently trained guards of Fairmount Park and the equally well trained guards of the city squares. Philadelphia has never had anything approaching the cold-blooded "clip joints" of New York or the gang wars of Chicago. When Al Capone made the mistake of coming to Penn's city he was promptly imprisoned in Cherry Hill. As in every other relationship, if you want to have a pleasant time in Philadelphia, you should be properly introduced.

Tolerance in great matters, if not in small, did persist and endure. The shadow of Penn and the Quakers fell across the city beneficently. Only once did the macabre witch-hunting of the seventeenth century, which swept Europe and parts of America, appear in Philadelphia, and then it was settled for good and all with a verdict which is a model of common sense and Quaker compromise, if the two are not often the same.

In 1683 Yeshro Hendricksen and Margaret Mattson, Swedish women, were accused of witchcraft and, with the strange psychological perversity of witch trials, pleaded guilty. The verdict in each case was, "Guilty of having the common fame of a witch, but not guilty in the manner and form as she stands indicted."

Quaker common sense and compromise were evident in numerous other ways. If you got yourself whipped, it cost you six shillings a whipping, and you paid it, not the city. On one occasion a very valuable Negro slave, committing a major crime, was returned to his master for safekeeping because his value and use to the community was too great for punishment.

This was a Negro named Jack who in September, 1700, shot and killed a white youth. The victim was buried in the Friends' burying ground at Fourth and Mulberry streets with this inscription on his tombstone:

> Here lies a Plant,
> Too many have seen it,
> Flourish't and perish't
> In half a minute;
> Joseph Rakestraw,
> The son of William,
> Shott by a negro,
> The 30th day of Sept,
> 1700, in the 19th year
> And 4th mo., of his age.

And although slavery existed in Philadelphia as everywhere else, and the early gazettes had their quota of advertisements concerning runaway slaves, Philadelphians never liked slavery any more than did the Mennonites of Germantown. This attitude, naturally, was also largely the result of the Quaker attitude and especially that of the Quaker preacher, John Woolman, who, born near Burlington in 1720, devoted the fifty-two years of his life to working for emancipation and to preaching among the Indians. It was Woolman whom Charles Lamb called "that beautiful soul". As early as 1696, eight years after the Germantown protest against slavery, the Yearly Meeting of the Friends in Philadelphia followed suit. Eighty-two years later this sentiment had grown to such an extent that in 1778 the Supreme Executive Council of Pennsylvania no sooner returned to the city after the British evacuation than it sent a message to the Assembly asking for the manumission of all infant Negroes and the prohibition of any further import; in this way eventually to "abrogate slavery, the opprobium of America". In 1780 a bill for gradual emancipation was passed, to the great astonishment of the Quakers, as George Bryan, formerly vice-president of the Executive Council, wrote to Samuel Adams, who "looked for no such benevolent issue" from a government at the moment dominated by Presbyterians. And so Pennsylvania was among the earliest of the states to abolish slavery.

At an early date Philadelphia also had had a salutary lesson in the terrors of brutality. In 1731 Catherine Bevan, together with Peter Murphy, her servant who had assisted her, were ordered to be hanged at New Castle, Delaware, for the murder of Catherine's husband. Peter Murphy's sentence was plain hanging, but Catherine was to be hung over a pile of faggots to be set nfire after she was dead. The fire was lit too soon, and reached the rope, parted it, and Catherine, fully alive, fell into the flames, screaming and struggling horribly.

The entire countryside was sobered for a long while.

And now we come to what, in a way, was the most sardonic escapade of all. Back in England only two years, William Penn felt the disgrace deeply, and, obstinate and loyal as usual, rather foolishly took his son's part.

On the 1st of July 1704 the grand jury had before it "some of the young gentry" for a riot at the inn of Enoch Storey in Combes' Alley. "The young gentry" had made so much noise that James Wood, constable, and James Dough, of the watch, had entered to find out what it was all about, and the young gentry had beaten them severely. The young gentry were: John Finney, sheriff, Thomas Gray, scrivener, James Ralph, afterwards a friend of Benjamin Franklin, and, believe it or not, John Evans, the brilliant and attractive young Welshman whom Penn had sent over upon his departure to act as governor, and William Penn, 2nd. Yes, no less. Moreover, not content with being drunk and disorderly, Penn 2nd had "called for pistols" to shoot James Wood and James Dough.

It is pleasant to record that Alderman Wilcox, attracted with numerous others by the disturbance, whipped William Penn, 2nd, over the head with his cane, "not knowing", as he said discreetly, "who he was".

William Penn, 2nd, was a foolish and arrogant fellow. On his return from England he brought with him a mysterious Lady Jenks, a young woman of great beauty, many accomplishments, and an expert horsewoman—all this "so it was said", for Penn for the most part kept her up in Bucks County, where, dressed as a man, she accompanied him on fox hunts.

There is something rather attractive about Lady Jenks—and a good, plain Welsh name at that! But she caused great scandal in the city.

CHAPTER IX

Quaker with a Plume

". . . but to all that speak of it say, I shall have no need to stay [in England] and a great interest to return."

LETTER FROM PENN TO JAMES LOGAN, JULY, 1701.

PENN DID NOT want to leave in 1701. He loved Pennsbury and his province despite the dislike his wife Hannah Callowhill and his daughter Letitia had for them, and despite his disagreements with the Assembly. But it was necessary for him to return to England. There was an increasing sentiment there, as well as in America, to consolidate all the proprietary holdings into Crown Colonies for the purposes of common defence and better administration, and a bill to this effect had been brought into the House of Lords. The shadow of coming events was falling athwart Europe and therefore America. Already the storm had broken once in King William's War, and soon there was to be Queen Anne's War, 1702–13, and King George's War, 1744–48, and the French-Indian War, 1756–63, or the wars of the Spanish Succession, the Austrian Succession, and the Seven Years' War, as they were called in Europe.

To the north of the colonies were the French in Canada, to the west were the French again with their great and tireless explorers: Joliet and Marquette, and others, on the Upper Mississippi, La Salle the whole length of it; Groseilliers and Radisson, west beyond Lake Superior. Who was to own North America?

Down in Philadelphia the Quaker Assembly thought that was none of its business. Pennsylvania was far from Canada and the Mississippi and would never be involved with either. For seventy years the Quaker Assembly tucked its head into the sand as much as possible, and when it did vote for the levying of troops or for funds to equip or maintain them, did so reluctantly, although this has been exaggerated by hostile historians. On the whole, however, it was against Quaker "principles and conscience to hire men to kill others", and until the French-Indian War this policy of do-nothingism was all right; but with the French-Indian War the smoke of burning farms and

MARKET STREET MARKET, 1836 (Kennedy)

Philadelphia
Juni 1876

WATER WORKS, FAIRMOUNT PARK, 1876 (Anon.)

the brown-red trickle of blood crept as near Philadelphia as Reading to the north, and to the west, Lancaster and the centre of the state. And all about Pittsburgh and in the forests was massacre.

This "peaceable" country of ours between 1690 and 1763 fought four wars, and each one of them had its source in Europe. And between 1775 and 1814 it fought three more wars, for we fought an undeclared war with Napoleon, and each one of them had its source in Europe. And between 1846 and 1944 we have fought five wars, and only two that had not their source in Europe. Two hundred and fifty-four years ago Americans should have learned, even the Quaker Assembly in Philadelphia, that there is no such thing as isolation.

On September 10, six weeks before his departure, Penn called the Assembly together and, despite considerable quarrelling, managed to put through some constructive measures. He appointed a council of ten to manage the province in his absence and gave Philadelphia a borough charter. On October 28 he handed in an amended Frame of Government containing the following new provisions: The Assembly was to be chosen yearly, four members from each county, and was to have all the privileges of the English House of Commons; the Council was no longer to be elected by the people, but was to be nominated by the governor, thus leaving the governor practically unhampered in executive control; and above all, the Assembly was to have the right to initiate laws. Under the original Frame of Government it had had the right only to amend or reject them. Freedom of conscience was again emphasized. Penn appointed Colonel Andrew Hamilton, former governor of West and East Jersey, deputy governor, and James Logan colonial secretary, and at the end of October set sail for Portsmouth, England, on the ship *Dalmahoy*, arriving in December.

Up on the shining Delaware, frost now on the trees and a morning mist above the broad river, Pennsbury the beautiful, its formal gardens, and its vistas and its vineyards at Springettsbury Farm superintended by an imported Frenchman, its brewhouse and its stables, was quiet except for an overseer and a handful of slaves and servants. And so it was to remain until the end, except for occasional visits from William Penn, 2nd, and other sons of Penn. The brewhouse stood until 1864; then it was torn down, but now a faithful replica stands on the original site, thanks to the Welcome Society, and so one more beautiful American house, if not saved, has at least been restored.

Minor disagreements are frequently more significant than major quarrels. The Assembly was blocking Penn in all his proposals, and after his departure it rejected his amended Frame of Government, but perhaps the most confirming evidence of the difference between Penn's idea of a "Holy Experiment" and the ideas of the colonists on the subject had to do with rum, Indians, Negroes, and illegitimacy. Where slaves are concerned, the less you bother them with marriage the greater their fecundity, and to the owners of slaves, slave fecundity is profitable. Selling rum to Indians is obviously profitable.

Penn believed that Negro slaves should be encouraged to legitimatize their unions, and he also thought that selling rum to Indians was bad. The Assembly thought both notions silly. It did not take very long for the "Holy

D

Experiment" to break down. When it comes to profits, Christianity has always had a weak team and no substitutes.

Almost everyone except Logan and a handful of faithful Quakers was glad to see Penn go—he was getting to be a nuisance. But the Indians came in by scores to say good-bye.

Penn was aware that he was regarded as a nuisance. He wrote in a letter of the time:

"What I have mett with here is without Example and what a Diadem would not tempt to undergoe seven years—faction in Government, and in property, almost indissolvible knots."

Back in England, however, he managed to save his proprietorship— there is no doubt about it that he had a way with kings and queens. Once he was in her presence, even the coldly high-headed Anne liked him again— and for a while he had a busy and profitable time. At first he resided once more in Kensington, and then in 1703 moved to Knightsbridge for a while. In Kensington he wrote a sequel to his *Fruits of Solitude,* called *More Fruits of Solitude,* and in Knightsbridge he wrote his *Life of Bulstrode Whitelocke,* the great Cromwellian lawyer and believer in religious tolerance. In 1710, after an interval in Brentford, he took up his final residence in a small house with a garden at Field Ruscombe, near Twyford. He had resumed his leadership of the English Quakers and of the English dissenters in general. Where, during his life, he ever found time to pick any of the "fruits of solitude" is a question.

And now the dark days were upon him. They had been on their way since 1705.

Philip Ford, a London merchant, Penn's English representative, had, over a period of years, managed to bankrupt Penn entirely except for the quit rents from his private holdings in Pennsylvania. Ford died, and his widow, through her son, put in a claim for a balance of ten thousand pounds. In 1707 she had Penn arrested for debt, and rather than pay what he considered an unjust demand he went voluntarily to jail. Shocked by this, some of the influential Quakers, and others of Penn's admirers, raised the necessary sum and he was released. But the episode had shocked him too, although while in prison, according to Isaac Norris of Philadelphia, who, being in England, visited him, he had his usual serene and social time; living comfortably, corresponding with his friends, seeing those who were in London, and holding meetings of his church.

During this period, the government in Pennsylvania also, as far as the relationships of the successive governors with the Assembly were concerned, was steadily going from bad to worse.

Andrew Hamilton, an excellent man, died suddenly on April 20, 1703; and after an interregnum during which Edward Shippen, Philadelphia's first mayor, acted as lieutenant-governor, Penn sent out in 1704 John Evans, the attractive young Welshman, a friend of William Penn, 2nd, who had been something of a figure at the court of Queen Anne. Evans arrived in the company of young Penn, and could not have been a more unfortunate choice. He was gay, dissipated, and tactless. He hated the Quakers and called them hypocrites and, whether true or not, was said to have been more than tender toward various ladies, Indian and white. At all events he was a leading figure in the riot at Enoch Storey's inn. James Logan, a young man himself at the time, was an intimate of Evans', and as a result even James Logan was for a while in bad odour.

Evans lasted only three years and in 1709 was succeeded by Charles Gookin, a retired British soldier. A "sober man", Penn wrote, of an "easy, quiet temper", who understood how "to command and obey . . ."

. . . of what you call a good family, his grandfather, Sir Vincent Gookin, having been an early great planter in Ireland in King James I and the first Charles' days, and he intends, if not ill treated, to lay his bones, as well as substance, among you, having taken leave of the war and both England and Ireland to live amongst you; and as he is not voluptious, so I hope he will be an example of thriftiness.

But Pennsylvania did not take kindly to the permanent settlement of Penn's emissaries. There was something about the Quaker Assembly which seems to have driven governors crazy. The Assembly started off by refusing Gookin any grants for his salary or living expenses—it said William Penn was rich enough to pay his own deputies. It had told John Evans the same. And then it proceeded to turn down Gookin's request to raise Pennsylvania's quota of one hundred and fifty men for the Queen Anne War, but obstinately continued its attempt to impeach the fine and loyal Logan.

Logan hurried over to England; Penn wrote a strong letter to Pennsylvania, and a more amicable Assembly was chosen which voted two thousand pounds to aid the proposed expedition to Canada. But a third Assembly, elected in 1714, renewed the quarrel, and in 1717 Gookin resigned. He ended up by kicking a judge and walking out on a committee of the Assembly. The Assembly, always charitable in its public ideas if not its private ones, decided he was suffering from a mental aberration, but it looks much more as if a sober man of "easy quiet temper" had reached the limits of his endurance.

Gookin was succeeded by Sir William Keith, the handsome, affable, adroit, and slippery Scotsman who governed the province from 1717 to 1726, and whose portrait—he wears the jointed steel cuirass of the time, and there is a lace ruffle at his neck, and supercilious eyes look out from beneath arched eyebrows and a curled, full-bottom wig—is almost as common in Philadelphia collections as the portraits of Penn and Franklin.

Sir William had been surveyor-general for the Carolinas.

Meanwhile William Penn, 2nd, back in Pennsylvania—he died in 1720 —had been doing whatever he could to complicate by his private life his father's already complicated public affairs.

"*He has wit*", Penn wrote, "*pretends much to honour, has kept the top of company, is over-generous by half, and yet sharp enough to get to spend. Handle him with love and wisdom. He is conquered that way.*"

And again in 1703, prior to William 2nd's return to Philadelphia in the company of John Evans, Penn wrote to James Logan:

"*Immediately take him away to Pennsbury, and there give him the true state of things, and weigh down his levities as well as temper his resentments, and inform his understanding. . . . Watch him, out-witt him, and honestly over-reach him for his good.''*

The pattern is a familiar one through the centuries.

William the younger was neither to be "out-witted" nor were his levities to be weighed down.

And by now Penn was getting to be an old man, old beyond his time—he was in his middle sixties—and the corpulence that often afflicts big men had taken hold of him.

In the spring of 1712 he suffered a paralytic stroke while on a visit to London, or, as it was described, suffered "a lethargic fit". In Bristol that autumn he suffered another. And a third in Ruscombe in 1713. All during 1713 and 1714 these fits came upon him, although in a milder form, and were sometimes followed by a total loss of memory. When fairly well, much of the great energy, the driving force, was left, and he saw people, and went to Meeting in Reading, and was refreshed and moved by the spirit, but now he would not allow Hannah Callowhill out of his sight.

He was "scarce ever easy", she wrote James Logan, "with or without company", unless she was at his elbow. And when feeling ill, all mention of the "Holy Experiment" depressed him immeasurably, despite the fact that when more himself, when "a little easy", he had "returning thoughts still alive in him of Pennsylvania, and frequently expressed his enjoyment in the Lord's goodness in his private retirements, and his loving concern for the good of his province". In 1714 he was "in pretty good health . . . not worse in speech than for some months before", and when thoughts of business were kept away from him, "very sweet, and comfortable, and easy, and cheerfully resigned, and takes great delight in his children, his friends, and domestic comforts".

Doubly hard, all this, of course, on Hannah Callowhill, for, a most capable woman, she was now managing entirely, and continued to do so until her death, the great and involved family holdings in Pennsylvania. In 1712 Penn, on the advice of everyone, including James Logan, had decided to sell his Lord Proprietorship to the Crown, but his illness interfered with this, and the Lord Proprietorship was held by the Penns until the American Revolution, when it was bought for £130,000. Much of the private holdings remained in the hands of the family, however, for generations to come. In fact, all of them were not liquidated until 1884.

Penn, when well, walked in his garden with enjoyment; when ill, he walked restlessly and endlessly.

One is haunted by the vision of the tall, corpulent man, once so beautiful, so vigorous and alive, walking endlessly and restlessly in the soft mists of the English winter or the gay, close, outer security of the English springs.

On July 30, 1718 he died and was buried August 5 at Jordan's Cemetery near Chalfont St. Giles, Buckinghamshire, the lovely county after which the lovely county in Pennsylvania that Penn was so fond of was named.

Just so long as he could, Penn wrote voluminously his charming and simple and affectionate letters. Here is one written from London in August of 1705, and a second from the same city in March of 1708. The first was written to John Sacher, his overseer at Pennsbury, and to Sacher's wife; the second to John Sacher alone:

Honest John and Mary:

My reall love is to you, and desire you and your little ones preservation heartily, and I know so does my dear wife and loving mistress. We are all, through the Lord's mercy, well, save little Hannah at Bristoll, whose arme has a weakness. She is a sweete childe, as Thomas and little Margaret.

I doubt not your care and good husbandry, and good housewifery, to make that place profitable to me, after the hundreds, yea thousands, yt have been sunk there from the beginning. Though if that could be lett, to one yt would not misuse it, and you upon a plantation for my deare Johnne, I should like it better, and pray tell James [Logan] so; for I think I have spent too much there already. Johnne grows a fine childe, tall, brisky as a bird, his mother's limbs, but my counte-nance, and witty, as others say, and as healthy as any of them. Let me hear from you how Sam and Sue attend, and if the black boy and little Sue begin to be diligent. The Lord be with you, and all his humble and faithful ones, on both sides the water.

Farewell: your reall friend,
Wm. Penn

John Sacher—Loving friend:

I had my letter with satisfaction, and glad to hear of thy and family's welfare. I am glad to hear of the good condition of poor Pennsbury, beloved of us all, and there, in the will of God, we wish ourselves. If thou leavest it, give J. Logan an acct. of ye fruit of thy labour, as acres cleared, and fence, and of both plow and sow land. Likewise, deliver all ye plate, linnen and household stuff into his posses-sion and care. I bless God, we are all alive and well, save for our dear sweete Hannah, whom the Lord took four months ago, at $4\frac{1}{2}$ years, the wittiest and womanliest creature that her age could show, but His holy will be done.

Thy loving friend,
Wm. Penn

In another letter to Mary Sacher, Penn speaks of Pennsbury, "poor Pennsbury", as "that place of my pleasure . . . which I like for a place better than I have ever yet lived at".

But he could be as urban as he was country-minded. In 1710 Dean Swift writes Stella that at Mr. Harley's he had met "Will Penn, the Quaker," and that they had had a delightful and entertaining evening in each other's company. And you had to be a witty man to entertain Dean Swift.

"We sat two hours," wrote Dean Swift, "drinking as good wine as you do."

There is also a charming story about that lovely Quakeress, Elizabeth Haddon, who founded Haddonfield, the quaint New Jersey town of old trees and old houses not far across the Delaware from Penn's own city. The story is probably not true, although all of Haddonfield believes it if few in Philadelphia have ever heard of it. It is such a charming story, however, that it bears repeating. Elizabeth is buried in the Quaker churchyard in Haddonfield, and a huge elm not so far away bears a brass tablet commemor-ating her "resolution, prudence and charity."

Elizabeth, so the story goes, early in life fell in love, although she never met him (why, is mysterious), with the young and dashing and godly—most of the time—Penn, and years later followed him to America, but by now determined never to meet him, settled at a discreet distance and worshipped from afar.   Prudence, if resolute, she had already married one John Estaugh.

And looking at the famous early portrait of Penn, the one painted when he was a young soldier in Ireland, a copy of which is in the possession of the Historical Society of Pennsylvania—the portrait where Penn, like Sir William Keith, is wearing a jointed cuirass and has a lace jabot at his neck —one doesn't blame Elizabeth at all.

She knew a handsome and interesting man when she saw one.

Historic figures pretty soon after death begin to assume the features desired by the community in which they functioned.   They become household gods to whom thoughtless incense is lit; sacrificial goats who wash away the sins of man.   Symbols of the especial virtues admired by that community. Virtues which, often as not, are vices, and which may or may not bear the slightest resemblance to the living man.   This also has happened to Benjamin Franklin.   Had Penn or Franklin been New York demiurges instead of Philadelphia ones, our present conception of them, for better or worse, would at all events have been entirely different.   Philadelphia has never especially admired gallantry, moral courage, the unexpected, the outer reaches of the imagination, or generous extravagance.   On the other hand, it does admire dignity, patience, benignity, thrift—except in city government—and the figure that comes with good living.   The average Philadelphia notion of William Penn—the notion of those who think of him at all—is of a man who was born at the age of sixty with a round stomach and a look of resigned kindness.   Undoubtedly a banker of some sort because of the number of trust companies and other financial organizations named after him.   Above all, a man who counted his pennies and drove a hard but Christian bargain, and whose idea of happiness was Sunday dinner with a second wife.

Penn, as a matter of fact, was one of the most imaginative, adventurous, and extravagant men of an adventurous and extravagant era.   A gallant man both physically and morally.   One of the great men of a great period. He was not in the least smug, demure, or resigned, and the one thing he was not was a good business man; and the other thing he was not was a sober- or thin-minded man.

He was a Quaker with a plume, a panache, just as he was a Quaker who wore a sash of light blue silk and was particular about his wigs and his hose. A Quaker who wrote his first deputy, his cousin, Captain Markham, to drink his Madeira, and his friend Thomas Lloyd to use the handsome wigs he had left behind in Philadelphia.   A Quaker who, while at Pennsbury, had his steward import butter from Rhode Island, candles from Boston, rum from Jamaica, wine from Europe—sherry, port, claret, and Madeira—gin from London; and from his own province, flour by the ton, molasses by the hogs- head, and everything else on an equal scale.   He overwhelmed the governors of Virginia and Maryland by the lavishness of his entertainment and gave away money right and left to any who asked him, including the Indians. All his life he made money, great sums, for he was a vivid entrepreneur with a long vision, and all his life he spent money and lost it as fast as he made it. The Ford scandal has been given a church and a local slant, and as a result the unfortunate Ford has achieved a reputation he probably did not deserve.

Penn borrowed continually from Ford, and as security attached his name to any sort of paper. Mrs. Ford, a widow, can hardly be blamed for the steps she took. She was held in contempt because she, too, was a "Friend". If on those grounds no Quaker had ever foreclosed a mortgage or brought a suit, half the business of Philadelphia would never have happened.

If you can sum a man up in a sentence or two, then perhaps the most significant symptoms of Penn's many-sided nature are the rectangular streets of Philadelphia and the bright blue sash he loved to wear. Here are his love of order and precision, his altogether opposite love of luxury and display. Penn hated anything "ascu", as he spelled it. He sent definite instructions that nothing at Pennsbury should be "ascu". Nothing was, except the expenditures.

That Penn was a charming companion we know; easy, affable, simple, and amusing. That he was witty, there are few signs. But he was humorous and human. He became a Quaker because he had great spiritual and social and political imagination and ambitions, and the thing was a flame and a sword to him, and not an extinguisher and a sheath. He would have liked the Quakers to go out to rescue the sick, the wounded, and the starving; he would not have understood the Quakers who refuse to take their own part and the part of God.

Vain? Yes—in a harmless way; but humble fundamentally. Self-centred? Most men with a great vision and a great object are. But Penn listened to people and was patient with their troubles and their causes. Imperious? Yes; mildly so. But so are most men with a great vision and a great object. It seems so easy to them for men to be sensible, and wise, and fairly happy. They become impatient with the way humanity, like a grinning clown, trips itself up with its own feet, as if deliberately.

After a while the trick ceases to be amusing.

Penn lay in the quiet graveyeard near Chalfont St. Giles, in Buckinghamshire, in England, and Sir William Keith, with his full-bottom wig, and his supercilious eyes, and his affable easy manners, and his adroit ambitions, governed in Pennsylvania. The city was now forty-two years old, almost half a century old, and the "Holy Experiment" was completely forgotten, never to be revived. It was a Sunday morning in October 1723, and up High Street, now called Market, looking curiously about him, as he always looked at anything new, walked a tall, bright-faced, badly dressed boy of seventeen, just arrived from Boston; a printer, a writer, and a poet. That night he went to stay for a while at the Crooked Billet inn near the wharf on Chestnut Street, and shortly after applied for work with Andrew Bradford, son of William Bradford—the famous William Bradford who, coming over as early as 1685, had established Philadelphia's first print shop and then had gone to New York. Bradford, having all the apprentices he needed, introduced the stranger to a fellow printer, Samuel Keimer.

The tall boy was Benjamin Franklin.

CHAPTER X

Port of Entry

"The Bank and River-Street is so filled with Houses, that it makes an inclosed Street with the Front in many places, which before lay open to the River Delaware . . . we have likewise wharfs Built out into the River, that a Ship of a Hundred Tun may lay her side to."

CAPTAIN RICHARD NORRIS, MARINER, DECEMBER 12, 1690.

THE MOTTO OF the Great Seal of the City of Philadelphia, approved February 14, 1874, and March 13, 1908, replacing the original seal of 1701, is "Philadelphia Maneto". *Maneto* sounds like an Indian word, but it isn't. It is the third person singular, future imperative of the Latin verb *maneo*, which means "to continue", "to remain", and the statement where Philadelphia is concerned is singularly appropriate, although the intended translation of the two words, "Philadelphia" and "maneto", in conjunction, is supposed to be —hog Latin and all—"Let Brotherly Love Continue".

As to brotherly love, that is a question, and has been almost from the beginning. It didn't last very long; at least, in any very great quantity. But the "continue", the "remain", are perfect.

Philadelphia has remained, and continued, mightily.

Many people, including some thoughtful and questioning Philadelphians, have asked themselves occasionally just why Philadelphia exists. Or rather, since towns and cities exist everywhere, especially where two rivers meet, the reason, not for Philadelphia's existence but for its greatness. What are the causes, despite many handicaps—the disposition of its inhabitants, their traditions, outside circumstances—for the city's ponderous inevitable growth? Why, with very little effort on its part, indeed, at moments with what seems almost suicidal intent, has this leviathan of cities remained securely among the four or five greatest cities of the country, most of the time the third, continuing its calm, not to say sluggish, way, obvious of suggestion or criticism from within or without?

The thing seems very much like a natural phenomenon; very much like the flow of a river itself, unconscious but assured. Like the flow of the broad Delaware past the city's doorstep.

And the question must occur daily to thousands of Americans to whom, slicing their way through the outskirts of the city on their journeys north or south, or from the west, Philadelphia seems merely a sprawling way station, little more than a whistle stop, between Chicago and Pittsburgh, or Washington and Baltimore, and New York. They wonder why so many people get on and off the trains. Probably in the entire country there is not a city through which such quantities of Americans pass without the slightest intention ever of seeing it. In its own especial way, Philadelphia is even more remote than Boston.

From the north the train, after leaving Trenton and crossing the Delaware, a broad swift-moving stream there, rocks sticking up in it—Trenton sits at the head of Delaware navigation—runs for a while through rural river country, charming and placid, often a pearl-grey mist across it, the Delaware, hidden by trees, off to the left—this is where Pennsbury was. But abruptly one begins to pick up the immense river suburbs of the city: Talcony, Bridesburg, Frankford, manufacturing suburb after suburb overlaid with the fierce, drab monotony of unplanned enterprise. Here and there are a few factories with the decency of grass and planting and modern airy buildings, and occasionally there is a pleasant residential quarter with trees and a park, but for the most part there is an endless waste of low-lying brick and streets with small two-family houses, porched and bay-windowed, stretching out indefinitely. Church towers, an unusual number of them, and their co-cathedrals, the factories and warehouses, alone break the horizonless sky-line.

And then the train stops at North Philadelphia, the junction for Germantown and Chestnut Hill, and Chicago and the West, and one has a glimpse of Broad Street, the longest straight street in the world, twelve miles without a curve, with the distant gigantic tower of the City Hall ending the view, before the train slides again between factories and breweries and warehouses. This time tall, sightless, close-pressing ones of brick, like the fortresses of mediæval *condottieri*.

But only for a little while; for suddenly, as if the train had come out of a tunnel, is one of the most beautiful city views in the world.

The train emerges from a deep cut between rocks and crosses a high bridge, and below, stretching as far as you can see, right and left, is the tree-shaded valley of a great park—Fairmount Park—and down-river, pearl and opal and faint blue, are the towers of the city itself; at that distance, even the tower of City Hall, graceful and glamorous. On the drives of the park, the East Drive, the West Drive, the tops and radiators of cars twinkle, and on the river single shells, two-oared shells, and an eight-oared shell or so, a coach's launch trailing, part the water into white plumes, their sweeps glistening. Philadelphia is a great rowing city.

After this, beyond the river—which is the Schuylkill, if you don't know —to the left is a far-spreading and famous Zoological Garden, where hartebeests and various horned citizens of Africa graze, and innumerable other foliage-obliterated animals, and where, interestingly enough, and perhaps significantly—this is statistical—they live longer than any other animals in captivity. And then you pass a maze of switching tracks, followed by another lovely glimpse of the river, the rose-brown Philadelphia Museum of Art sitting up on top of its small hill, before you come to an impatient stop at the white neo-Greek temple of the Pennsylvania Railroad.

Just why all the major stations of the Pennsylvania Railroad are neo-Greek would make an interesting psychological research. Plato would be surprised, and so would Benjamin Franklin.

This is not a terminus, definitely not. The terminus is a mile farther into the city, into the very heart of it, across the Schuylkill again until you come to the ancient shabbiness of Broad Street Station, with its pigeons and its labyrinthian underground suburban adjunct where the stranger, like a

D*

bewildered Attic maiden sent as a sacrifice to Minotaur, loses himself help
lessly.   That is the terminus, smack up against City Hall and its plaza; so
much of a terminus that there is the ancient Philadelphia story of the old
Quaker lady, unused to trains, who asked the conductor if the one she was on
stopped at Broad Street.

"If it doesn't, madam," said the conductor, "you'll get one hell of a
bump."

But now Broad Street Station is only a terminus for the suburban trains
and the faithful every-hour-on-the-hour trains to New York and a few submerged, shy trains to Chicago or the South.   The big traffic is routed through
Thirtieth Street or North Philadelphia, and the passengers on the crack trains
pass through Philadelphia without a bump—physical, historical, or spiritual.

The better-informed have a vague recollection that there's a Liberty
Bell somewhere.

From the south the entrance to the city—now a pseudo entrance, like
all of them—is considerably simpler.   You merely traverse—from Wilmington
and Chester on—endless miles of factories and occasional shipyards, and end
up with a view of the Schuylkill at its worst and the dump-heaps of the University of Pennsylvania, like the careless backsides of an absent-minded
professor.   While the entrance from the west, equally simple, is astonishingly
beautiful.

Chicagoans and other Westerners must have an exaggerated notion of
Philadelphia's comeliness; Washingtonians, Baltimoreans, and Southerners,
an exaggerated idea of its ugliness.   New Yorkers and New Englanders
should have a more moderate, fifty-fifty point of view.

From the west the train slides out of the small blue distant hills of Lancaster County, the neat little "Pennsylvania Dutch" towns, the huge typical
stone barns and fine stone houses, grey, white, or yellow, into unbroken mile after
mile of green, great-treed suburbs; big houses or little, sitting back on their
hedged lawns.   This is American landscape at its best.   This would have
pleased William Penn, although he approved more of making such greenness
and neatness a city matter rather than a suburban one.   Anyway, these have
been called the "most beautiful suburbs in the world".   Certainly they are
among the richest, and the only ones that were deliberately and cold-bloodedly
made by a railroad and which take their nickname from this fact.   This is
the famous "main line", the place where the original Welsh settlers lived
—St. David's, Radnor, Bryn Mawr, Haverford, Narbeth, Merion.   And
this, in passing, and similar suburbs like Chestnut Hill and White Marsh,
is also the index finger of Philadelphia's mortmain; the dead hand which
grips the city in a vice of trust funds, absentee landlordism, with its consequent
"rack-renting", and political and municipal irresponsibility.

The people who live on these endless rolling acres control, more than is
the case with any other American city, a major share of Philadelphia's wealth,
power, tradition, and enterprise, or lack of it, but they neither live in the
city nor vote in it, nor any longer care much about it.   They merely go into
it to conduct their business.

But no matter from what direction you approach the city—north, south,
west, or east, coming over the suspension bridge across the Delaware from

Camden and southern New Jersey—you are still haunted, despite the city's immense size and far-flung industries, by the question of why it is so great. And why it has always been great, almost from its first small beginning. And why it shows every sign of so continuing.

If you live in the city—actually live in it—the question is even more pressing.

The answer is simple. It has already been partially given.

Philadelphia, to be sure, is not the metropolis of the Mason and Dixon line, of the upper South, as is Baltimore. Nor is it the metropolis of New England, as is Boston. And if it once was the metropolis of the Middle States, New York, with the opening of the Erie Canal in 1825, and its better harbour, long ago pre-empted that position. Moreover, nowadays, with railway transportation, Pennsylvania products and minerals can be taken over the mountains as easily to New York, or, the mountains missing, even more easily to Baltimore. The province no longer runs downhill to the junction of the Delaware and the Schuylkill. Nonetheless Philadelphia still has a greater variety of advantages than any other city in the country.

It may no longer be supreme in most of these, but it has more of them. And the more important were there to begin with.

To begin with, Philadelphia is a great inland city, but it is also a great seaport, a not too usual combination. In the second place, it stood at a cross-roads and filled a strategic need between the older colonies to the north and to the south: New York, New England, Maryland, Virginia. Here had been to all practical purposes a wilderness, and now here, abruptly, was a town. Finally, Penn's declaration of tolerance and his description of the natural wealth of the country resulted at once in an influx of skilled men from all north European countries.

Six factors account for the early growth of Philadelphia, far surpassing that of any other American city, and for Philadelphia's baffling but continuing solidity: its port, its strategic position inland, iron, anthracite coal, manufacturing and tolerance. While Philadelphia was permitting every man to think as he liked, even, after some initial reluctance, a Roman Catholic —the first Roman Catholic church in Philadelphia was St. Joseph's in Willing's Alley, 1733, but almost from the start Mass had been held—Connecticut, a fairly informed colony, as late as 1705 was passing Acts like this:

All who shall entertain any Quakers, Ranters, Adamites, and any other Hereticks, are made liable to the penalty of five pounds, and five pounds per week for any town that shall so entertain them; that all Quakers shall be committed to prison or sent out of the colony; that whoever shall hold any unnecessary discourse with Quakers shall forfeit twenty shillings [and so on].

Tolerance, looking at it from its lowest level, is, as Mr. Castleman said, profitable.

For unknown centuries great Indian trails, with their subsidiary branches, like the trail of the Iroquois Nation of the North to the Cherokee Nation of the South, marked the loneliness of North America. The Indian followed the trails made by the game, and when the white man came he followed the trails of the Indian, and so it can be said that most of the great concrete highways of to-day were laid out, not by engineers, but by elk and buffalo.

The game of America were our original highway commissioners.

One such great trail ran from New England and eastern and lower New York and, crossing the Delaware near Trenton, skirted the peninsula of Coaquannock.

At first the white man's trail was a narrow, muddy and dangerous pack-horse trail, and if people travelled at all, they travelled in numbers for safety. The white man with his pack-horses ruined the smooth silent foot-trails of the Indian. Then the horse-trail widened a little into an equally muddy, or dusty, wagon-road. Finally, around the middle of the eighteenth century, this rutted road evolved into a coach-road or highway, but still an unbelievably rough and uncomfortable one. As a matter of fact, travel in this country, save for the tranquil interregnum of the canal period in the early 1800's, was a pretty grim business until a comparatively little while ago, unless one travelled strictly *de luxe*; and then the clock went round, and now we travel as comfortably as the Indian did three hundred years ago, but more swiftly. But there was no travelling *de luxe* in the eighteenth century unless one had one's especial equipage, as had Thomas Jefferson, and even that was none too good.

As late as 1795 it took two days to go to Baltimore from Philadelphia, and there was no conveyance but a rough mail wagon, and although the time between New York and Philadelphia had been cut to a long day, the journey was an ordeal. You left New York before four in the morning and did not arrive in Philadelphia until well after sunset, having changed stages five times and having crossed the Raritan and the Delaware on scows prepared for the purpose. Those—and there are many—who are disagreeable before breakfast must have been something to travel with, for breakfast was not to be had until you reached New Brunswick at the end of the third change, or stage.

The first regular stage line between New York and Philadelphia was started in 1757—before then there had been a bi-weekly mail wagon—and the journey required two days. When this was bettered, the pride of the stage company was such that it christened its new coach the "Flying Machine". The pack-horse trail, the wagon-road, the coach-road followed the Indian trail, and in 1835, when the first railroad was built connecting Philadelphia and New York, it more or less did the same, as it does to-day. On June 13, 1910, one hundred and fifty-four years after the "Flying Machine", the first aeroplane flight on schedule—Hamilton's—soared above this historic route. Hamilton arrived in Philadelphia in one hour and fifty minutes, just as he said he would. This was five minutes faster than the fastest train of the moment between the two cities.

No wonder then that Philadelphia almost at once became a great town for inns and taverns, and remained so until the coming of the railroads. Even the removal of the Federal Government to Washington in 1800, and of the State government a year before, first to Lancaster and then to Harrisburg, did not affect it greatly in this respect. Until the 1830's it remained the principal stopping-off place between the North and the South, and hardly had it been founded when ships from all over the world began to haunt its harbour, and travellers from all over the world, and from all the colonies, began to frequent it; a fact that added to the city's cosmopolitan attitude, but, since it was Philadelphia, increased the kindly local feeling of superiority toward strangers.

As early as 1683 many immigrants from New York and New England, from Maryland and farther south, had come over the muddy pack-horse trail to settle in Penn's tolerant town, and all during the decade others followed. Philadelphia soon became a shopping centre as well as the principal port of entry for the colonies, and therefore a place of fashions. Increasing wealth meant an increasing flow of imports, many of them goods of luxury. By the middle of the eighteenth century Philadelphia houses were as beautifully furnished and many of them as handsome as the houses of England. All this meant, as well, a steady bolstering of the Quaker and Church of England, not to mention the Mennonite, Lutheran and Moravian, love of good food and wine. It meant a great many other things, too, including the attracting to the city of men of taste and ambition. The hanging signs of the inns and taverns of Philadelphia were as famous as the inns and taverns themselves. The names, the signs were legion.

The Plume of Feathers, the Pewter Platter—where John Evans and William Penn, 2nd, disgraced themselves—the Crooked Billet—where Benjamin Franklin stayed—the Indian Queen, the Indian King, the London Coffee House, the Wigwam, the Prince Eugene, the Queen's Head, the Lion. Horses of every shade, of course; the White Horse, the Black Horse, King George on Horseback; Peg Mullen's Beefsteak House, the Swans, the Three Crowns, the Lemon Tree, the Queen of Hungary, the Bear and Highlandman, the Star and Garter, and so on indefinitely. On the outskirts of the city pleasant inns with gardens sprang up, where strangers stayed or Philadelphians went for supper. By 1744 the increase of taverns and licensed houses of the lower sort was so great that Benjamin Franklin became alarmed. There were over a hundred of such places in the city, in one section so many that it was called "hell-town".

Sixty years after its birth the "green countrie towne" was well away on its career of breath-taking slums. A pre-eminence—one of the few—it has managed to retain even up to to-day.

There is a tradition that the sign of the King of Prussia, the ancient inn built in 1709 and still standing in the outskirts of Philadelphia, was painted by Gilbert Stuart in one of his penniless moments on condition that his name be not used.

The tavern-keepers, imaginative fellows, fostered the inventiveness of the sign painters. The Quiet Woman, for instance, showed a picture of a woman without a head; the Man Full of Trouble, man walking wearily, his wife hanging on his arm, a monkey perched on his shoulder, a parrot on his hand, the wife carrying a bandbox on top of which sat a cat. The XIOU8, translated, meant the Extenuate. The Man Making His Way in the World, depicted the head and shoulders of a man emerging from a terrestrial globe. The Four Alls bore this early communistic inscription: "King: I govern all. General: I fight for all. Minister: I pray for all. Labourer: And I pay for all." Some of the tavern-keepers were poets. "The Widow" Sarah Brown, who ran the Huntsman and Hounds, advertised her establishment with this quatrain:

> Our hounds are goods, and the horse too;
> The buck is near run down;
> Call off the hounds, and let them blow,
> While we regale with Brown.

While William McDermott, simple and direct, merely said:

> I, William McDermott, lives here;
> I sells good porter, ale, and beer;
> I've made my sign a little wider
> To let you know I sell good cider.

The tavern-keepers of Philadelphia anticipated with their signs the "Bar B Q" and hot-dog stands and saloons of to-day, but they were intelligent enough to make their signs artistic and amusing and their places in many instances delightful. There is a charming description of the Yellow Cottage, which stood in Southwark to the south of the city, with its garden going down to the Delaware, and it is pleasant to relate that the misogynist who owned the Quiet Woman in the same district—he had bought it from a Frenchman who had called it the Purple and Blue Tavern—had to change the new sign speedily. His patrons, spoken to in no uncertain terms by their wives, began to go elsewhere. In their own unobtrusive fashion the women of Philadelphia have always had a great deal to do with the affairs of their city. Nor have they been so markedly unobtrusive.

But even Philadelphia's strategic inland position, both for inland travel and inland goods, would have amounted to little had it not been for Philadelphia's port.

The port of Philadelphia was the underlying secret of the city's growth, and despite many vicissitudes, and several natural disadvantages, and long periods of neglect, the port continues to be one of the principal assets of the city. Nowadays a hidden one, and one of which the majority of visitors to Philadelphia are totally unaware, and one of which even the majority of Philadelphians, perhaps, have little knowledge. One can live in Philadelphia all his life and not know that it is a seaport. No great seaport anywhere has less of the sea about it than Philadelphia. Because of the number of United States sailors always on its streets, Philadelphia is constantly reminded of League Island, the historic navy base, the largest naval shipyard in the world, at the southern tip of the town, but unlike New York, or Boston, or Baltimore, or New Orleans, with its ever-present sense of the Mississippi and the Gulf, Philadelphia definitely has the feeling of an inland city.

There is no salt in its air, and no sea-breeze ever blows across it, and in the early 1800's the city began to move away from the Delaware and the docks, and the lovely old brick houses, with their iron grillwork, of the merchants and statesmen and mariners on Second and Third and Fourth and Fifth streets, and is now—the centre of it—fourteen or more blocks to the west, or, as they call them in Philadelphia, to the mystification of everyone else, squares. Furthermore the blocks, or squares, of Philadelphia are long— exactly twice as long as the blocks of New York. And finally all the roads out of Philadelphia except one, the road over the Delaware River suspension Bridge to Camden and southern New Jersey, lead away from the sea and strike out into the hinterland.

To discover the port of Philadelphia, a man, unless he has business there, has to make a pilgrimage.

If he does, suddenly he steps from a huge and bustling self-contained inland city into a port, as if he had stepped across an invisible but definite line. Everything abruptly has to do with the sea: ship chandlers' offices and ship warehouses, and a custom-house, and marine insurance officers, and huge drays drawn by huge horses. And fishmongers, and saloons and restaurants, for sailors, and venerable importing firms for wines and cigars; all the endless paraphernalia and colour of a most especial trade. The look of the people changes, and there are many sailors and merchant-marine officers; and there is the smell of wharves and ships and distance; and everywhere there is the quiet restlessness, the elation, and the ever-changing permanence of the sea.

As for the history of the port, no one is more ignorant than the average Philadelphian, and no one more astonished when you tell him some salient facts about it: its magnificent past, its none too meagre present; despite all manner of discouragements, Philadelphia almost from its beginning in 1682 until around 1812—for a hundred and thirty years, that is—was the principal port of this country, of the colonies, of the new and struggling United States. Philadelphia was responsible for two famous models: the Humphreys frigate, which revolutionized frigate building, and the Philadelphia China trader, which was probably the most beautiful sailing ship ever built in the history of the sea, as fine if not finer than the tall ships of the Honourable East India Company. Philadelphia was the birthplace of the American navy and of the Naval Academy. Philadelphia's privateers both in the War of the Revolution and in the War of 1812 acquitted themselves nobly. Philadelphia had one-third of the China trade; a fact which will astonish most New Englanders. And even when the China clippers of the 1830's and '40's and '50's, the *Witch of the Wave*, the *Nightingale*, the *Cutty Sark*, the *Sea Cloud*—dozens of them with their lovely names and their spread of sail —challenged the more beautiful but slower China trader, Philadelphia managed to hold some of its own.

Tea from China, silk and sugar from the Indies, hemp from Russia, spices from Java and Batavia, gum copal from Zanzibar, coffee from Arabia, hides and ivory from Africa—and black slaves—cork, olives, olive oil, and wines from Spain, port and Madeira from Portugal, sugar from the Philippines, India and the West Indies, lacquer and laquered furniture from the Orient, pepper from Sumatra—and yet who has ever spoken of a "Philadelphia sailor" or a "Philadelphia master", although there have been, and are, thousands of them? And who finds in Philadelphia houses the sea chests and the smell of spice that still haunt the houses of Salem and Boston and Newburyport and New Bedford? A few ivory fans, a few pieces of yellowed ivory. That is all. Old Philadelphia houses have a smell of their own, and a pleasant one, but it is the smell of Europe and Pennsylvania, and not the smell of the sea or of the Orient.

CHAPTER XI

The Shrouds and Masts of Ships

"Long since, when all the docks were filled,
With that sea beauty man has ceased to build."

JOHN MASEFIELD: "SHIPS:"

BUT WHAT A port Philadelphia was, and still is! For two hundred and thirty years the Seven Seas have known the city and its ships.

Not only did Philadelphia originate the Humphreys frigate and the magnificent Philadelphia China trader, but it also designed a famous steamship model out of the yards of the Lynns, the Vaughans, and George Burton that was used on those early New York ships, the Black Ballers. Philadelphia built the first four iron ocean liners to fly the American flag, for twenty years the only American merchantmen to call regularly at western European ports. Philadelphia shipbuilding is as famous to-day as ever, even if the port is no longer supreme. The Cramp Shipyards—originally Grice-Bowers-Cramp—held in collateral, then direct succession from 1760 to 1927, when for a while they were closed to emerge under different management—built during the nineteenth century most of the American navy and a considerable portion of foreign navies as well. To-day they, and the other Philadelphia shipyards, or the neighbouring ones, the New York Shipbuilding Company across the river at Camden, the Sun Shipbuilding and Drydock Company down the river at Chester, a dozen more, large or small, are busier than ever, and not until this war (World War II) is over will their total construction and their new designs be known.

Philadelphia opened up the South American trade with the ship *John* in 1799, or some say the *Fabius*. During the years 1801 to 1802, of the forty-four American ships to enter the Rio de la Plata, fifteen were from Philadelphia. Philadelphia held the record across the Atlantic for sailing ships. In 1809 the *Rebecca Sims*, Bowers-built, Captain Brinton in command, made the trip between the Delaware Capes and Liverpool in fourteen days. Philadelphia also set the coastwise record to Mobile Point—the brig *Huntress*,

1837, nine days, and the record to New Orleans, the bark *Gazelle*, eight days. And the record to Rio de Janeiro, the ship *Roanoke*. Philadelphia built the first ice-breaker in 1835, and a little later, with its fleet of ice-breakers named after various Philadelphia mayors—a great cleansing for the names of some of them—designed a model that has been used since all over the world, and is now being used by the Soviet Government. The first ice-breaker, named candidly the *Ice Breaker*, is still in use carrying molasses from Cuba to Brooklyn. Its bows were, and probably still are, twenty feet thick. Philadelphia even —in 1753—sent a schooner, the *Argo*, by private subscription to continue the search for the North-West Passage.

Henry Hudson would have liked that.

Philadelphia had its own "tea party", but a fairly orderly and quiet Quaker one, although determinedly threatening. Philadelphia heard the echoes off the Delaware Capes of the pirates, the buccaneers, of the end of the seventeenth century and the beginning of the eighteenth. For a hundred years privateers with their letters of marque used the Delaware. Philadelphia built a major portion of the American navy during the War of the Revolution, or the War of Independence, to give it its less formidable name; six frigates, fifty-four craft of all kinds for the Pennsylvania State navy; a great quantity of private armed vessels. Decatur, Barry, John Paul Jones, Truxtun, other great ones, at various times sailed out of Philadelphia, and Barry and Truxton were Philadelphians. Or rather, Barry was an Irishman, born at Tacum-shane, County Wexford, and Truxtun was born on Long Island, but both became Philadelphians. There is a statue of Barry in Independence Square. The first American naval expedition—American, not colonial—weighed anchor from Philadelphia. And finally "Old Ironsides" was—is—a Philadelphia ship.

Yes, she is.

She was built in Hartt's shipyard in Boston, one of the first three frigates of the young United States, her keel laid in 1794, her launching in 1797, but the soul and mind of her were Philadelphian; "Old Ironsides", the United States frigate *Constitution*, whose nickname was given her by her sailors on that hot August afternoon of 1812 when the round-shot of the *Guerrière* bounced back from her live-oak ribs. Her sailors lined her side and cheered as the *Guerrière* struck her flag. All the rest of that famous first fleet, with its resounding names, was Philadelphian, too: the *President*, the *Congress*, the *United States*, the *Constellation*, the *Chesapeake*, although, with the exception of the *United States*, they were all built elsewhere. Everyone, however, was a Humphreys model, even if in some cases, as in the case of the *Chesapeake*, the design was changed to the disadvantage of the ship.

The frigate *Philadelphia*, more distinguished for its misfortunes than any-thing else and the fact that, captured by the Barbary pirates, it was retaken and burned in the harbour of Tripoli in February of 1804 by Stephen Decatur on the first of his expeditions to end the shameful tribute to North Africa, was, like the *United States*, not only Philadelphia-designed but Philadelphia-built.

Joshua Humphreys, "the father of the American navy", believed in fast, heavily-armed ships, but ones stoutly enough built to take the most severe of punishments. He was one of the first naval architects to balance properly speed, power, and defence. He was also one of the first of Americans to realize that America was destined to be, in fact had to be, a great naval power. He urged constantly a powerful navy. And Joshua Humphreys was not only a Philadelphian, but what is even more interesting, a Quaker, born in Delaware County, the son of one of the original settlers. To add further to the interest, his son Samuel was chief of construction to the United States Navy, and his grandson, General Andrew Humphreys, West Point, 1831, was one of the most distinguished engineers and combat officers of the Civil War. Subsequently, until retired in 1879, chief of engineers of the United States Army.

The more you read or see of Quakers, the less you find them innately pacific. There is something queer about them. You may have noticed it yourself. When they fight—and nowadays most of them do—they make peculiarly tenacious soldiers. They are stout folk with a good deal of hidden choler. Wrestling with the "spirit" seems to make them as strong, not to mention obstinate, as wrestling with the angel made Jacob.

Philadelphia also saw the first American steamboat—the boat of the unfortunate John Fitch—which puffed up and down the Delaware, its engines exploding to the horror of some and the derision or amusement of the majority, who thought it at best merely a dangerous toy. This was almost twenty-five years before the Hudson saw Robert Fulton and his *Clermont*. Or, to give its full name, *The North River Steamboat of Clermont*.

Let New Yorkers take notice of this, although, when told, none but the more instructed believe. And let New Englanders take notice of this.

Not only was Philadelphia from 1784 to 1850 responsible for one-third of the American China trade, but there is fairly conclusive evidence that Philadelphia started that trade. At all events, it was Robert Morris, financier of the Revolution, signer of the Declaration of Independence, and, together with Thomas Willing, founder in 1754 of Philadelphia's first great firm of merchants, Willing and Morris, who was the moving spirit of the group of Philadelphia, Boston, and New York shipowners who, shortly after peace was signed in 1783, sent a ship to China to see if the dominance of the British East India Company could be broken. They found that it could be to the tune of about twenty-five per cent profit per voyage, and so at once Thomas Truxtun, John Donaldson, Nalbro Frazer, John Pringle, and Tench Coxe dispatched the tactfully-named *Canton*. Shortly after this, other Philadelphians—Fishers, Dales, Walns, Brinkers, Hazelhursts—did the same, and it was a Philadelphia ship, the *United States*, that opened up the American trade with India by entering the port of Pondicherry.

Philadelphia also had its own submarine, Belton's of 1778, although there is nothing particularly original about that, as in 1775 Sergeant Lee of the Continental Army, in David Bushnell's "Turtle", had attempted to torpedo His Majesty's ship *Eagle* in New York Harbour, and might have done so had the screw attached to his torpedo been strong enough to penetrate the *Eagle's* copper-lined bottom.

Submarines have been in the minds of men for many generations, and if not so long as Icarus and the first thought of the aeroplane, at all events, as early as 1620. In that year Cornelius van Drebel, a Dutchman, exhibited the first model—his—to a none too interested James I on the Thames in England. By 1727 fourteen patents for submarines had been taken out. More noteworthy was the fact that a Pennsylvanian invented what looks like the first amphibian tank, and that Philadelphia first witnessed its successful demonstration. This was Oliver Evans' "Orukter Amphiboles" of 1804. Designed by Evans as a dock-cleaning machine, it was mounted on wheels and carried a five-horse-power engine, and when Evans put it in the Schuylkill, and then the Delaware, and attached a paddle-wheel to its stern, after taking it across land on its wheels, it went up and down both rivers successfully; sixteen miles up the Delaware, "leaving all the vessels that were under sail full halfway behind. . . ." But what was more remarkable, the "Orukter Amphiboles" was really amphibian, for it had first, before taking to the Schuylkill, circled Centre Square, and then had proceeded in a stately fashion out Market Street.

On July 13, 1805, there appeared this advertisement in the Philadelphia *Gazette:*

To the Public:

In my first attempt to move the Orukter Amphiboles, or Amphibious Digger, to the water by the power of steam, the wheels and axle-trees proved insufficient to bear so great a burden, and having previously obtained the permission of the Board of Health (for whom this machine is constructed), to gratify the citizens of Philadelphia by the sight of this mechanical curiosity, on the supposition that it may lead to useful improvements, the workmen who had constructed it voluntarily offered their labor to make, without wages, other wheels and axle-trees of sufficient strength, and to receive as their reward one-half of the sum that may be received from a generous public for the sight thereof—half to be at the disposal of the inventor, who pledges himself that it shall be applied to defray the expenses of other new and useful inventions which he has already conceived and arranged in his mind, and which he will put in operation only when the money arising from the inventions already made will defray the expenses. The above machine is NOW to be seen MOVING AROUND CENTRE SQUARE at the expense of the workmen, who expect twenty-five cents from every generous person who may come to see its operation. But all are invited to come and view it, as well those who cannot, as who can conveniently spare the money.

Oliver Evans

The author of the above breath-defying sentences was one of the most distinguished of American inventors, now, strangely enough, almost forgotten except by engineers. Oliver Evans, a farm boy born near Newport, Delaware, in 1775, at the age of twenty-two invented a machine for carding wool and cotton, and from then on various other labour-saving devices, and before long turned his attention to the steam engine. He was the first steam-engine builder in the United States, and by 1812 ten of his high-pressure engines were in use in Florida, Louisiana, Kentucky, Mississippi, Ohio,

Pennsylvania, and Connecticut. But, as is usually the case with inventors, he was looked upon as being slightly insane by most of his contemporaries, especially when in 1804 he bet $3,000 that he could "make a carriage go by steam on a level road faster than any horse", or could build carriages "to run on a railway at fifteen miles an hour". No one offered to bet against him, however. Steam was beginning to be taken seriously. A little later he accurately described the railways that before long were to make their appearance. He predicted they would run at the incredible rate of "fifteen to twenty miles an hour". A carriage would "leave Washington in the morning, breakfast at Baltimore, dine at Philadelphia, and sup at New York on the same day. . . ."[1]

Nor is this all; Philadelphia also saw the birth of the United States Marines. Here it is—on a bronze tablet over a garage at the back of the present Merchants Warehouse, halfway between Chestnut and Walnut, on Water Street down by the docks:

This tablet marks
The site of Tun Tavern
The birthplace of the
United States Marine Corps.
Here in 1775 Captain Samuel
Nicholas, the first Marine
Officer, opened a recruiting
Rendezvous for the Marine
Battalions authorized by
Resolution of the
Continental Congress
November 10, 1775.

The Tun Tavern was a favourite meeting-place. On the wall of the same garage is another bronze tablet commemorating the organization of the first Masonic lodge in America, an event which took place at the Tun Tavern on St. John's Day (June 24), 1732.

Philadelphia, at least its historians, knows these things, but with the Quaker reticence which affects, and often afflicts, the city, makes small mention of them. In addition to what is surely known, there are a couple of other important "firsts" which Philadelphia suspects it might claim, but about which it is not entirely certain.

It is just possible, for instance, that the whaling industry of America began on the Delaware and not an Nantucket or New Bedford. At all events, whalers were at work in the river as early as 1633, seven years before the first New England whalery. Moreover, it is likely that Philadelphia had a great part, never acknowledged, in the development of that beautiful and symbolic ship the American clipper. In 1719 Jonathan Dickenson designed

---

[1] Both science and invention are blind gods. Neither the scientist, nor the inventor, nor anyone else, knows whether discovery will benefit the world or not. Man has a way of twisting good things into bad; and then, surprisingly, twisting bad things into good. Oliver Evans, excellent if curious man, invented machine-made flour and so for generations robbed American bread of the vitamins, just recently restored.

a "sharp built" sloop that embodied exactly the same ideas as those used by Donald McKay and William Webb a hundred and thirty years later. But Philadelphia does not need these laurels, for it can stand alone and unchallenged with its memory of the China trader. The clipper ships may have outsailed the China traders, but they were no more beautiful and not as majestic. With the opening up of the American trade with the Orient in 1784, for three decades and longer the tall ships of Philadelphia could have tied brooms to their fore-trucks as Admiral van Tromp tied them to the fore-trucks of his fleet as he swept up the Thames.

One after another the China traders took to the seas: Commodore Thomas Truxtun's *Canton;* Commodore John Barry's *Asla;* Samuel Archer's *Coromandel;* Willing and Francis' *Bengal;* Jesse Waln's *William Penn;* Stephen Girard's *China Packet* and his *North American* and *Superb,* and then, from 1790 on, his major fleet named after philosophers: the *Rousseau,* the *Montesquieu,* the *Helvetius,* the *Voltaire.* Prior to 1822 twenty-five or more great China traders were sailing to China or India. Around 1822 fifteen or so were added. Altogether there were close on fifty of these magnificent ships. Philadelphia ships were enduring, too. Stephen Girard's *Rousseau* was in service for ninety-three years. Built in 1801, she was not retired until 1894. The *Truelove,* built by the Eyres in 1764, came back up the Delaware like a homing pigeon in 1873, a hundred and ten years later, by then a whaler out of Hull, England. Endurance, speed, and, overlaying them, great beauty distinguished these ships, for Philadelphia has always been a city of craftsmen. By 1785 the Boston and Baltimore and New York newspapers were advertising ships "built of the best white oak and finished off in the neatest manner on the Philadelphia plan." And to add the finishing touch, Philadelphia figureheads became as famous as Philadelphia ships. Many of these figureheads were carved by the sculptor William Rush.

When the China trader *Ganges* entered for the first time the harbour of Calcutta, a Rush figurehead, the "River God", at her bow, the peasants followed her in boats or knelt along the shores as she passed, thinking an avatar had come to visit them.

In the very first year of Penn's arrival, 1682, he was able to write Lord North in London: "Twenty-two sail more have arrived since I came. . . . Since last summer we have had about sixty sail of great and small shipping, which is a good beginning." In 1696 the ubiquitous Gabriel Thomas set down this description:

Now the true reason why this fruitful country and flourishing city advance so considerably in the purchase of lands is their great and extended traffique and commerce, both by sea and land, viz., to New-York, New-England, Virginia, Maryland, Carolina, Jamaica, Barbadoes, Nevis, Monserat, Antego, St. Christophers, Barmudoes, New-Foundland, Maderas, Saltetudeous, and Old-England; besides several other places. Their merchandise chiefly consists in horses, pipestaves, pork and beef, salted and barreled up, bread and flour, all sorts of grain, peas, beans, skins, furs, tobacco and potatoes, pot-ashes, wax, &c., which are bartered for rumm, suger, molasses, silver, negroes, salt, wine, linen, household goods &c.

By 1752 these exports had grown annually to 125,000 barrels of flour, 86,550 bushels of wheat, 28,338 tons of wheat biscuits, 90,743 bushels of corn, 3,431 tons of bacon, 925 tons of beef, 4,812,943 staves, 57 boxes of ginseng root, 4,491 tons of bar iron, 9,865 hogsheads of flax seed, 305 boxes of furs and deerskins.

The item of ginseng root is a curious one. Before the Revolution the farmers around Philadelphia and along the Susquehanna grew considerable ginseng root for China, where, as you remember, it is supposed to promote fertility and the birth of boy children.

The Rev. Israel Acrelius, the Swedish missionary who wrote so charmingly of the Swedish settlers along the Delaware, in speaking of the port of Philadelphia in the middle of the eighteenth century, states that in a single day of October, 1754, one hundred and seventeen large ships were at the docks or in the river.

To the West India Islands are sent [he says] wheat flour, bread, Indian corn or maize, beef, bacon, cheese, butter, staves, bar-iron and cedar shingles. There is brought thence rum, Muscavado sugar, syrup, Spanish gold or silver coin, and exchange upon England. . . . To the Bay of Honduras are sent all kinds of provisions and thence are brought various kinds of wood—mahogany, lignum-vitae, logwood, Brazil wood. . . . From the Gulf of Mexico, called the Musqueto shore, buffalo hides are brought. . . . With Rotterdam has sprung up a very profitable commerce in the transportation of German and Swiss immigrants. The ships go to South Carolina, where a cargo of rice is taken in, and duty paid to England; after which they go to Rotterdam. . . . Each person has to pay £70 (copper coin) for the passage. Those who have no means . . . are sold to service for three, four, or five years.

This Rotterdam trade, and similar immigration from other European ports, was an enormous factor in the early shipping of Philadelphia and in the settlement of the city and the province. Between 1702 and 1727 it is estimated that at least 45,000 or more Palatinate Germans—Moravians, Amish, Mennonites, Dunkards, Schwenkfelders, Lutherans, in addition to those already there—immigrated to Pennsylvania. Between December 1728 and December 1729 alone, 6,400 persons, Germans, Irish, a few Scots and Welsh, arrived. In the year 1728, 4,500 immigrants, mostly Irish, landed at New Castle, Delaware. James Logan—even James Logan the wise and tolerant—became alarmed at the influx of these Celts and complained lest they take over the city: "It looks as if Ireland is to send all its inhabitants hither. The common fear is that if they continue to come, they will make themselves masters of the place. It is strange that they thus crowd where they are not wanted". In 1755 Douglas, the historian, shares James Logan's alarm. "This colony", he writes, "by importation of foreigners and other strangers in very large numbers, grows prodigiously; by their laborious and

penurious manner of living, in consequence they grow rich where others
starve, and by their superior industry and frugality may in time drive out
the British people from the colony."

Xenophobia is an interesting malady, isn't it?—the fear and hatred of
foreigners and new arrivals. "Foreigners" are merely people who are not
born where you were born. The words "rival" and "river" come from the
same root, and a rival is merely a man who lives on the other side of the
river and is therefore, *ipso facto*, an enemy and a "foreigner". We shall
come later to the anti-Irish, anti-Roman Catholic, Native American, Know-
Nothing riots that disgraced Penn's "Holy Experiment" in the 1840's. It
is well for all whose nationalities have gone into the making of every great
country to remember that at one time or another each ancestor they had, late
or early in coming, was also a rival and an enemy and a "foreigner". William
Penn was a "foreigner" to the Indians.

On the other hand, Americans of more ancient lineage should take no
shame should they find in their family tree a "redemptioner"; a "bond
servant" or two, male or female. If they are really interested, they should
first find out on what charge the young man or woman in question was committed. In the eighteenth century in one day alone some twenty or so young
women were hung in a row in London for stealing a loaf of bread each for
their starving children. Apparently they had not enough influence to become
redemptioners. Even in the colonies, except such liberal ones as Penn's
province and Maryland, you could get into trouble with the greatest of ease.
In North Carolina, for instance, a province settled largely by hardy and free-
dom-loving Scots, there were over fifty offences for which you could be hung;
occasionally also, if you were a slave, you could be burned. Many of the
redemptioners were ambitious, adventurous, discontented young people, or
skilled mechanics, who worked out their passage money in this way. Others
were indicted for the most minor of misdemeanours, or through the machinations
of enemies. Some were the cream of the country, political rebels. After
the Monmouth Rebellion thousands of his followers were sent out to various
parts of the world as bond servants. In 1728 there appeared in Philadelphia
this advertisement:

*Lately imported, and to be sold cheap, a parcel of likely men and women
servants.*

The school of history which for the last three decades has concentrated
on making Americans apologetic for their past and ashamed and fearful of
their present, argues from biased grounds, largely personal, and exhibits
great lacunæ, either deliberate or unwitting.

We are still the children of a dream.

CHAPTER XII

Tides and Currents

"Men travel far to see a city, but few seem curious about a river. Every river has, nevertheless, its individuality, its great silent interest. Every river has, moreover, its influence over the people who pass their lives within sight of its waters."

H. S. MERRIMAN.

WITH THE FORESIGHT that distinguished him in everything but his finances and the raising of his children, William Penn had foreseen what the great hardwood forests on the upper reaches of the Delaware would mean to Philadelphia. They would mean ships and they would mean lumber both for export and domestic use. Man lives off the soil but most of the time forgets it. The forests of England had been exhausted by the end of the sixteenth century, and England could not live without ships. "The hearts of oak" began to some extent to be imported. Scientific forestry did not come to England until 1919, after the last war had taught England that no great country can live without forests. William Penn advertised in his early prospectuses directly for shipbuilders and shipping men of every sort, and the response was large. As a result, shipbuilding became a hereditary profession in Philadelphia, and all that went with it: pilotage, ship ownership, the merchant marine.

One of the earliest settlers was William West, master shipwright, who, with William Penn as a silent partner, had hardly arrived in Philadelphia before he laid the keel of a vessel. The name of this first Philadelphia ship is unfortunately lost to history, but there is a tradition that it was called the *Amity*, in honour no doubt of the ship which had recently brought over Surveyor-General Thomas Holme. William Penn gave William West a plot of ground on the Delaware at the foot of the present Vine Street as a site for his enterprise, and so began the initial Philadelphia shipyard: the small but sturdy ancestor of the huge Cramp and other shipyards of to-day. By the turn of the century—within eighteen years, that is—there were, as has been said, four shipyards.

Down from the upper reaches of the Delaware came the logs, and these were either used in Philadelphia, or processed there, or sometimes made into huge ship-rafts that were sent up and down the coast to other colonies or even across the Atlantic. Hardy mariners must have sailed them, although they were constructed in the shape of ships. Some of these rafts contained as many as eight hundred logs, enough to build six ships of two hundred and fifty tons each, and some time before the Revolution it was said a ship-raft of five thousand tons was dispatched to England. This was called the *Baron Renfrew*. The last ship-raft reached England just before the Revolution.

For over a hundred years Philadelphia, then, among other things, was a logging town. All that while the forests were disappearing; but as they disappeared, the rich cut-over lands were turned into farms, so at an early date Philadelphia became an exporter of grain and flour as well as logs and lumber. But the best export, and, as always, the best advertisement, was Quaker honesty. One of the earliest officers of Penn's "Holy Experiment", and one who seems to have done his duty, was the "Searcher and Packer of Flour and Bread and Regulator of Weights and Measures". Quaker flour became famous; Philadelphia bread, wholesome, and almost equally well known. Benjamin Franklin, upon his arrival from Boston, was amazed at the amount of good bread he could buy for a penny.

William West was shortly followed by other shipwrights: Bartholomew Penrose, son of a Bristol shipwright; James West, a relative of William's; Hermanus Wiltbank, who had arrived in Pennsylvania in 1665, seventeen years before the founding of Philadelphia, and others. The Society of Free Traders constructed numerous whaleboats for their whalery at Cape May. William Penn had his sons William, 2nd, and Springett instructed in the craft of shipbuilding. Richard Castleman, the observant and pleased, but not always accurate, visitor, said that by 1710 over three hundred ships had been built in Philadelphia, in addition to numerous small craft, "which may give us," he observed, "an idea of the Opulency of the Place".

No accurate records were kept until 1772, but between 1772 and 1774 forty-two large vessels—large for the times—were built, and as early as 1692, Jonathan Dickenson, a very accurate observer, wrote: "We are Rarely without ten or twelve Vessels on ye Stocks—Ships, Brigantines and Sloops, haveing orders from Bristol and London to Build for Merchants there." In 1718, twenty-six years later, he wrote again: "Here is great employ for shipwork from England. It increases and will increase, and our expectations from the iron-works forty miles up the Schuylkill are very great." With the exception of Massachusetts, Pennsylvania became the leading shipbuilder of the colonies. The growth was steady for the quality was high, and all through the eighteenth century the fame of Philadelphia ships increased. It reached its height in the three decades following the Revolution, just as did the activity of the port. Brissot de Warville mentions the fineness of Philadelphia ships and shipyards, saying they were the best in the United States; and Colonel Champion, Member of Parliament, who had been in the colonies, told the House of Commons in 1784:

An American ship will pay for herself in six years, whilst the British ship will not accomplish it in less than ten. New England has supplied about two-fifths of the whole number of American ships employed in Great Britain. But the most beautiful are those built in Philadelphia where this art has attained to the greatest perfection equal, perhaps superior, to any other part of the world.

One thing leads to another, and where there is any flowering of a craft or science, subsidiary discoveries or improvements are constantly being made. In 1730 Thomas Godfrey, a glazier by trade, and a self-educated astronomer, invented his quadrant, an epoch-making improvement on the one then in use.

By the time of the full blossoming of Philadelphia shipping, by the time of that apogee, the period of the tall Philadelphia China trader, Philadelphia ships were in demand all over the world as they had been in demand in England from the start.   Philadelphia built for the Czar of Russia, the King of Spain, the Dey of Algiers.   For the last it even built corsairs: the *Hamdullah*, the *Leila Eisha*, the brig *Hassan Bashaw*.   "Bad medicine", for in the later expeditions of Decatur and Bainbridge against the Barbary pirates following the War of 1812, Algiers and Tunis figured as well as Tripoli.   Two Philadelphia naval constructors, Samuel Humphreys and Samuel Bowers, showed a high degree of patriotism, and one, Bowers, an early sense of our modern knowledge that the world is closely knit and that therefore it behoves all men to let their right hand know exactly what their left is doing.

The King of Spain asked Bowers through the Spanish ambassador to become chief naval architect of the Spanish navy, then engaged against the English under Lord Nelson, and Bowers refused, dryly remarking that he did not wish to know any better the two leading traits of the Spanish character, "treachery and assassination".

Humphreys, son of Joshua Humphreys, refused a similar offer from the Czar of Russia because he felt it his duty to stay with the navy of his own small and struggling country.   The Czar had offered him ten times more salary than the United States was paying, a town house in St. Petersburg, a country house, a coach, servants—any extras he wanted.   Sixty thousand dollars a year was the salary offered, plus all manner of other allowances.

Fine men, Bowers and Humphreys!   Modern cartel makers should look them up.   Down-river at Wilmington, Eleuthère Irenée du Pont de Nemours, royalist refugee from France, who had started powder mills, in 1831 refused to sell ammunition to the secessionist leaders of South Carolina, "the destination of this powder being obvious", and a little later, before the Mexican War, declined in a similar manner to have dealings with President Santa Anna, who in a few years was to become the slaughterer of the Alamo.   This attitude, of course, was exactly what Penn had meant by his "Holy Experiment".

Generation after generation the Philadelphia shipbuilders wrought, and along with them the carvers, riggers, sailmakers and artisans who built the figureheads and finished the fine interiors and set the masts and spars and furnished them.   Rope-walks were numerous.   It came to be a saying that the finest ship had a Boston bottom and a Philadelphia top.   William Rush, born in 1756, son of a Philadelphia ship carpenter, became the most famous figurehead sculptor of his day.   Apprenticed as a boy to the great Edward Cutbush of London, he came back to Philadelphia to design his "River God" for the *Ganges*, his "Indian Trader" for the *William Penn*, his "Montezuma" for the *Montezuma,* and scores of other figureheads.   He was the first carver ever to use a walking attitude for his figures, as if they too were going along with the ship, or rather, leading it.   Heretofore all figureheads had rested athwart the cutwater.   In his grimmer moments, Rush made statues of William Penn, Voltaire, Franklin, and other famous men—very good statues, too—and among his better-known works was a heroic female statue called "Commerce".   Why?   Female, that is.   And a group, "Leda and the Swan", sometimes called more chastely, "The Nymph and the Swan", which he managed to get through the Philadelphia censorship of the time—

1809. This was first erected in Centre Square, now the site of the City Hall, and subsequently removed to Fairmount Park. In a doubly allegorical mood he designed another well-known group, two recumbent figures—male: "The Schuylkill in an Improved State"; female: "The Schuylkill in Chains". This, too, was first erected in Centre Square and then removed to Fairmount Park.

Perhaps the most famous shipbuilding family of Philadelphia's days of sail was the Penrose family, descendants of Bartholomew, son of the Bristol shipwright, just as the Cramp family were the most famous shipbuilders of Philadelphia's days of steam. Joshua Humphreys, "father of the American navy" was an apprentice of James Penrose, grandson of Bartholomew.

Bartholomew, with William Penn (back in England), William Penn, 2nd, and William Trent as partners, and James Logan as bookkeeper, launched his first ship, the *Diligence*, one hundred and fifty tons, May 24, 1707. Until 1845, one hundred and thirty-nine years in direct succession, the Penrose family built ships, and the women were as good as the men despite William Rush's statue of "The Schuylkill in Chains". In the middle of the eighteenth century Ann Penrose "shipwright", was in charge of the family fortunes. The Lynn family were master shipwrights from 1717 until 1860. There were other ship-building firms in which the business was handed down from father to son through many generations. The Cramp Company, originally Grice-Bowers-Cramp, later changed to Cramp & Sons, built ships in collateral, and then direct succession from 1760 to 1927. Outside of scores of naval vessels and ocean liners, Cramp & Sons built the first *Corsair*, progenitor of those yachts so famous that one becomes confused as to whether the Morgans sailed the *Corsairs* or the Corsairs sailed the *Morgans*.

Perhaps the most momentous ship built by the Cramps—and they built many—was the U.S.S. *Mississippi*, the man-of-war on which, on July 14, 1853, Commodore Matthew Calbraith Perry opened up the hidden empire of Japan.

Shipping families were as well confirmed in succession as were the builders; outside of those already mentioned were the Emlens, the Willings, the Mordecai Lewises, the Simses, the McCreas, the Bories, the Gurneys, the Ridgeways, to mention only a few. And the growth of the port kept pace with its ship-building.

By 1805 arrivals from foreign ports had grown to 547; clearances, 617. Coastwise arrivals, 1,196; clearances, 1,231. A total tonnage of around 110,000. In 1793 the exports of Philadelphia exceeded those of all New England by $1,717,572 and those of New York by $2,934,370. In that year, 1793, the total of Philadelphia exports was $6,958,736, one fourth of the total for the entire country. With steam, despite a series of disasters and increasing handicaps, the port, unbowed, if definitely bloody, continued to hold its head up.

As early as 1821 Thomas Cope, Philadelphia shipowner, established a line of regular sail packet-boats to Liverpool which eventually changed to steam. The *Lancaster* is supposed to have been the name of the first sail liner. In 1832 the Boston and Philadelphia Steamship Company was formed, and in 1842, the Clyde Line, which, at first with only a single small steamer between Philadelphia and New York, developed later into one of the great coastwise and West Indian companies of the country. The Boston and Philadelphia Line became known as the Winsor Line from the name of its owners, and it too developed into a great and far-spreading line. In 1844 the Ericcson Line—Philadelphia to Baltimore—started operations, and in 1871 the famous old Red Star Company—Philadelphia to Antwerp—was founded. A year later Philadelphia saw the birth, under the auspices of the Pennsylvania Railroad, of the American Line, with its four original steamers, *Pennsylvania, Ohio, Illinois,* and *Indiana.* These were the liners already mentioned—the first four iron ocean liners made in the United States.

In 1893 the International Navigation, which was the parent of the International Mercantile Marine, succeeded the American Line. Two 10,700-ton liners, the *St. Louis* and *St. Paul,* were built by Cramp's and were put into service in 1895. In 1902 the 12,500-ton steamers *Kroonland* and *Finland,* also built by Cramp's, joined the fleet. These were later transferred to New York, but in 1902 the International Mercantile Marine put into the Philadelphia–Queenstown–Liverpool service the steamers *Meriom* and *Haverford,* names dear and familiar to all Philadelphians, and although the *Merion* was sunk in the Dardanelles early in World War I, her sister "suburban liner" maintained service until 1924. Then she was broken up for junk.

With that, the history of Philadelphia as a passenger port for Europe ended. At least for the time being.

During its biggest era of steam—the biggest, that is, with the exception of the 1914 war and the present one—statistics of which are enormous but as yet unknown, during the 1890's and the early decades of the 1900's, twenty-three steamship lines, large, small, coastwise, deep-water, freight or passenger, either had Philadelphia as their home port or maintained services there.

To take some recent figures: in 1935, the port of Philadelphia, no longer, and not for almost a century and a quarter, the premier port of the country, but sunk now to eighth place—in 1910 it was fifth; in 1920 it had climbed back to fourth; in 1933 it sank to eighth—had a shipping business of 32,378,567 tons, worth a little short of a billion dollars. The custom receipts for that year were $24,105,718. The next year these increased over $4,000,000, a sign that shippers, both foreign and domestic, were beginning to take a renewed interest in the Delaware. For the eleven months and seven days ending December 7, 1941, the last figures available, Philadelphia's exports and imports had risen to 44,948,882 short tons. In 1941 arrivals at Philadelphia were 7,992; clearances, 8,015. Included in this is the traffic, mostly coastwise, of the lower Schuylkill.

Most people overlook the fact, including the majority of Philadelphians, that the lower Schuylkill is a great port in itself. It does not look like a port, or even the possibilities of one, as you cross it on the bridges of the city; the Walnut Street Bridge, the South Street Bridge, the Chestnut Street Bridge, and so on. It just looks small, dirty, and disreputable. But in 1935 the commerce of the lower Schuylkill alone was 10,066,667 tons, with a value of $116,047,297. And it is from the lower Schuylkill that most of the oil-tankers depart for the oil ports of Texas and still, to some extent, Mexico. Oil-tankers deserve a note in themselves, for they are neglected, and they are strange. Go aboard one the night before sailing and you are in a bewildering inferno of huge rubber hose, and the remnants of black oil, and dirty men in sea boots working apparently without order under arc lights. But stay aboard and see what happens, for within a day the tanker, out at sea, is sliding through the waves as neat and shining and serene almost as Kipling's "lady", the liner.

Like a tide, but with none of the regularity of a tide, the fortunes of the port of Philadelphia rose and fell with what was happening in the colonies; the young United States; the rest of the world. After a while—in another ten thousand years or so—men will get through their heads, possibly, that humanity, red, white, yellow and black, is connected. In the 1930's dust from the Dust Bowl blew across Philadelphia and turned the sunsets of the "main line" red. Famine in Montana sits down to supper with a Philadelphia stevedore.

And here an interpolation must be made lest there be misunderstanding: Philadelphia ranks eighth among the ports of the country, but if all the neighbouring ports, Wilmington, Chester, and so on, are counted, the total traffic of the Delaware ranks a good second. That figure is often used, but it is not altogether fair.

Philadelphia's period of sail can be divided into three main epochs: one small, two large. First, the meagre but steadily growing era of shipbuilding for the province itself and for England, and the steadily growing export of flour, grain, lumber, and so on, with the accompanying import of English goods. Second, the heavy trade with Europe and the flamboyant trade with the West Indies during most of the eighteenth century. Third, the great and colourful period of the Philadelphia China trader and the India trade, begin ning after the War of the Revolution and continuing at its full height until around 1812, and after that, although diminished and competing with steam, vigorous until 1850.

Pennsylvania products, naturally, became equally varied and voluminous. They were no longer mostly "flour, grain, and staves".

All during the eighteenth century we were in far closer touch with the great crescent-shaped, fourteen-hundred-mile-long sub-continent of sub-merged mountain peaks known as the West Indies than we have ever been since. "The Islands", as yet undevastated by yellow fever and slave insur-rections, were at their richest, so much so that in Paris there was a phrase, applying particularly to the sugar barons of Haiti, "as rich as a Creole". Nowadays "the Islands" have become remote and exotic, the objective mostly of cruise ships; but during the eighteenth century there was constant inter-course and exchange with this country, especially with Antigua and Barbadoes, and this applied even to the interchange of families. All one has to do to discover the latter fact is to look into the history of Philadelphia, or Charleston, or New Orleans, or visit the lonely live-oaked cemeteries of certain of "the Islands", Spanish moss throwing black shadows on the headstones. This trading to and fro of residence was accelerated greatly, of course, by the War of the Revolution and the exodus from "the Islands" during the slave insurrections that marked the beginning of the nineteenth century. Of the sixty thousand or so loyalist families that left this country after the Revolution—the majority of loyalist families didn't—many settled in the West Indies. Of the indefinite number of families that left the West Indies when Toussaint L'Ouverture and other slave chiefs struck, a number immigrated to this country. And all during the eighteenth century, until the China and India trade came along to make a fourth, there were three great trade routes out of Philadelphia and the rest of northern America.

The first was up and down the coast and to the West Indies. The second was across the Atlantic to England. The third, farther south, was across the Atlantic by way of the Azores and Madeira—the "wine islands" as they were called—to Portugal, Spain, and the Mediterranean. It was from this third route that Philadelphia acquired its taste for Madeira wine. Philadelphia traded wheat and flour, cattle and sheep, barrels and lumber for the rice and indigo of South Carolina, the tar and shipmasts of North Carolina, the tobacco of Virginia and Maryland, the codfish of Massachusetts. From the West Indies came sugar and rum. Often the West Indian run was triangular.

The American ships unloaded their native products at various of "the Islands," took on rum and sugar for England, and in England took on silk, wool, tea, furniture, and other staples and luxuries for the home run. This proved to be enormously profitable. In 1748 it was estimated that a cargo out of Philadelphia worth £11,900, translated into rum and sugar for England, and there translated into goods for the colonies, brought a return of £61,500. By 1768 a cargo worth £50,400 brought a return of £432,100, almost 900 per cent. No wonder Philadelphians began to be wealthy, and at an early date. American walnut was in especial demand by the great cabinet-makers of eighteenth-century England, and so a great deal of the beautiful furniture brought to this country saw its birth in the forests of America; a sort of "return of the native". Before long American cabinet-makers began to be pretty good themselves, including William Savery of Philadelphia; and in the 1820's, the great Duncan Phyfe.

Meanwhile, none need worry lest these triangular runs to England deprived the colonies of their much-needed rum, that historic American drink.

Outside of what was manufactured at home from the sugar directly imported from the West Indies, Philadelphia's record for imported wines and rum was heroic. Between March 25, 1711, and February 6, 1713, a scant two years, the figures are: "Wine: 459 pipes, 15 hogsheads, 25 quarter casks, or 59,579 gallons; rum: 574 hogsheads, 360 tierces, 185 barrels, 1 kilderkin, 200 gallons, 1 pipe, 19 casks, 2 puncheons, and four gross bottles, or 60,345 gallons." In 1753 the population of Philadelphia had grown to a scant 14,563; the annual importation of rum from the West Indies was 400,000 gallons. It is only fair to add, however, that Philadelphia was the principal distributing point for this product, and that a great deal of it went to the Indians. By this time the "Holy Experiment" had taught the Indians a lot about drinking. Tedyuscung, last great chief of the Delawares, prominent around the 1750's, and when sober as fine a man as his predecessor, Tammany, of William Penn's time, was drunk for months on end; gloriously, steadfastly, and Amerinded-ly drunk: a condition the Philadelphians took advantage of in their dealings with him. Tedyuscung was notorious for his habits even in what might most conservatively be called a drinking town and a drinking century, and was finally, in 1763, burned to death by Indian enemies while lying drunk in his cabin.

There is a very fine statue of Tedyuscung, sober, on a hill overlooking Wissahickon Drive in Fairmount Park.

Tedyuscung and Tammany are the Indian deities of Philadelphia, but Tedyuscung had his revenge when, a hundred and fifty-six years later, Prohibition came to bedevil Penn's town as well as the rest of the country. The author of *Ten Nights in a Barroom and What I Saw There*, a book that sold even more copies than *Uncle Tom's Cabin*, and had an equal influence, and is still selling, alas, was a Philadelphian, or rather a Baltimorean who spent most of his life in Philadelphia. The house of Timothy Shay Arthur is a Philadelphia landmark at 721 South Tenth Street, and annually a number of disagreeable-looking people reverently visit it.

Before long another and a sinister run was added to the triangular run to London. This was often a quadrangular run that carried American goods to the West Indies, loaded rum and sugar for West Africa, and returned with slaves for "the Islands", from which, after "sweetening" and temporary removal of certain between-deck bulkheads, rum and sugar were carried north. As often as not, this run was also triangular, bringing the "black cargoes" directly back to the colonies. Both these runs were very popular with New England and especially Rhode Island, but they were not so popular with Philadelphia due to Quaker sentiment, although as late as August 15, 1756, there appeared this advertisement in the *Pennsylvania Journal*:

Just imported in the ship Granby, Joseph Blewer, Master, Seventy Gold Coast Slaves, of various ages and both sexes. To be sold aboard said ship at Mr. Plumstead's wharf by Willing & Morris.

Except for the triangular runs, the trade with England was not as favourable to the balance of the colonies as were the other routes. England was still largely self-supporting, and English staples and luxuries were worth more than the cruder products of America. As a result of this, Pennsylvania gold fled to England; so much so that Sir William Keith, the governor, and young Benjamin Franklin advocated and put through a paper-currency measure much to the alarm of James Logan and the more conservative Philadelphians. The expedient worked well until the complete financial collapse of the Revolution. It could not help working well with the hidden wealth, year by year being discovered, the increasing population, and the expanding economy of Pennsylvania. One of the strangest superstitions that has haunted the minds of "practical" and "factual" men since the invention of money is the notion that money is real; as real, let us say, as a horse or a pig or, for that matter, a man. Money, of course, gold or paper, is merely an invention for the purposes of convenience; a symbol; and its only values are the credit back of it and what you can buy with it. These two values, in either a natural or a properly controlled economy, function apart from the gold, the paper currency, or their representative, the cheque.

On a desert island gold is worth no more than a dollar bill—and both are worth nothing. In a shrinking economy paper money is dangerous; in a growing and self-confident economy it is as good as gold and a lot more convenient to carry. Benjamin Franklin and Sir William Keith were right, although Benjamin Franklin, dismayed by what happened during the Revolution, later regretted his original standpoint.

Wise man that he was, he nonetheless confused war with gold, and they are not the same.

English interference with the West Indian trade, one of the causes leading to the Revolution, hampered Philadelphia's port to some extent, and during the English occupation the port and its shipbuilding for a while came to a standstill. The Delaware and its wharfs were deserted except for English men-of-war, the rope-walks, the shipyards were quiet. Following the evacuation of Lord Howe in June 1778—

there was not a vessel of any kind at them [the Philadelphia wharfs], for the British during their stay had destroyed all the sea vessels and nearly all the River craft they could put their Toarch to Wherever they could get at them. But one Square Rigged vessel escaped to my knowledge—a large ship belonging to the Cliffords which lay on the Jersey Shore . . .

This abeyance, however, was temporary. Hardly had the British left when the port began to hum again with activity, and for three decades flourished as never before, and then five factors in succession damaged it, two of them —the last two—permanently.

These were: President Jefferson's Embargo Act of 1807, the War of 1812, the Battle of Waterloo, whether you've thought of that before or not, the Erie Canal, and finally steam—steam at sea, and steam on land in the shape of the railroads.

The embargo of 1807 made, for a while, graveyards out of all the American ports. And yet what could the small and struggling republic do? Seldom has there been a case of clearer predestination to confirm the Presbyterian soul. American was damned if she did and damned if she didn't. England, locked in a death struggle with Napoleon, claimed the right to stop and search all American ships for sailors of English nationality. Nor were the English commanders very careful, either. France said that if the American ships permitted this, French ships would sink or capture them; an attempted practice that led to a small, undeclared, but brisk Franco-American war, now almost entirely forgotten. Hardly was this over when the War of 1812 began.

For a few years, released from the embargo, the shipbuilding of Philadelphia had flourished temporarily. In 1810 its tonnage had risen to over 100,000 tons; 9,145 tons of which, valued at a million dollars, had been launched that year. Not until eighty or so years later did the tonnage of the port in this respect reach again such figures. The War of 1812 with its close blockade of the American coast called for swift, low-lying ships to slip through the British men-of-war. The Philadelphia China trader was too

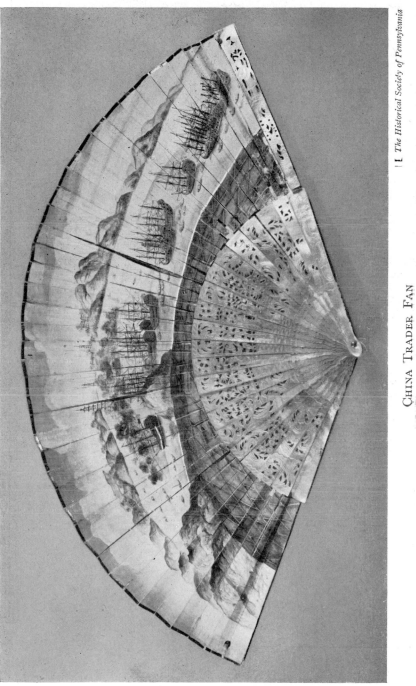

China Trader Fan

ROBERT MORRIS, by Otis and Sully

slow, and Baltimore came forward with the famous Baltimore clipper. Philadelphia also began to build clippers, but the trade had gone to Baltimore.

The Battle of Waterloo, and the peace that followed, so far as American shipping was concerned, proved to be the paradox that peace often is. American shipowners and shipmasters heaved a sigh of relief, only to discover that the entire merchant fleet of Europe had been restored to commercial purposes and so to overwhelming competition. But the port of Philadelphia would have recovered, as did all the other American ports, from these temporary set-backs had it not been for the Erie Canal of 1825 and the practical application of steam to paddle- and driving-wheels.

The Erie Canal opened up New York's splendid harbour to the entire Middle West, and across northern New York is a water-level route. There are no formidable barrier mountains, as there are in Pennsylvania. Philadelphia struck back gallantly—the last time, incidentally, it has struck back gallantly about anything. It built its own canal systems to the west, but the mountains made them expensive, both in the building and for traffic. Better still, Philadelphia, turning its eyes inland, decided to make use of the new method of transportation that ran on rails behind a puffing engine.

If the Erie Canal was responsible for making New York the premier port of the country, it was also responsible for the Pennsylvania Railroad, in some ways the greatest railroad system in the country. And the Pennsylvania Railroad, was, to begin with, a Philadelphia product and a Philadelphia vision, if nowadays, like a small-town boy grown to be a millionaire, it is somewhat forgetful of its origin and the "home folks". The Pennsylvania Railroad has not been an unmitigated blessing to Philadelphia, although its stocks and bonds have on the whole been magnificently solid, and its trains are beautiful, and there is a tradition that at one time young Philadelphia mothers used to tell their children to add this to their prayers: "And O dear God, please bless the Pennsylvania Railroad, the Girard Trust Company, and the Republican Party".

The Pennsylvania Railroad, begun as the Columbia Railroad, started in 1832, soon began to spread all over the state and then into New York, incorporating the Camden and Amboy and various other railroads, such as the Philadelphia, Wilmington and Baltimore, and so on. Its original object was to maintain Philadelphia's position as a premier port of export and import, but although its main offices are still in Philadelphia, and its president and leading officers live there, and sentimentally it is still a Philadelphia institution, affectionately known as "the Pennsy", its heart long ago succumbed to the Delilah of the Hudson. Meanwhile, with its beautiful "main line", the first developers of which, incidentally, were the officers of the road; and its "Chinese Wall", the impenetrable brick fortification that cuts the city in two between the Schuylkill and Broad Street Station, and which is always to be taken down, but never has been; and its magnificent neo-Greek, thirty-million-dollar station at Thirtieth Street, which was to start a new city centre, but never has, Philadelphia's favourite railroad has been one of the leading agencies in the destruction of Philadelphia real estate, the underlying sickness of the city's entire financial structure.

E

Nor has this great local system by any means been completely an aid to the city's port.

Freight differentials, those mysterious computations known only to railway men, have for many years worked a hardship on Philadelphia. Occasionally some courageous Philadelphian, like the late Mayor Wilson, who was not a Philadelphian but, like most courageous Philadelphians, was born elsewhere, has spoken of these in no uncertain terms. Whatever the facts may be, for a long while it has been cheaper to haul Pennsylvania products, as well as all other products, to New York or Baltimore rather than to Philadelphia. Bulk exports, slow-traffic exports, go to Baltimore; luxury goods, fast-traffic goods, go to New York. Philadelphia takes what is left. And this is too bad in more ways than one, for so far as dock equipment is concerned, Philadelphia has one of the finest ports in the country. Among other things it has the largest crane in the United States, the largest grain elevator, the largest coal tipple, and two of the largest oil-handling piers on the Atlantic seaboard, and also a total water frontage of thirty-seven miles, twenty of it along the Delaware, seventeen on the Schuylkill. It has somewhere around 267 wharfs of various sizes, or a total berthing space of 190,000 lineal feet, 51,000 feet of which can berth ships of heavy draught. One hundred deep-draught steamers can be docked at Philadelphia at one time. Moreover, during the past few years there has been steady improvement of the port and river, and there are several large projects along this line awaiting the end of the war.

Perhaps Philadelphia will come back as a port. Perhaps not. In any event, it manufactures so enormously that its port from now on cannot help but grow, and in all honesty it must be said, in extenuation of shippers and railways—and this will sound odd after the laudations just bestowed upon it—the port of Philadelphia was not, to begin with, among the best in the country. It, and the long harbour of the Delaware, have several natural disadvantages that only persistence, money, and modern science have been able partially to conquer.

One of them cannot be conquered except by passengers who like the sea and slow liners, and by freight equally indifferent to speed.

Philadelphia is a semi-tropical city by latitude if not climate. It faces Spain and Portugal and North Africa, not England and Holland and Sweden. The mouth of the Delaware Capes lies at latitude 38° 55′ 59″, which is a little south of Valencia in Spain. Added to this is the length of the Delaware, 110 statute miles from the Capes to Philadelphia, and the strange fact that although New York is around ninety-nine miles to the north-east of Philadelphia, it is nonetheless one hundred miles nearer Brazil. One would expect New York to be nearer Liverpool, but Brazil——!

From Philadelphia to Rio de Janeiro is 4,800 miles, from New York to Rio de Janeiro, 4,700 miles. From Philadelphia to Liverpool is 3,300 miles; from New York to Liverpool, 3,100.

Distance, however, has not been the main handicap of Philadelphia's port. By a topsy-turvy process, it was only because Philadelphia was a great city that its port for so long was a great port. Reversing the usual rule, when you come to examine it closely you see that Philadelphia made the port more, in reality, than the port made Philadelphia. Perhaps after all the basis of the whole thing was Penn's proclamation of tolerance.

People had to come to Philadelphia to find tolerance. And the only way they could get there from Europe was on ships. And having got there, they needed ships to import what they wanted and export what they made or grew.

Upon final analysis, ideas have a curious way of proving themselves as being of major importance.

In the first place, and this is another paradox, considering Philadelphia's semi-tropical latitude, the Delaware is the most ice-ridden river on the Atlantic seaboard. No one would suspect as much, but it is so. The fresh-water upper reaches of the Delaware used to freeze over on the slightest occasion, and now are kept open solely because of the invention of the ice-breaker. Fantastic as it may sound, the only other Atlantic ports equally troubled with ice are Montreal and Quebec. You remember the two early ships, filled with Quaker immigrants, that accompanied the *John and Sarah* in 1681 and were caught in the ice at Chester and had to remain there all winter? In the winter of 1809–10 seventeen vessels were lost in the Delaware because of ice, and as late as 1863, even after the advent of ice-breakers, the ship *John Trux* was cut in half and sunk, a total loss, at the foot of Race Street. In the same winter, and in many other winters, numerous other vessels were lost in the same way.

This had depressing and far-reaching subsidiary effects. Shipping often came more or less to a standstill during the worst winter months, unemployment was periodic, and Philadelphia merchants fell into the habit of re-routing their cargoes through New York. In fact, at one time there was a movement among Philadelphia merchants and shippers to pull up stakes entirely and move down-river to Chester or Wilmington, where the waters of the Delaware become salt.

Philadelphia has conquered its ice problem, much to the loss of romance, for during the first half of the 1800's the Delaware was a favourite place for skating, sleighing, and ox roasts. The city has three-quarters of a million dollars' worth of ice-breakers. And Philadelphia and its neighbouring down-river ports have also conquered the harbour's second handicap, the lack of protection at the Delaware Capes. The entrance to the river was an open roadstead, beautiful but dangerous. It had none of the natural advantages of other harbours along the Atlantic coast, and during a storm was dreaded by mariners. Between 1801 and 1821 it was calculated that over two hundred and fifty-five ships on their way to Philadelphia had had to put out to sea again after entering Delaware Bay, and in 1821 fifty-one were wrecked almost in sight of the Capes. Even pilot boats were constantly being lost, and the almost irreplaceable members of that notable guild were being drowned; a guild, so far as Philadelphia is concerned, founded on October 4, 1788. For a long while, to be a Delaware pilot was to pursue a peculiarly dangerous calling. Even to-day Delaware pilots are known as the most skilful pilots on the coast. They have more to learn.

The situation was impossible, and in 1821 a committee of Philadelphians waited upon Congress. Even then there seemed to be a disposition to treat Philadelphia as the Cinderella of American cities, but when the committee of citizens brought evidence to bear that Philadelphia's sea commerce represented one-fourth of the entire Federal income, and whereas, in the case of other ports, one-twentieth of the annual receipts was frequently turned back for harbour improvements, in the case of Philadelphia never more than one dollar out of every hundred had been returned, Congress acted. William Strickland, a famous Philadelphia engineer, was selected for the undertaking, and the Delaware Breakwater was begun, an immense stone pier extending out into the bay, against which the Atlantic can do its worst without avail.

Hundreds of thousands of rocks were used, and Philadelphia has now as safe an entrance and lower bay as any in the country.

One problem remained to be solved, and it still exists to some extent, although millions have been spent upon it and the work has been going on for almost two hundred years. Between Philadelphia and the sea are one hundred and ten miles of a powerful, tortuous, and shifting river. Philadelphia has won the contest, but the river is a strong and sleepless adversary, requiring constant watching. Henry Hudson with his trained eye noted this fact, and that is probably why he did not try to find the North-West Passage by way of the Delaware. In the log of the *Half Moon*, entered by Hudson's mate, following that August day of 1690 spent between the Delaware Capes, is this note:

. . . *the Bay we found Shoal; we were forced to stand backe again. Steered away to the Eastward on many courses for it is full of shoals. He that would discover this Bay must have a small Pinasse that draw but foure or five foot water to sound before him.*

The Dutch were the first to begin to chart and mark the Delaware. In 1658 they set out some wooden buoys on the more dangerous shoals, and after Penn arrived the Provincial Assembly, for the purpose of continuing this work, laid a tax on vessels entering the river, although nothing much was done until five years later. From then on the work has been continuous. In 1756 Joshua Fisher completed his famous survey for "the Merchants and Insurers of the City of Philadelphia, This Chart of Delaware Bay and River, containing a full and exact description of the shores, Creeks, Harbours, Soundings, Shoals & Bearings", and Fisher's chart, at first suppressed by the Provincial Assembly for fear that it might fall into the hands of the French, became, when released, the standard for the river until the United States Coast Survey map of 1846.

In 1725 the first lighthouse on the Delaware was erected at Cape Henlopen, a small affair whose light was visible for only four miles or so. This is said to have been the second lighthouse on the Atlantic coast. In 1765 a stone tower seven stories high was built on a sand dune over a mile from the sea, and this stood until 1926, when the sea, cutting into the shore, finally reached it. In 1778 when the British evacuated Philadelphia they tried to burn this lighthouse, and in 1813 they shelled it, but it stood for a hundred and sixty years. To-day the Delaware has two lightships, six lighthouses, and hundreds of shore markers, shore lights, and buoys between Philadelphia and the sea. There is now from Philadelphia to the Capes a 35-foot deep-draught channel, the dredging of which was completed some ten years ago, and from Philadelphia to Trenton, the head of navigation, is a narrower channel.

But for all this, and all that the port is doing now in its tremendous war-time awakening, and all that it will do when peace comes again, Philadelphia long ago, sometime around 1830, lost the mentality of a seaport town and adopted that of a great inland manufacturing, mercantile, and financial city. Stephen Girard, that master shipowner, whose mind was a most delicate business barometer, ran up the first storm signals of this change when in the early decades of the 1800's he began to turn from his first love, his tall and mighty ships, to banking.

Now on quiet foggy nights in the winter when you awake, sometimes, far off, no matter where you are in the city, you can hear the bull-like calling of steamers feeling their way up the Delaware and Schuylkill. And down by the docks on Walnut Street there is still one of the finest sea-food restaurants in the world, Bookbinder's. And not far away there is an ancient firm that has been dealing in wine, olive oil, spices, and cigars for generation after generation, father to son—a reminder of the "wine islands" and the great Madeira and Mediterranean trade of the eighteenth century. In its cigar vaults, kept at a proper temperature by the now built-over and submerged waters of Dock Creek, whose angling underground course is responsible for one of the few aberrational, Boston-like streets in Philadelphia, are thousands of cigars, bought and stored there as reverently as stocks and bonds by what cigar connoisseurs are left in the city. Every now and then they go down, and examine them, and smell them, and when the occasion arises, withdraw a few, later on to waste them on a cigarette-smoking generation.

A visit to these cool caverns is like a visit to a cathedral dedicated to the god of taste, and when you are in them you are very close to the waters of the small creek William Penn saw when he first landed.

Certain members of a one-time shipping family, the Bories, who came to Philadelphia at the turn of the eighteenth century from France by way of San Domingo and its revolutions, make still from a family recipe a most delicious and exotic, and also famous, flavouring for soup. It is called "Scotch Bonnet", and it comes in a tiny bottle, and you use only a few drops of it, for it is very hot, and it is that rare thing, a flavouring that does not change the taste of a soup, but merely heightens it and sharpens your palate. The recipe is a secret, but the basis is Madeira wine in which are steeped for a year or so peppers and various West Indian herbs.

The peppers and herbs are the descendants of plants and seeds brought by the Bories almost a hundred and fifty years ago and planted in their gardens.

CHAPTER XIII

Honesty is the Best Policy

"*That I may be preserved from atheism and infidelity, impiety and profaneness, and in my addresses to Thee carefully avoid irreverence and ostentation, formality and odious hypocrisy,*—Help me, O Father!

"*That I may be loyal to my prince and faithful to my country, careful for its good, valiant in its defence, and obedient to its laws, abhorring treason as much as tyranny,*—Help me, O Father!

"*That I may to those above me be dutiful, humble, and submissive; avoiding pride, disrespect, and contumacy,*—Help me, O Father!

"*That I may to those below me be gracious, condescending, and forgiving, using clemency, protecting innocent distress, avoiding cruelty, harshness, and oppression, insolence, and unreasonable severity,*—Help me, O Father!

"*That I may refrain from censure, calumny, and detraction; that I may avoid and abhor deceit and envy, fraud, flattery, and hatred, malice, lying and ingratitude,* —Help me, O Father!

"*That I may be sincere in friendship, faithful in trust, and impartial in judgement, watchful against pride and against anger (that momentary madness),*—Help me, O Father.

"*That I may be just in all my dealings, temperate in my pleasures, full of candour and ingenuity, humanity, and benevolence,*—Help me, O Father!

"*That I may be grateful to my benefactors, and generous to my friends, exercising charity and liberality to the poor and pity to the miserable,*—Help me, O Father!

"*That I may avoid avarice and ambition, jealousy and intemperance, falsehood, luxury, and lasciviousness,*—Help me, O Father!

"*That I may possess integrity and evenness of mind, resolution in difficulties, and fortitude under affliction, that I may be punctual in performing my promises, peaceable and prudent in my behaviour,*—Help me, O Father!

"*That I may have tenderness for the weak and reverent respect for the ancient; that I may be kind to my neighbours, good natured to my companions, and hospitable to strangers,*—Help me, O Father!

"*That I may be adverse to talebearing, backbiting, detraction, slander and craft and overreaching, abhor extortion, perjury, and every kind of wickedness,* —Help me, O Father!

"*That I may be honest and open-hearted, gentle, merciful, and good, cheerful in spirit, rejoicing in the good of others,*—Help me, O Father!

"*That I may have a constant regard to honour and probity, that I may possess a perfect innocence and a good conscience, and at length become truly virtuous and magnanimous,*—Help me, O Father!

"*And foreasmuch as ingratitude is one of the most odious of vices, let me be not unmindful gratefully to acknowledge the favours I receive from Heaven.* . . .

"*For peace and liberty, for food and raiment, for corn and wine and milk, and every kind of healthful nourishment,*—Good God, I thank Thee!

"For the common benefits of air and light; for useful fire and delicious water,—
Good God, I thank Thee!

*"For knowledge and literature and every useful art, for my friends and their prosperity, and for the fewness of my enemies,—*Good God, I thank Thee!

*"For all Thy innumerable benefits; for life and reason and the use of speech; for health and joy and every pleasant hour,—*My Good God, I thank Thee!"

BENJAMIN FRANKLIN, "PETITION AND THANKS", 1728

THE FUTURE IS an odd thing, even more curious than the past, for it is the past added to what is to happen.

The tall boy walking up High Street that Sunday in October—Benjamin Franklin, aged seventeen—the clothes he was wearing stuffed with what possessions he had, an extra shirt, socks, was a modest boy as most imaginative persons are, so he could not have had the slightest idea where his imagination, his brains, and his charm were to take him. He did not know that he was to become the leading citizen of this new strange town, and a leading citizen of the world, and one of the great men of a new nation as yet undreamed of. Nor did he know that he was to become a national folk-figure totally at variance with what he had thought and tried to do all his life.

Had he known the last, he would have been depressed.

Nor could he, inspecting the small brick town, have realized what was going to happen to that, either.

With his life, a long one—he died when he was eighty-four—he was to span the emergence of that town from a town into a city. He was to witness sixty-seven years of that emergence and growth: And he was to see this small brick town become for a while the centre of the country; politically, intellectually, physically, commercially, and socially. Furthermore, he was to span with his life practically all of the eighteenth century—that crucial century when the past really began to become the past and the present began to take shape.

There must have been some half-conscious prevision; that intuition, largely unwitting, which, almost like the migration of birds, brings to the place where great events are going to happen so many of the men who help to make them. Certainly as yet Philadelphia was only a small provincial town and the youngest of them all. Only forty-one years had passed since Penn had sailed up the river on his ship, the *Welcome*.

Boston, 1630, was almost a hundred years old. New York, 1615, was over a hundred years old. Philadelphia was a new-comer. Many of the founding fathers were still alive, some of them, like James Logan, not too elderly men at the height of their powers. The Quaker Assembly, beleaguered by the churchmen on one side, the Scottish-Irish on the other, the Mennonites and other Germans in between, was fighting doggedly to retain what authority it had and quarrelling as usual with the governor, still Sir William Keith of the wig. Queen Anne's War was over. It had ended in 1713, and Philadelphia had taken very little interest in it. The thunderheads of King George's War, 1744–48, were gathering on the horizon. All the while Philadelphia, despite its smug self-sufficiency, was coming close to war.

The question of the proprietary interests of the Penns was to the fore locally, where it remained until settled by the Revolution. The estate paid no taxes to the province. Hannah Callowhill, in England was managing the estate well, but neither she nor her sons knew that they were dealing with a nation. They had the blithe self-confidence of rich absentee landlords; all except Thomas Penn. Thomas Penn took a great interest in his province and was a good administrator. While he was to the fore, the proprietorship reached a higher degree of popularity and acceptance than at any other time.

In 1723, the year of Franklin's arrival, Philadelphia had somewhere around 10,000 inhabitants. In 1753, the first accurate count made, it had 14,563. By 1769 these numbers had grown to 28,043. By 1800, ten years after Franklin's death, the population was 41,200.

But this is not altogether fair, for all around Philadelphia were little towns and villages, their elbows nudging the central city, and after the consolidation of 1854 the city suddenly jumped from 93,665 in 1840 to over half a million in 1860. So, although there were only 10,000 people in the central town, Franklin did not come to a village; he came to a busy port and a busy market-place, the magnet for a large territory. But the central town was just beginning. One has only to look at Peter Cooper's primitive painting of the Delaware water-front in 1720 to realize what a small place it still was. Brick houses and docks and a few warehouses huddled along the river; a couple of church towers broke the sky-line. Once more, however, the lure of tolerance, so astutely remarked upon by Mr. Castleman, was at work to Philadelphia's benefit.

Tolerance was what had brought Benjamin Franklin south.

Boston was an older town, Boston was a richer town; at the moment, it was a bigger town, but Philadelphia was more hospitable, more alive, and more liberal. Moreover, despite the Quaker influence, it was gayer; a quality that attracted Benjamin Franklin to the end of his days, never, however, to the injury of his concentration, his industry, and his ambition. That is where he was such an extraordinary combination. No man ever thought more, did more, enjoyed more, savoured more, and worked harder, producing thereby a prototype which, badly mauled and largely misunderstood, has remained, by and large, the most popular one of his country. Here, unless you look more carefully into it, is the almost perfect extrovert; the man who absorbs everything, but never too much, and who, successfully, can turn his hand to anything. Here is the barefoot boy—well, practically. The Horatio Alger hero—save for some discreet and well-controlled lubricity, which after all is rather endearing and amusing, since we are human ourselves. Here, in short, is the typical American hero, at least the typical post-Civil War American hero who, starting with nothing, through thrift and application and frugality works his way up to the highest position obtainable.

Did he not say all this himself in *Poor Richard?* But the picture, of course, is not yet complete, and does not yet satisfy the somewhat wistful national ideal.

Having made his fortune, having secured himself, this epitome turned to literature, dabbled in science, took part in civic good works, and mixed in politics and government,. that final and dubious avocation of the broad-minded, charitable citizen not wise enough to retire to golf.

The older America—not colonial America, but the America of the 1800's and early 1900's—had, and still has—what is left of it—a deep and desirous respect for the things of the mind and.spirit so long as they are kept in their proper place. So long as they do not interfere with what is really important. And anyone who studies the country will misunderstand it unless he bears this fundamental respect in mind. America is not a nation of materialists, as are so many European nations; it is a nation of poets forced into materialism by the Procrustean demands, first, of the frontier, then of unprecedented expansion and opportunity. This split in personality is what causes the wistful respect; its contrary, the swift and often brutal action.

You respect the things of the mind and spirit, but you don't indulge in them, at least not seriously, and not as a profession. You should know about them, however—as soon as you have the leisure. And you should patronize them—as soon as you have the wealth. And meanwhile, if you have a little talent, you may even indulge in them occasionally, but harm-lessly and strictly as an amateur. You render unto Cæsar, in other words, the things that are Cæsar's, and you do this wholeheartedly. You render unto God the things that are God's, but in their proper place. You never make the mistake of thinking God's things more important than the things that belong to Cæsar.

History is studded with paradoxes. Nothing is more certain than that America, which was formed in the eighteenth century, has retained, until recently, far more than most parts of the world, the eighteenth-century mind, especially in pools of tradition like Philadelphia. And the eighteenth-century mind was a matter-of-fact, deistical mind, and yet at the same time, within its limits, a most imaginative and appreciative one, and, above all, brilliantly inquiring. The eighteenth century, in revolt from the mysticism of the seventeenth, tried hard to keep its feet on the ground, and yet it also knew music, literature, painting, philosophy, and science. It was *par excellence* the century of cultivated amateurs; of gentlemen farmers and merchants and even tradesmen who read Latin and Greek. Benjamin Franklin at an early age studied French, Italian, Spanish, and Latin. James Logan before he was sixteen had taught himself four languages: Greek, Latin, Hebrew, and French; and he wrote Latin as easily as he wrote English.

But in its love of the well-rounded man the eighteenth century never put the cart before the horse as the nineteenth century, overwhelmed by the Industrial Revolution, and the machine, and a mistaken idea of democracy, did; or as the twentieth century, overwhelmed by mere size, is still doing. The eighteenth century took its art, its science, its politics hard. They were not avocations but vocations, and of the utmost importance and dignity. The things of the mind and spirit came first, not second, and at the heart of the wide circle of appreciative and, often, performing amateurs was invariably a large, hard nucleus of immensely respected professionals.

When, around forty-five, Benjamin Franklin more or less retired from active business, he wasn't retiring, he was beginning; he was entering upon what really interested him. Then began the great decades of his life.

E*

As with William Penn, the picture Philadelphia has of this greatest of its citizens is understandable only if you bear in mind, as with Penn, the psychology of the sacrificial goat and the common human desire to compensate for one's own stupidities and indifference by attaching them to a legendary figure. The popular portrait of Franklin is of an obese and canny old man —born old; tolerant, humorous, equivocal, playing his cards close to his chest, too sensible and cautious for wrath, even if righteous; a master of intrigue and personal relationships. A good patriot, but a careful one. In short, a man with an eye, honest but shrewd, always open to the main chance. Undoubtedly, as in the case of Penn, by nature a banker or a real-estate promotor, since so many institutions of business are named after him.

A very cool hand, indeed, so Franklin appears in the popular portrait of him. An amiable sceptic. Didn't he present Deborah Read with an illegitimate son, later to become the Tory Sir William Franklin, shortly after he married her in 1730—or, as he himself said, "took her to wife"? Weren't most of his statements dry and pragmatical, in keeping with his conclusion that "a single man resembles the odd half of a pair of scissors", and so on? Not a "service club" sits down to its Wednesday or Friday luncheon without the memory of this matter-of-fact deity lurking somewhere in the background. There is no portrait in the American mythology more disastrous or more grotesque.

Service clubs are excellent institutions and do a lot of good. They would do more, and their members would be happier, if they put the horse before the cart. Benjamin Franklin was exactly not what most people believe him to have been. And it doesn't make the slightest difference how many pragmatical things he said or wrote. He lived in the eighteenth century; a century of apothegms and moral sayings. Nor does it make the slightest difference that he was an extremely successful business man in a modest way, with branch printing and publishing houses in Antigua, Jamaica, and Charleston, South Carolina. Nor that he was, first, a good postmaster for Pennsylvania and, later on, the first Postmaster-General for the colonies to turn in a profit from that bureau. Nor does it matter that early in life, having written many poems, he came to the conclusion that it was all right to "amuse oneself with poetry now and then, so far as to improve one's language, but no further".

None of these things, and hundreds of others like them, are as important as what a man does in a crisis, or as the whole tenor of his life. Men living in a certain environment and certain decades of a certain century say many things if they are sententious and articulate as was Benjamin Franklin. What they fundamentally mean is shown by what they fundamentally do. And so, to begin with, Benjamin Franklin was a rebel, and remained one all his life.

That's the first thing to remember about him: he was a rebel.

He left Boston because he was a rebel, and hardly had he got to Philadelphia when he began to oppose the dominant element, the Quakers. He also opposed the Penns, and their proprietary interests. Moreover, along with Sir William Keith, he flew in the face of all conservative opinion by advocating a paper currency. Nor would he leave anything alone. He was always improving, petitioning, scolding, upsetting. He must have been a most annoying and disturbing citizen to those who believe in the *status quo*, and frequently he was in ill favour with the more securely placed. He made Philadelphia pave to some extent its filthy and muddy streets; he organized Philadelphia's first fire company. He was responsible for the first insurance company in the country, the "Hand-in-Hand," so named because of its disk of two disembodied hands firmly clasped, or, to give it its formal title, the Philadelphia Contributionship for the Insurance of Houses from Loss by Fire, founded in 1752, which, for two hundred years short of eight, has given its directors, in lieu of a fee, an annual dinner featured by pickled oysters and Philadelphia gingersnaps in the shape of an S.

The Contributionship, however, would not insure if a house were near a tree, so the Mutual Assurance Company, the Green Tree, was formed later on by bolder spirits, and its sign, a metal oval with an embossed tree, is equally visible on many older Philadelphia houses.

Most important of all, as it turned out to be, this busy man organized Philadelphia's first social and debating and intellectual club of any importance, the Junto, to begin with a club composed mostly of young mechanics and inventors and restless spirits. And he did this after he had been in Philadelphia only four years and when he was only twenty-one. Out of the Junto came two of the most important institutions in America, let alone Philadelphia, where the development of the country is concerned: the American Philosophical Society (1743), first of its kind in the country; and the Library Company of Philadelphia, founded in 1731, sometimes called familiarly "Mr. Franklin's Library", the first circulating library in America. To-day the Library Company of Philadelphia possesses probably the finest collection of Americana in existence and a priceless collection of other books and manuscripts, some 300,000 in all. Franklin was equally concerned with the public health and was one of the founders of the Pennsylvania Hospital, 1751, oldest hospital in the United States. He drew up the first set of rules of that magnificent and venerable institution for "sick and distempered strangers", still standing far down on Spruce Street in the beauty of its colonial architecture and ample trees. Finally, Franklin was responsible for all of Philadelphia's higher learning with his "Academy and Charitable School of the Province of Pennsylvania", the ancestor of the present University of Pennsylvania.

Nor were his earlier activities solely those of peace.

One forgets that he was among the few citizens of Philadelphia always ready to defend his city.

The Quakers were pacifists, the Germans were timorous, and also, the new-comers among them were suspected of being pro-French because so many of them were Roman Catholics. In addition to this, the Moravian missionaries working with the Indians wore white crosses, a sure sign of subversiveness. The rest of the town, save for a few like Franklin and a succession of unfortunate governors, was indifferent. Even the Penns, over in England, who came—one or another of them—as visiting proprietors or lieutenant-governors, showed singularly little interest in the safety of their province. Thomas Penn, who arrived as proprietor in 1732, and his brother John, "the American", two years later. And a second John, grandson of the founder, in 1763, when he was two times, at intervals, lieutenant-governor. And Richard Penn as governor in 1771. Franklin wasn't like that. He was constantly alert. By means of the Junto, the Freemasons, and his other friends in Philadelphia, he helped organize a militia. In 1745 it was largely at his urging that the Delaware was fortified. In 1753 he was a member of the commission that conferred with the Indians at Carlisle concerning a treaty to protect the western frontiers of Pennsylvania. In 1754 he was the commissioner from Pennsylvania at the meeting at Albany, New York, with the chiefs of the Six Nations to assure their help against the French.[1] A year later, at his own risk—nobody else would—he organized the unfortunate Braddock's supply train when that general moved against Fort Duquesne. And abruptly, and for the same reason, at the age of forty-nine, he suddenly transformed himself temporarily into a military man, and as a colonel superintended the building of a string of forts along the north-western line of the province.

When the French and Indians were close to Philadelphia, raiding down the Lehigh Valley, it was Franklin who marched out at the head of his troops and stopped them. After which, as speedily as he had become a soldier, he became a civilian again.

As a matter of fact, if it had not been for Franklin, Philadelphia—shivering at its own shadow, torn by internal quarrels; the Quakers, although they had both in King George's War, and this war, appropriated money and reluctantly raised levies, still obstinately pacific; the "Pennsylvania Dutch" and other farmers pouring into the city for protection—might have acquired as heavy a French accent as New Orleans.

Those who quote the famous sentence from the letter to Josiah Quincy, written in 1783, "For in my opinion there never was a good war or a bad peace", a sentence Franklin repeated in various forms many times, forget what he did when he had to make war; in the French-Indian War, in the War of the Revolution.

Franklin hated war; no man more. When he had to, he made it.[2]

But none of this is the ousstanding symbol that displays the gallantry of this supposedly cautious and worldly-wise man. The symbol was visible when mortal, final war came to the colonies. And by then Franklin was a man of seventy; an age when, if ever, one is supposed to be permitted a certain leisure of wariness, of caution, even of timidity. Franklin was the

---

[1] Carl Van Doren, and correctly, in his definitive biography of Franklin, points to the training Franklin received for his later international career through his dealings with the Indians; this "forest diplomacy". Good manners, intelligence, fairness, are the same everywhere.

[2] All through history wise men, even wise generals, have hated war, the belief in it, that is, its acceptance as a necessary evil, and have inveighed against it as did Franklin. All through history wise men, realizing the world as it has been, have believed in proper preparation against war and in taking time by the forelock. Wisdom is largely the ability to reconcile theory with what is imperative; or, in simpler terms, the ability to put two and two together. The wise man recognizes the short arc of immediate and necessary action, and this recognition does not damage his equal knowledge of the long arc of intelligent theory, eventually to become a fact. Let it be noted that among the many projects of William Penn was a proposal for a League of Nations, so wide and so intelligent that it included seventeenth-century Russia and seventeenth-century Turkey. And yet William Penn took drastic steps against the pirates in Delaware Bay. Also Franklin, despite his pacificism—and who isn't a pacifist?—organized the first police force in Philadelphia. Two hundred years ago, an organized civic police force was regarded with the same uneasy fears as an organized international police force is to-day. To-day the world to all intents and purposes is little larger than the Philadelphia of 1751.

oldest member of the Continental Congress. And just before that, despite his English connections, despite his dear and admiring English friends, despite his love of England, despite his patient attempts to settle all problems within the circle of peace and understanding, the die cast, he shows himself, while still in England, as forthright and unswerving an American as this country has ever seen. He had always been a resolute one. And no bones about it, either, the final decision made. No looking back over the shoulder. No man has ever been a more two-fisted, tireless, fighting American than Franklin. Moreover, something frequently overlooked, he happened also to be a real democrat in the modern sense of the word. Most of the "fathers" weren't.

Citizens of an agrarian, small-town country, they did not realize the full implications of what they were doing. But Franklin did, and a few others. Franklin believed in universal suffrage. He was too wise a man not to trust the people in the slow arc of their desires, eliminations, and eventual solidifications. He realized the full implications of democracy as much as Thomas Paine did; much more than did the agrarian Jefferson, great theoretical democrat as Jefferson was.

We are inclined to overlook the major operation Franklin performed upon himself when most men are beginning to retire from active life. He had spent his happiest years in England. As a young man he had gone there first, sent by Sir William Keith to finish his education in printing and to collect what material he needed to establish his press in Philadelphia. In 1757 he was sent to England again to represent the province in its quarrel with the Penns. He was now a man of fifty-one. He stayed in England five years, returning to Philadelphia in 1762. Again in 1764 he was sent back to England, and there he stayed until 1775, the very eve of the Revolution, battling ceaselessly for his country but also, up to the last moment, for peace. His position was paradoxical, and for a while he was unpopular with the more extreme on both sides. He was an ardent American, no man more so, and yet at the same time he was a faithful subject of the Crown and a loyal British citizen. He just missed being tried in England for treason, and, called before the Privy Council in January of 1774, he was insulted by Wedderburn, England's attorney-general, who denounced him as a thief.

And this was the England Franklin loved and where, altogether, he had lived for eighteen years. Really lived, too. England had bestowed upon him extraordinary honours: a degree from Oxford, a degree from the University of St. Andrews. For a long while he had been a member of the Royal Society. In 1753 the Royal Society had given him its Copley Medal for his experiments with electricity. Among his more intimate friends were many of England's leading men, men of every kind; men of science, of politics, of fashion: Priestley, Sir John Pringle, the king's physician, Sir Grey Cooper, the elder Pitt, Lord Shelburne, that distinguished rake and brilliant diabolist, Sir Francis Dashwood, later Lord de Despenser. What could have been easier or more reasonable, and in his case more forgivable, than for Franklin to have remained in England, withdrawing in a dignified manner from the entire quarrel?

He could have said, "I have done my best. I can do no more. I am a loyal Englishman, and I am also an old man."

Hundreds of colonists with far less at stake and much less excuse said just that in one way or another. But Franklin didn't. Quietly and firmly he came home and, a man well over the allotted span of life, began his greatest years, the last fifteen.

Life begins at forty? Life for Franklin began every time he entered a new decade or took up something new.

Perhaps his most brilliant years were the nine years he spent in France from 1776 to 1785, and he began these when he was seventy and ended them when he was almost eighty. In those days the mere crossing of the Atlantic was no small undertaking for a man of his age. And Franklin dreaded his final trip home, and says so in his biography. Once again, he could have stayed so easily in Europe, in France. France had honoured him as greatly as England; he was a member of the French Academy of Science; he was honoured and, the adverb is not too large, rapturously beloved in France. He was one of the dozen or so greatest figures in the French galaxy. When he died, the French Assembly went into mourning for three days. France understood even better than England, and far better than his own country, the combination he was of learning, wit, vitality, romance, simplicity, glamour, and realism. This was Gallic. And Franklin had come to love France as well as he had loved England. Better, perhaps, for he found himself in a country where young and beautiful women have never considered a man's age, but solely his personality and his achievements; a great factor in putting off death and keeping a man young.

When Franklin died, he died quietly, but no man in history has wanted more to live fully up to the very moment of death.

Nothing but his passionate love of America and Philadelphia, his longing for them, could have brought him home. He was nostalgic. He came. And the last five years of his life were as active and multifarious as any. In 1787, to show how his mind worked, he wrote a treatise, *Observations on the Causes and Cures of Smoky Chimneys*, and another treatise, his famous pamphlet on the abolition of slavery.

Nor was he, when he came back from England in 1775, the sort of man not to know fully the risks he was taking. He had weighed them with his accurage intellect. He knew it was a hanging matter. He and "Mr. Washington", for the English refused the title of general, and all the rest were going to be hung if caught. Every one of them was attainted of high treason. Franklin is the man who is supposed to have said to a quarrelling Congress—the story has never been verified: "Either we hang together, or else we hang separately." But true or not, it was what he thought, and he knew the risks. He was no swashbuckling young cavalryman like "Light-Horse" Harry Lee; no young empire-maker like Alexander Hamilton. He was a retired business man, and it was something to be an American in 1776. It wasn't the fashion as it is now, and you had no huge implacable country back of you. Merely thirteen small, separate, quarrelling colonies. We are inclined to forget this. We are also inclined to overlook the status of the men who, if caught, got hung.

These were no rabble. These were men of property and position, like Franklin. Many of them men of maturity. Washington was forty-four, and for four generations his family had lived in peace and prosperity and dignity under English rule. Consider that! That's your father, grandfather and great-grandfather, and would take your family back to about 1827. That was how long the Washingtons had lived in America before one of them led a rebel army. And when he did, for eight years the war dragged on, most of it defeat. In addition to this, if you were a rebel, many of your lifelong and most respected friends and neighbours were against you. Fine men, honest men; reasonable and convincing men, these men, and they were against you. The Fairfaxes in Virginia, where Washington was concerned; Joseph Galloway and dozens like him in Philadelphia, where Franklin was concerned. At least half of the better people in New York and Pennsylvania, in contradistinction to the South, were loyalists, although nowadays there is a tendency to exaggerate this. But at all events it was difficult and sad, and enemies were all about you. As much about you as they are now; open or secret, or unconscious of what they are doing. For the War of the Revolution was as much of an ideological war as the present one.

But Franklin did not waver, nor did the others: ". . . we mutually pledge to each other our lives, our fortunes, and our sacred honour."

It was something to be an American in 1776.

So that's the first thing to remember about Franklin: he was a rebel. And the second thing to remember about him is that he was a poet, if the terms are not synonymous.

He was an eighteenth-century poet, to be sure, and so that means he was not a lyric or romantic one, but he wrote a great deal of poetry, and he lived poetry, and he gives a charming description of how he and Charles Osborne and James Ralph, and others of his young friends, when he first came to Philadelphia, used to walk out to the Schuylkill on Sundays, "into the woods, where we read to one another, and conferred on what we read", and compared the verses each had written.

Franklin started as a poet and essayist and evolved into a scientist and philosopher, a natural evolution, especially in the eighteenth century, but natural anyway, since poetry is the most analytical and scientific of the arts except music and therefore leads to science, philosophy, and the science of politics. Nothing escapes the eager and questioning mind of the poet, and most poets have been amateur politicians. Count them! Pamphleteers, too. Milton, Shelley, Wordsworth, Byron, Goethe, Heine, Victor Hugo, Tennyson, Whittier, Whitman; scores of others. The basis of poetry, like the basis of all art and science, is profound inquiry. So naturally the poet is never willing to leave the world as he finds it.

The enigma of electricity was to the fore; Musschenbroek and his discoveries, the Leyden jar. Franklin was the first to prove the identity of lightning and electricity. He was interested in ventilation, in earthquakes, in thermodynamics, although the science was not yet invented. As a result of his knowledge of air currents, he invented one of the most graceful and efficient heating apparatuses known, as good to-day as ever—the Franklin stove. He invented the lightning rod; the stool that turns into a ladder, used in all libraries. He invented numerous other useful appliances, including bi-focal glasses, the initials of which, incidentally, are the same as those of the inventor. One has only to glance at a few of the titles of the books and pamphlets Franklin published or wrote during his twenty-one years of printing and publishing to realize the range of this curious and extraordinary mind:

Essay on the West India Dry Gripes; Essay on the Iliac Passion—these by Dr. Thomas Cadwalader; *Plain Truth, or Serious Considerations on the present state of the City of Philadelphia and Province of Pennsylvania,* 1747, B. Franklin; *Experiments and Observations on Electricity made at Philadelphia in America* (1751)—three of these. *Supplemental Experiments, etc.,* in 1753; *New Experiments, etc.,* in 1754. It was for these pamphlets that Franklin was elected to the Royal Society and received its medal. *Proposals for Establishing an Academy,* 1743. *Plan for a Union of the English Colonies in America,* 1754. This plan was turned down both by the colonies and in London: had it gone through, there might have been no American revolution. *Some Account of the Success of Inoculation for the Smallpox in England and America,* 1760. The same year: *Parable Against Persecution.* And so on endlessly. Also let it never be forgotten, Franklin published the first novel ever published in America, a reprint of Richardson's *Pamela* in 1744.

So first he was a rebel, and then he was a poet, and then he was a statesman, and then he was a scientist and a philosopher, and then he was a democrat, an inventor and an educator.

He thought science nonsense unless—whenever possible—it went as directly as it could to the comfort, health, and happiness of man. After two hundred or so bitter years, science is beginning to flirt with that idea again. He thought education should teach a man to handle himself in his life and through the deep knowledge of his own tongue open to him the gates of all knowledge. The classicists and formalists fought him and for a while defeated him, but Franklin's ideas on education are as modern and controversial as ever, for they were not based on manual training and vocational training, as many have thought them, but fundamentally on the proper use of language— English, with all that that implies.

Finally, in the distorted and popular portrait of the man, his infinite charm, his wit and good looks are minimized, or else entirely forgotten. His gaiety; his powers of persuasion.

We know that it was his charm, backed by intelligence, that first interested Sir William Keith and made Sir William Keith his patron, shortly after the tall, unknown boy had come to Philadelphia. And it was his power of persuasion, more than anything else, that caused the repeal of the Stamp Act in 1766, although this repeal was followed almost immediately by the equally unpopular Townshend Act of 1767. And it was his power of persuasion that brought the French in on our side in 1778, although the French, naturally, were looking for an excuse to make trouble for England, and the American victory at Saratoga was the determining argument. And certainly Franklin's charm and powers of persuasion were evident all through his life in his relations with other people; in the way he could organize groups like the Junto and make them do his bidding; in the way he could stir people and communities out of their lethargy. And this charm, this persuasion, are nowhere more clearly to be felt than in Franklin's innumerable letters to friends all over the world, and after he was fifty, to the women, old and young, who adored him.   Like most busy men he seemed to have time for everything and on the slightest provocation was witty, advisory, tender, and sententious.

To read Franklin's letters is like lifting the top from a jar of pot-pourri; a potpourri of herbs, pungent from the sun.

Shortly after he came to Philadelphia, his brother James, up in Boston, in trouble over the *New England Courant*, in fact, in jail because of it, got young Benjamin, safe in Philadelphia, to take over ostensibly the saucy sheet, Boston then, as now, dreaded the naked truth more than any other form of nakedness.   The *Courant* in its issue of February 11, 1723, the first under its new suppositious editor, announced this as its policy:

The present undertaking . . . is designed purely for the diversion and merriment of the reader.   Pieces of pleasancy and mirth have a secret charm in them to allay the heats and tumours of our spirits, and to make a man regret his restless resentments.   They have a strange power to tune the harsh disorders of the soul, and to reduce us to a serene and placid state of mind.   The main design of this weekly paper will be to entertain the town with the most comical and diverting incidents of humane life.

But there was also to be "a grateful interspersion of more serious morals" drawn "from the most ludicrous and odd parts of life".

The ever youthful side of Franklin loved his hoaxes and satires, his *jeux d'esprits*, such as his *An Edict of the King of Prussia*, 1777, his *Letter of the Count de Schaumberg to the Baron Hohendorf Commanding the Hession troops in America*, 1782, and his fictitious *Supplement to the Boston Chronicle* of 1782.[1] While he was in France he wrote the charming and delicate small essays called *Bagatelles*, some of which he dedicated to Madame Brillon, the wife of the French financier, who had playfully adopted him as her "father"— a dangerous thing to do; others of which, with his usual tact, he dedicated to the equally beautiful Madame Helvetius, widow of the philosopher.   He did not wish either lady to be jealous.

But he was not all sweetness and light and tact.   He could hate as well as William Penn could, and speak as sharply.   Of Thomas Penn he wrote: "I was astonished to see him thus meanly give up his father's character, and conceived at that moment a more cordial and thorough contempt for him than I have ever felt for any man living. . . ."   And there were numerous other instances when his words crackled as they did here.

As for his appearance—there is the portrait painted in London in 1767, when he was sixty-one, by David Martin.   And it is a fine portrait, and not a grotesque one like the portrait when he was forty-two, which is now in the Fogg Museum of Art at Havard.   The unknown artist of 1748—the name is

[1] Times change, new inventions are made, or rather, not "made" but come into being, for all inventions are the results of much trial and error and the age-long imagination of men. The Greeks thought of the aeroplane, and so did Leonardo da Vinci and numerous others.   But good brains don't change; they remain the same through the ages.   In these hoaxes of his, Franklin anticipated modern psychological warfare, just as in other ways he anticipated aerial warfare. Franklin was the Francis Bacon, the Da Vinci, of America, and in any other country but America, with its strange lingering, provincial, lack of appreciation of its real virtues, this would be known.

in dispute—had a passion for dish faces, insolent eyes, and prognathous, if weak, jaws. The Martin portrait shows an extremely handsome and witty-looking man—with a beautiful bony structure to his face—and a fashionably dressed one, too. Franklin didn't begin to wear his fur cap until late in life, and then it wasn't because of indifference to dress, but because of erysipelas of the scalp, although a fur cap seems a strange emollient. The French loved the fur cap, however, as further proof of the classic, yet Paul-and-Virginia simplicity of this delightful "frontiersman". The frontiersman, incidentally, who is supposed to have said when chided by a French lady with the statement that she was "the only woman at the French court" to whom he had not "made love": "Madame, this is July. I am waiting until the nights are longer".

The popular conception of Franklin has been very bad for the mentality of the United States: the myth of the frugal, slow-moving, ultra-conservative, rather mean-minded man. And this myth has been used by the ignorant or the cunning to cloak a multitude of the exact sins that did not make America and could not have made it. It is wryly amusing too, this myth, for although Franklin, like Penn, was a good money-maker, he wasn't much better as a money-keeper. He was extravagant, he liked to entertain, he was frequently in debt. And although he was given to writing out régimes and self-disciplines and theoretically loved order as much as Penn, he admitted that after drawing up an elaborate card index to keep his papers and desk neat, he found it much easier to forget it, and just hunt for things.

The French gave us a famous ship—the first lend-lease—the *Bonhomme Richard*. And John Paul Jones sailed her into eternal glory. The French named the ship in honour of Franklin, for "Bonhomme Richard" is their translation of "Poor Richard", although it isn't a very good one, for *bonhomme* in French means, "A simple fellow. Sweet. Without malice. Easy to abuse." And the *Bonhomme Richard* was not "sweet" or "easy to abuse", and neither was Franklin. The *Serapis* didn't think the *Bonhomme Richard* "sweet". But the name was more symbolical than the French knew. Under his tact and winning manners and graceful ease, Franklin carried full broadsides.

The worst thing Franklin ever did for his own reputation, and the only injury he ever did his country, was to publish the *Poor Richard Almanacks*, although they were extremely profitable. And the *Poor Richard Almanacks* were by long odds the least original of his writings. Practically everything in them had been said years before by the Greeks, or the Romans, or the English of Elizabeth. But those who saw the first issue might have suspected that they had hold of a bigger fish than was obvious. In the *Pennsylvania Gazette* of December 19, 1732, appeared this advertisement:

Just published, for 1733. An Almanack, containing the Lunations, Eclipses, Planets' Motions and Aspects, Weather, Sun and Moon's Rising and Setting, High Water, etc; besides many pleasant and witty verses, Jests, and Sayings; Author's Motive of Writing; Prediction of the Death of His Friend, Mr. Titan Leeds; Moon no Cuckhold; Bachelor's Folly; Parson's Wine and Baker's Pudding;

Short Visits; Kings and Bears; New Fashions; Game for Kisses; Katherine's Love; Different Sentiments; Signs of a Tempest; Death of a Fisherman; Conjugal Debate; Men and Melons; The Prodigal; Breakfast in Bed; Oyster Lawsuit, etc.

By Richard Saunders, Philomat.   Printed and Sold by B. Franklin.

But, luckily for us, and for the country, and for the town, the first thirty years of Franklin's life in Philadelphia, the formative years, were a comparatively quiet time both for him and the city; a time of steady growth and the busy ways of peace.   A man could think, and solidify his point of view, and make his modest fortune, and so be ready for the greatness of the future. King George's War, when it came, did not come too close, although by declaring war against Spain in 1741 Pennsylvania had Spanish as well as French privateers hovering off the Delaware Capes, and even on one occasion coming as far up the river as to be able to fire on New Castle and Salem. Philadelphia replied by building some privateers herself.   The *Tartar*, for instance, the biggest ship yet built in the Philadelphia shipyards, and destined to a curious fate.   On her first voyage down the Delaware in entirely calm weather she capsized, drowning all but three of her crew.   The *Marlborough.* The *Cruiser*.   The *George*.   The *Wilmington*.   The *Trembleur*, and others.

The *Wilmington* took five vessels in September.   The *Trembleur* secured four thousand pounds sterling from one French schooner.

The Quaker Assembly had at length appropriated four thousand pounds for supplies for the army up in Canada, and under Franklin's urging, and that of James Logan, who was no complete pacifist despite his Quaker beliefs, had fortified the Delaware as well.   Cannon were brought down from Boston; many young men went north to the war and came back Louisburg veterans. Seven companies of home militia were formed, the "Association Regiments". But on the whole, King George's War was not an intimate war; not a neighbouring one, as it was to New England.   Philadelphia and Benjamin Franklin could go ahead with their local projects.

Christ Church was rebuilt in 1727; the Junto—no one knew how powerful it was to be, least of all Franklin—took shape in the same year.   In 1731, the library.   In 1736, Franklin's fire company, the Union, the first official volunteer fire company in the world.   And in 1740 the town built its first almshouse and, with the "Academy and Charitable School of the Province of Pennsylvania", laid the foundations of the University of Pennsylvania.[1] In 1743 the American Philosophical Society was organized, and in 1749 Philadelphia, despite its tradition against "masks and revels", and despite Quaker opposition, saw its first theatrical performance; a performance of Addison's *Cato* by a company of strolling players in William Plumstead's warehouse on Water Street—the same Plumstead who auctioned slaves and who, the next year, was to be elected mayor.   While, in 1734, John Penn, "the American", had returned to be greeted by the firing of cannon and a

---

[1] It is necessary to emphasize the clause "laid the foundations," and perhaps even that is exaggerated.   There is only a misty connection between the Charitable School and the subsequent University of Pennsylvania; about the same connection as between Princeton University and the Log Cabin College of 1727.   Princeton has decided to lean backward in the conservatism of its claims, and so has set 1747 as the date of its founding.   As late as 1748 there were only four colleges in the colonies granting degrees: William and Mary, Harvard, Yale, and Princeton.

State dinner that cost forty pounds, a sum which shocked many of the more conservative Quakers.

Yet it had not been all beer and skittles. In 1740, '41, and '49 yellow fever had struck again. In 1699, "Barbadoes" distemper. In 1730 and 1756, small-pox. In 1741 and '54, Palatine distemper, which was probably scurvy. In 1746, "putrid sore throat", probably diphtheria. And in 1747, "malignant fever".

Philadelphia was building up its reputation, which it maintained until somewhere around 1900, of being one of the least sanitary of cities, populated by an extremely healthy people. Outdoor life and the survival of the fittest accounted for the latter.

Under Franklin's stimulus, however, the city in 1751 replaced its volunteer night watch, established in 1704, by paid constables — the beginning of Philadelphia's police force—and in the same year lighted its streets. But not until 1768 did it let its first municipal garbage and street-cleaning contract; the second part of which contract has never yet been fulfilled. The first part of which—garbage collecting—was to furnish Philadelphia, over a hundred years later, its quaintest, and in some ways most colourful, "czars", the Vare brothers.

Philadelphia has always had the dirtiest streets of any large city in the country. Every now and then the citizens, tired of wading through old copies of Benjamin Franklin's *Pennsylvania Gazette*, discarded somewhere around 1730, arise in their wrath, but not for long. A thousand years from now Philadelphia will present an interesting midden for antiquarians. Mean-while its streets, when a wind blows, furnish much practice for its skilful opticians, just as its climate makes it a Golconda for nose and throat specialists, and a world centre for that branch of medical research. No Philadelphians can pronounce their R's, owing to lifelong post-nasal difficulties.

From 1720 on there had been growing complaints of the way butchers threw their offal outside their shops and other citizens their slops from second-storey windows, and there had been considerable street paving done—large flagstones, bringing relief from the accustomed mud and dust. There had been, as well, considerable complaint about the morals of women, or rather, the lack of them; always a sign of peace and growth and prosperity. Further-more, there had been too much noise at night: slaves, and others, gathering together and singing. Most outrageous. A curfew law was passed, to which apparently no one paid any attention. Women were very much out of hand—they usually are. They were "cutting and drawing down their hair on their Foreheads and Temples", and were using fans and even—they and their males—carrying snuff-boxes to Meeting, which diverted their minds from "inward and spiritual exercise".

One couldn't, alas, do much about the proud and flaunting daughters of the Church of England, but one could admonish the Quaker maidens— in fact, one could not only admonish them, one could forbid them—not to lay aside their aprons, sign of worthy womanhood, nor pleat their caps, nor wear striped shoes, and, above all, not to succumb to the "immodest fashion of hooped Petticoats". But the ladies had taken to even more evil habits, or, worse, were confirmed in them. They were stoutly lined up beside their men in what was, to say the least, a drinking age. Westbrook Pegler would have been shocked, with his belief that women and liquor never met until a few years ago, and even Benjamin Franklin, liberal as he was, in the *Pennsylvania Gazette* of 1733, warns that women, instead of just taking one big satisfying glass of ale in the morning, were ruining their appetites by indulging in "two or three drams".

Mr. Black of Virginia, the young gentleman who liked so much the look of the girls in Christ Church, lingered in Philadelphia in the year 1744 in a happy mist of entertainment and the drinking of healths.

There was bread, cider, and punch for lunch, rum and brandy before dinner, Madeira, port, sherry, and punch with dinner, liqueurs and bounce with the ladies, and then wine and rum until bedtime. Mr. Black went to soirées where there was a fine lemon punch that would have "swimm'd half a dozen young geese", and everywhere liquor was as liberal "as an apple-tree of its fruit on a windy day in the month of July".

Meanwhile, at Fifth and Chestnut streets, a most important thing had been happening; far more important than anyone at the time knew. The most historic building in America had been built.

In March 1729 the Assembly had passed an appropriations bill for £30,000, and of this, £2,000 was to be used for a Provincial State House. Work was begun in July 1732, and the central portion was about done by 1736; enough, at least, for a State banquet, the first, to be given in the East Room.

Franklin's *Pennsylvania Gazette* speaks of this as the "most grand and elegant entertainment that has been made in these parts of America".

Fourteen years later, Isaac Norris, being Speaker, it was suggested that a bell be hung in the tower and a clock be affixed to the tower wall. The bell, cast in London, arrived in 1752 and, when tested, cracked. Two young brass founders, John Stow and John Pass, who had a foundry on Third Street above Market, or High, offered to break up the bell and recast it, adding an ounce and a half of copper to each pound of the old bell. On April 17, 1753, the new bell, found satisfactory, was raised into place.

Four blocks away, diagonally across the State House square, not yet called Independent Square, and then across another open space, not yet called Washington Square, ground was being readied for the building of the Pennsylvania Hospital. When the corner-stone of the main building was laid in 1755, this was carved on it:

> *In the year of Christ MDCCLV,*
> *George the second happily reigning,*
> *(For he sought the happiness of his people)*
> *Philadelphia flourishing*
> *(For its inhabitants were public-spirited)*
> *This building*
> *By the bounty of the government*
> *And of many private persons,*
> *Was piously founded*
> *For the Relief of the sick and the miserable*
>
> *May the God of Mercies bless the undertaking.*

Twenty-one years later, across the intervening squares, across the whole town, across the entire country and the world, the bell of the State House clamoured its denial of the pious corner stone of the Pennsylvania Hospital.

But unfortunately for tradition—and why does this have to happen so often, for tradition as a rule is so much more right, philosophically and dramatically, than the facts?—it was not the great bell, now known as the Liberty Bell, which Isaac Norris had ordered from London, and John Stow and John Pass had mended, which rang. To the contrary, it was a smaller bell, which now hung in the tower of the State House, and which was known as the "Province Bell".

The big bell had rung for the last time before the Revolution, in 1765, when it had called the citizens together to protest against the Stamp Act. But even by then it had become a symbol, and a name, and a tradition. During the British occupancy of 1777-78 it was taken north to Allentown for safekeeping, being returned to Philadelphia later.

About the Liberty Bell, you see, there was an odd occurrence, a coincidence, an eerie second sight. Around its top ran these words:

"Leviticus xxv, 10—'*Proclaim Liberty throughout all the Land unto all the Inhabitants thereof.*"

And Isaac Norris had ordered the bell in 1750, twenty-six years before the Revolution.

That's interesting, isn't it?

After all, it makes little difference which bell actually rung so long as the big one, the great full-throated one, and the verse from Leviticus, still ring in the hearts of the American people. It seems to me they do.

CHAPTER XIV

Growing Pains and Progress.

"*Whatever ye do, let virtue be cherisht.*"

WILLIAM PENN, 1685.

THE UNFORTUNATE Sir William Keith went the way of most of Pennsylvania's early governors, which, so far as one can make out, was either mildly or violently insane. There is a psycho-historical treatise to be written on the cumulative effect upon any energetic executive, of Quaker passive resistance and the silent obstinacy of those in direct communication with "the spirit". Novelists, transferring this into more personal terms, could also find provocative themes. The submerged stories of many of Philadelphia's better-known families are not without dramatic significance. Although there are only about fifteen thousand professing Quakers now left within the actual limits of the city, the Quaker strain is a strong one, no matter how long the bearers of it may have gone to Mass or to such High Episcopal institutions as St. Clement's. Wives, without a single overt act, can drive their husbands to distraction by violently refusing to lose their tempers. Husbands can do the same to wives. And this is equally true of parents where their children are concerned.

Sir William Keith did not kick a judge or turn his back upon the Assembly, but his governorship toward its end steadily deteriorated, and finally in 1726 he was superseded by Major Patrick Gordon, a bluff and honest veteran of the British army. Gordon died ten years later, still in office, and for eleven years, Colonel George Thomas, a former Antigua planter, took his place. After that came a succession of governors, each one of whom found himself caught like a fly in the same baffling web of proprietary interests, Quaker pacifism, and the desire to be left alone on the part of increasingly rich merchants and shipowners of all faiths. James Hamilton, Pennsylvania-born son of Andrew Hamilton, the distinguished and wealthy lawyer who had been lieutenant governor in 1701, succeeded, after an interregnum of a year, Governor Thomas, to be himself succeeded in 1754 by Robert Hunter Morris, son of Lewis Morris, former governor of New Jersey. By now native Americans were coming into high office. Morris lasted only two years, and his place was taken for three years by William Denny, a gentleman of much colour, high temper, and a quietly lurid private life. He and the Rev. Richard Peters, who also had had a quietly lurid and similar private life never mentioned in Philadelphia annals, hated each other. But the Rev. Richard Peters had left his "private life", a winsome lady, definitely in London, whereas Governor Denny imported his. There is considerable difference. The Rev. Richard Peters is not to be confused with his nephew, Judge Richard Peters, who during the Revolution was for a while secretary of the Board of War.

After Governor Denny came James Hamilton again until the return in 1763 of the Penns, this time in actual political office; John Penn, grandson of the Founder, as governor for eight years; Richard Penn, his brother, in 1771, for two years; John Penn again in 1773 until September 1776 and the Revolution. It is said that when John Penn landed from England on a Sunday afternoon at Ches-nut Street wharf Philadelphia experienced its first recorded earthquake—a severe one.[1]

John Penn lingered in America until 1784 and built Solitude, one of the lovely colonial country seats along the valley of the Schuylkill, all of them now incorporated as historic monuments in Fairmount Park. Solitude stands in the grounds of the Philadelphia Zoological Gardens, where the animals live so long, and which, until recently, thought itself, with the exception of the London Zoological Gardens, the only zoological garden in the world the proud possessor of a male and female gorilla. The *dénouement* proved to be a zoological and civic tragedy, for the young, supposedly female, gorilla

[1] Philadelphia has had other earthquakes, but so far, since the time of John Penn, only mild ones. The last was in 1937. One of Philadelphia's most eminent scientists happened at the moment to be in the bathroom, an experience he will never forget, for, as he says, it turned him into "a sort of human seismograph".

turned out, when the time came, to be another male. All hopes of a dynasty were shattered. Gorillas hide their sex with the shyness of true forest lovers.

John Penn, back in England, died and left Solitude to his younger brother, Granville Penn, and in the early 1850's Granville Penn's son, Granville John Penn, occupied it during his stay in Philadelphia. In 1867 it was sold by the estate, the last piece of land owned by the Penns in the province their ancestor had dreamed of and begun.

Governor William Keith, after being eased out of office, got himself elected to the Assembly, where he hoped to combat successfully his enemies and make a name for himself. He was known as a firebrand of oratory, but neither this nor his ambitions got him anywhere, and finally he went back to England, leaving a penniless wife and daughter in Philadelphia. In 1749 he died, a debtor, in the Old Bailey in London, a sad death for a gallant and bewigged gentleman who, whatever his faults, had at least great imagination and enough sense to pick out at first sight young Benjamin Franklin as a boy worth helping and educating.

Lady Keith died in 1740, and her grave is in Christ Church burying ground at the corner of Fifth and Arch streets. Meanwhile, to make a tragic story better, the daughter Sir William Keith had left in Philadelphia had done well by herself by marrying Dr. Thomas Graeme, the eminent physician.

The difficulties the pre-Revolutionary governors of Pennsylvania experienced were practically insoluble. They were indeed on the horns of a dilemma—a three-horned one. To begin with, they were representatives of the proprietors, the Penns, and the Penns, like most proprietors, wanted receipts, not expenses. Secure in their pleasant English country life, they thought that their provincial friends should pay for their own protection and development. But these provincials, in addition to the Quaker dislike of aggressive protection of any kind, were steadfastly determined, if they did have to raise money, to force the Penns to pay their share of it. This produced half a century of deadlock, and in the meantime, danger, scalp-locked and tomahawked, was coming down from the north. Year by year it came closer. Danger that slipped through the forests and struck with blood and smoke. And Philadelphia and Pennsylvania, by means of rum and dishonest dealings, were doing all they could to increase this danger.

The peaceable Delawares of Tammany and William Penn were growing more and more sullen. French agents and the news of French victories did not help. Nor were the Lenni-Lenape, the Delawares, the completely virtuous Indians painted by most historians of Pennsylvania. They, too, had their faults and were often inclined to be factious and unreasonable.

John Penn, "the American", son of the Founder, and not to be confused with the later John Penn of the governorship and Solitude, in 1737, together with his brother Thomas, had put through the none too righteous "Walking Purchase". This was based on a supposed deed granted to William Penn by his Indian friends in which William Penn was entitled to further purchases of land along the Delaware "as far as a man can go in a day and a half". Good! A great opportunity for a clever white man. Also the Delawares were having their usual trouble with the Iroquois. So John and Thomas Penn said they would protect the Delawares if they would let the "Walking Purchase" go through. Meanwhile the Penns hunted up three of the hardiest and most expert woodsmen in the colony, and when the day came, these woodsmen covered sixty-five miles in the allotted time. Nor did they walk, as the Delawares had expected, but heel-and-toed, and when they had exhausted the Indians selected to accompany them, they are said to have run.

The same thing happened more or less on Long Island with the famous "Bull" Smith purchase. The original Smith of Smithtown, astute man, arranged with the Indians to purchase all the land around which he could ride a bull between sunup and sundown. A bull is a slow animal, but Smith of Smithtown took a young bull, conditioned him, trained him, and when the day came, galloped him. Ever since the family name has been hyphened colloquially to "Bull-Smith".

Actually, neither of these episodes was as clever as seemed at the time. Indian psychology is a mysterious affair. Thousands of scalps, red and white, have been the results of misunderstanding it. The Indians are Orientals, and everything Indian goes by "face". William Penn, Onas, knew this, and would never have permitted the "Walking Purchase". If you can outwit an Indian honestly—and this is no contradiction in terms—it is all right, and you can shake hands and laugh. But if you outwit him by taking advantage of what he thinks is an understood bargain, Death, vulture-like, ruffles its wings. Moreover, out to the west, in the centre of the province, and beyond in the still virgin-forested Alleghanies, were the Scottish-Irish, grim fellows and confirmed in their belief that "the only good Indian is a dead one".

Who, pray, was an Indian to interfere with predestined Presbyterian real estate?

But this much must be said for Thomas Penn, despite the "Walking Purchase" and Benjamin Franklin's opinion of him. He was by far the ablest of Penn's descendants, and he made a real effort to be an actual Lord Proprietor and to understand both the Delawares and the Iroquois. In this he was ably assisted by Governor George Thomas, late of Antigua. Governor Thomas was the wisest of Pennsylvania's provincial governors when it came to the Indians; while as for Thomas Penn he was, to begin with, as much trusted by the Indians as his father had been, and in some respects he knew them better, as did Governor Thomas.

William Penn had always cautioned his agents to treat the Indians with the utmost gravity under all circumstances. Numerous other white men, with the best of intentions, have made the same mistake. Once more, "face" should be the guide in such matters. In council, with strangers, the Indian is a grave and reticent fellow. He loves ceremony and ritual, and you transgress his sense of dignity where these are concerned at your own risk. But, on the other hand, when at his ease, there is no man who loves a "party" more than an Indian, or who enjoys more a feast and boisterous humour and practical joking. An Indian camp or village when relaxed is like an assemblage of jackjaws. Thomas Penn and his deputy, Governor Thomas, appreciated this fact, whereas William Penn apparently did not. It must also be remembered that Thomas Penn was called upon to meet far graver Indian problems than his father. The white man had been in Pennsylvania for several decades, and the longer the average white man—especially the land-hungry English—stays in Indian country, the more vexing the problem. The Founder had worked in what was practically virgin territory, untroubled save by the amicable and wise Swedes. The Lenni-Lenape, the Delawares, still thought white men some sort of beneficent gods, as all Indians are inclined to regard white men until they learn better. By Thomas Penn's time they had learned much better.

Nor was it any easy task to adjudicate between the conflicting claims of the Iroquois and the Delawares. It is never an easy task to adjudicate between overlapping claims, especially when they are as vague as Indian claims necessarily are, and the Iroquois were not only cleverer than the Delawares, but they were infinitely better organized and more powerful, and so much more to be wooed as potential allies.

At all events, and this added more fuel to the smouldering fire, at the Albany conference the Penn brothers made a further deal with the Iroquois whereby they purchased all Pennsylvania lands west of the Susquehanna. Once more the Delawares denied that the Iroquois owned an inch of Pennsylvania lands.

The provincial governors of Pennsylvania, one after another, realizing what was happening, fought for appropriations and levies of troops, and year after year the Quaker Assembly met them with obstinate refusal and, when forced to pass appropriations, invariably slipped into the bill, not without justice, a clause taxing the Penn estates in due proportions. Then the governor, mindful of his obligations to the Lord Proprietors, would send the bill back unsigned. This began to have all the aspects of a contrapuntal dance; the decorous bowing and backing and advancing of a minuet. In 1754 Pennsylvania was called upon to furnish three thousand troops, subsistence and transportation. In answer, the Assembly voted fifty thousand pounds for public defence, but as usual with the Penn proviso included. Governor Morris refused to sign the bill, and the upshot was that the Assembly borrowed fifteen thousand pounds, and the Penns, moved to unwonted generosity, and with some appreciation of the danger, made a contribution of five thousand pounds, but this was in the shape of a gift—a bonus—and so the precedent of a non-taxable Lord Proprietorship was maintained.

The governors, however, were not always punctilious and politely contrapuntal. Occasionally they lost their tempers, as sorely tried executives have done all through history. Next to mosquitoes—the female ones, for the males do not bite—nothing is so badgering as recalcitrant legislators, especially in times of crisis. And those are always the times, of course, when recalcitrant legislators choose to be recalcitrant. Danger stirs them blindly, as a wind does their winged counterparts.

Governor Morris to the Assembly, 1755: "Your very tedious message is of such an inflammatory nature, that did not the duties of my station, and justice to the people, require me to take some notice, I should deem it beneath my notice as a gentleman."

Governor Denny to the same, 1758: "Though moderation is most agreeable to me, there might have been a governor who would have told you the whole tenor of your message was indecent, frivolous and evasive."

The same to the same, 1757: "I have the less reason to regret such usage, since it is obvious from your conduct to those before me, you are not so much displeased with the person governing, as impatient of being governed at all."

Quarrels between the executive power and the legislative, however, are not new and should worry no one. To the contrary, it is upon this stress and strain, this check and counter-check, that democracy is based.

As an interesting side-note of the times, when Governor Denny arrived at Trenton on his way to Philadelphia, the guard of honour waiting to escort him consisted of Colonel Jacob Duché's dragoons and "Colonel" Benjamin Franklin's Regiment. "Colonel" Benjamin Franklin!

If, however, the white man has been foolish in his dealings with the Indian, the Indian has been equally foolish in his reprisals. Nothing so annoys the white man as to be awakened at dawn by massacre.

Tedyuscung, not yet chief of the Delawares but a man of power among them, was doing the best he could to prevent war, despite his habit of drinking a gallon of rum a day and sometimes staying more or less drunk for a year. He and the other chiefs threatened to take the Delaware grievances straight to London and the Crown. It is a pity they didn't. Instead of this, a delegation of Delawares were received at the new State House in 1755 and there, surprisingly enough, delivered the first "Declaration of Independence" known to the world. They did this twenty years before the vague and never proven Mecklenburg Declaration of North Carolina, twenty-one years before the great and thoroughly proven one of Philadelphia. Some of the finest state documents in America have been written or spoken by Indians.

And then, on July 9, 1755, came a disastrous thing: Braddock's defeat at Fort Duquesne.

Foolish, red-faced General Braddock! He did more than any other man to make Pennsylvania a shambles; and while doing this he also made the most potent rebel who ever fought the English crown. Tall, young, not very articulate Colonel Washington never forgave the insolence, stupidity, and arrogance of the British regulars. When the Braddock campaign was over, young Colonel Washington came to Philadelphia and was fêted as a hero; then he returned to Virginia and the quiet life of a gentleman farmer. When he saw Philadelphia again it was nineteen years later, the end of the summer of 1774, and this time he came as a delegate to the First Continental Congress. The next time he came, ten months later, it was in the uniform of an American general.

The echoes of the ambuscade that killed Braddock had hardly died away when the Indians struck. All the west and centre and north of Pennsylvania burst into flames, and in the west the flames came as near to Philadelphia as the Susquehanna, and in the north they crept down as close as Berks and Lehigh counties, and eventually even to the outskirts of Bethlehem and Nazareth. Sunbury on the Susquehanna was the scene of the first massacre, and the Indians wiped out the settlement completely, killing or capturing twenty-five whites. To show how completely removed Pennsylvania had been until then from the dangers of the other colonies, Richard Peters, at the time secretary of the Council, was able to state that Sunbury was "the first inroad ever made upon the Province since its first settlement". In November the Moravian community of Gnadenhutten was treated as Sunbury had been treated, and eleven of the brethren and a boy of sixteen were slain as they were sitting at their quiet communal supper. This was too bad, for of all the innocent whites in the province the Moravians were the most innocent. The Moravians, like the pelican, were "wounded in their piety", for Tedyuscung was one of their converts, known as "Brother Gideon". A gently, godly people, the Moravians, invariably kind and just to the Delawares.

In a panic—an angry one—five hundred "Pennsylvania Dutch" farmers moved upon Philadelphia, coming mostly from Berks County, and numerous other farmers, Quakers, from the nearer counties, Chester and Delaware, did the same. The farmers were received politely in Philadelphia and were assured by the Assembly and Governor Morris that they would be protected. But the defence bill passed by the Quaker Assembly had a lot of catches in it.

All conscientious objectors were automatically relieved of any responsibility, even financial; no Quaker could be drafted; no one under twenty-one could be called; no one could be forced to take part in any campaign lasting more than three days; and no troops could be held in service longer than eleven months.

This deviousness paid no better than deviousness ever does pay in the long run. Because of this bill, and what happened as the result of it, the Quakers lost the support of the Germans, incensed the rural settlers everywhere, and pleased only their enemies, the Scottish-Irish and the governor, glad to see the Quakers fall into a pit of their own digging. The massacres continued. Somewhere around forty villages were burned, and threescore or more of farmers and their families were killed. Presently a grim and convincing procession passed through the "green countrie towne": the most dramatic procession Philadelphia has ever witnessed. The "Pennsylvania Dutch" brought in their dead, the blood black and congealed on them, and paraded them through the streets of the "Holy Experiment". The badgered and angry governor lost his head and issued his famous "scalping decree". But no one need have thought it original.

Scalping is an old and honoured custom, as much white as red. Herodotus mentions it as a practice among the Scythians, and American frontiersmen have always been given to it. A couple of decades after Governor Morris' decree, British General St. Clair, raiding down through the Mohawk Valley in New York, offered identical bounties, although far less liberal, to his Senecas, or anyone else. The Continental Congress replied by setting a bounty on the scalps of "blue-eyed" Indians, since as numbers of General Clair's Scots had fallen into the habit of stripping, dyeing themselves, and shaving their heads into warlocks in order better to release their inhibitions. Governor Morris' earlier and more generous offer was one hundred and thirty pieces of eight for every Indian scalp, male, female, and child over twelve, and the same amount for every female or child captive. No age limit on the latter. As for males, you were not supposed to make them captives.

In this instance, however, Governor Morris' offer, atrocious as it was, seems to have had speedy results, for in three months the Delawares were suing for peace with the provisos that the "Walking Purchase" be rescinded and the Iroquois authority over the Delaware be declared void for ever. Governor Denny, who had taken Governor Morris' place, refused both these demands, and eventually, largely through the adroitness and knowledge of Conrad Weiser, the pack-horse trader and interpreter, and the good offices of an honest and trusted young Moravian missionary, Frederick Post, Tedyuscung and the Delawares were bought off for four hundred pounds.

Four years later Tedyuscung met his ignominious death. But he got his statue on the Wissahickon. Philadelphia has erected a number of statues to worthies whom, during their lives, it mistrusted and usually mistreated.

It was about time for the Indians to settle down, anyway. As always, the white man, once he had made up his mind, was defeating them. General Forbes, dying but able, friendly and gallant, had come up from the South, where he had been in command of the British troops stationed there, to take Braddock's place. The French lost Fort Duquesne and Pennsylvania, and the Indians, wherever come across, were annihilated. Forbes of the Scots Greys, affable and successful, never saw England again. He came back to Philadelphia and died in what had once been Penn's official residence, the "Slate Roof House", now a superior sort of boarding-house, and was buried near the altar of Christ Church. All those who believe in Anglo-American friendship should make of this grave a shrine, for Forbes was a good friend of America. Near him lies another historic grave, the grave of Bishop William White, first bishop of Pennsylvania, first duly consecrated American Protestant Episcopal bishop, and first presiding bishop of the Protestant Episcopal Church of the United States. Bishop White, more than anyone else, was responsible for the name "Protestant Episcopal".

After the ending of the French-Indian War, Penn's "green countrie towne", save for the outbreak of the "Paxtang Boys", savage and dreadful, in 1764, settled down again to a decade of peace, but it was a troubled one, for now the War of the Revolution was rising like a stormy moon above the horizon. The ways of peace go on, however, despite wars; also the perpetual quarrels of peaceful men.

All during the French and Indian troubles, and before them, Philadelphia had been behaving like a normal city.

The eloquent George Whitefield, that great "Billy Sunday" of the eighteenth century, who had begun life by assisting, as a boy of fifteen, at the bar of his father's tavern, the Bell Inn, at Gloucester, England, paid his first visit to America in the late 1740's, and lingered in Philadelphia and preached, and troubled mightily the soul of the city, although, as the canny James Logan predicted, only temporarily. Franklin printed his sermons, and was an intimate of his, and took an active part in getting a chapel built for him. *Poor Richard* was appearing annually, and Franklin, by no means a frugal man himself, thought *Poor Richard's* dry suggestions as to thrift were doing the citizens of the province great good. Had Pennsylvania and Philadelphia taken them literally to heart, there would be no present-day Philadelphia millionaires. As it is, there are lots of them.

Thrift is the most static of all the virtues.

Four or five jealous imitators of *Poor Richard* had sprung into being, and for a while Philadelphia was deluged with almanacs. Also, for a while during the Indian war, the 62nd Royal Americans had been quartered in Philadelphia, under command of Colonel Henry Bouquet, that scholarly and excellent Swiss mercenary in the English service who had so much to do with the final conquest and pacification of the Pennsylvania frontier. The 62nd Royal Americans worried Philadelphia; smallpox crept through the barracks, and the troops did not have enough to eat. Philadelphia would have been even more worried had it known that in twenty years the 62nd Royal Americans, the "American Rangers", still a famous British regiment, was to be the most deadly Tory regiment of them all.

Many a fine young American lost his life or his citizenship by belonging to it.

In addition, of course, were the perennial religious controversies, and as well, an early example of American devotion to European impostors. The American drinks in devotion to European impostors with his mother's milk.

A strange and silent Oriental calling himself Sheik Sisi, Emir of Syria, arrived on horseback, entered the State House, and presented a letter from the governor of New York. The combination of New York and fictitious royalty were too much for Philadelphia, and so the "Emir" had a wonderful time and received numerous valuable presents, including—and no one could imagine anything more fantastic—a substantial sum of money subscribed by Quaker friends. Getting to be something of a nuisance—part of the pattern —the "Emir" wandered tactfully off to the West Indies and was never heard of again, but religious controversy stayed at home, as it always does.

In 1737 a correspondent writing to the *London Magazine* had been very much alarmed. He writes:

> As I join with you about the Quakers, I shall give you a small specimen of a notable step taken towards the Propagation of Popery abroad; and as I have it from a gentleman who has lived for many years in Pennsylvania, I confide in the truth of it; let the Quakers deny it if they can. In the Town of Philadelphia, in that Colony, is a Publick Popish Chapel, where that Religion has free and open exercise; and in it all the superstitious Rites of that Church are as avowedly performed as those of the Church of England are in the Royal Chapel at St. James.

Philadelphia is to-day a great Roman Catholic city, seat of a cardinal, His Eminence Denis J. Dougherty, Archbishop of Philadelphia, and there are over 2,500,000 Roman Catholics in Pennsylvania. A further interesting fact is that Pennsylvania was shown by the census of 1936 to have more churches of every denomination than any other state in the Union, although there seems to be the usual gap between faith and performance, since Pennsylvania during most of its history has been a curiously wicked state politically and socially. Smug about it, too. None of the continual unrest of New York; little of the sporadic striving toward honesty and better government that has distinguished numerous of the other states.

Like a great sluggish carp, shadowy at the bottom of an opaque pond, Pennsylvania stays fat on the bread Nature has thrown it.

Nor, in these times of comparative peace, had the Church of England, by now the dominant party and comprising the majority, perhaps, of the leading and more energetic citizens, been idle. In 1753 the steeple of Christ Church was completed, erected through money raised by the "Philadelphia Steeple Lottery", and by this time, also, Christ Church was beginning to acquire some of its famous pews and tombstones. Adams, Franklin, Lafayette, the Penn family, Robert Morris, the Hopkinsons, Benjamin Rush, Washington, and Betsy Ross had pews in Christ Church, and in its churchyard are buried Robert Morris, General Charles Lee, of the Continental Army—no great honour to the plot of sacred ground—Peyton Randolph president of the First Continental Congress, and James Wilson, signer of the Declaration of Independence, the great Scotsman who became an American and tried to be a good Philadelphian, and whose body should have been left in Edenton, North Carolina, where he died in the home of James Iredell after Philadelphia had treated him so badly.[1] Until 1840, General Hugh Mercer, killed at the Battle of Princeton, was also buried in Christ Church graveyeard, but in 1840 his body, appropriately enough, was removed to Princeton. In the supplemental Christ Church Burial Ground, a few "squares" away at the corner of Fifth and Arch, are buried Benjamin Franklin, his wife Deborah, his son Francis Folger, who died at the age of four, Franklin's daughter, Sarah Bache, her husband, Richard Bache, and Deborah Franklin's father, John Read.

In Christ Church is the silver communion service presented by Queen Anne in 1708, and the eight bells that joined the Liberty Bell (the "Province Bell") when the Declaration of Independence was read to the people on July 8, 1776. The central chandelier of the church dates from 1749. Above the altar is Philadelphia's first stained glass window.

And then in 1755 something sad and wistful happened. Philadelphia received its first formal contingent of refugees, the exiled Acadians of Nova Scotia; despairing and bewildered folk. They were unhappy and at a loss what to do, and Philadelphia did not want them. Many of them stayed and were absorbed into the population; others moved on toward the south. It was in the Quaker Almshouse, according to Longfellow, that Gabriel and Evangeline finally met.

---

[1] The body of James Wilson, Signer, was brought back to Philadelphia from Edenton in 1907, with much ado and ceremony. All the "City Fathers" and other worthies attended the belated funeral. Some hundred and twenty-five years earlier, after the Revolution, Wilson had been almost mobbed in the streets of his adopted city, and his house had been assaulted by the militia and a crowd of hoodlums. Only the prompt action of prominent citizens and better-trained troops—Captain Leiper's Troop of Light Horse and Colonel Baylor's cavalry—saved an ugly situation from becoming worse. As it was, Captain Campbell, one of the group of gentlemen gathered at Wilson's fine house, known as "Fort Wilson", with its high wall and garden at Third and Walnut streets, was shot by the mob and fatally wounded.

Wilson, who had been a staunch patriot, and who was the most unswerving of democrats, had made the mistake of defending, as a lawyer, some of the, by now, helpless loyalists.

It is a psychological wrench to turn from Christ Church to the "Paxtang Boys" of 1764; their nucleus, militiamen of Paxtang Township on the Susquehanna.

Possibly the "Paxtang Boys", about two thousand active ones when they got started, and all the other Scottish Presbyterians of the frontier and the central part of the state, had just cause to become angry with the Quaker pacifism of Philadelphia, the nonchalance of the new governor, John Penn, and the urbane indifference of Philadelphia's rich merchants and shipowners, but they took a mistaken and savage way of showing it.

The "Paxtang Boys" were not urbane; they were fierce riflemen, and as they marched they gathered up the ragamuffins that lynchings always attract. Led by Lazarus Stewart, the "Paxtangs" started from the Susquehanna intent upon killing and scalping every Indian they met and capturing Philadelphia—yes, seriously, and they nearly did it. They intended to hold the city until the governor and the Assembly assured them of adequate protection. On the way they murdered indiscriminately Indian men, women, and children, and to have two Indian scalps was the same to the "Paxtangs" as a modern service ribbon. Meeting seven friendly Indians on a country road on their way to church, the "Paxtangs" murdered them, which was typical. The "Paxtangs", moreover, had an especial dislike for the Moravians, because the Moravians treated the Indians so well and went among them as friends and missionaries, and this hatred was transferred to the Moravian Indian converts who fled to Philadelphia for protection. The "Paxtangs" thought Indians had been spoiled by the Moravians.

The "Paxtangs" began their bloody history by what is known as the "Conestoga Massacre". Conestoga, home of the Conestoga wagon, the ancestor of the covered wagon, was at the time a small village near Lancaster, and there on the banks of a creek lived a tiny colony of entirely peaceable Indians, fishermen and basket weavers. Shortly after Christmas the "Paxtangs" fell upon this colony and murdered seven of its members. The survivors —fourteen in all—fled to Lancaster and the protection of its jail. They were well known in Lancaster, for it was there that they sold their baskets. In Lancaster, also, was a company of regular troops. But the "Paxtangs" marched on Lancaster and, with the regular troops and the citizens looking on, stormed the jail and lynched the Indians, Lazarus Stewart screaming, "Kill the vermin in their nest!" Then the "Paxtangs" continued on their way to Philadelphia.

By this time the city was thoroughly alarmed, even the nonchalant John Penn, so it proceeded to call out its militia and fortify itself. Stewart and his "Paxtangs" came by way of Germantown, and first they were met by three clergymen who reasoned with them and got their consent to wait for a further parley before entering the city, and next day a delegation headed by the inevitable Franklin talked further with them. The "Paxtangs" agreed upon peace if the Assembly would assure them protection for their farms and settlements. To this the governor, John Penn, and the Assembly agreed, although at the moment it was the Indians more than the "Paxtangs" who needed protection.

PORTRAIT OF BENJAMIN FRANKLIN, by Robert Feke (?)

PHILADELPHIA: THE BENJAMIN FRANKLIN PARKWAY

The peaceful Moravian converts who had fled to Philadelphia for protection had already been shipped off to New York under guard of British regulars stationed in Philadelphia. New York would have done of them, claiming the whole affair was Pennsylvania's business, so the British regulars and their charges had started back and were at the moment, fortunately and vaguely, lost somewhere in New Jersey.

New Jersey has always been a useful "no man's land" between the arrogance of New York and the obstinacy of Pennsylvania. The time it takes to traverse it diagonally permits a cooling off, coming or going.

Meanwhile, the more warlike Indians, bewildered because they thought the war was ended, and enraged by the "Paxtangs", and claiming, not without justice, that Tedyuscung had as usual been drunk, and had been made drunker, when Conrad Weiser and the others had dealt with him, had struck back and killed a score more of settlers. Again the frontier fires were lit, nor did they actually die down for many years. The Delawares moved west into Ohio, but their war-drums went with them to join the war-drums of the Ohio tribes.

And meanwhile, as if there were not enough trouble as it was, the so-called Yankee-Pennamite Wars, which were to continue intermittently right through the Revolution, and indeed, so far as litigation was concerned, up to 1807, broke out in 1763 between the fellow-Americans of Connecticut and Pennsylvania.

Whenever they were relieved temporarily from fighting Englishmen, Tories, and Indians, Pennsylvania and Connecticut fought each other.

CHAPTER XV

Coal

"Every basket is power and civilization. For coal is a portable climate. It carries the heat of the tropics to Labrador and the Polar Circle; and it is the means of transporting itself withersoever it is wanted."

EMERSON.

IT WAS BY the merest chance, or rather, to put it better, only because of the ultimate good sense of English-speaking Americans, and that Fate which seems to have intended, anyway you look at it, that there should be such a country as the United States, that northern Pennsylvania did not become western Connecticut, and that Connecticut is not, instead of Pennsylvania, the great anthracite coal state of the Union. So far as the legality of prior claims and prior documents is concerned, Hartford should be the anthracite capital of the country, and not Philadelphia.

Also, one continues to wonder why, once the Revolution was out of the

F

way, the thirteen colonies did not disintegrate into the Balkans of the West. It looks as if a common language, and an eminently intelligent and reasonable one at that, was to be thanked more than anything else. As it is, it is interesting to reflect that the Pennsylvania coal towns of Wilkes-Barre, Pittston, Plymouth, Kingston, and so on, are not Pennsylvania towns at all, but New England towns, founded by Connecticut "Yankees", although it is reasonable to suppose that, had Connecticut continued to hold them, they would be considerably neater than they are to-day.

Even Connecticut, the most southern of New England states, and made bawdy toward its west by the huge and sprawling neighbour, New York, retains an inherent neatness unknown to the more casual inhabitants of the middle or south of America. Anyone who knows the Western Reserve of Ohio, part and parcel of the same claims Connecticut had upon northern Pennsylvania, realizes how well this neatness and frugal beauty have been planted and are preserved.

Certainly Connecticut had a prior charter, for it was granted in 1662, twenty years before Philadelphia was founded, and in 1681, when Penn was looking into the territorial rights of his proposed province. Sir William Jones, the English Crown attorney, admitted that there was a real conflict and that there was weight in Connecticut's contention. From then on, with what might be called a certain typical blandness, Pennsylvania thought it best to ignore Connecticut's claims. If you forget about something, perhaps other people will, too. But New Englanders have long memories, and so in 1753 Connecticut formed the Susquehanna Land Company, and the year following purchased from the Six Nations all rights to the territory in question. The Delawares were as usual ignored.

Owing to the outbreak of the Seven Years' War, Connecticut's plans for colonization were delayed, and so it was not until 1763 that there was any chance of their being put into effect. In that year a few Connecticut pioneers settled at Mill Creek in what is now Luzerne County. These were almost immediately driven away by the Indians, but the obstinate New Englanders came back with more settlers and a few troops, and by 1768 were fairly well established. Pennsylvania, thoroughly alarmed, had already begun to move. In the same year—1768—Pennsylvania delegates, led by the Penns, also saw the Six Nations and got them to repudiate the Connecticut agreement and purchase of 1754, and shortly after this Pennsylvania troops moved upon the Mill Creek blockhouse and took possession of it and of the frontier settlement surrounding it.

The Iroquois were astute real-estate men of the older and less ethical school.

Connecticut, naturally, felt aggrieved and showed no intention of relinquishing either its claims or its settlements, and for seven years, from 1768 to 1775, the First Yankee-Pennamite War lingered on intermittently, and finally ended, Connecticut on top. Practically in the middle of the Revolution, Pennsylvania and Connecticut fought a battle, not a very serious one, at Rampart Rocks on December 25, 1775. Bunker Hill had been fought six months earlier. Philadelphia was in the throes of national indignation and suspense. But Pennsylvania and Connecticut were nonetheless at war.

The Second Yankee-Pennamite War broke out in 1784, the Revolution just over, following the unanimous decision of the Continental Congress in 1782 that the territory belonged to Pennsylvania. Pennsylvania, triumphant, had begun to administer the territory with such cruelty and arrogance on the part of its agent, Alexander Patterson, that the Connecticut settlers rebelled. This time the arms of Pennsylvania were victorious, and the rebellion was settled amicably by the removal of the offending Patterson and the confirmation of all titles. But although actual fighting ceased, the quarrel lingered on in the courts until 1807, when the United States Circuit Court finally decided in favour of the larger state. Common sense and geography were on the side of Pennsylvania; legality, on the side of Connecticut.

To us, looking back—those of us who have ever heard of the Yankee-Pennamite Wars—these strange fraternal pioneer conflicts have a trace of *opéra bouffe* and seem absurd and incredible. It is almost as if to-day New York and Connecticut should go to war as to who owned the New York, New Haven & Hartford Railroad, and fortunately, so far as actual bloodshed was concerned, the Yankee-Pennamite Wars were comparatively harmless. Both sides showed a desire not to be any more deadly than could be helped, although a few soldiers and settlers did manage to get themselves killed. Frequently both Pennsylvania and Connecticut behaved like the king of France who "marched up a hill, only to march down again". Constitutionally and historically, however, these disputes were of immense and final importance in the forming of America, and possibly may be of equal importance in the forming someday of a more sensible world. To the future of the United States they were as determining as, in its way, Hamilton's *Federalist*.

Robert Livingston told Lafayette that when the United States of Europe were eventually formed, the peaceful settlement of the Yankee-Pennamite Wars would be cited as a precedent and, in fact, this peaceable settlement was cited at the Hague Tribunal in 1907. When the trial at Trenton in 1782, the first trial involving war-provoking issues between the states, was settled by adjudication, the implications for the future were enormous and were immediately recognized by James Wilson and all the other great lawyers present. This trial, as was the subsequent one, was much more than a trial between Pennsylvania and Connecticut over bounderies, important as those were; it was a trial of the new Union. Had it failed—the peaceable agreement, that is, between the contestants—there would have been no Union, or at the best, a sadly weak and crippled one. And during the Revolution the actual fighting between Pennsylvania and Connecticut, minor as it was, came as near to preventing future union as any of the quarrels between the diverse colonies.

Few historians have recognized the vital importance of the Pennamite Wars. They were indeed a crucial event in the history of this country: a deciding factor, a turning-point. They are worth a volume or two by themselves. And involved with them was one of the most dreadful episodes in the long history of Penn's province.

In the hot summer of 1778 the Connecticut men and women in Pennsylvania's Wyoming Valley must have regretted the fact that they had ever left the shores of Long Island Sound.

Down from New York came Walter Butler and his Tories and his Senecas, and with the Senecas was beautiful Esther Montour, said to have been the quarter-breed granddaughter of the great Count de Frontenac.

Over the hills and down through the forests lying between New York and Pennsylvania they came, twelve hundred of them, and there in the Wyoming Valley, fertile with its ripening crops, occurred the bloodiest massacre of the Revolution save for the Cherry Valley Massacre up in Walter Butler's native state, also the work of Walter Butler.

Connecticut men and Pennsylvania men fought side by side in those July days and nights to hold their blockhouse, and when it fell, and in the desperate flight afterwards to reach safety, some four hundred or more men, women, and children were killed or died from privation. Esther Montour tomahawked with her own hand six helpless captives because in the first day's fighting her son had been slain.

John Butler, Walter Butler's father, had led the Wyoming Valley expedition, but Walter Butler came down in time to assist. Walter had even a prettier taste in massacres than his father.

History is tied together. It is indeed "out of the cradle endlessly rocking".

In their slow creaking saga across the plains, the covered wagons, first conceived in Conestoga, Pennsylvania, were to see other massacres of peaceful Indians as ruthless as that conducted by the "Paxtang Boys". And they were to see massacres of peaceful white men as cruel as those of Wyoming Valley and Cherry Valley.

In this respect there has been little to choose between white man and Indian. Cruelty knows no colour.

As has been said, the Yankee-Pennamite Wars were also in another way far more important than either Pennsylvania or Connecticut realized at the time, or most American historians realize to-day:

In 1806, a year before the final decision of the United States Circuit Court, there had occurred in Philadelphia, at a Delaware River wharf, an inconspicuous and unheralded and subsequently derided arrival. An "idealist" named William Turnbull, one of those fellows who won't let well enough alone, had floated down the Lehigh, and then the Delaware, on a home-made flatboat, on its deck a rough box of lumber containing ten tons of a black, shining "rock-like" substance. Turnbull, fanciful fellow, said the black "rock-like" substance would burn, and the Centre Square Water-works in Philadelphia had been foolish enough to undertake the experiment. Naturally, it was a failure—naturally, because there were no proper grates. Indignantly the Centre Square Waterworks threw the trash out on the dump pile, and William Turnball, now known to be a swindler, went back in disgrace to where he had come from, which was near Mauch Chunk. But the next year Joshua Malin discovered a way of making the "black rocks" burn, and with that, the immense anthracite coal-fields of Pennsylvania, at one time so nearly in the possession of Connecticut, began their subterranean existence.

Once more, Nature had been kind to Penn's province.

Within a short time coal began to be transported regularly down the Delaware, although six years after Malin's discovery, three hundred and sixty-five tons were still sufficient to meet Philadelphia's demands for a year. And then suddenly the entire country, and the world, awoke to what anthracite coal meant. Another giant, steam, was in the offing; steam on tracks, steam on the sea, steam in stationary engines. The swiftness and the power of the world poured out, and at the source of this pouring, where North America was concerned, sat Philadelphia.

In 1822 four coal ships left the port of Philadelphia for the north. By 1827 this fleet had increased to 397 vessels carrying 39,000 tons. By 1837, 3,225 coal ships were clearing the greatest number of ships ever to clear up to that time, and 350,000 tons of Turnbull's "rocks" were leaving Philadelphia annually. Just as with the Pennamite Wars, there is a book to be written—a history; a sad one—about the men who first discover things. They are the saddest men in history, the discoverers, whether it be a new form of beauty, or a new form of wealth, or a new form of goodness, or even a new continent. The world does not like newness, for newness hurts, even if it is no more than the newness of a new shoe. Newness upsets preconceived notions. It makes you use your brain and heart, always a painful process. The discoverers as a rule die poor, achieving only oblivion, and, while alive, only obloquy. It is the men who come afterwards who are the famous ones.

William Turnbull had predecessors where coal is concerned. Marco Polo saw in the Orient "rocks that burned". Marco Polo was a great liar. Everyone laughed. Somewhere in the eighteenth century a backwoods girl out in what is now West Virginia also saw "rocks that burned". She just missed getting into serious trouble. People said she was a witch. John Fitch, real inventor of the steamboat, after his heartbreaking experiments in Philadelphia between 1785 and 1790, during which the Pennsylvania legislature refused him any aid whatsoever, but during which he actually ran a steamboat on regular schedule up and down the Delaware, although occasionally the boiler exploded, went to France. The French laughed at him as had the Americans.

Drunken, distracted, and utterly hopeless, John Fitch came home and went to Kentucky, where he owned some lands, his only hope of income. He found that they had been pre-empted during his absence by squatters, and he could get no redress. On July 2, 1798, he died penniless at Bardstown, some say by his own hand. But a hundred and twenty-nine years later everything was made right—Congress erected a statue to him near Bardstown.

That, of course, evened the score, and balanced the account, and left the Present free to crucify its own geniuses.

The day of Fitch's first experiment, the President, General Washington, did not even go down to the river to watch.

Paul du Chaillu, great French African explorer, and discoverer of the gorilla, lived in Philadelphia for a long while toward the end of the last

century. He became to all intents and purposes a Philadelphian. He was
a source of great amusement to those who knew him. He was a little fellow,
talkative. What "preposterous stories" he told about "monkeys bigger
than men"!

And all the while, Indian Wars or no Indian Wars, Pennamite Wars
or not, one of the most vexatious and burning questions in Philadelphia
had been the theatre. Men and women fought about it, parents and children.
And the stricter Quakers were much saddened by its growth.

This really "vital" quarrel—much more "vital" than whether someone
got scalped or not, or whether Connecticut obtained all the north of Pennsylvania—continued unabated until the Revolution, when theatre-going
became a settled custom—among, that is, the less godly.

The strolling players of 1749 with their production of Mr. Addison's
Cato had started something.

CHAPTER XVI

Masques and Revels

*"That popular Stage-plays are sinful, heathenish, lewd, ungodly spectacles,
and most pernicious Corruptions; condemned in all ages as intolerable Mischiefs
to Churches, to Republics, to the manners, minds and souls of men."*

WILLIAM PRYNNE, "HISTRIO-MASTIX."

SO SAID WILLIAM PRYNNE, graduate of Oriel College, Oxford, lawyer, parliamentarian, and one of the most unflagging and vindictive of Cromwellians.
He said more; he attacked as well the morals of all ladies interested in the
drama, even from the reverse side of the footlights.

"It hath evermore been," he wrote, with the vigorous pleonism and
obscenity of a certain type of reformer, "the notorious badge of prostituted
strumpets and the lewdest Harlots, to ramble abroad to Plays, to Playhouses;
whither no honest, chaste or sober Girls or Women, but only branded Whores
and infamous Adulteresses, did usually resort in ancient times."

Lawyer Prynne was inclined to put the cart before the whore; most
"strumpets" are prostituted. It is worth recording that William Prynne
died a bachelor.

Yet in a gentler fashion, although with equal conviction, all professing
Quakers felt exactly as William Prynne did. It is curious then, and noteworthy, that Philadelphia should have been, more than any other city, the
home and shrine of the American theatre, and for over a century and a half,

until somewhere around 1890, a great theatre town. Perhaps there is a perverse influence which directs things to where they are not wanted, for certainly the performance of Addison's *Cato* in William Plumstead's Warehouse on Water Street caused an immediate rumpus. The Quakers were shocked, the Church of England men pleased, and a number of the young Quakers, male and female, quietly interested. The leaven of the flesh was working within them.

There had been premonitions, of course. Shocking things of this kind seldom happen out of a clear sky. In 1724 the *American Weekly Mercury* made note of the performances of a band of itinerant acrobats on the outskirts of the city at the New Booth on Society Hill, Society Hill being a quarter of the city down on the Delaware between Pine and Union streets; a mild elevation now almost obliterated. Among these strolling acrobats the ungodly took especial delight in a female child of seven "who danced and capered upon a strait roap, to the wonder of all spectators". A year earlier James Logan, then mayor of the city, had expressed alarm because a group of wandering players had set up a stage just outside the city limits which "the sober people" wished him to suppress. He did not do so because, to his embarrassment and that of all "the sober people", the governor, Sir William Keith, liked plays and attended the performances.

The early theatre of Philadelphia is deeply indebted to the liberalism of two of the colonial governors, Sir William Keith and Governor Denny, and, finally, to George Washington, who was an inveterate playgoer.

The female child "who danced and capered upon a strait roap" was followed twenty years later by a puppet show, *Punch and Joan* (1743) which was presented at the Sign of the Coach and Horses, but meanwhile the town had not been without its public amusements, for an eight-legged cat had been exhibited, a leopard, "a beautiful creature, but surprising fierce", and a moose, spelled "mouse" in the advertisements. Addison's *Cato*, however, was the first formal performance, and the Common Council of the city at once took steps to prevent further scandals of the kind.

The Recorder than acquainted the board that certain persons had taken it upon themselves to act plays in this city, and, as he was informed, intended to make a frequent practice thereof; which, it was to be feared, would be attended by very mischievous effects, such as the encouraging of idleness and drawing great sums of money from weak and inconsiderate people, who are apt to be fond of such entertainment, though the performance be ever so mean and contemptible.

Whereupon the board unanimously requested the magistrates to take the most effectual measures of suppressing the disorder, by sending for the actors and binding them over to good behaviour, "or by such other means as they should judge proper".

With what seems premonition, but which was probably no more than propinquity, the strolling players departed for the less righteous city of New York, just as nowadays Philadelphians who have the money much prefer to go to the theatre in that city rather than support what their own town has to offer—two theatres, now, and for the most part "try-outs".

It is more expensive to go to the theatre in New York, and lots more trouble, so, naturally, it is "gayer". More trouble? Theatre-going to-day in New York resembles nothing so much as an antarctic expedition.

When the strolling players departed, they took with them Miss Nancy George, who seems to have been the first Philadelphia girl to join the professional stage. She must have been a brave girl, for from that time on most of her old friends refused to speak to her. Nonetheless, despite William Prynne, and even the wise, if mistaken, James Logan, there were other respectable young women who, if they did not adopt grease paint, at least exposed themselves to it. John Smith in his journal, now preserved in the Ridgway Library, writes:

John Morris and I happened in at Peacock Bigger's and drank tea there, and his daughter being one of the company going to hear the tragedy of 'Cato' acted, it occasioned some conversation, in which I expressed my sorrow that anything of the kind was encouraged.

Peacock Bigger is a delightful name. There could be a chapter written on early Philadelphia names. During the Revolution there was a Major Philip Pancake, an ardent patriot, and during the bloody anti-foreign, anti-Negro, anti-Roman Catholic riots of the 1830's and 40's there was for a short while a "Colonel" John Pluck, a hostler who was voted to supreme command of the "Bloody Eighty-fourth" militia regiment, with the threat on the part of its "bloody" members that anyone who didn't vote for "Colonel" Pluck would be assaulted. Dr. Philip Syng Physick, "father of American surgery", one of Philadelphia's most distinguished early physicians, had a name almost unbelievably appropriate, and on the list of the Philadelphia Dancing Assembly of 1757, those famous and sacrosanct balls, now known as "The Assemblies", begun in 1748 and still flourishing, there was a Miss Sober, first name not given.

This name is undoubtedly a mis-spelling of Shober, a distinguished Philadelphia name.

Michael Welfare, belonging to what was known as the "Christian Philosophers of Conestoga", was also for a time much on the streets of the town.

With the advent of Lewis Hallam's company, an English company from London, in 1754, the Philadelphia theatre can be said actually to have begun. Hallam presented the tragedy *The Fair Penitent* and, anticipating trouble, distributed on the streets of the city a small pamphlet setting forth the virtues of the stage, entitled:

Extracts of Several Treatises,
Wrote by the Prince of Conti;
With the Sentiments of the Fathers,
And some of the Decrees of the Councils,
Concerning Stage Plays.
Recommended to the Perusal, and Serious Consideration of the
Professors of Christianity, in the City of Philadelphia.

The "professors of Christianity" probably did not know what all this was about, and if they did, were further antagonized by the foreign name of "Conti", but fortunately Governor Denny was as much in favour of the stage as his predecessor, Sir William Keith, had been. Also, William Plumstead, now mayor of the city, seems to have been an equally enlightened man.

After the production of *The Fair Penitent*, the theatre continued to live in the doldrums for five years longer, and then, in 1759, David Douglas reorganized Hallam's company and, under the patronage of Governor Denny, to whom Douglas had promised a benefit for the new Pennsylvania Hospital, built a theatre just outside the city at what is now South and Hancock streets. As he had been refused permission to build within the city, Douglas built this theatre of the faubourgs secretly. It was called the Society Hill Theatre and was Philadelphia's first. When word of it got out, the church leaders descended upn the Assembly and an Act was passed prohibiting all theatres both within the city and near it, but Governor Denny adroitly delayed the enforcement of this Act, and from June until the following December the Society Hill Theatre functioned. It was there that Philadelphia saw its first performance of *Hamlet*, *King Lear*, *Romeo and Juliet*, and *Richard III*. *Hamlet* was the benefit performance given for the Pennsylvania Hospital. Seven years later, by 1766, the demand for the theatre had grown to such an extent that Douglas in full view of everyone could build the Southwark Theatre almost within the limits of the city on South Street west of Fourth. Here on April 24, 1767, occurred a momentous event, the first performance of the first American tragedy, *The Prince of Parthia*, by Philadelphia and America's first playwright, Thomas Godfrey, Jr., second son of Thomas Godfrey, inventor of the Godfrey quadrant and noted maker of glass.

Thomas Godfrey, Jr., one of Benjamin Franklin's circle of intimates, as was his father, was also Philadelphia's first poet of worth. A few years later, as an officer of the Continental Army, he was killed in the Carolina fighting.

The British occupation during the Revolution gave a great impetus to the Philadelphia theatre. Lord Howe and his officers liked the stage, and two of them, the charming and unfortunate Major John André, who was to be hanged at the age of twenty nine, and Captain De Lancy, the young New York Tory, not only acted as comedians but painted scenery and designed costumes. Colonel "Charley" O'Hara was also a constant patron. Following this, with the young republic, and the "Republican Court", Philadelphia saw not only the most brilliant seventeen years of its history, but also, in certain ways, the most brilliant decade and a half of its theatre.

Owing to the President's liking for the stage and his frequent occupancy of a box, the theatre became almost official. To suit this new dignity, the first Chestnut Street Theatre, at Sixth and Chestnut streets, the latter name at the time usually spelled "Chesnut", was built in 1794, and here audiences of two thousand frequently attended performances to the starlike candlelight of "a profusion of chandeliers".

From then on for a century Philadelphia's theatre grew in dignity and power.

In 1809 the Walnut Street Theatre was built, still standing and now

F*

the oldest existing theatre in America; but in 1820 the original Chestnut Street Theatre was burned to the ground, and a new one, by the same name, long famous in American theatrical annals as "the Old Drury", took its place. Here Jenny Lind, "the Swedish Nightingale", sang under the management of P. T. Barnum, and Forrest, and Booth, and Jefferson, and Laura Keene played. In 1855, with the city's mania for destruction, this historic edifice was pulled down under the assumption that the brand-new Academy of Music, at the corner of Broad and Locust streets, would present unmatchable competition. This fear proved to be unfounded. The Academy of Music, not an academy at all, but so named because the mores of the city still could not permit so pagan a name as opera-house, turned out to be a place of extraordinary acoustics and strange dignity, perfect even for Wagner, equally good for orchestras, and excellent for public gatherings and public speakers who, unlike children, should be heard—possibly—but never more than dimly seen. Its huge stage and auditorium, however, swallowed up the average play completely, and so pretty soon a third Chestnut Street Theatre arose on Chestnut Street west of Twelfth, and stood until just before the last war.

Very simply and succinctly—perhaps it was the Quaker influence— most Philadelphia theatres were named after the streets upon which their façades fronted; that is, until the turn of the century, when such names, equally famous in theatrical annals, as Garrick and Forrest came along. Between Locust and Spruce streets until recently there was the charming bijou theatre, the Broad Street.

Far down on Arch Street was erected in 1828 the most famous Philadelphia theatre of all. Here for thirty years, from the Civil War until 1892, played one of the most celebrated stock companies in the country, that of Mrs. John Drew, Sr., and here in 1873, her son, John Drew, 2nd, made his début at the age of twenty in *Cool As a Cucumber*. For fifty-four years he was to rule the American stage as the epitome of the well-bred American. Because of the Arch Street Theatre, Philadelphia was the birthplace of the second and third generations of the Royal Family of the same American stage, the Drew-Barrymore family. Ethel Barrymore is a Philadelphian; so is her brother, Lionel; and in 1882, the "Sweet Prince", John, who could have been the greatest actor of his time, was born. From their father, Maurice Barrymore, whose real name was Herbert Blythe, an Irish actor who stirred mightily the hearts of audiences two generations ago, and from their mother, Georgiana Drew, this generation inherited an extraordinary combination of talent and charm.

Their grandmother, Mrs. John Drew, Sr., was one of the great ladies of the stage and while she lived in Philadelphia was a major figure in the life of the city. So far, then, in a hundred and forty years had the "Holy Experiment" come from the female child "who danced and capered upon a strait roap".

Philadelphia was not only the birthplace of the American theatre, but, as has been said, for considerably more than a century it was a great theatrical city; for a long while the greatest in the country, and then, for an equally long while, second. At one time there were something like twenty first-class theatres in Philadelphia. There is even every reason to suppose that Philadelphia also saw the inception of that peculiarly American form of entertainment, the minstrel show; at least, this statement was made by William Whitlock, who should have known, since, together with Master John Diamond, he appeared as a blackface minstrel at the Walnut Street Theatre as early as 1842. Seven years later, the Buckley Serenaders gave a minstrel show in Musical Fund Hall, and in 1853 the first regular Minstrel Opera House, Sanford's, was opened on Twelfth Street below Chestnut. For sixty-seven years, from 1862 to 1929, Philadelphia was the home of the most famous minstrel troupe in the country, Carncross and Dixey's, whose small and exciting theatre was on Eleventh Street near Market. Here Raymond Hitchcock, Eddie Foy, and Henry E. Dixey had their start.

Carncross, like Miss Nancy George, the eighteenth-century dissident, was a member of a prominent Philadelphia family, a Quaker one as well. His brother was one of the first great oculists of the United States, but in those days you couldn't be a minstrel, "wandering" or otherwise, and maintain your place in society. For years the two brothers lived in Philadelphia and never spoke. Strange, to disinherit a man because he has a talent!

"Carry Me Back to Old Virginny", inappropriately enough, was first sung in Philadelphia in 1846, introduced by the minstrel, Jim Sanford, at what was known as the Chinese Museum. Practically all songs now taken to the bosom of the South were written by northerners and first sung north of the Mason and Dixon line.

Another famous Philadelphia stage family were the Davenports, and Philadelphia has had more than its share of famous, or well-known, actors and actresses, three of whom, besides the Drews and Barrymores and Davenports, were world famous.

Edwin Forrest was a Philadelphian, born in 1829 at Spruce and Fifth streets, and so was James Edward Murdock, born in 1811, and who for a hundred and ten consecutive nights played Shakespearean rôles at the Haymarket Theatre in London. Joseph Jefferson was a Philadelphian. The first Joseph Jefferson, an English actor, the great Joseph Jefferson's grandfather, settled in Philadelphia in 1796. Francis Wilson was a Philadelphian; like Carncross, a Quaker. Janet Gaynor is a Philadelphian, and so are Ed Wynn, Eleanor Boardman, Jeannette MacDonald, W. C. Fields, Minnie Palmer, Nelson Eddy, George Bancroft, Charlotte Greenwood—dozens of others. It is interesting to set down a list like this, considering Philadelphia's initial prejudice against the theatre.

Forrest was the hero of one of the most curious, and, as it turned out to be, deadly incidents of the American stage, if we except theatre fires. Forrest made two tours of England, one in 1836 and the other in 1845. The English critics and audiences did not like him and did not treat him well. This caused great anger in America, where Forrest at the time was the most popular actor. In 1849 William Macready, the great English actor, arrived in this country and opened in *Macbeth* at the Astor Place Theatre, in New York. A riot followed and twenty-two men were killed and over two hundred injured.

One took one's theatre seriously in the days of our great-grandfathers.

Philadelphia has also had its quota of playwrights: Clifford Odets, George Kelly, Edward Childs Carpenter, John Cecil Holm, Langdon Mitchell, son of a peculiarly Philadelphia product, Dr. S. Weir Mitchell, America's first great neurologist, but at the same time a distinguished novelist; Richard Harding Davis, Thomas Fitzgerald, John Luther Long, author of *Madam Butterfly;* several more. John Luther Long, like Weir Mitchell, wrote as a side issue and was a Philadelphia lawyer, and what makes *Madam Butterfly* even more interesting is that John Luther Long never saw Japan; in fact, seldom left Philadelphia. He was a busy lawyer; he got his information, such as it was, from a sister who lived in the Orient.

Philadelphians began to write plays early. Following Thomas Godfrey, Jr., there came a succession of playwrights, good or bad: Charles Jared Ingersoll, David Paul Brown, Mordecai Noah, John Augustus Stone—whose *Metamora*, Forrest's favourite play, still survives—Robert Montgomery Bird, and so on. In the middle of the nineteenth century appeared George Henry Boker, who might have been a great playwright and writer had he not laboured under almost crushing handicaps. He was known as "the handsomest man in America". He belonged to a fashionable Philadelphia family. He was a diplomat—at one time minister to Turkey, at another, minister to Russia. And he was one of the founders of the Union League.

A man might have struggled successfully against one or even two of these, but four is too many. Nonetheless, Boker did write two excellent plays, *Anne Boleyn* and *Francesca da Rimini*, the latter of which first made Lawrence Barrett famous, and which was revived as late as 1901 by Otis Skinner.

Langdon Mitchell wrote two excellent plays, *The New York Idea* and *Becky Sharpe;* George Kelly wrote *Craig's Wife;* Edward Childs Carpenter, *The Bachelor Father* and *Whistling in the Dark;* Clifford Odets, *Golden Boy* and *Waiting for Lefty;* John Cecil Holm, *Three Men on a Horse*. But all these latter playwrights went to New York, and there they are, and there they will stay, and there all future Philadelphia playwrights will go, unless, and it is unlikely, Philadelphia revives its theatre.

Each year, like the youths of Britain, hostages to Rome, the talented young of this country's third greatest city, and certainly its most historic, leave the city, never to return. Nor does the city care much, or do anything about it. And this is bad for the city, and bad for the country, and not too good for the talented young, for great art is indigenous, and springs from the soil and the love of it, and is a deep-rooted thing, not too readily transplanted.

Great art, in a large sense, not the usual one, is provincial and local. Most of it is interwoven, however cosmopolitan its final outcome, with the unconscious web of folk material, or at least with the unconscious webs of folk feeling. The passionate love of their cities is what made the Greeks great artists, although each artist spent most of his time upbraiding his particular city. The passionate love of locality is what made the English great novelists and poets.

Only a bedraggled ghost of Philadelphia's theatre is left; a couple of legitimate theatres, playing mostly "try-outs" for New York, or else New York successes a year or so old. Burlesque theatres are unhampered, since there is no stern mayor as in New York. Plump young women remove their clothes generously, but not in the tradition of Forrest, Jefferson, and the Drews. On the other hand, there is a strong and healthy little-theatre movement which is a good sign.   The "Plays and Players" is an excellent organization, and there are several similar ones.   Down on Walnut Street, meanwhile, and not so far down as not to be readily accessible, is one of the loveliest theatres in America and the most historic ; yet, as with so many other things, Philadelphia, as has been said, when it wants to go to the theatre, goes to New York.

Why, it is not so easy to see, as has been said before.

Philadelphia has a population of over a million and a half.   Going to the theatre in Philadelphia has for a long while been far pleasanter than going to the theatre in New York.   If you live in the centre of Philadelphia you can walk easily to any of the theatres; take your time, be leisurely.   If you live away from the centre Philadelphia has the quickest and easiest street transporting system of any city in the country, and the most convenient: its famous and often laughed at, but priceless, "trolley" system.   If you live in the suburbs, the stations of the city are within ten minutes of any theatre. Finally, in Philadelphia you don't dress much for the theatre, only for the opera, and a stiff shirt and art are not compatible.[1]

Art is not a fashion, or shouldn't be.   For the artist it is hard and grimy work; for the audience it should be an attempt to capture, unhampered, a mood and an experience.   You should wear comfortable clothes, you should sit in the dark, you should not be pushed about by crowds; you should sit, receptive and attentive, relaxed in the darkness, waiting to be served, to learn, to be moved.

Music in Philadelphia is different.

Music in Philadelphia is healthy, and always has been.   It is indigenous, its roots well watered by the early Welsh and German settlers and by the later Italian ones.   Even some of the wealthier Quakers succumbed fairly early, and to-day many of their descendants are accomplished amateurs and among the most earnest supporters of music in the city.   Music in Philadelphia has for a long while been not only a fashion but a custom.   As for the working musicians and students, they have perhaps the best school of music in the country, the Curtis Institute, and as an inspiration and place to go, the loveliest opera-house in America, the Academy of Music.   Lovely and inspiring because, in addition to its acoustics, it has tradition, a stately Victorian dignity, and an atmosphere of breath-taking *pastiche*.   Singers sing better, and actors act better, when they tread the boards great predecessors have trod, and their audiences are better, for the ghosts of history watch in the darkness and affect without their knowing it even the most unaware.

Philadelphia has a good Metropolitan opera season and, in addition, a

[1] Philadelphia's trolley system is a lesson in the fact that haste not infrequently makes waste, and that the tortoise is often quicker than the hare.   See *Æsop's Fables*.   While all the other American cities were tearing up their trolley tracks in order to make boulevards for buses, Philadelphia, unmoved, simply ordered new and streamlined and beautiful trolley cars that have been proven by statistics to be boons to the weary shopper, or business man or woman. Then came the war, with the result that Philadelphia now has one of the few adequate—or almost—transportation systems in the country.

How the speed at which the new, upholstered delights of Philadelphia could stop and start was determined by the city's transportation experts, is a fascinating story, but one, unfortunately, which cannot be told here.   The next time you meet a transportation engineer, ask him.

good opera company, at popular prices, of its own, and for many years it had the finest symphony orchestra in the country led by one of the few conductors who can turn an assemblage of musicians, men and individuals, into one great and eerie instrument. The Friday afternoon and Saturday night concerts of the Philadelphia Orchestra are still as sacred to Philadelphians from all parts of the city as the Eleusinian mysteries were to the Greeks. The Orpheus Club, now 74 years old, is one of the finest and most traditional of American male singing clubs.

But the surest sign, perhaps, of Philadelphia's liking for music is in the spring, for in the spring, when the windows are open, in many quarters of the city, and all about you, you can hear pianos being played and people practising singing, and that is very nice and reassuring, and the final test of a city. If you add to this the fact that Philadelphia is the farthest city north that sells flowers on street corners, you will see why, in the spring, the narrow streets, with the warm damp sunshine, are so pleasant.

Jonquils and violets, tulips and hyacinths, and roses—Philadelphia is like Charleston in that respect, or a foreign city. And there are women selling lavender, too. You forget the newspapers blowing about, and the torn-down houses, and the empty spaces looking like the sockets of extracted teeth, and the signs of "To rent". Despite the Quaker interdiction, music began in Philadelphia almost as soon as the city was laid out. The Welsh sing as naturally as throstles, the Germans play instruments and love *lieder*, the Scots and the English have folk-songs. It is hard to keep a man from singing or whistling. Philadelphia's first formal concert seems to have been a romantic one. It consisted of the playing of viols, trumpets, and oboes by the "Monks of the Wissahickon", or to give them their official name, the Brothers of the Society of the Woman in the Wilderness.

The Woman in the Wilderness, if you remember, is mentioned in the Book of Revelation, and the "Monks of the Wissahickon" expected to meet her "as she was to come up from the wilderness leaning on her beloved". For this event—prospective spiritual bridegrooms—they began to prepare themselves. They laid aside "all other engagements, because being hermits"; and they "trimmed their lamps" and adorned themselves "with holiness, that they might meet the same with joy" in the manner in which the "so beloved" had behaved in an earlier wilderness.

Nothing in the early history of Philadelphia is more colourful than the story of these German Pietists, fifty in number, mystics, and most of them men of education and position, who, under the leadership of John Kelpius, of Sieburgen in Transylvania, came in 1694 to settle along the slopes of what was then the lonely and forested gorge of the Wissahickon. They called themselves familiarly, and others called them, the "Hermits of the Wissa-hickon", and Hermit's Lane in Germantown attests to their memory, since it led down from that neat and not unmaterial small town to the forest retreat of the more solitary and mystic brethren. The monks, in the shadows of the tall chestnuts and tulip poplars and elms that line the stream, lived in log huts and caves and dug-outs, although there is a tradition that eventually they built a stone monastery, still standing. They began as celibates; but after a while some of them married, weary of waiting for the Woman in the

Wilderness, and this substitution of the more substantial charms of near-by Germantown maidens resulted in bitter disagreement. Over the question of celibacy the colony broke up.

A few of the monks—the married ones—drifted back to ordinary life; some went up toward Lancaster to join the Palatinate monastery at Ephrata, culturally an even more extraordinary gathering; a handful remained, faithful to their wilderness. But before celibacy reared its ugly head, the Wissahickon seems to have furnished, at least once, the first Philadelphia Orchestra.

The next forward step in music was the installation in 1728 by Christ Church of an organ, and in 1743 the manufacture of spinets by Gustavus Hesselius—a date which marks the beginning of the pianoforte in America. Philadelphia seems also to have witnessed the birth of the oldest German choral club in the country, the Mænnerchor Society, founded in 1835.

Meanwhile, the American Company had introduced opera (light) to the city by the presentation in 1766 at the Southwark Theatre of the operettas *The Sailor's Return* and *Thomas and Sally*, and in 1786 "a grand concert" of fifty instruments and two hundred and thirty voices had been held at the German Reformed Church. In February 1857 the Academy of Music, just finished after five years of building, saw its first opera, *Il Trovatore*. But for a hundred years the city had taken pains with its singing and its instruments, and there were numerous private concerts and some chamber music, and young women were taught among their other accomplishments to play the spinet, and later on the piano, and also, in Victorian days, the harp. And young people sang together, as Mr. Black relates.

Now, all summer, there are many outdoor concerts, and in winter all the music a man can need. Pennsylvania is a musical state. Up at Bethlehem in the Lehigh Valley, at Easter, are the world-famous Bach Festivals, inaugurated at dawn by the blowing of golden-throated trumpets from the church tower; a custom and festival that the Moravians duplicate each year in North Carolina, where, a century and a half ago, some of them founded Winston-Salem. Philadelphia is also beginning to send out its great, or fine, singers, operatic or otherwise. Marian Anderson is a Philadelphian; so are Dusolina Giannini, Henri Scott, Nelson Eddy. These, and many more. David Bispham was a Philadelphian; so was James Huneker, one of the greatest music critics America has ever known, and a brilliant writer. No man set forward more the standards of American music.

And with this we can come to Philadelphia's own especial "mask", or "revel", as curious a "mask" or "revel" as any in existence, and perhaps, here and there, in some respects a somewhat gruesome one. Once a year, on New Year's Day, all day the city witnesses, to the puzzlement of uninformed strangers, and even some of its citizens, this annual "mask" or "revel", the annual Mummers', or Shooters', Parade.

All day the parade marches down Broad Street, the longest straight street in the world, and as always when Philadelphia parades, the city is cut in two, much to the agony of visitors in downtown hotels, such as the Adelphia and Benjamin Franklin, who have to catch a train, since, with the exception of the Reading Terminal, all Philadelphia stations are to the west of Broad Street. In a stand in front of the Union League, to the right of whose bulky brownstone Victorian portico and club-house is a statue of a charging soldier of Pennsylvania's "Bucktail Regiment" of the Civil War, prominent Philadelphians and city officials review the parade.

The parade is enormously colourful and expensive, and for the twelve months between each parade the members of the various Mummers', or Shooters', clubs spend a great deal of time thinking up new ideas and new costumes. One could see the parade's shimmering length better were it not for the interrupting bulk of City Hall.

Year by year the gorgeous procession goes by, club after club—the Joseph A. Ferko String Band, the Frank A. Collins New Year Association, the Silver Crowns, the Klein Club, the White Caps, the League Island New Year Association, the Zu Zus, the James J. Brown Comic Club, and so on endlessly —competing for the substantial prizes put up by the city. Prizes for "the best-dressed club", "the most expensive costume", "the most comic club", "the most gorgeously dressed 'female'," etc., although all the marchers are men; about twenty thousand of them. They go past, kings, queens, clowns, tumblers, ballet girls, harlequins, devils, twisting and capering, bands braying, and disappear into South Philadelphia, where the majority of the clubs come from, and which was the original home of the custom, although now many sections of the city are represented. With their going, the city, with a sigh of relief, resumes its business, glad such "madness" happens only once a year. Also visitors, unimpeded, catch their trains.

Through parading, the Mummers give New Year dances and hold open house in their clubhouses, as the whole city once did on that date. In all history it is doubtful if there ever was a more demure—at least, on the surface —"mask" or "revel", or if the "Abbot of Unreason", or the "Lord of Misrule" ever behaved more decorously and officially. One rather wishes that the entire city, masked, would take part for a week. It would make for social cohesion and refreshed nerves. At all events, nowhere does a municipal celebration so little affect a city as a whole, and nothing could more aptly express the difference between the spirit of Philadelphia and the spirit of New Orleans.[1]

By now the majority of Philadelphians regard this parade as an immemorial custom and are vaguely proud of it because of its antiquity, but as a matter of fact, officially it is comparatively recent. Officially it is only forty-two years old. Before 1902 the masking and parades were neighbourhood affairs, confined to the localities where the clubs had their homes, and the police looked askance at them. It was not until 1902 that the parade became official and that permission to march down Broad Street was given, and that the city put up prizes; all this largely due to the Vare brothers, the extraordinary "pig-men", tribunes of the people, who for thirty years or so owned and ran Philadelphia. As one has every reason to suspect, most of the clubs are strongly tinged with politics. But on the other hand, the Mummers—the Shooters—are extremely ancient spiritually; they are the direct spiritual descendants of the Christmas waits and the Twelfth Night revellers of Eliza-

[1] It is an interesting comment on the Mummers' Parade that there are now so many out-of-town participants. Perhaps it is not altogether a good thing. During the term of the late Mayor S. Davis Wilson, who died in office, a determined effort was made to make this curious Philadelphia festival purely local again. It failed. Many of the clubs said, no visitors, no parade.

bethan and an infinitely older England. The Philadelphia Mummers are the spiritual descendants of the Druids and pre-Druids, as Mummers are all over the world.

Once a year—sometimes twice—as a rule, near the time of the winter solstice, or on St. John's Eve in summer—there stirs in the human breast, like the yeast in wine, the runic spirit of festival. The earth and saturnalias are ancient and inevitable things. In the small red-brick town of Penn, young people, and those who refused to become old, around Christmas-time rang doorbells, and asked for "doles", and sang in the streets, and danced, pursued by the volunteer watch and to the scandal of the more sedate. These malefactors also shot off firecrackers, hence the name "Shooters", an Anglo-Saxon Christmas custom far antedating the use of the Christmas tree, an idea imported from Germany only a hundred and fifty years or so ago.

In the South they will shoot off firecrackers at Christmas and the New Year, greatly to the mystification and impatience of northerners who think the southerners don't know what they're doing and have mixed up January with July.

In any case, as H. Bart McHugh, one-time councilman and a leading spirit among the Mummers, remarked, "Once a South Philadelphian, always a Shooter".

Philadelphia has another celebration, a weekly one, but it is not a saturnalia, although it is even more famous than the Mummers' Parade; it is known everywhere as the "Philadelphia Sunday". On Saturday the majority of visitors to the city, including all chorus girls, take early or late trains to New York as if fleeing from a plague. As for Philadelphians, on Sunday mornings thousands of them go out into the country, and those who remain go to church, eat a soporific Sunday dinner, and then read the comic supplements of the Philadelphia *Record*, or the Philadelphia *Inquirer* until they doze off. A good many, however, go out to the Zoo, or to Fairmount Park, or view the wonders of the Franklin Institute. Until recently there were blue laws in Philadelphia prohibiting Sunday baseball and Sunday motion pictures, and still, unless you carry a flask, or have friends, or belong to some sort of club, nowhere on Sunday can you get a drink in Philadelphia. Philadelphia even has the distinction of having passed toward the end of the eighteenth century a law providing for the chaining off of all streets on either side of churches while services were going on. This law was in effect for thirty years or so, to the great inconvenience, once more, of those who had to go somewhere else.

And yet, for those who like it, the "Philadelphia Sunday" is a sweet and peaceful and nice-smelling affair, to be looked forward to. The narrow streets are quiet. The squares are green and shady, or bright with sun-shot ice. There is a great clear clamour of bells, and the asphyxiant of carbon monoxide is for one day absent. One recaptures a little—for a few hours—the "Holy Experiment". There are still in every quarter remnants of "church parades": families slowly walking back home; wives and husbands; people stopping to talk to each other; although no longer do those who have not been at church sit at parlour or drawing-room windows, nodding to those who have been.

Nor is the Philadelphia "busybody", the double-paned reflecting glass attached to second-storey window-sills, and which enables one to see what is going on in the street without being seen, any more very visible. There are a few left, but not many.

And now for some odds and ends.

It is not only to the legitimate stage that Philadelphia made such a major contribution. Strange as it may seem, especially if one considers the climate, Philadelphia was the pioneer motion-picture city of the country. In 1898 Sigmund Lubin, a Philadelphia optician, started a studio for making motion pictures on the roof of a Philadelphia business building and a year later opened at Seventh and Market streets what seems to have been the first motion-picture theatre in the United States. For a long while the Lubin Studios were a feature of Philadelphia, until California beckoned them. Nor was this all. In 1860 Dr. Coleman Sellers, a Philadelphian, made the first photographs of motion, and it was upon his invention that the later developments of Edison were based, and ten years later, on February 5, 1870, Henry R. Heyl displayed at the Academy of Music his "plasmatrope", a machine "designed to give to various objects and figures upon the screen the most graceful and life-like movements". In 1894 C. Francis Jenkins used for the first time flexible films at a demonstration given at the Franklin Institute.

Philadelphia has also had a long and honourable history of marionettes of the puppet stage, that delicate midget sister of the legitimate stage which lives a sequestered fairy-like existence of its own. The first recorded puppet show was given in Philadelphia in 1742, and in 1786 Charles Dusselot, a young retired officer of Louis XVI's Guards, established a regular season. Madame Dusselot, who had a pleasing voice, sang behind the scenes.

Philadelphia's large population of Italian descent still sees to it that Philadelphia's puppet stage is healthy.

Perhaps the most unexpected and paradoxical event in Philadelphia's long history of the stage was the production some fifteen years ago of Aristophanes' *The Lysistrata*. It is, as you remember, not exactly a chaste play. The *Encyclopædia Britannica*, in describing it, contents itself with this demure note: "As the men can do nothing, the women take the question into their own hands, occupy the citadel, and bring the citizens to surrender."

Quite so!

The version of *The Lysistrata* in question had for some years been the property of the family of famous Shakespearean scholars, the Furnesses, and shares in it had been taken by numerous friends, many of them of the purest Quaker descent, if not themselves still members of "the Meeting", but most of whom, it is to be assumed, had not read *The Lysistrata*. Finally, in the middle of a dull season, it was decided to produce the play in a more or less amateur fashion, against the better instincts of some of the shareholders. The début, amid cheers and blushes, was a smashing success, and after a long run in Philadelphia *The Lysistrata* went on to New York to become a sensation.

One wonders what James Logan would have thought.

CHAPTER XVII

Golden Vessels

"You, O Books, are the golden vessels of the temple . . . burning lamps to be held ever in the hand."

RICHARD DE BURY, BISHOP OF DURHAM, "PHILOBIBLON," 1345.

PHILADELPHIA HAS ALWAYS taken its education and its charities seriously, and this is a natural evolution, for however inept the Quakers may have been politically, owing to their pacifism and desire to evade worldly issues of the kind, they have been invariably magnificent and beautifully generous in their desire to train the mind and to alleviate human suffering. The early Quaker almshouses of Philadelphia were models of their kind; small, charming brick houses, each in its garden, so that honest poverty need know no shame. Quaker tolerance has also made any locality where there is Quaker influence singularly open-minded intellectually, if not socially.

James Logan, who dominated the thought of Philadelphia from its beginning as a small settlement until well into the time of Franklin, had one of the best-trained minds of the eighteenth century—a century of well-trained minds. In his fine country seat, Stenton, he began the collection of the famous Loganian Library, over two thousand volumes at the time of his death in 1751, now about fifteen thousand volumes, which, after some vicissitudes, became a part of the Library Company of Philadelphia, to be sequestered, unfortunately, in the upper galleries of the Ridgway Branch, that huge Doric tomb of priceless books, remotely situated on South Broad Street.

Philadelphia has a habit of hiding its light under a bushel; a charming habit, but a self-defeating one.

The Loganian Library is known to scholars all over the world, but it must take considerable sangfroid for the ordinary citizen to pass between its formidable stone columns and ask, let us say, for the latest book of Ludwig Bemelmans.

Moreau de St. Mèry, the West Indian Frenchman—he was born on Martinique—who, after presiding over the Revolutionary Assembly and exercising so much power that Louis XVI had to appear before him as a suppliant, fled to Philadelphia in 1794 to escape Robespierre and the Jacobins, and who for several years kept a Philadelphia bookshop, speaks of there being at least five thousand volumes in the Loganian Library when he visited it in 1794, so greatly had it grown since the death of its founder. Amongst its numerous treasures are the first Caxton to come to America, Voragine's *Golden Legend*, London, 1483; a Book of Hours, printed on vellum and illustrated in colour, Vèrard, Paris, 1508; Pliny's *Historia Naturalis*, printed on vellum at Venice in 1472; and Dante's *Divina Commedia*, printed at Venice in 1491 by Benali and Mattheo di Parma, and illustrated with woodcuts. The Pliny has illuminated borders and initial letters and was presented by the printers to Don Lodovico of Aragon, grandson of Ferdinand, King of Naples.

These are only a few of the Loganian jewels, all of the above donated by William Mackenzie, an intimate of Washington's, who lived on High Street, and who was a very charming and well-bred man, to judge from his portrait painted by John Neagle. Below the powdered peruke are long and arched eyebrows above steadfast and discerning eyes. In his hands Mr. Mackenzie holds his Caxton edition of the *Golden Legend*. He was a great book collector and, unlike many of his kind, seems to have prized what was inside a book as much as its print, date, and binding. Among other presents he made to the Loganian were a first edition of Byron's *Childe Harold, Canto IV*, in its original boards, and a copy of the first treatise on political economy ever written by an American, also a Philadelphian: *Ways and Means for the Inhabitants of Delaware to Become Rich*, by Francis Rawle, Philadelphia, 1725. *Ways and Means for the Inhabitants of Delaware to Become Rich* was the first book set up in type by Franklin, and he set it up himself. Sometimes one wishes that Francis Rawle had also been the last American economist.

Franklin had learned during his first visit to London, whither he had gone under the patronage of Sir William Keith, the value of clubs and men's gatherings, and to this knowledge can be traced the formation of the Junto, or the Leathern Apron Club, as it was scornfully called to begin with by some of the richer and more conservative Philadelphians, since its members, with one exception, were young and poor artisans or tradesmen like Franklin himself. The one exception was Robert Grace, who, as Franklin says in his biography, was "a young gentleman of some fortune, generous, lively and witty; a lover of punning and his friends". The others were such young men as Franklin's partner in the printing business, Hugh Meredith, William Parsons, a cobbler, William Naugridge, a joiner, Joseph Breintnall, a scrivener but also a poet, William Coleman, merchant's clerk, Thomas Godfrey, famous mathematician to be but at the moment a glazier, Nicholas Scull, surveyor, and so on. Many of these young men, especially energetic and ambitious, surrounded as they were by the opportunities of early Philadelphia, became extremely well-to-do later on in life and founded, as Franklin did, families still distinguished in the life of the city. Presently, as the Junto became more powerful, other young men, some of them, like Robert Grace, young men of means, joined, as Franklin observes, "for the sake of diversion, mutual aid and a rest from their wives".

As the Junto grew to greater seriousness and dignity, Franklin, with the attractive and lovable mind he had, dreamed of forming another club more like the Junto in its earlier and less formal days, the Free and Easy Club, but he never got around to it.

To begin with, the Junto was an informal debating and literary club which met every Friday night at some tavern and discussed all subjects under the sun, but principally natural philosophy and morals. The members were sworn to love the truth for its own sake, to love mankind, to respect and aid each other, and to uphold freedom of opinion. Pretty soon Robert Grace, the "young gentleman of some fortune", offered the club for its meetings his house in Pewter Platter Alley, and pretty soon the Junto began to discuss politics and civic questions in addition to more abstract subjects and became increasingly a major force in both. Within two years of its founding in 1727, Franklin printed privately Ralph Sandiford's tract on Abolition, *Practice of the Times*, which Sandiford distributed free on the streets of Philadelphia, and the same year Junto backed Franklin in his stand for paper currency, a move that so angered James Logan, although he liked and admired Franklin personally and thought him an "ingenious young man", that he called the members of the Junto "base and lying lackeys" of Sir William Keith.

James Logan, like William Penn and like most leading Quakers, had an excellent command of strong words when he thought them necessary.

Franklin, with his sense of social comfort and gaiety even in the most serious matters, had, when drawing up the rules of the Junto, made it obligatory that at certain intervals there should be pauses "while one might fill and drink a glass of wine", and with his admirable balance he always saw that the Junto never forgot the good things of the body while they pursued the good things of the mind. When the Library Company was first founded, directors absent from a meeting were fined one shilling, but Franklin presently hit upon a better scheme; instead of being fined a shilling, the deliquent director had to send "two bottles of good wine" in time for the meeting: a magnificent example of how absence can make "the hearts—of those not absent—grow fonder". The monthly meetings of the Library Company, which was soon to grow out of the Junto, had a repast consisting entirely of a tub of oysters and punch—a gourmet's dream—the directors standing around the tub with their hats on.

Franklin, with his directness of vision and forthright opinions concerning education and culture, his belief that in reading lay the foundation of knowledge, went straight to the heart of the matter as soon as the Junto was formed. What the Junto needed was books, so Franklin suggested that all the members pool their resources in this direction and assemble them for the common use of the members in the room in Robert Grace's house that they had come to call "Pewter Platter Hall".

In that way the Library Company of Philadelphia, the first circulating library in America, began.

Before long it was obvious that more books and money to buy them with were needed, and the Library Company was formed, shares were subscribed, and officers and a librarian elected. James Logan, generously forgetting his anger with the Junto, offered his wide knowledge in the selection of books, and many men of prominence joined: Francis Rawle, author of America's first treatise on political economy; a justice of the peace; Dr. Thomas Cadwalader; Thomas Hopkinson, recently arrived from England and a young lawyer of great talents, and the father of a signer of the Declaration of Independence; and so on. Benjamin Franklin, Thomas Godfrey, William Parsons, Robert Grace, Dr. Thomas Cadwalader, Philip Syng, Thomas Hopkinson, Anthony Nicholas, John Jones, and Isaac Penington were the first board of directors. William Coleman was made treasurer; Joseph Breintnall, secretary.

Wise endeavour reaches out across the world and makes friends, just as evil does, unfortunately. It is a race between them. In any case the one thing that gains no followers is sitting still.

Word of the Library Company went abroad, and from many places came books and donations. In June of 1738 this letter arrived from Antigua, in the West Indies, from a Dr. Walter Sydserfe, an elderly physician, until then totally unknown to the board of directors: "Sirs, the noble Design and most commendable Emulation of the young Gentlemen of your Province in erecting a public Library for the Advancement of Learning, promises so much Good to Mankind, that I cannot withhold from contributing my Mite." Enclosed was a draft for sixty pounds, or the equivalent then of about a thousand dollars.

This was the first gift of money to the library.

London, too, was extremely friendly to this new venture in the most English of all cities, save Boston, across the seas. For almost three decades Peter Collinson, of Gracious Street—and a most appropriate name—acted free of charge as the Library Company's foreign agent, sending new books as they came out. When Franklin went to England he also was an energetic agent, combing the London bookstalls. It was through Franklin that the list began to be leavened by fiction and poetry, and it was through Logan, a great admirer, interestingly enough, of Swift and other satirists, that the library began to acquire its notable collection along this line.

Peter Collinson was a fascinating man: a Quaker, a book collector, an antiquarian, a botanist, and a gardener; enthusiastic, burningly interested, easily ruffled. He had heard of John Bartram, Philadelphia's great botanist, and for years corresponded with him, although the two never met. They exchanged information on the flora and fauna of England and Pennsylvania, and quarrelled in a friendly manner, or agreed about the habits of birds and the virtues, or lack of them, of this plant or that. ". . . The mysteries of 'the sensitive Tippitiwichet' . . . the respective merits of the Sweet White Narcissus and the Double Sweet Daffodil", as Mr. Austin Gray, Cambridge man, and son of the master of Jesus College, Cambridge, and until recently scholarly and witty Librarian of the Library Company, records in his book *Benjamin Franklin's Library;* the best book written about that venerable institution. Collinson fell, unfortunately, into the habit of sending a miscellany of other things along with his assignments of books: seeds to his friend John Bartram, leather breeches for John Bartram, clothes for Bartram's son, Billy Boy, microscopes for James Logan, gifts for other friends in Philadelphia. After almost thirty years of this, the directors of the library foolishly, since Collinson was donating his services, objected, and Peter Collinson, of Gracious Street, never forgave them. From then on he sent no more books, although the Library Company dispatched a letter of apology.

The Penn brothers, the Lord Proprietors, behaved in their usual strange fashion. No wonder Philadelphia wanted to be rid of them. One of the handicaps of the human race is the impossibility of maintaining the breed. Dogs are simple problems compared to men. William Penn would have been mortally ashamed of his sons; even, at times, of Thomas, the best of them.

Thomas Penn had just come out to the province, and so on May 14,

1737, the Library Company, recently formed, sent him its first catalogue and a petition which began, "May it please your Honour—All the good people of Pennsylvania rejoice in your Arrival and Residence in this your Province . . ." and which ended, "May your Philadelphia be the future Athens of America! May plenty of her Sons arise, qualified with Learning, Virtue and Politeness! . . ." Thomas Penn received this obvious appeal for funds with, so it is written, "great Civility and Kindness", and promised "a parcel of books", which never arrived. Not discouraged, the board of directors in 1738 wrote to John Penn, Thomas' brother, who was then in London. John Penn was equally "Civil and Kind". He congratulated the directors on being the first to encourage "Knowledge and Learning" in his province and sent them, of all things, an "Air Pump", accompanied by one Samuel Jenkins, "a Gentleman well acquainted with Natural Knowledge and Mathematics" who would show them how to use it, all this being "both natural and pleasant".

The directors accepted this handsome and "noble Present", as they called it, with gratitude, and it is still in the possession of the Library Company, encased in a much more valuable wooden case designed by Franklin, and which is a beautiful example of early Philadelphia craftmanship.

History falls into four simple categories—wise men, good men, bad men, and fools. Lincoln spoke to the point when he said you could not evade it —history.

If life lives on after death, it must be depressing to go through eternity laughed at, not only by your fellow ghosts, but even by the living marplots and traitors of each succeeding generation, unwitting of their own similar fate. All men seek some sort of renown, however humble. The renown of the man who mishandles the present is pinned like a dusty butterfly to the records of the future.

The small and self-important Lord Proprietors were unaware that when dealing with Franklin they were being permitted the honour of dealing with one of the great men of all times. But the Penns eventually did give the Library Company a plot of land—having so much—although the Library Company had to collect the rents.

The most charming story of the Library Company is that of the book taken out by an English officer, Major Trent, during Lord Howe's occupation of the city and not returned until ninety-nine years later; an exceptional instance of English honesty that might well be remembered by borrowers of books, private and public.

The book was Crantz's *History of Greenland*, London, 1767, and Major Trent took it with him when the British evacuated Philadelphia in June 1778. In 1876 the book arrived from England with no explanation and no name attached.

During Howe's occupancy, and subsequently, during Sir Henry Clinton's, the Library Company was much used by the British officers, especially, so the lists show, Lord Cathcart, Colonel Charles O'Hara, Lord Wrottesley, and the charming Major André, who, by being what he was, has become, despite his execution as a spy, as much of a romantic figure in American eyes as in English ones. When Lord Howe was relieved, Sir Henry Clinton taking his place, Colonel O'Hara and Major André, experts on the theatre and pageants, as has been said, haunted the library, looking up costumes and historical references for the *meschianza*, the grand festivity lasting all day and most of the night, given in Lord Howe's honour. The Library Company has the best collection of André relics, papers, and letters in existence, presented in 1889 by the family of General John Meredith Read.

Just before the Revolution, the last gift of books was from John Wesley, dispatched from England.

Perhaps the strangest episode in the history of "Mr. Franklin's library" was that of Mr. Henry Cox, who signed himself as "of the Kingdom of Ireland," and who appeared at the library on a March day of 1799 carrying a black box. Mr. Cox, a distinguished-looking man, tall and dressed as a Quaker, said that in the box were certain documents of value which he had inherited from a grandfather; papers and documents, as the inventory showed, having to do with Irish history in the reigns of Queen Elizabeth and the Stuarts. He wished to leave the box with the Library Company for safe-keeping. Mr. Cox then went to York, Pennsylvania, accompanied by his wife and children, presented himself to the Friends' Meeting there, introducing himself by means of a letter from the Friends' Meeting in Dublin, and for eighteen years lived quietly, first on a farm he purchased near York, later on a larger farm in Chester County. All his family worked on these farms, and he prospered despite the fact that to begin with both he and his family were obvious amateurs. He took much interest in Quaker affairs, preached often in meeting, and was valued on account of his worldly advice. His Quaker friends, however, were puzzled. Somehow, he wasn't quite like a Quaker, and at moments, forgetting himself, was known to address this or that Quaker conference as "My Lords".

Then in 1817, Henry Cox suddenly sold his farm in Chester County and went back to Ireland as abruptly as he had appeared.

It turned out that his name was not Cox at all, but Hamilton, and that he had been an officer in the English army and had changed his name to Cox upon inheriting from an uncle, Dunmanway, an estate in County Cork. Unfortunately Dunmanway was heavily encumbered with debt, so Mr. Cox, or Mr. Hamilton, had left it in charge of capable agents, had changed his faith temporarily, and come simply and frugally to America. When the debts on Dunmanway were paid off and the estate was once more solvent, he returned to assume his place as a country gentleman. Also, he re-entered the Anglican Church and proceeded to write poetry; the last resulting in a volume of versess called *Metrical Sketches; by a Citizen of the World*, in which, in a poem entitled "Pennsylvania Georgics", he described his experiences as an American "dirt-farmer". He especially loved clover, "Best plant, tho' latest known, Columbia's pride . . . ," and well he might.

All of which is interesting enough, but the point of the story is the black box. The black box remained for almost forty years more with the Library Company; Mr. Cox had forgotten it. Then it was opened. It was found to contain a priceless collection of state documents and papers pertaining to Irish history—letters signed by Queen Elizabeth, by James I and James II, the correspondence of various statesmen, cardinals, and lord deputies, addresses

from the Privy Council, the memoirs of the Marquis of Clanricarde, the Jaco-
bite leader, and so on. The Library Company was delighted and proudly
displayed these letters and documents until 1866, when an English historian,
visiting Philadelphia, identified them as some missing from the archives of
Ireland since 1690. How they came into the possession of Mr. Cox's grandfather no one ever knew, but once this discovery was made there was no other
course, naturally, except for the Library Company to return Mr. Cox's box
to the English Government, where it was gratefully received by the Master
of the Rolls.

Bread on the water, however, returns. In reward for this fair dealing,
in 1897 the manuscript volume of the *Log of the Mayflower*—of which the
correct title is *Of Plimouth Plantation*—which had just been discovered in the
library of the Bishop of London, was presented to America, under a decision
of the English Court of Consistory, and in addition an especial gift of copies
of valuable English state papers was presented to the Library Company itself.

For over two hundred and fifteen years the Library Company of Philadelphia has had a more than distinguished and, at times, dramatic history.
In 1740, Pewter Platter Hall being found too small, the Library moved to a
second-storey room of the new State House, destined thirty-six years later to
change its name to Independence Hall. In 1773 the directors rented two
rooms "in a new Building called the Carpenters' Hall, in the centre of the
new Square where the Friends' School stands"; one room for their books,
one for their collection of various objects, including the air pump, known
as the "Philosophical Apparatus". In 1789, Bishop White presiding, the
directors decided to have a home of their own, and a plot of land was bought
on Fifth Street below Chestnut, where a lovely Palladian structure was
erected. Franklin did not live to see its completion, but his statue in a Roman
toga, as he wanted it, was ensconced in a niche over the main doorway,
and he wrote the inscription for the corner-stone:

Be it remembered
In honour of the Philadelphian Youth
(Then chiefly Artificers)
That in MDCCXXXI
They cheerfully
INSTITUTED the PHILADELPHIA LIBRARY
which tho' small at first
Is become highly valuable
And extensively useful:
And which the Walls of this Edifice
Are now destined to contain and preserve;
The First STONE of whose FOUNDATION
Was here placed
The thirty first Day of AUGUST
An: Dom: MDCCLXXXIX

In 1880, following the tendency of the city to move westward, the Library
Company migrated again, this time to the corner of Juniper and Locust

streets, just east of Broad.   Just back of the new building, in its back yard,
was the little vacant plot of ground Philadelphia preserves for any visiting
Indian who wishes to camp out.   The statue of Franklin in his Roman toga
was taken along, to be put in place above the new doorway, and the corner-
stone was also moved, to be sunk in the wall of the ascending double stairs
that led up from Locust Street, where for sixty years it was read by passers-by.
A couple of years ago even this building was torn down and is now a parking
lot.   Meanwhile the lovely original building on Fifth Street had first been
purchased by a bank and then destroyed, and meanwhile the forbidding
Doric temple of the Ridgway Branch of the Library Company, on South
Broad Street, between Christian and Carpenter, had been completed in 1878
under the will of Dr. James Rush, gentle recluse, book collector, student,
husband of Phœbe Ann Ridgway, Madame Rush, daughter of Jacob Ridgway,
shipowner and merchant, and powerful rival of Stephen Girard.   Dr. Rush
died childless in 1869, twelve years after the death of his beloved but so totally
different wife, and left his large fortune, inherited from his wife and father,
to the Library Company on condition that it build a separate branch named in
honour of Madame Rush.

A simple will and a simple request, but Dr. Rush as time went on added
some confusing codicils, and the resultant legal quarrel, too long to describe
here, which lasted for almost a decade, is one of the most interesting and
amazing of Philadelphia stories, and a brilliant example of how a good man's
obvious desires can be mutilated by obstinate trustees and technicalities.
Dr. Rush, solitary, hardly ever seen by his old friends, died in state in the huge
house, the Rush Mansion, or, as it was called, the Rush Palace, built by Madame
Rush in 1843, far up on Chestnut Street, between Nineteenth and Twentieth.
For a long while afterwards this great brick house was a small hotel called
the Aldine, and then that was torn down, and now a motion-picture theatre
of the same name occupies the site.

And now, also, the newest building of the Library Company, at Juniper
and Locust streets, has been torn down, too.   This happened a couple of
years ago, and where the "new" library stood is a parking space.   For the
time being you can look right into the Indian camp ground.   The potential
campers have no privacy at all.   While as for the Library Company, it is
confined to the Ridgway Branch, and pretty soon will be forgotten except
by scholars who seek out the latter formidable pile.   "Mr. Franklin's Library"
will no longer have any influence in the city where for over two hundred years
it meant so much.

Certain old buildings should not be torn down, and wise cities do not
permit this to happen, even if the saving of these buildings requires subsidies
and city appropriations, and possibly their use as museums, or in other ways.
Certain old buildings—libraries, theatres, opera-houses, private houses, even
certain quarters of a city, certain public buildings—are more than bricks and
mortar; they are also history.   The sum total of all the great who have ever
used them, entered them, or walked their streets.   How can you duplicate
visible history?   And how can you inculcate the love of your country's and
city's past, and hence a sense of their honour and your own, if you tear down
all visible signs?   Can you learn from books alone?   The very ones who

need most the past in order to live properly the present and prepare for the future, do not read.

The new Library building at Juniper and Locust streets was an ugly building, and after all, only sixty years old, but it was acquiring dignity and a certain air, and many famous ghosts had been transplated from Fifth Street, along with Franklin's statue and his corner-stone. Moreover, the new building was acquiring memories of its own.

Thomas Jefferson, Alexander Hamilton, George Washington, Moreau de St. Mèry, Talleyrand, William Cobbett; Lorenzo da Ponte, Mozart's librettist for the operas *Don Giovanni*, *The Marriage of Figaro*, and *Cosi fan Tutte*, and a strange temporary resident of Philadelphia; Bayard Taylor, Edwin Forrest, Thackeray, Edgar Allan Poe; Karl Almquist, one of Sweden's most famous authors, and a fugitive from a charge of forgery and attempted murder; Walt Whitman, Washington Irving; Frank Stockton—a Philadelphian; Richard Harding Davis, also a Philadelphian; Owen Wister, author of *The Virginian*; Dr. S. Weir Mitchell; Horace Howard Furness, America's greatest Shakespearean scholar, and one of the two greatest Shakespearean scholars who ever lived; Dr. Furnival of England was the other—those are a few of the many who used the original building or the newer one. And what are you going to do about them?

Where can they go now in Philadelphia?

Thackeray, although he was in Philadelphia only a short while, was so impressed by the building and books on Fifth Street that he wrote back, mentioning especially the "dear old library"; Washington Irving spent many days looking up Major André.

The Junto, a fine impressive name, since it means in Spanish a cabal, a joining together of people for a purpose, was an excellent example of what can be accomplished by earnest intelligent young men as yet unimpeded by the mental arthritis which overtakes so many as their purses swell. The Junto came close to fulfilling Shakespeare's wistful desire, a desire all of us have felt at one time or another, "Would we were of one mind, and one mind good". Recently the Junto has been revived in Philadelphia with surprising success, and now has many hundreds of members representing all parts of the city.

Philadelphians are sturdy folk spiritually, with deep and vigorous roots. All the roots need is an occasional good hard rain of common purpose.

CHAPTER XVIII

That Benignity of Mind

"With the whole should be constantly inculcated and cultivated that benignity of mind which shows itself in searching for and seizing every opportunity to serve and oblige, and is the foundation of what is called good breeding."

BENJAMIN FRANKLIN ON EDUCATION.

EDUCATION AND LEARNING—books, that is, and how to implement them— are a part of Quakerism, and so Franklin found a fertile seed-bed for his theories and his energies along these lines in Philadelphia. Franklin and his Junto cultivated the garden. Quite naturally, and by inheritance, Philadelphia became what it is to-day: one of the major educational centres of the country. As for Franklin, he believed that books were the foundation of education—books and the personalities of the men who taught through them —an opinion shared by the very latest leaders in the revolt against the rigid yet sentimental vagueness of the German theory of electives and stated examinations and Ph.D.s, introduced into this country in the 1870's.

Hardly had William Penn landed for the first time on the shores of Coaquannock, when the Council sent for Enoch Flower, which the Council spelled "Enock flower", an experienced schoolmaster, and asked him to begin. "Enock flower" acquiesced on the following terms:

"To Learn to read English 4 shillings for the Quarter, to learn to read and write 6 shillings by the Quarter, to Learn to read, Write and Cast accts., 8 shillings by ye Quarter; for Boarding a Schollar, that is to say, dyet, Washing & Scooling, Tenn pounds for one whole year."

Six years later the Quakers opened a school for coloured youth.

Philadelphia's spelling has improved over that of its first schoolmaster. Over that of George Washington, too, let it be recalled. And of even the most cultivated men of the eighteenth century. But Enoch Flower, despite his spelling, deserves more fame in his city than he achieved. He was the ancestor of everything in an educational way that it has at present. The Adam in the innocent educational Eden of Penn's tiny town. The great-great-, and so on, grandfather of the magnificent University of Pennsylvania; the almost equally fine, if not so historic, Temple University; of the two small but solid Quaker colleges on the outskirts of the city: the Orthodox college, Haverford, the Hicksite college, Swarthmore; of Bryn Mawr, and all the other great schools, cultural, medical, dental, law, and manual-training, of Penn's metropolis.

It is fascinating how many experts, many of them world famous, many of them esoteric, live in or on the outskirts of the modern "Holy Experiment", although it is equally fascinating how few of them affect the life of the city, or are generally known to it. They stand like undiscovered stars around the perimeter of an unenthusiastic moon.

In 1749 Franklin, backed as always by the Junto, wrote his *Proposals*

Relating to the Education of Youth in Pennsylvania, and the movement toward higher education in Pennsylvania, long pending, actually began. The Rev. William Smith, a brilliant, active, and although no one knew at the time, bitterly combative young Scotsman, was summoned from New York, largely because of a pamphlet he had written called *The College of Mirania, which* had attracted the favourable attention of Franklin and others. The Rev. Mr. Smith—destined to be later on the first provost of the University of Pennsylvania—arrived, and the "Academy and Charitable School of the Province of Pennsylvania" began to function in a humble way in a two-storey building at the corner of Fourth and Arch streets. Franklin was the first president of its board of trustees. In 1753 the first charter was granted.

Harvard had been founded in 1639; William and Mary in 1693; Yale in 1702; Princeton in 1746; so Philadelphia gave birth to the fifth most venerable institution of its kind in the country, and the one which of all others had, to begin with, the most stormy history.

Philadelphia was indeed a fertile seed-bed, but it was also well manured for quarrelling of any kind between Quakers and Church of England men; and education, which is supposed to encourage open-mindedness, has always been an excellent excuse to close one's mind. Dr. Smith, a fiery churchman who hated the Quakers, was exactly the hot wind needed to bring the ugly crop to full bloom. Braddock's defeat gave him an opening, and he wrote two papers in which he charged everything that had happened to the neglect of duty and the cowardice of the Quaker Assembly. The Indian massacres, he said, were entirely the result of criminal Quaker kindness toward red savages, and he concluded by the statement that it would be a benefit to the world if Quakerism were wiped entirely off its surface.

Hardly a tactful way to begin one's career in Philadelphia.

Dr. Smith also found grounds to quarrel with Franklin, who might otherwise have supported him. Smith was a confirmed classicist and a believer in church influence. The new school had received many gifts and cordial endorsement from English clerics and admirers of Smith in England. Franklin believed in non-sectarian education, of course, and, there being so much to study, that the classics, if taught at all, should be taught from translations. Dr. Smith, adding further seditious statements to those contained in his pamphlets, was clapped into jail for libel, and the town was at once split three ways. An exciting time was had by all. Dr. Smith demanded a writ of *habeas corpus,* stoutly refused to apologize, and announced that he would appeal directly to the Crown. For the eleven weeks he remained in jail he had as revivifying an experience as William Penn had had in the Old Bailey, but a more noisy one.

His enthusiastic adherents called upon him, a beautiful young Philadelphian (all women in history if they behave romantically are set down as "beautiful", although homely women have been known to behave in the same way) fell in love with him, and shortly afterwards married him, and the trustees of the college ordered the students to attend classes in jail as if nothing had happened. Dr. Smith, released, and re-arrested, and released for the second time, took his grievances to England, where he was received as a popular hero.

The universities of Oxford and Aberdeen gave him degrees, the Church of England and the Bishop of London, his immediate superior, treated him as a martyr, and he moved through a round of dinners and applause, reaffirmed by the Privy Council, which severely censured the Quaker tyrants back in Philadelphia. Dr. Smith returned to that city in full control, to take up his disagreement with Franklin, and to become twenty-five years later a leading patriot, despite his initial reluctance, shared by so many other earnest Americans, including Franklin, to encourage a final break with the mother country.[1]

This furious internecine quarrel, however, had done the cause of education in Philadelphia no good, and for a while a rival school was started, but in 1779 differences were adjusted, the rival factions coalesced, and the charter of the College of Philadelphia was vested in "the Trustees of the University of the State of Pennsylvania". Professional schools, at first distinct from the college, were organized, and already the first medical school in America had opened its doors. This was followed in 1789 by the first law school in the country. In 1792 all these were merged with the college under the title of the University of Pennsylvania. Meanwhile two of the most venerable boys' schools in the country had been founded, the Friends' Public School, now the William Penn Charter School, in 1689, and in 1761, Germantown Academy. The steeple of the old Main Building of Germantown Academy still carries at the top the English Crown.

Philadelphia was also to the fore in the training of women for medicine. The Female Medical College was opened in 1850.

Coaquannock had come a long way from the times of Enoch Flower and Jan Peterson, barber-surgeon, who had attended the ills of the Dutch and Swedes along the Delaware before Penn's arrival, or even the more skilled services of John Goodson, chirurgeon, who had been sent out by the Society of Free Traders to settle in Upland, now Chester, and who had moved up the river when the *Welcome* dropped anchor, to become one of Philadelphia's earliest practising physicians. In the same year, 1682, Drs. Thomas Lloyd, Thomas Wynne, and Griffith Owen, all three from Wales, disembarked, and hardly had they done so when they met for Philadelphia's first consultation.

It is worth while to mention some of the salient features of Franklin's theories of education; they are still refreshingly valid. First were the physical aspects of the perfect academy or college: proper and attractive buildings, "if it may be, not too far from a river, having a garden, orchard, meadow, and a field or two". And then there was to be a library, "with maps of all countries, globes, some mathematical instruments, and apparatus for experiments in natural philosophy and mechanics; prints of all kinds, prospects, buildings, machinery, etc."; while as to the health and bodies of the students, the scholars were to be "frequently exercised in running, leaping, wrestling, and swimming".

Franklin, an expert swimmer himself, made an especial point of the last, both from the point of view of health and of safety.

The members of the corporation should:

[1] Merely as a matter of interesting comment, Provost Smith's great-great-great-grandson, a lieutenant in the American army, was with the U.S.A. Troops in occupied Germany. He has good combat blood in him.

make it their pleasure, and in some degree their business, to visit the academy often, encourage and countenance the youth, countenance and assist the masters, and by all means in their power advance the usefulness and reputation of the design; [they should] look on the students as in some sort their children, treat them with familiarity and affection, and when they have behaved well and gone through their studies and are to enter the world, zealously unite and make all the interest that can be made to establish them whether in business, offices, marriages, or any other thing for their advantage.

Meanwhile the students were to be taught "everything that is useful and everything that is ornamental", but since "art is long and time is short, they had best learn those things that are likely to be most useful and most ornamental, regard being had to the several professions for which they are intended".

"All should be taught to write a fair hand, and swift, as that is useful to all. . . . Drawing is a kind of universal language, and understood by all nations." Arithmetic and the first principles of geometry, astronomy, and accounting were imperative. English was fundamentally important, and was best taught by grammar (How true, if one adds rhetoric!) and by study of the masters. History was equally important because by means of it the past, the customs of ancestors, geography, and the sense of time could be understood. No one should be compelled to learn Greek, Latin, or modern foreign languages, "yet none that have an ardent desire to learn should be refused; their English, Arithmetic, and other studies absolutely necessary being at the same time not neglected". Visits were to be made to neighbouring farms and estates to learn agriculture, horticulture, and management, and to the shops of artisans and mechanics.

Above all, what was to be constantly cultivated and inculcated was the underlying virtue, the name of which heads this chapter: "that benignity of mind which shows itself in searching for and seizing every opportunity to serve and oblige".

The great university that Franklin and the Junto helped to found, the University of Pennsylvania, has almost everything that Franklin desired, and infinitely more, including his spirit of complete tolerance and candid research; the only thing it hasn't is "a river, a garden, orchard, meadow, and a field or two"; all of which Franklin, as well as William Penn, knew to be infinitely important in forming the minds and hearts of men. As a result, Franklin's university has never altogether gathered to itself the passionate love and loyalty so many similar institutions enjoy, and which are so needful, and its influence on Franklin's city has been considerably less benign and considerably more material than Franklin would have desired.

The great light has been colder than necessary. The botanical and other gardens are where few students can see them; the meadows are non-existent; and the river—the Lower Schuylkill—resembles nothing so much as an open sewer. A little way up the Schuylkill, above the Fairmount Dam, are the lovely stretches of the park, and here, to be sure, in the autumn and spring a group of Franklin's scholars bend to oars in varsity or class boats; but they are a handful, and have to be especially strong and tall.

Rudolph Blankenburg, born a German, and one of Philadelphia's few good mayors since the Civil War, a "reform mayor" it goes without saying, once remarked that Philadelphia, "unlike most cities, has two rivers, and, unlike most cities, makes use of neither".

From the strong loins of Quaker good sense and Quaker charity, professional schools, hospitals, and almshouses sprang as inevitably as did academies and libraries. Not only was Philadelphia the birthplace of the first American medical school, but it was also the birthplace of modern dentistry, which means, of course, not solely an American event, but a universal one. Philadelphia practically discovered teeth, and for years "Philadelphia dentist" was synonymous with excellence, and Europe blossomed with framed degrees, many of them fictitious, from the various dental schools of the city. Philadelphia is still the dental centre not only of the United States but of this planet, and it is interesting to note that among the myriad things it manufactures, false teeth are a major item. More false teeth are manufactured in Philadelphia than in any other place in the world.

In 1852 the Philadelphia College of Dental Surgery was founded, and in 1863 the Philadelphia Dental College, now a part of Temple University. Fifteen years later a dental department was added to the University of Pennsylvania. All those who have ever had trouble with their teeth should each evening at dusk take out their prayer rugs and kneel down reverently in the direction of Philadelphia. While as for dentists, for some reason, they seem to be peculiarly adventurous and romantic souls. There is a book to be written about the Philadelphia dentists who have gone out across the Seven Seas, some even to become powers behind various thrones. A man with a drill in his hand is in a position of influence. Dr. Evans, who engineered the escape from Paris of the Empress Eugenie, was a Philadelphian.

Following Drs. Lloyd, Wynne, and Owen, and John Goodson, chirurgeon, came a great flight of good, or distinguished, men, many of whose descendants are still practising: John Kearsley, Thomas Graeme, William Shippen, Sr., and Jr., John Morgan, Lloyd Zachary, Thomas Bond, Phineas Bond, Adam Kuhn, William Cadwalader and his son Charles, Benjamin Rush, and Philip Syng Physick—he of the beautifully appropriate name—and many more. Dr. Thomas Bond was the "father of American clinical practice". Dr. Physick, of American surgery. Dr. John Morgan was a man who "made people proud to say, 'I have seen him'". Coming out from London, he was also one of the first Philadelphians to use the new-fangled invention, the "umbarilloe". And these early Philadelphia doctors had plenty of practice, some of it baffling and terrible enough, considering the recurrent and varied plagues that swept down upon the city; plagues that gave them plenty of opportunity to display the courage and steadfastness of their profession.

When the Revolution came they had gangrene as well, and the dreadful naked unanæsthetized operations of those days, and prison fever, and all the other horrors of war; and yet, until 1789, the degree of Doctor of Medicine did not exist in Philadelphia except when imported. Until then Philadelphia doctors were Bachelors in Physic, although the larger degree had first appeared in Europe in the fourteenth century.

CHRIST CHURCH (Strickland, 1811)

SOUTH-WEST CORNER OF WALNUT STREET AND WASHINGTON SQUARE, 1824 (Kennedy)

As early as 1732 a hospital department was added to the Philadelphia Almshouse, and in 1811 the first medical textbook ever published in America was written by Dr. Caspar Wistar, who, among his many other excellent deeds, introduced into this country the Chinese shrub wistaria, often erroneously spelled wisteria.   And at this point it should be told to those who do not know their Philadelphia that there are two ancient Philadelphia families: the Wisters and the Wistars, and that they do not like to be confused, although they frequently are, even by some of the more thoughtless of their fellow citizens.

Dr. Caspar Wistar introduced wistaria to America; Owen Wister wrote the best book yet written about the early Far West, *The Virginian.*

At all events, *a* or *e*, it is singularly appropriate that the white, or violet, heaven of bees and dripping perfume, wistaria, should now be so common about Philadelphia and its environs.   In the spring, even countless Philadelphia backyards are sweet, and never a Philadelphian anywhere who does not associate in his memory wistaria with his city.

He can hear the bees and see the cascading loveliness.

For over a hundred and twenty-five years Philadelphia was the fountain-head of American medicine, just as it still is of American dentistry, and although numerous other cities now equal it in the former respect, none as yet has surpassed it.   Both medicine and the law are hereditary professions in Philadelphia, and this builds up through the generations a mysterious something, a texture, an instinct.   It is almost as if channels in the brain had been formed.   A great many Philadelphia lawyers and doctors look like lawyers and doctors, a distinction in this heterogeneous age.   And there are so many famous legal and medical families in Philadelphia, father to son straight down from colonial days, that when you meet a hitherto unknown member of one of them you are fairly sure he is a lawyer or a doctor, and usually you are right.

Just as Philadelphia is a lean place for the arts, save music, and possibly painting, this partly due, there is no question, to Quaker tradition and influence, so, for the same reason, it is the most sympathetic of environments for the more learned of the professions.

The Quakers did not believe in any unnecessary or adventitious beauty, except the beauties of Nature, and in those they believed beautifully; but they did believe in curing the sick and in trying to keep the well as honest as the well can be kept.   William Penn, disapproving of litigation, as do all Quakers, nonetheless provided for courts which were to prove "a terror" to all those who, having had the chance, "failed to agree with their adversaries while in the way with them".   And Philadelphia lawyers, like Philadelphia doctors, have had a lot to practise with.

The law of the commonwealth is old and intricate and embossed with precedent.   Many Philadelphia ground rents, for instance, going back to earliest colonial days, call for payment in "Spanish dollars; true weight"; a difficult provision if one wants to make a point of it.[1]   And because of this

---

[1] There is an ancient firm in downtown Philadelphia which still has a quantity of "Spanish dollars" and which specializes in just such transactions.   The Spanish dollars are rented for the occasion and then returned to the owners.   This is a good story in itself.

G

provision occurred one of the nicest legends of the Philadelphia bar; a real David and Goliath story.   The controversy was between a midget lawyer, who looked as if he had stepped out of Dickens, and that lion of the law, John G. Johnson, who with his roaring and incisive voice, his huge frame and brilliant minds dominated Philadelphia legally for twenty years.

Mr. Johnson was a ruthless man; he was also one of the most delicate and discriminating collectors of art America has ever known.   When he died, he left his priceless collection to the city.   While he lived—a widower —he occupied a house on South Broad Street so stacked with masterpieces against the walls, even of the bath-rooms, that visitors wondered how Mr. Johnson dared to take a shower.

Mr. Johnson and his midget opponent quarrelled through the years, and the quarrel grew more acrimonious; and since Mr. Johnson administered a ground rent on which a client of his diminutive enemy had a building, the material of further incident was ever present.   Mr. Johnson fell into the habit of being annoying every time, semi-annually, the ground rent was paid.   He would send it back with this quibble or that.   Finally, his midget opponent, remembering the clause, "Spanish dollars; true weight," had an idea.   During the six months that followed he hunted everywhere for pieces of eight, and having procured a sufficient quantity from antiquarians and coin collectors, he sent the ground rent up Chestnut Street in a stout canvas sack, carried by his office boy, who happened to be a hunchback.

Mr. Johnson received the rent grimly.   In a few days he sent it back. It was not "true weight".   Ancient coins lose considerable intrinsic value through handling and the inevitable "sweating" of the years.   Mr. Johnson's opponent found a small Spanish coin, added it to the rent, and for the third time sent the office boy and the sack up Chestnut Street.   For the third time Mr. Johnson refused the sack.   The small coin, naturally, was not gold. Mr. Johnson's opponent started suit.   The first court decided in his favour. Mr. Johnson took the case further up.   The next court decided in the same way.   Mr. Johnson appealed to the Supreme Court of Pennsylvania, the Supreme Court dismissed the case in the Latin terms, whatever they may be, that "the case was below the dignity of the Court", and bade Mr. Johnson desist. Triumphant, his opponent sent the sack up Chestnut Street for the fourth time.

By now Mr. Johnson was in a temper.   As his opponent's office boy timidly entered the lion's office, Mr. Johnson roared, seized the sack, and threw it at the messenger, hitting him between the shoulders.   The office boy sued Mr. Johnson for assault and battery, and collected a pleasant sum in damages.

There are doubts as to whether this is a true story.   But you can look it up in the famous legal magazine, the *Green Bag*.

The Johnson era followed not so long after that of another great "lion of the Philadelphia law", Richard Vaux, who was mayor of the city in 1856 and '57, and who not only behaved like a lion but looked like one—a handsome and dignified lion.   Mr. Vaux, who was known as "the Bourbon war horse" —there seems to be a confusion in similes here—was further distinguished by a beard, the length of which no one ever knew except himself, since he kept it tucked inside his vest.

He arose at five o'clock in the morning, took an ice-cold shower, never wore an overcoat, walked like a young man until the day of his death, and never entered a street-car.

In the same fashion as Philadelphia lawyers, Philadelphia doctors have also been permitted and encouraged to develop their individualities in a way similar to the great doctors of London, but a way that is often lost in a less personal city than Philadelphia. As a result Philadelphia has had many urbane and, generally, learned doctors, and many choleric ones as well.

The stories about them are legion. There was, for instance, the distinguished general practitioner who, being extremely absent-minded and forgetting his stethoscope, called one night late on his rounds upon a lady patient to whose heart he wished to listen. Leaning down and listening, he fell asleep, and remained in that position for almost half an hour, the lady thinking it no more than an especially thorough examination. One of the city's present most distinguished throat and nose specialists, Dr. Francis R. Packard, is also a world-famous authority on Shakespeare's medicine, or lack of it. In correspondence with fellow practitioners in England he has for a number of years been trying, among other things, to determine whether England's Henry IV died of leprosy, syphilis, or ergotism, that dreadful medieval disease due to diseased wheat, now happily almost extinct.

The opinion leans toward ergotism.

Dr. S. Weir Mitchell was a brilliant example of this catholicity. Dr. Mitchell was not only America's first neurologist—admission that nerves can cause illness is a comparatively recent event, although it is obvious that both Eve and her husband suffered from them immediately after eating the apple—but he was also America's pioneer in the toxicology of snake-bites. At the same time he was a hard-working novelist; a professional novelist, not an amateur one. One of the few professional novelists in Philadelphia's history.

No one ever knew how he did it. But in extreme old age, and suffering from palsy, he was seen on a train between Philadelphia and Washington, working continuously on a manuscript.

Dr. Mitchell was the real hero of the story, now folk-lore and attached to many doctors, in which a leading specialist, suffering temporarily from his own speciality, goes to see a European authority who does not recognize him.

Dr. Mitchell was in Vienna. The great Austrian whom, unheralded, he saw, said after much reflection: "In your own country is the man who can do you most good. His name is Dr. S. Weir Mitchell of Philadelphia."

Because of this tradition, this intellectual inheritance, Philadelphia physicians and lawyers have always been peculiarly prominent in forwarding the music and painting of Philadelphia, as well as all other public-spirited enterprises. There was, as an example of this, the famous doctor who never failed to lend his authority to every worthy list. Like Abou Ben Adhem, his name was always first, in addition to, in a generous hand, the promise of ten thousand dollars, on the understanding, however, known only to the necessary few, that the sum was never to be paid but was to be transferred to the head of the next worthy list.

This was indeed what is known as a revolving fund, and the tradition is that it never failed to achieve its purpose.

In the long, but not simple, annals of the Philadelphia law, perhaps the most interesting criminal case is that of the attractive lady in the early decades of the nineteenth century who, having quite obviously murdered her husband by means of poison, walked out of the court as free as air because the jury had been dismissed for "a non-essential reason" and she could not twice be placed in jeopardy of her life. The "non-essential reason" was that an elderly gentleman on the jury had fainted after being locked up for twenty-four hours without food. At that time no provision was made for feeding a jury or taking them out for air, and the superior court, reviewing the case, decided that the elderly gentleman's behaviour was entirely non-essential.

Evidently a man of no stamina. But the acquittal in question marked the beginning of the feeding of juries in Pennsylvania.

One becomes embarrassed after a while calling attention to the innumerable "firsts" in Philadelphia's history. If Oxford, England, is "the home of lost causes", Philadelphia is "the home of lost firsts". No other city in the country comes anywhere near to approaching it. Even the mushroom has its place. The mushroom is as much identified with France as the *Marseillaise*, but so far as America is concerned, the mushroom was first domesticated in the little town of Media on the outskirts of Philadelphia, and although there is no connection here, unless one picks the "Angel of Death", the deadly *Amanita phalloides*, or something of the kind, Philadelphia also lays indisputable claim to the founding of the first College of Pharmacy in America, founded in 1821. And since we are more or less on the subject of sanitation and health, one becomes embarrassed, but not from boasting, at mention of another Philadelphia "first"—municipal water-works.

In 1801 Philadelphia built the first municipal water-works in the United States, and so far as any layman can discover, had never built another since, although there are rumours that this had been done several times. In any case, every ten years or so the enraged citizens arise and demand action. They do the same about the condition of the streets. These latter movements are known as "Clean Streets Campaigns", and it is interesting that as early as the 1720's wits began to play on Philadelphia's name and call it "Filthy-dirty". No one who has not seen a garbage collectors' strike in Philadelphia knows what garbage is. The narrow alleys of the city, such a distinctive feature, and which bisect all the residence blocks, are designed to make garbage strikes poignant. It is there that the garbage is put for collection, and when it is not collected the alleys become as surrealistic as the paintings of Salvador Dali. They are then an extraordinary visual and nasal phenomenon.

Meanwhile the strange mephitic liquid which comes out of Philadelphia pipes, and which, one is assured, is no longer dangerous, bears no resemblance to the water of any other great American city, or even of the small ones. It is a strange combination of food and drink, and makes you nostalgic for Paris. The nicer Philadelphians think it bad form to smell it. Nor was it harmless until 1900, or thereabouts. Until then it killed hundreds of Philadelphians annually. Typhoid poured down the Schuylkill from all the farm and coal towns of eastern Pennsylvania; while as for to-day, safe or not, Philadelphia is the only great city in the country the majority of whose citizens drink bottled water, or else make pilgrimages with demijohns to the springs of Fairmount Park.

You can see them standing in long queues.

Water is as fruitful a subject for conversation in Philadelphia as the weather is in London. The city is divided into two camps: those who square their shoulders and look brave and frank, and say, "Why, of course I drink it! Nonsense!" and those who cast down their eyes and shudder.

But in Franklin's time the town still drank from wells, and these were comparatively palatable.

Philadelphia remains, section by section, quarter by quarter, despite its huge size, a delightfully personal city.

There is a well-known chiropodist who, examining a patient's foot, is given, after long reflection, to such remarks as this:

"Hmm! Very interesting! . . . Have you ever by any chance seen Mrs. Penn Witherspoon's big toe?"

CHAPTER XIX

The Athens of America

"The city is large and elegant, but it did not strike me with the astonishment which the citizens predicted. Like the rest of Mankind, they judge favorably of their own place of residence, and of themselves, and their representations are to be admitted with some deductions."

OLIVER WOLCOTT.

OLIVER WOLCOTT SPOKE with the reserve of a New Englander, and also possibly with a touch of malice and jealousy, although what he said of the complacency of natives everywhere is true, and truer perhaps of Philadelphia than most places. At all events, at a very early date—they may have brought it with them—Philadelphians began to display that quiet, well-mannered, not-to-be-argued-with satisfaction with their estate which has been for many decades the despair of the rest of the country and not a few of the more restless inhabitants of the city itself.

Philadelphians do not consider themselves the chosen people of the

United States. That would be pretentious, and rude, and an unnecessary exercise of the will and imagination. They merely think that other Americans have been hasty in their choices.

And it is this attitude which has been partly responsible for the fact that, next to Brooklyn, Philadelphia has been the most belaboured and ridiculed great city in the United States. Ridicule mixed with a degree of wistful envy on the part of the more knowing, for along with its failings, Philadelphia has numerous inherited advantages. But if you don't defend yourself, others will attack you, and for a long while somnolence has been supposed to be a synonym for the Quaker City; paradoxical, when you come to think of it, applied to the greatest and most varied manufacturing town in the country and, among many other things, the home of the country's most powerful publishing house. But even this attitude has certain advantages, for it explains why, for two hundred years, visitors or citizens, in print or from platforms, have been able to say to Philadelphia audiences whatever was in their minds and have found, in return, Philadelphia audiences the most charming, witty, and sympathetic audiences there are, save those of London. The ability to take punishment good-naturedly, if tactfully applied, is a sign of urbanity and leads to mutual wit, but it is also a sign of a certain self-satisfaction.

After all, it is provocative to hear what the less fortunate have to say about you, and comfortable not to be disturbed by any intention of taking their advice.

Like an intelligent, self-analytic old lady, Philadelphia is well aware both of its virtues and its vices, and on the whole is inclined to like both, or at least settle down with them, assured that the combination makes for character and flavour. Streamlining is not in the city's mood.

But in Oliver Wolcott's time the "Holy Experiment" had a right to be proud of itself in almost any way you choose to look at it. To begin with, less than a hundred years old, to end with, not much more than that, Philadelphia, first as a colonial city, then as the capital of the United States, was the second English-speaking city in the world. And this does not mean in population alone, or merely as a seaport, or commercially, or financially, but culturally as well—scientifically, artistically, and in the urbane intelligence and life of its inhabitants. During the sixteenth and seventeenth centuries Mexico City, Guatemala City, and Lima, Peru, had borne this relationship to old Spain; during the eighteenth century Philadelphia bore it to England.

Across the panorama of that century, where Philadelphia is concerned, the figure of Franklin bulks so large that one is likely to forget that he was only one, the most distinguished and energetic, to be sure, but only one, of many learned and energetic men, also women, some of them in their own ways equally distinguished. One swallow does not make a summer; and one great man cannot make a period, although he may influence it greatly. Nor does greatness, any more than discovery or invention, spring out of nothing. It has a background. One reason of many why, if one wishes to live in a great period, one should try himself to be a little bit great.

Franklin was indeed a focus, a burning glass, an energizing force, but from the standpoint of historical perspective he was also something of a bright obliterating midday. His fame has been unfair to eighteenth-century

Philadelphia. It is too much taken for granted that he was eighteenth-century Philadelphia. Nor did Franklin step into a virgin field. James Logan was there before him, and Franklin was the spiritual foster son, if a more liberal and more modern one, of the sage of Stenton: a Stenton, incidentally, which had a secret stairway, a "priest's escape", although why a Quaker should have wanted that has never been explained.

James Logan, that benign and learned man, had already gathered around him, and encouraged, and loaned his books to a flock of brilliant young men, many of whom were to become coadjutors of Franklin. David Rittenhouse, for instance, the astronomer; Thomas Godfrey, glazier to start with, famous mathematician to end with; John Bartram, whom Linnæus was to call "the world's greatest natural botanist". And not long after Franklin arrived in Philadelphia and walked up High Street such men emerged, or came into their full stature, as Francis Rawle; William Allen, chief justice of the province; Anthony Benezet; the Shippens; George Ross; Richard Tilghman; Dr. Thomas Graeme, who married the daughter of Sir William Keith; Joseph Galloway; the Hamiltons;[1] John Dickinson, of the famous "Farmers Letters"; the Hopkinsons, father and son; the Rev. Mr. Peters, rector of Christ Church, and his nephew, Judge Richard Peters, and William Peters; William Logan, son of James; the Chews of Cliveden; Robert Proud, schoolmaster and annalist; the Muhlenbergs, father and three sons; the Tennents, father and three sons; the Rev. Jacob Duché, dandified parson, a real "macaroni", with the young men about him, and intelligent, too, but also a great fool. Benjamin Rush; the Cadwaladers; James Wilson, the great lawyer; and so on endlessly.

During the Revolution, and just previous to it, save for the months of British occupancy the city saw, of course, all the great men of America. John Adams, down from Massachusetts as a delegate to the First Continental Congress, wrote to his wife of the elegance, the food, and the entertainments, a combination that almost killed him. And after the Revolution, as the centre of a new, small, struggling, but most important country, more significant as a portent than a fact, for over fifteen years the city was a world capital.

The coaches of ambassadors rolled through its narrow streets: the coach of the President, its occupant a stately man in black satin small-clothes; the carriages or coaches of the statesmen of the republic. A few used sedan chairs. And several of the women of the city, Mrs. Bingham in particular, had definite salons; something that has now about gone out of the world. Thomas Jefferson was there for a while, and Alexander Hamilton, and the great Philadelphia merchants, Robert Morris and William Bingham; and Thomas McKean, come up from Delaware but now a Philadelphian; and James Madison. And Jacob Ridgway and Stephen Girard, and many of the fighting commodores and generals. During the French Revolution, a new strand was woven into the colour of the town, the French refugees; first the royalists, then the discredited republicans, among the latter even a terrorist or two. The French kept coming after the first flight had gone home.

---

[1] Andrew Hamilton, most distinguished and gifted lawyer, who is credited with the design for the State House, is also credited with having originated the phrase, "Philadelphia lawyer".

In the second decade of the nineteenth century the city, no longer either a state or national capital, but settling down to its long career as a provincial commercial and manufacturing centre, saw other French refugees, the Bonapartists, including some members of the imperial family itself. But long before that the "Holy Experiment" had blossomed, first, in the steady sun of colonial prosperity and of especial tolerance, and then, despite war and revolution, in the sun of ideas, of trade, of politics, and the great adventure of being independent.

Not far west, at Elizabeth Furnace in Lancaster County, and then even nearer, in the same county at Manheim, Henry William Stiegel, miscalled "Baron" Stiegel—he had no need of titles—had in 1762 begun to blow glass; the most beautiful glass America has ever seen, and as beautiful as the world has ever known.[1] A priceless collection of it, together with all kinds of other glass, is now in the Philadelphia Museum of Art, left to the museum by that collector of glass, George Horace Lorimer, the great editor of the *Saturday Evening Post*.

Until 1774 Stiegel prospered greatly, and then the war shut his glassworks down, leaving him practically bankrupt. But from many parts of the world he had imported glass experts, with the result that Pennsylvania is still one of the great glass-blowing sections of the country.

Meanwhile, at Ephrata, the learned and gentle Ephrata Brethren, Palatinate Seventh Day Adventist monks, in their extraordinary monastery, were making their illuminated manuscripts, wood-blocking their exquisite penmanship, and spreading all through eastern Pennsylvania the love and knowledge of good printing. Toward the end of the eighteenth century there were over a hundred skilled printing houses in a radius whose outer edge was not so many miles away from Philadelphia.[2]

Nicholas Ludwig, Count of Zinzendorf and Pottendorf, the romantic leader of the Moravians, and a stormy petrel of religion, had come to Philadelphia in 1742 with his daughter, Benigna, and then had gone up to Bethelem, founded the year before by Zinzendorf's missionary bishop, David Nitschmann. Count Zinzendorf stayed a couple of years in this country. Like so many other prophets he was a man of strong words when aroused. The following letter to some erring members of his flock is dated December 26 of the year of his arrival!

To the copper, F. Vende, in Germantown—I take you both—man and wife —to be notorious children of the devil, and you, the woman, to be a two-fold child of hell. Yet I would have your damnation as tolerable as possible. . . . If that sevenfold devil which possesseth you will permit—then consider and leave your daughter with a congregation.

[1] Interestingly enough, "Baron" Stiegel apparently had no idea what he was actually doing, for Stiegel glass was made for the most ordinary trade—what today would be the cheap-store trade. So much is this so, that one of Philadelphia's best-known collectors of glass, guided more by his knowledge than his eyes, refuses to have Stiegel glass in his collection. *Suus cuique mos.*

[2] Printing, as a matter of fact, was Philadelphia's first industry, and the first book wholly manufactured in America—types, paper, authorship, everything—was printed in Philadelphia in 1776. In this way, as in so many others, spiritual as well as material, Philadelphia led and others followed. The monastery at Ephrata is now being restored by the State, and authorities say it is the only frame building in America in the mediæval tradition.

Nicholas Ludwig was temperamental. According to contemporaries, the Vendes were estimable and quiet people, and their enraged leader had often stayed with them. There is a tradition that even Zinzendorf's religious fervour was the result of temperament. Travelling as a gay young nobleman through Germany, he fell in love, while in Castell, with his cousin Theodora, but his mother not approving of the match, Theodora married Henry of Reuss. Nicholas Ludwig took this as a sign that God had called him to especial work.

Should this happen to all young men, churches would lack no ministers.

David Dove, born in England, but who came to Philadelphia in 1758 to be the town's best-known school-teacher, was equally temperamental. David Dove was, in addition, a poet and satirist. Judge Richard Peters, who as a boy studied Latin under David, puns upon his name with fierce distaste. "A sarcastical and ill-tempered doggereliser," he wrote, "and was called Dove ironically—for his temper was that of a hawk, and his beak was that of a falcon pouncing on innocent prey."

Judge Peters himself was an exceedingly gay, witty, and intelligent man, also a most useful one; his one fault, if it is a fault, was a love of punning. He was one of the founders of that most useful organization, the Society for Promoting Agriculture.

Out at Kingsessing, on the road to Darby, on the lower Schuylkill in what is now West Philadelphia, John Bartram, Quaker yeoman, was studying his beloved plants and shrubs, collecting specimens in various journeys through the colonies, and starting the first botanical garden in America. It is said that he turned to botany because, turning up daisies with his plough, he began to wonder about them. When he died he was known the world over. Before the Revolution he was appointed Royal American Botanist to George III. In 1731 he built the simple but lovely stone house still standing in its gardens, one of its few historical buildings Philadelphia has preserved. The botanical gardens are a public park. Over one of the windows of the library is a stone bearing this inscription:

It is God alone, Almyty Lord,
The Holy One by me Adored.
JOHN BARTRAM. 1770

In his simple but lovely stone house John Bartram, simple Quaker but world famous, lived in miniature feudal state. His servants and his slaves ate at the same table with himself and his wife Ann and his twelve children, but all were arranged "according to the salt". John Bartram, quiet Quaker, also always carried and used his simple and excellent coat of arms. Simple because it was old. He was the direct descendant of a knight who had come to England with William of Normandy.

Craftsmanship of all kinds, a sure sign of increasing elegance and civilization, was also evident throughout the city and province, in addition to the glass of Stiegel and the printing of the monks of Ephrata. The unofficial boycott against foreign goods that began to spread through the colonies around 1761 gave domestic crafts of all kinds a great impetus. Edward

G*

James, Benjamin Randolph, Thomas Tufft, Jonathan Gostelowe, and others were turning out fine designs which culminated in the "Philadelphia Chippendale" of the late years of the eighteenth century, and a Philadelphia "School of Painting" was beginning to be visible.

Despite what has been done to it, despite the wrecking that has been going on since the turn of the century, Philadelphia is still a painter's city; the atmosphere soft, and often grey, yet luminous; the fact that Philadelphia, unlike New York, still has a horizon, a sky-line, you can see without standing on your head. The way the sky-line builds up or diminishes—a church steeple here, a tall building there, a low one next to it. Down almost every street, if you raise your eyes for a moment, is a lovely vista. There is none of the terrible and beautiful rigidity of New York. And everywhere are all sorts of small streets for studios and for living. These in addition to Philadelphia's tradition of painting and its fine art schools. And here is another curious and little-known fact: Despite the destruction of the magnificent trees —horse chestnuts, maples, limes—that once lined the city's streets, Philadelphia, counting Fairmount Park, is still the greatest urban forest reserve in the world, greater even than Paris. From the windows of high office buildings, everywhere you look in spring or summer, Philadelphia is still Penn's "green countrie towne". These trees are in the city square, in small unspoiled streets, and especially in Philadelphia's back yards.

It is a pity that the city does not replant its principal streets as New York is doing, so that the citizens can once more have the numerous benefits of trees and see them without taking an elevator.

John Meng, Matthew Pratt, William Williams, Benjamin West's first instructor, were among the earliest of Philadelphia's painters, and presently many more were added to their number. Eugene du Simitière, miniaturist and naturalist, much involved with Franklin's American Philosophical Society; James Claypole, another miniaturist, who with Philadelphia's instinct for high-grade amateurism, was also for a while sheriff of the city; and Gustavus Hesselius, father of John Hesselius, an equally well-known painter, who came from Sweden in 1711 and who later on was to make the first organs and spinets in the colonies. Hesselius was a man of many parts; he was also an excellent ecclesiastical architect and designed several churches. In the Historical Society of Pennsylvania are six Hesselius the Elder portraits, perhaps the first painted in Philadelphia: one of Colonel Patrick Gordon, a self-portrait of the artist, one of his wife, one of James Logan, and two of the Indian chiefs, Tishcohan and Lapowinsa. Also belonging to the Historical Society are four portraits by John Hesselius (1728-78): that of Mrs. William Penn (Hannah Callowhill); Mrs. Thomas Penn (Margaret Freame); Robert Morris, Sr.; and Mrs. John Redman.

The Quakers did not believe in any sort of painting except portrait painting. Anything else might lead to unworthy divagations. But it is as hard to suppress the pictorial instinct in man as to suppress his instinct for music, and toward the middle of the eighteenth century Philadelphia began to develop a distinguished school of its own that anywhere else would be known by the

place of its origin.   Not in Philadelphia, however; that would be immodest
and possibly disturbing, and so who has ever heard of "the Philadelphia
School of Eighteenth Century and Early Nineteenth Century Portraiture"?
But, on the other hand, what other American city had a Benjamin West;
four Peales (father, three sons), and an uncle, Gilbert Stuart, for eleven
years; Matthew Pratt; John Neagle, given much less credit than he deserves,
and whose portraits are now a feature of the Players' Club in New York;
and a Thomas Sully; not to mention numerous lesser lights?   To see how the
reverse is done, one has but to consult the *Encyclopædia Britannica,* where
Benjamin West is set down as an "English historical and portrait painter",
and Bostonian John Singleton Copley is claimed in the same fashion.

However, the English, God bless them, think "Way Down upon the
Suwannee River" is an English folk-song.

Benjamin West, to be sure, did go to England when he was only twenty-
two, to become eventually, upon the death of Sir Joshua Reynolds, the favourite
court painter of George III and second president of the Royal Academy,
but back of him was a stout Quaker ancestry—he was born at Springfield,
Pennsylvania—and several years of work in Philadelphia and New York;
nor did he ever forget his American ancestry.[1]   He kept in close touch with
American painting and influenced it greatly, especially Philadelphia painting.
As for Copley, he did not emigrate to England until he was thirty-
eight.

Americans have always been inclined to be humble, or not humble, in
the wrong places; Philadelphia, the most American of all our greatest cities,
has carried this confusion to its extreme limit.

It is the fashion now to laugh—or shudder—at Benjamin West, especially
in Philadelphia, which feels a sort of proprietary right to amusement, and
which also, it must be admitted, did suffer for many years from the gigantic
Wests, classical or historical, that took up most of the walls of the inner galleries
of the Academy of Fine Arts, to the terror of generations of Philadelphia
children.   "Death on a White Horse" has had a very sombre effect on
Philadelphia imaginations, which are often inclined to be sombre to begin
with.   So had "The Death of General Wolfe".   And the huge painting
of a supposititious Penn, evidently a glandular case, signing his Treaty beneath
a supposititious Treaty Elm, has had a disastrous influence upon local historical
thought, but nonetheless West was an outstanding draughtsman and one of
the great portrait painters of a portrait-painting period.

It is a pity he did not heed the admonitions of his forebears and confine
himself entirely to portraits.

---

[1] It took a Russian, William Sawitzky, to recognize Benjamin West as the very fine painter
he was and to allocate properly his different periods.   West's gigantic and frightening canvases
were painted after he went to Europe and fell under the influence of European academic traditions and was subjected to the essential vulgarity of an eighteenth-century court.   West's great
talent and original and indigenous quality is best exhibited by his portrait of Thomas Mifflin as
a boy, painted while West was still almost a boy himself.   It is one of the great eighteenth-
century portraits.   As is so often the case, it takes a non-American—in this case a Russian—
to point out to Americans, with their strange inverted snobbishness where art and letters are
concerned, the fact that America has had not only a memorable spiritual past, but has an
equally memorable spiritual present.   Matisse laughed at this curious attitude of Americans
on his last visit to the U.S.A.

Even more important to Philadelphia painting than Benjamin West, because they became Philadelphians and remained such, was the famous Peale family: Charles Willson Peale, 1741–1827, and his three sons, so named that they could have been nothing else but artists—Raphael, 1774–1825, Rembrandt, 1778–1860, and Titian, 1800–85. Raphael confined himself mostly to still life; Rembrandt, like his father, was a portraitist and at the age of seventeen painted his portrait of Washington, the general giving him three sittings; Titian was an excellent animal painter and executed most of the plates of Charles Lucian Bonaparte's *American Ornithology*. Mrs. Rembrandt was no mean painter, either, although she spent most of her life copying her husband's portraits. His highest compliment was to tell her he couldn't distinguish her paintings from his.

The Peale family were vigorous patriots as well, as artist of all kinds are likely to be. Charles Willson was captain in the Revolutionary army, and his most famous portrait of Washington was begun at Valley Forge, continued calmly at New Brunswick a couple of days after the Battle of Monmouth, and completed in Philadelphia. James Peale, brother of Charles, himself an excellent painter, was an officer of the Continental Line. Generation after generation, Philadelphia's most famous family of artists continued to paint. The last as a painter was Miss Alice Peale, a charming old lady with Angelica Kaufman ringlets and the demure defensive reserve of Victorian career women, who survived into the first decade of this century. Charles Peale, the patriarch, had twelve children, to many of whom he gave the last names of famous painters; in addition to Rembrandt, Titian, and Raphael, or Raphaelle, there was a Rubens. Charles, who did sixty portraits of Washington, at the age of seventy-eight invented a velocipede which he rode to the alarm of his family.[1]

Copley, before he too, like Benjamin West, emigrated to England, was also probably in Philadelphia off and on, although the only records are some Philadelphia portraits. But in 1794 down from Rhode Island came

[1] The Peales were as extraordinary a painting family as the history of art has ever recorded. A round dozen of them, sons, other descendants, wives, were painters of varying degrees of excellence. The patriarch, Charles Willson, was a sort of American Leonardo da Vinci, interested in everything. His house was a madhouse of half-completed inventions, cooking herbs and medicines, and collections of stuffed birds and animals. In the midst of this, and the comings and goings of his huge and steadily increasing clan, the patriarch painted calmly and prodigiously. At the age of eighty-one he painted a large canvas, "Christ Healing the Sick at Bethsaida", and at the age of eighty-three he did a full-length portrait of himself. Two years later, on Washington's Birthday, 1826, he died at the age of eighty-five, still going strong. One of his first acts upon arriving in Philadelphia in 1777 from Maryland, where he had been born in 1741, son of a country schoolmaster, was to get himself elected to the Committee of Public Safety. Then he aided in raising a company of militia and served with it at Trenton, Princeton, and Germantown, first as lieutenant, then captain. While with the army he frequently cooked for his troops, made shoes out of rawhide for their freezing feet, and painted miniatures of his officers in order to keep up their morale, which they sent to their families. Upon his return from the war he served as a member of the Pennsylvania Assembly, voted for Abolition, and immediately freed his own slaves, which he had brought with him from Maryland. Just to show his varied interests, in 1801, largely at his own expense, he undertook the excavation of the skeletons of two mastadons in Ulster and Orange counties, New York; in 1802, established the Philadelphia Peale's Museum; and in 1805, helped to found the Pennsylvania Academy of Fine Arts. So far as can be discovered he never heard of "the ivory tower". One of his soldiers during the Revolution said of him, "He fit and painted, painted and fit".

Gilbert Stuart to study the President close at hand and to remain for over a decade. Stuart is supposed to have made a hundred and twenty-four sketches of the President, including the portraits of that dignified gentleman. Stuart was a prodigious worker and a most eccentric man, as he had a right to be, and he worked on over a thousand canvases during his life. As for the general, he was also a prodigious worker, and, in addition, a prodigious sitter. In nothing did the Father of His Country show more his indomitable will, not even at Valley Forge, than in the number of portraits he allowed to be painted of himself.

By birth Stuart was half Philadelphian; his mother, Miss Anthony, was a Philadelphian.

Finally, in 1810, there arrived in the city a young man of twenty-seven, Thomas Sully, to remain there all the rest of his life until he died in 1872 at the age of eighty-nine.

Sully, whose parents were actors, was born at Horncastle, England, in 1783, but when he was nine his parents brought him to this country, settling in Charleston, South Carolina, and there he had his first lesson in art from a French miniaturist. Afterwards he studied in Boston under Gilbert Stuart, and, in 1809, the year before he came to Philadelphia, he was with Benjamin West in London.

The reputation of Philadelphia as a painting centre was well established by 1800. Charles Willson Peale had long cherished the idea of a school of art, and in 1805 a number of those interested gathered in Independence Hall and drew up a petition for a Pennsylvania Academy of Fine Arts. The charter was granted the next year—the first organization of its kind in the country—and the Academy began operations in a house on Chestnut Street between Tenth and Eleventh. In 1870, just at the worst period, the present hallowed, hideous, and slightly inaccessible building was erected. By that time Philadelphia was indeed a place of painters, many of them already there, many of them yet to be born; a goodly number of both, the already born and to-be-born, destined to become world famous. The Pennsylvania Academy of Fine Arts has sent painters out to the four quarters of the globe. Its only fault is that it has not kept enough of them resident in the city. Here are a few of the better-known: Thomas Moran, born in England but brought to Philadelphia when he was nine by his parents, and, like West, a much better painter than he is given credit for being; Mary Cassatt; Cecilia Beaux; Robert Henri; Henry Tanner, the Negro painter; William Frost Richards, the marine painter; Edwin Abbey; George Luks; John Sloan; Daniel Garber; Birge Harrison; Robert Susan; Daniel Ridgeway Knight; Adolphe Borie; Hugh Breckenridge; Franklin Watkins; George Biddle; Virginia McCall; Henry McCarter; Edward W. Redfield and the other landscape painters of the "New Hope School"; Leopold Seyffert, and the greatest of them all, the really great Thomas Eakins. Thomas Eakins lived the life of the complete artist; an epitome of how an artist should live. After studying at the Academy of Fine Arts he went to Paris for a while and worked under Gérôme and Bonnat, and then he came home and lived quietly in a small and ugly house up on Green Street, painting endlessly.

Art is a dedication. One reason why America is so rich in unfulfilled promises is that Americans, a restless folk, dislike the monasteries of their own minds.

But Philadelphia did not make painting easy. Philadelphia has never made any kind of art easy, once you get away from portrait painting. The city has ever been a severe test of the spirit.

Thomas Eakins, remote as he was, got into a lot of trouble. A great anatomist, his famous picture, the "Agnew Clinic", a group portrait of the distinguished surgeon, Dr. Hayes Agnew, operating, aroused a storm of protest. A similar group portrait, the "Gross Clinic", did the same. Somewhere around 1900 Thomas Eakins was practically kicked out of the Academy of Fine Arts because of his support of Impressionism, although he was the least impressionistic of artists himself. As for the human body, it has always, until recently, had a difficult time of it in Philadelphia; which is odd, considering the present prosperity of Philadelphia's burlesque theatres.

Where anatomy is concerned, Dr. William Shippen, Jr., when in 1762 he made Philadelphia's first dissection of the human body, was nearly mobbed; where art and sculpture are concerned, Philadelphians had a milder but no less effective way of showing their distaste.

We already know about William Rush and his allegorical figures now in Fairmount Park.[1] Adolph Ulric Wertmuller, a Swedish painter who settled in Philadelphia in 1794, had a scandalous time with his "Dane," as innocent a nude as can be imagined. But his financial rewards were as great as his artistic shame. Forbidden to exhibit "Danæ" publicly, Ulric began a series of private exhibitions which for a long while netted him a handsome income.

Around 1805, some classic statues coming to Philadelphia, ladies were allowed to see them on no other days but Fridays, and then only when they had been draped in long white sheets.

One is describing, of course, a dead and buried Philadelphia, and yet, not always so dead. Every now and then the ghost has an odd way of reappearing. At times, lurking in remote corners, one still finds the attitude of the old Philadelphia lady of an earlier period who, when told that Mary Queen of Scots had been the mistress of Rizzio, remarked, "How unnecessary."

The Academy of Fine Arts has also turned out some famous illustrators:

[1] Recently the Fairmount Park Commission, fearful perhaps that Philadelphians might think too much about democracy and discover what it is, declined to permit a statue of Thomas Paine to be erected within the confines of the park.

As for the female allegorical figure, "The Schuylkill in Chains," of that excellent sculptor and famous figurehead carver, William Rush, there is more to its history than even the fact that it was coyly removed from Centre Square to Fairmount Park. Mr. Rush, with the convictions of an artist, believed that a woman without clothes was a woman without clothes, a very shocking idea to numerous Philadelphians of his time, and so he insisted upon doing his work from living models. His wife, a woman of equal determination, rather than argue with him about this, merely took her knitting to his studio and sat close to the model during all the hours of work, thus killing two birds with one stone. This determination on the part of Mrs. Rush has been immortalized by Thomas Eakins in one of his nudes, few despite his love and knowledge of anatomy. You see William Rush at work, you see Mrs. Rush knitting, and you see "The Schuylkill in Chains" standing on the model stand. Oddly enough, the young lady who posed for the statue was a Miss Vanuxem, daughter of a leading merchant, which adds even more to the story. Just why Miss Vanuxem in that period of the world's history decided to do this is puzzling, but then we must remember the extraordinary revealing women's costumes of the time.

Felix Darley, Howard Pyle, Nathaniel Wyeth, Maxfield Parrish; and some equally well-known sculptors: Charles Crafly, Daniel Chester French, Alexander Stirling Calder, and others. Joseph Pennell, the great etcher, was a Philadelphian. Daniel Claypoole Johnson, "the American Cruikshank"; Bass Otis, the first American lithographer, were also Philadelphians.

Despite various quirks and attitudes, by the middle of the eighteenth century Philadelphia was in every detail a complete city, even if its population by 1776 had reached only 40,000, including "the Liberties". But then most eighteenth-century cities were small according to modern standards.

Bristol, the second city of England itself, boasted of no more than 36,000 inhabitants; Edinburgh in Scotland, Dublin in Ireland were only a little larger. And Philadelphia, although there were only 40,000 Philadelphians, was nonetheless suddenly treated to that final sign of civilization, the gossip columnist, America's first. The by-line of this worthy was "Palinurus Peeper", or "The Pennsylvania Spy", and he claimed to be a member of the American Philosophical Society. "Palinurus" was thoroughly modern; he missed no gossip and covered everything. There were by now many coffeehouses in Philadelphia, so far as gossip was concerned, the great-great-grandfathers of the modern night clubs, although their clientèle was strictly masculine. Philadelphia by now also had an active press: the *American Weekly Mercury*, the town's first paper and the third in the colonies, founded by Andrew Bradford in 1719; the *Pennsylvania Packet*, founded in 1728 by John Dunlap; the *Pennsylvania Gazette*, Franklin's paper, founded in 1728 by Samuel Keimer, eccentric printer and Franklin's first employer. Keimer is the man whose claim to distinction largely lies in the fact that he thought that Franklin did not amount to much. During the year he ran his venture before selling it to Franklin and Hugh Meredith, he called it by the winning title of the *Universal Instructor in all Arts and Sciences and Pennsylvania Gazette*.

In addition to these were several other gazettes and periodicals, including the *Pennsylvania Magazine*, or *American Monthly Magazine*, owned by Robert Aitken, which Thomas Paine edited. In 1783 the first trade journal in the country, the *Price-Current*, edited by John Macpherson, was added to the list.

"Palinurus Peeper", like all gossip columnists, was inclined to bite the hands that fed him, and, like all gossip columnists, was a sort of reverse-English moralist; but on the whole he was fairly mild compared to his modern counterparts. Perhaps the most interesting thing we learn from him are the names of the popular tunes of the moment: "Lovely Nancy", "Cruel Tyrant Love", "Coronation Anthem", and "Rule Britannia"; these, and the interest in a new musical instrument, the barrel organ, recently introduced from England, on which they were played.

A tart, anonymous lady, however—thought by many to be Mrs. Ellenor Fitzgerald, the fashionable milliner—grew weary finally of "Palinurus", as women all through the ages have done with the pontifications of men, and took him and his sex to pieces in a letter to the *Pennsylvania Gazette*. "Men", said the lady, could be "divided into three sorts, the rattle, the honest lover, and the sober, sly deceiver". The first barked like a dog, but was fairly harmless; the second did you little harm if you left him alone, and might prove useful; the third was the one to watch. He would "creep to your heels before you are aware of him" and would "certainly bite you" if he could.

Mrs. Fitzgerald, or whoever it was, then proceeded to give a perfect eighteenth-century description of what our own young call "a patient wolf", or, as they sometimes add, "the synonym for a perfect gentleman".

"The cool, temperate deceiver," wrote the tart lady, "is by much the most dangerous of the whole pack. These are the worst sort of poisonous creatures, for they are of a pleasing countenance. . . . I will give you some marks by which you may be the better able to distinguish them". She then goes on to say that they are "over-furnished with officiousness and assiduity and pretended friendship and modesty and honour". They bend the knee, have a sigh ready, tears if necessary, and when suitable, tremble before they speak. "Beware of all men," she warns, "but chiefly of those who are most extravagant in your praises." In fact, "All young women should look upon the men in general with a penetrating eye, Nature has furnished them [the men] with a strong desire of insinuating themselves into our favour, and, in return, has furnished us with more art and cunning".

The Rev. Jacob Duché had also taken to column writing under a pseudonym, "Letters of Tamoc Caspipina", the secrecy of which he managed to preserve for some time, although "Tamoc Caspipina" is the simplest sort of acrostic for "The Assistant Minister of Christ Church and St. Peter's in Philadelphia in North America". "Tamoc Caspipina" was considerably more acidulous than "Palinurus Peeper" and greatly concerned with the behaviour of his fellow citizens, male or female. The young women thought of nothing but dress; the young men danced away their youth until such riotous hours as eleven at night, thus rendering themselves unfit for any work next day. "Tamoc" attacked many thing: the conditions of the streets of the city (O ancient lamentation!); the quality of the teachers at the College of Philadelphia, which was to become eventually the University of Pennsylvania, and where he had classes himself. He also mentions "bundling", that quaint, but for the most part harmless, colonial substitute for central heating. Displaying a by no means charitable mind, he puts the harmlessness down, at least where Philadelphia and its environs are concerned, to "the cold, slow, indolent disposition" of Pennsylvanians; a large assumption.

But in another place there is even a larger assumption, for he calls Philadelphia "the last refuge of virtue", and states that in all Philadelphia there were at the time only two unfaithful wives.

The Rev. Jacob Duché was an odd character. The grandson of a Quaker of French descent who had come to Philadelphia with the first waves of immigration, Duché was one of the most fashionable of Church of England parsons, renowned for his florid oratory and his meticulous appearance. Miss Sally Eve (another lovely early Philadelphia name!) in her diary inquires with sly malice as to why Mr. Duché has to sit so long every day to have his hair curled and powdered.

With the Revolution, Duché became an ardent patriot, deleting at once the prayer for King George from the Liturgy and preaching fiery sermons, which were printed and widely distributed. He was made chaplain of the First Continental Congress, and his ardour increased until Lord Howe began to march upon Philadelphia. With Lord Howe's advance, the ardour steadily diminished until, with the British occupation, there was none left at all. Duché was imprisoned for a night, had a revelation, and came out the next morning as earnest a loyalist as a little before he had been a patriot. Indeed, he became such an earnest loyalist that he wrote Washington, up at Valley Forge, one of the most impertinent and presumptuous letters in American history, which is saying a good deal. He advised Washington to surrender, and throw himself upon the clemency of the British. This was the Duché who had prayed for the deliverance of "our American states" fleeing "from the rod of the oppressor" and who had delivered the funeral oration at the grave of that great Virginia gentleman and patriot, Peyton Randolph.

Duché's letter, delivered to Washington by Mrs. Elizabeth Fergusson, a parishioner, whose husband, Hugh Fergusson, a British subject, had just returned to Philadelphia with Lord Howe, is worth dwelling upon for a moment. It is the kind of letter that is timely to repeat in any crisis, for it is an epitome of a type of mind, cowardly, material, and snobbish, which, unfortunately, persists in every generation.

Washington promptly transmitted it to Congress, with this note: "To this ridiculous, illiberal performance, I made a short reply by desiring the bearer of it, if she should hereafter by any accident meet with Mr. Duché, to tell him I should have returned it unopened if I had had any idea of the contents." Francis Hopkinson, Duché's brother-in-law, answered Duché with bitter scorn, and in words that are well to remember. He told his brother-in-law that his letter had been distorted and false in every respect; foolish, scurrilous, and ill-judged. "You have ventured to assert many things at large of the affairs of England, France and America," Hopkinson wrote, "which are far from being true, and which, from your contracted knowledge in these matters, it is impossible for you to be acquainted with. . . . You presumptuously advise our worthy General, on whom millions depend with implicit confidence, to abandon their dearest hopes."

How modern it sounds!

Duché had written Washington that the Continental Army was a rabble—a note still popular with many American writers—cowards, unprincipled, and mainly fellows of the baser sort. The officers were no better. "Take away those that surround your person," he said; "how very few are there that you can ask to sit at your table." Congress was no better. All the gentlemen had left it. Washington must be "greatly hurt" by the quality of the remaining Virginians, as Duché was by the quality of the Pennsylvanians. From New England there was hardly a member remaining, except possibly Hancock, with whom Washington would care to associate. England was rich, determined, and united; France would never come to

America's aid, no matter what Benjamin Franklin said. Duché had just heard the last from a Frenchman in Philadelphia.

Nothing, of course, could have been further from the truth. One has only to examine the names of the men in Congress to realize how false Duché's charges were against that body, and one has only to glance at the files of the Continental Army to discern how libellous were his statements about its officers.

This was in 1777. Within a few months—April 1778—the treaty with France having been signed, a French fleet sailed from Toulon for the thirteen colonies.

Duché, upon the return of the Americans to Philadelphia, fled to England, deserting his wife. And here is an odd and interesting speculation: If you will look through history you will find that again and again traitors desert their wives. What connection there is, if any, can be left to further research. In England, Duché, managing to get an odd job here and an odd job there, preaching and teaching, was miserably unhappy and homesick. After the Revolution he wrote again to Washington, begging to be allowed to come home. This request was granted with quiet disdain, and Duché returned to Philadelphia to die obscure and little lamented.

Traitors invariably die so miserably that it is strange that any man would assume the rôle.

Philadelphia, just before the Revolution, also had its celebrated and fashionable murder case, a further sign and seal of confirmed urbanity; a comparatively simple and uncomplex murder compared to similar ones of to-day, and yet, in its psychology, a wistful and a shocking one.

John Bruleman, a young Philadelphia gentleman, recently a subaltern in the Royal Americans, but discharged on suspicion of having been connected with a gang of "coiners", shot and killed Captain Robert Scull, another Philadelphian, whom he did not know, and without the slightest provocation. On the afternoon of August 27, 1760, young Mr. Bruleman entered the famous Centre Tavern, which faced on Centre Square, the present City Hall Plaza, carrying a musket. West of the tavern at the time, all the way to the Schuylkill, there was nothing but woods, fields, and farms, where people were in the habit of shooting squirrels and rabbits, so nobody thought anything of Mr. Bruleman's musket. He set it against a wall and had a drink, and then watched a billiard game in which Captain Scull was one of the contestants.

Captain Scull made a particularly good shot, and everyone applauded, whereupon Mr. Bruleman picked up his musket, exclaimed, "Sir, you have just made a good stroke, but I will shew you a better," and shot Captain Scull, wounding him mortally. The captain, still holding his cue, staggered a few steps, crying out:

"The villain has murdered me!"

Mr. Bruleman, leaning over the prostrate captain, then said, according to the *Gentlemen's Magazine* of the date, "Sir, I had no malice or ill will against you, for I never saw you before. But I was determined to kill someone that I might be hanged, and you happened to be the man, and as you are a very likely man, I am sorry for your misfortune."

The innocent captain lingered for three days, dying August 30, and exhibiting, as reported by Benjamin Franklin's *Pennsylvania Gazette*, a singularly Christian character. "He was so far from shewing the least resentment against Bruleman, that he often prayed, we are told, for his Forgiveness. His Burial, the next Day, was attended by a great Number of People."

Young Mr. Bruleman during his trial explained with logical insanity his behaviour. "No man should remain in the world," he said, "who has lost his character." Lacking the will to commit suicide, he had for a week or so sought a victim. The first person he had met was the aged Dr. Cadwalader, whose grandson, General John Cadwalader, was soon to become famous in the Revolutionary War, but Dr. Cadwalader had spoken to him so courteously and had doffed his hat so politely that Bruleman had not had the heart to kill him. The next person he addressed, a stranger, had been equally polite—a recommendation for politeness in general. The third person had been a shooting companion, but just as he was about to raise his gun, John Bruleman had reflected that there were no witnesses and that the murder might be set down as an accident. Then the Centre Tavern had occurred to him. There would be plenty of witnesses there.

The miserable young man was hanged on October 8, his wish fulfilled. A few nights before the murder he had walked down the street. It was a warm August evening—one of those hot, still Philadelphia summer evenings, the smell of trees thick in the air. On the steps of his house was sitting—a universal Philadelphia custom until some fifty years ago—Mr. Charles Biddle and Mr. Bruleman's not as yet selected victim, Captain Scull. Young Mr. Bruleman, fashionably dressed, was walking thoughtfully, abstractedly, tossing his cane up into the air and catching it dexterously. Captain Scull was curious about this odd behaviour.

"What strange fellow is that?" he asked.

Mr. Biddle, who knew Bruleman, explained his history. "Since his discharge from the army, he is supposed to be a trifle deranged," he added.

Captain Scull did not know until some days later that Death, in the guise of Mr. Bruleman, had walked down the street, tossing his cane.[1]

[1] Early Philadelphia seems to have had an unfortunate effect upon certain young officers. In 1782 a young French officer, Major Galvin, deranged, like Lieutenant Bruleman, by his discharge from the army, and disappointed in a love affair with a beautiful and wealthy Philadelphia widow, arranged his estate, spent the day conversing gaily at a coffee-house with fellow officers, and then went to his room, dressed himself in full regimentals, wrote a letter, which is in the possession of the Historical Society of Pennsylvania, and shot himself.

CHAPTER XX

Iron

"Gold is for the mistress—silver for the maid—
Copper for the craftsman cunning in his trade."
"Good!" said the Baron, sitting in his hall,
"But Iron—Cold Iron—is the master of them all."

RUDYARD KIPLING, "COLD IRON."[1]

TRADE FROM THE port, craftsmen and merchants in the town, the black wealth of anthracite coal lying to the north, within a few decades to release power and wealth, and already iron, coal's grim and relentless brother, and one of the main factors of Pennsylvania's prosperity, discovered and at work.

Tobacco and iron made the thirteen colonies and the port of Philadelphia; and iron and coal made the commonwealth of Pennsylvania and the United States.

As early as 1568 an expedition sent out by Sir Walter Raleigh had found iron ore in North Carolina, and in 1640 the first successful iron works in the colonies were established in the Massachusetts Bay colony by the "Company of Undertakers for the Iron Works", the leading spirit of which was John Winthrop, Jr., son of Governor Winthrop. In 1644 this company was incorporated and obtained a monopoly for twenty-one years, and expert iron men were brought out from England, and furnaces and forges were established at Braintree, outside Boston, and at Lynn. Presently the industry spread to New Jersey and Maryland and Pennsylvania, and of all the colonies the last was destined to be, in this respect, by far the greatest.

With the exception of Joseph Hergesheimer, by long odds the most distinguished of Pennsylvanian novelists, but not a Philadelphian, since his home is in West Chester, few writers, historians or otherwise, have realized the romance of the Pennsylvania iron industry which flourished for over a century and a half until the consolidation and large-scale capitalism which followed the Civil War ended it. This was as distinct and colourful a life as the life of the great tobacco plantations of Virginia, of the rice planters of South Carolina, of the patroon families of New York, and like these it produced its own style of architecture, suitable to the countryside and using its especial materials: in the case of Pennsylvania, square dignified stone houses, made of Pennsylvania stone, set in their gardens and fish-ponds, the houses usually in small valleys surrounded by wooded slopes of chestnut and hickory and maple. In the winter the great ironmasters and their families came into Philadelphia, where they had town houses, and their presence added much to the colour and texture and peculiar character of that city.

The life was a feudal one, and the outlook of the ironmasters was feudal, too, and that affected as much in its own way the thinking of Philadelphia

1 From *Rewards and Fairies*, by Rudyard Kipling. Copyright, 1910; reprinted by permission from Mrs. Bambridge and Doubleday, Doran & Company, Inc.

and Pennsylvania as the influence of Quaker merchants and shipowners and farmers; or the Church of England influence of men of the same type as the ironmasters; or the influence of German Moravians and Mennonites; or that of the later coal barons of the Lehigh and upper Schuylkill. Near the "great-house" were the offices and shops and smaller stone houses, often whitewashed, of the overseers and foreman, and at not too great a distance was the village of still smaller stone houses where the workmen lived, for the most part men of English or Welsh origin, who generation after generation remained with "the furnace". The life was as self-contained as the life of any castle. Practically everything, even some of the coarser clothes, was made on the estates, many of them huge and covering thousands of acres, and there was continuing intimacy between successive owners and their workmen. Many of the owners had their own packs of hounds, and this formed another thread in the ancient tradition of eastern Pennsylvania fox hunting.

Philadelphia has always been one of the great fox-hunting centres of the country, and within a radius of sixty miles or so of the city are a score or more of packs, large or small, as various as the fashionable Radnor out along "the main line", with its crowded "fields" and stiff post-and-rail jumps, or the more indigenous, farmer-beloved Rosetree to the south. Hundreds of Philadelphians, business or professional men, are born to fox hunting and take it as naturally as they do their breathing.

The first bloomery forge in Pennsylvania was built in 1716 by Thomas Rutter, near what is the present city of Pottstown, and four years later Rutter and his friend Thomas Potts built the first furnace in the colony and named it Colebrookdale. By 1771 there were over fifty forges and furnaces in Pennsylvania, and by 1800 these had increased greatly and iron plantations had crossed the Alleghanies and had extended down into West Virginia and eastern Ohio. Reading—originally spelled Redding—Birdsboro, Warwick, Hopewell, Coventry, Stowe, Durham, Elizabeth, Joanna, Hibernia, Spring Grove—these were some of the great furnaces and villages, and their names show the English or Welsh origin of most of the ironmasters, with the possible exception of the name Hibernia, although this was owned by an English family named Brooke.[1] Englishmen like John Ross, William Bird, Thomas Rutter, the Brookes; Welshmen like James Old, Thomas Potts, James Morgan; a few Germans like John Lesher, were among the leading ironmasters; and the English or Welsh origin of most of the ironmasters furnishes a provocative historical reflection.

It has often been said that the long rifle won the War of the Revolution, and certainly it was also a major factor in winning the early frontier. The long rifle was a Pennsylvania invention, first made by Swiss gunmakers at Lancaster. But equally important for Washington and his troops were the furnaces of the same province, for they made the cannon balls, the guns, the chains to put across the rivers to hold back the English fleets, the rims for the wheels of caissons and wagons, and yet most of the ironmasters of

[1] Hibernia in Pennsylvania, near West Chester, and one of the later iron manors, was named after the earlier and more famous Hibernia in New Jersey. This magnificent old house is still standing.

Pennsylvania were of British descent; of English descent, but also hard-working patriots. If you look at the names of the majority of men who were the most earnest Americans during the Revolution, you will find the same thing: they also were of British descent or recent British immigration —Englishmen, Scotsmen, Welshmen, Irishmen. And this is natural after all, for a sense of liberty, individual or otherwise, is in the breed. When it comes to a question of freedom it usually takes an Englishman to lick an Englishman, although it takes an Irishman to make that remark.

It would be better to say that six things won the War of the Revolution: the long rifle, the furnaces of Pennsylvania, and Englishmen, in a broad sense; these together, with, of course, the French, the size and roughness of the country, and the stupidity of English generals who had not become Americans.[1]

Nor were the great ironmasters all men. As was the case with ship-building and "Ann Penrose shipwright", so it was with ironmaking, and occasionally a woman, widow or daughter, became an ironmaster. The best known of these was Rebecca Lukens, 1794–1854, "Mistress of Brandy-wine", who, left a widow at thirty, operated until her death what is now the Lukens Steel Company, and became the most famous woman executive of her age. The Lukens Steel Company, as did so many Pennsylvania steel companies, began as a small furnace, Rokeby, on Buck Run, Chester County, in the year 1793.

A further interesting historical note is the number of young British officers who, after the War of the Revolution, attracted by the life of these iron estates, married the daughters of the owners; a handful, perhaps, in their total numbers, but enough to be of importance. American historians seldom mention the Englishmen and Hessians who, after having fought Americans for eight years, became Americans when peace was declared. Washington's coachman was a Hessian.

The great iron plantations are a thing of the past. Many of the fine square houses and the villages have fallen upon evil ways, although some of the villages have become towns, and a fair number of the "great-houses" are still used as country seats by the original families; and one furnace, Hopewell, six miles south-east of Birdsboro, in Berks County, has been restored and made a national historic site by the National Park Service, together with the French Creek Recreation Area of nearly six thousand acres. Most of the iron families are still in the business and are still active in the life of Philadelphia, but they are now steel families, and the way they live is different. They are no longer pools of self-contained, English-customed existence surrounded, as were those in Berks and Lancaster counties, by the entirely different and equally self-contained "Pennsylvania Dutch". Everywhere along the blue Juniata, and in the Susquehanna Valley, and especially up along the Schuylkill, you find these old furnaces, some of them no more than ivy-covered ruins.

America has produced several magnificent ways of life, among them the plantation life of the South, the life of great ranches in the West, the life of

---

[1] The long rifle is most wrongly called the Kentucky rifle. It should be called the Pennsylvania rifle. It was a Pennsylvania invention and one of the great steps forward in warfare. The British, when they first came up against it, didn't know what to make of it.

the patroons of New York, the life of the ironmasters of Pennsylvania. Most of these earlier ways of living are gone, except for the ranches of the West, but not altogether.

Six years ago at Reading, at the Reading Country Club, occurred a picturesque and momentous dinner. The Philadelphia papers, with their interesting habit of overlooking more colourful local events, did not mention it, although the family in question is a Philadelphia family. The dinner was given by the foremen and workmen of the great Birdsboro Steel & Machine Company in honour of the Brooke family, celebrating the Brooke family's one hundred and fifty years' ownership of the Birdsboro "furnaces". The Birdsboro Iron Works, however, are actually older than this; they are now two hundred and four years old, for they were founded by William and Mark Bird, two brothers after whom the small town was named, in 1740 on Hay Creek, a stream which runs into the Schuylkill.[1] In 1788 Captain John Louis Barde, late of the English army, first rented and then bought them, and in 1805 Captain Barde's daughter Elizabeth married Matthew Brooke III.

And that is why the dinner was given.

The Birdsboro Iron Works are one of the three businesses in the United States older than a century and a half that have come down in direct succession, father to son, which in itself is historic enough. But this is why the dinner is even more interesting, for at the dinner were some six hundred or so foremen and workmen and their wives and thirty or so members of the Brooke family, the latter gathered together from all over the country and even London, and after the dinner, man after man got up and spoke, whose father, grandfather, and great-grandfather, or even great-great-grandfather, had worked for the Brookes. Or, to put it better, had worked along with them. And during all that time there had never been a strike. Everyone had lived in the small and, let it be remarked, charming iron village of Birdsboro, and everyone had known one another intimately, and everyone had always called one another by their first names.

There is a comment here for the "industrial relations" engineer.

Captain Barde was one of the young Englishmen who after the Revolution became Americans. He was the aide of Sir Robert Fermour, or Farmer, last British governor of Florida. But he did not marry an American; he left that to his daughter. He himself married Sir Robert Farmer's daughter and brought her up with him from the South, and upon his death in 1799 this English girl, this daughter of Florida's last British governor, became, like Mrs. Lukens, a Pennsylvania ironmaster. For ten years, until her own death in 1809, she ran the Birdsboro Iron Works, after which her son-in-law, Matthew Brooke III, took over.

When Washington was at Valley Forge, the Birdsboro Iron Works, just up the river, and still under the control of William and Mark Bird, sent him down cannon balls.

The legends of the ironmasters survive throughout the iron country; to the north, to the west. Curtis Grubb, master of Cornwall Furnace, near Lebanon, and a Rochester, save for the absence of Jane Eyre, in the dark of the moon still hunts a phantom pack of hounds near the Welsh Mountains.

[1] James Wilson married into the Bird family.

You can hear them and the unearthly hallooing of Curtis and his huntsmen. Curtis, cruel and dissolute, was a great fox hunter and inordinately proud of his hounds. From Philadelphia on one occasion he brought up some supercilious guests to see his hounds perform. On that day alone the hounds hunted badly. Curtis, furious, hunted and whipped them straight into the fiery mouth of the furnace, even Flora, his favourite bitch, who had twice saved his life. Before obeying his command, Flora came and laid her head on his booted foot and looked up at him.

Years later to the bedside of Curtis, dying lonely and raving in his "great-house", came the ghost of Flora, and beyond his windows the rest of the pack went by. Now, willy-nilly, Curtis hunts when the moon is down.

There is a splendidly flamboyant Gothic folk ballad about Curtis. No one knows who wrote it.[1] As it is fourteen pages long, it cannot be repeated in full. This is how it begins:

> Colebrook Furnace in Cornwall stands
> Crouched at the foot of the iron lands,—
> The wondrous hill of iron ore
> That pours its wealth through the furnace-door,
> Is mixed with lime and smothered in wood,
> Tortured with fire till a molten flood
> Leaps from the taps to the sow below,
> And her littered pigs that round her glow.

To those who do not know iron the "sow" is the long fat conduit into which the metal pours from the furnace, and from it into the squat oblong moulds to make the "pigs". The whole bears some resemblance to a sow and a sucking litter, hence pig-iron.

The ballad goes on to describe Curtis's habits while he was still in good health:

> Howbeit, this devil's labor rolled
> Back on the Squire in floods of gold.
> Gold and hunting and potent drink,
> And loud-tongued girls that grin and wink,
> Over the flagon's dripping brim,
> Those were the things that busied him.
> Strong of sinew and dull of mind,
> He blustered round like a winter wind.
> You could hear his laugh come on before,
> While his hounds were off a mile or more;
> And in his wassail he stormed and roared,
> Clashing his fists on the groaning board,
> Or clutched his trulls till their young bones bent. . . .

[1] Arthur C. Bining, in his *Pennsylvania Iron in the Eighteenth Century*, published by the Pennsylvania Historical Commission in 1938, ascribes this ballad to George H. Boker. Bining relates that a similar legend is told about Peter Marmie of Jacob's Creek Furnace. Marmie, a Frenchman, was at one time Lafayette's private secretary.

Try the last line aloud. It is magnificent.

But the Grubbs were not all like "Uncle" Curtis. To the contrary, they were a very distinguished iron family, and one of them, a collateral descendant of Curtis, and a distinguished soldier, was named General E. Burd Grubb.

Inventions, discoveries that change the history of the world, are strange, mysterious; and hardly one of them but is credited to a man whose right to the honour, upon research, cannot be challenged.

Since we are upon the subject of iron—of steel—the history of the Bessemer process contains one of the most fascinating of these byways. The Bessemer process, as its name would indicate, is generally accredited to Sir Henry Bessemer, English engineer; that is to say, the process of decarbonizing cast iron by forcing a blast of air through it so that the iron is converted into malleable iron in a perfectly fluid shape. The first public announcement of this discovery was made at the Cheltenham meeting of the British Society for the Advancement of Science in 1856. But there is every reason to suppose that Horatio Gates Spafford, a New England-born American inventor, had discovered this process exactly forty years before, and that if the American Philosophical Society, Franklin's child and Philadelphia's pride, had been a trifle more attentive and imaginative, also the United States Government, largely in the shape of Thomas Jefferson and James Madison, with whom Spafford corresponded, America would have been making steel in quantity long before England.

In 1816 Spafford's manuscript, *Cursory Observations on the Art of Making Iron and Steel*, was read before the Philosophical Society and referred to a committee and, after four months' study, sent back to him, accompanied by a gentle, but not encouraging, letter on the part of that ripe scholar, Peter Du Ponceau. Nor were the Philosophical Society, nor Jefferson and Madison, altogether to blame. Spafford was almost insanely secretive and suspicious, and deliberately did not make clear what he had discovered. In fact, he was such a strange fellow that General Stephen Van Rensselaer wrote to John Kent Kane of Philadelphia:

"If you converse with Spafford for half an hour you will perceive that his mind is stored with a great deal of knowledge original & acquired & there is no possible pretence for supposing that he is deranged."

On the other hand, the American Philosophical Society throughout its long and invaluable history has not been infallible by any means. It listened with a weary ear to Jefferson's plea for scientific expeditions to the Far West and so missed the honour of promoting and helping to finance Lewis and Clark, and it allowed to languish unwelcomed by it that extraordinary scientist, college president, and voluminous author, Constantine S. Rafinesque (1783–1840), whose importance is just being recognized. The Philosophical Society found him eccentric, physically dirty, and unconventional, all of which he probably was. But then so was Diogenes.

Near to the city in the direction of Germantown, and beyond into White-marsh and Huntingdon valleys, but once more, especially along the wooded slopes of the Schuylkill in what is now Fairmount Park, another sort of country life and another type of country house had been developed; a most gracious type of country house, many still standing, the stone or brick walls as a rule covered with yellow stucco. These were the houses, girdling the city like stately jonquils, of the rich merchants and shipowners and professional men of Philadelphia who drove out to them when their day's work was over. Among these was Cliveden, still standing in Germantown, the seat of Chief Justice Benjamin Chew, and one of the few of these old houses still in the possession of the original family.[1]

Cliveden has a tragic place in American history, for Cliveden stemmed the tide of American victory at the Battle of Germantown and sent—in the mist and confusion of that morning, when American troops fired in the fog on American troops—Washington and his army reeling back to Valley Forge. Colonel Musgrave with six companies of the Fortieth Foot made Cliveden a fortress—dark blood is still on its polished floors—proving then, what has so often been proven since, that an ordinary house and an ordinary city are far harder to take than a fortress.

The name Cliveden seems fated to be unfortunate. Strange, isn't it?

Near Cliveden is the old Wister house, also still in the possession of the original family, where that fine Englishman, General Agnew, taken there mortally wounded, died, his last thought concerned with the safety of a terrified Wister serving-maid. Agnew is buried in Germantown. And in the same general direction were, or still are, numerous old houses like Fairhill, the home of Isaac Norris and afterwards of John Dickinson; Bush Hill, the country seat of the Hamiltons; Walnut Grove, the house of the Whartons; and Landsdowne Mansion, built by John Penn, grandson of William, the Founder. Nearer the city was Stenton, James Logan's country seat, now a city historical monument.

Fairhill was famed for its English gardens of clipped box and yew; it was destroyed during the Revolution. Walnut Grove, home of a grave Quaker, Joseph Wharton, nonetheless was the scene of that quaint and gay and gaudy spectacle, the *meschianza*, given by Major André and the other British officers in honour of Lord Howe when that pleasant, stout, and good-natured man was relieved of command of the city. But of all these, Landsdowne House possibly had the most spectacular history. John Penn sold it to William Bingham, the great West Indian merchant, and Bingham, who

---

[1]Other signs of increasing urbanity and worldliness were everywhere evident; for one, the custom of the European "Grand Tour". The brilliant young Quaker Francis Rawle seems to have initiated this, so far as Philadelphia is concerned, in the year 1748. Also, as was the custom in Virginia among the planters, and in Boston among the merchants, many sons of wealthier Philadelphians were sent to Oxford or Cambridge to finish their education, or to the Inns of Court. Philadelphia also began at an early date to collect paintings and statuary, as well as beautiful furniture. James Hamilton, of Bush Hill, was the most distinguished of these early collectors. His collection began with a Murillo, "St. Ignatius", sold at action as the result of a successful privateering expedition against the ships of His Most Christian Majesty. No doubt the Murillo was designed for a church or convent in South America. Hamilton acquired this in the '40's and by 1763 had an admirable collection, including, as Du Simitiére wrote, "*quelques bonnes peintures copiées par un nommé West*," to wit, Benjamin, and a "Venus" by Titian, "*toute nue!*"—how else would Venus dress? And an Annibale Caracci, "Venus Lamenting over the Body of Adonis". Chief Justice Allen was also an eminent collector of paintings, as was Colonel Joseph Shippen.

married Ann Willing, the sixteen-year-old daughter of Judge Thomas Willing, made it his country place. After the Revolution, in the stately years that followed, young Ann Willing was destined to be the most famous hostess Philadelphia has ever known; noted for her beauty, her distinction, her gowns, and her entertainments. Englishmen and Frenchmen were equally impressed. Mrs. Bingham also had a town house surrounded by a garden of three acres, in which were set out orange trees, and other exotic plants, in tubs; inside the house was a marble grand staircase leading to a ballroom and drawing-rooms on the second floor. And there were English carpets, the pile inches deep. And French wallpaper. And Italian frescoes and paintings. Some of the sterner Quakers and some of the starker democrats didn't like all this, nor did they like what they called "the Court Party" —the particular clique, including the Binghams, who saw most of the President and Mrs. Washington. How odd are the minds of the envious, or the fanatic, or the mischievous! Washington, who had so sternly and contemptuously dismissed the plot among some of his officers to make him a king, and who remained so staunchly a republican under all manner of temptation, was nonetheless constantly attacked because he preferred dignity, and direct action, and a decent way of life. No president was more wilfully maligned during his presidency, or more scurrilously libelled by the opposition Press when he left office; not even Jefferson or Abraham Lincoln. Even that great patriot, Thomas Paine, lost his fiery head and wrote back from France, where he was a prisoner of the Jacobins, a stupid letter upbraiding Washington as a tyrant and a snob. Paine had perhaps some excuse; he thought Washington and the American Government were not doing what they should to get him out of the clutches of Robespierre, but it was this ill-judged letter, more than anything else, that ruined Paine.

The beautiful Mrs. Bingham died young, and her grieving husband went to France to live. Joseph Bonaparte while he was in America occupied Landsdowne House for several years. On July 4, 1854, it was destroyed by a fire started by fireworks.

Along the Schuylkill, one of the loveliest places in all the world to build, a bevy of fine houses were erected before the Revolution, or shortly after. Most of them are still in existence, although, like Stenton, they are now city monuments. There is Belmont, for instance, built by William Peters, brother of the Rev. Richard Peters, rector of Christ Church, in 1743, and left by William to his son, Judge Richard Peters, Secretary of War for a time during the Revolution. And Woodford, reconstructed by William Coleman in 1756. And Cedar Grove, built in 1721, the original country seat of the Morris family, but Morrises not related to "the financier of the Revolution".[1] And Ormiston, the estate of Joseph Galloway, an excellent man, but the most disliked and unfortunate of local Tories. In 1778 he was attainted of treason and all his properties were confiscated. He spent the next ten years drawing up various constitutions for the British Empire, which anticipated the empire

---

[1] As with the Wisters and the Wistars, there is constant confusion over the Morrises in Philadelphia, only more so, since they all spell their name the same way. There are three distinct and ancient and distinguished Morris families in Philadelphia. Prolific, too. Philadelphia is filled with Morrises.

of to-day. Hatfield House and Mount Pleasant, the latter built by Captain John Macpherson, soldier of fortune and astute business man, somewhere around 1761; Strawberry, the country seat of William Lewis, noted lawyer and friend of Washington, who called the place originally Summerville Farm; Lemon Hill, Robert Morris' country house; the Randolph Mansion, built before the Revolution by Francis Rawle, but in 1828 purchased by Dr. Philip Syng Physick, "the father of American surgery", as a wedding gift for his daughter, Mrs. Randolph—these are some of the older houses. Immediately after the Revolution, or, in the case of one, during the Revolution, similar stately country seats were erected.

Others were: Rockland, which George Thomson, a wealthy merchant, built in 1810; Sweetbrier, built in 1797 by Samuel Breck, the Philadelphia merchant who drafted the bill establishing the public-school system of Pennsylvania; Solitude, already mentioned, built by John Penn in 1784, and now surrounded by the long-lived animals of the Philadelphia Zoo.

Mount Pleasant, called by John Adams in 1775 "the most elegant seat in Pennsylvania", was in some ways the most historic house of all. Built by Captain Macpherson and first named Clunie, after the seat of the Macpherson clan in Scotland, it was purchased by Benedict Arnold in 1779 as a gift for his bride, Peggy Shippen, when the general, still a shining hero in American eyes, was military governor of Philadelphia after the English evacuation. But the general never lived in Mount Pleasant, and had no chance, with his bride, to exercise his love of lavish entertainment. His treachery catching up with him, Mount Pleasant was returned to Captain Macpherson, who sold it again. For a while it was occupied by Baron von Steuben, "drillmaster of the Continental Army". Mount Pleasant is now completely refurnished as a colonial and Revolutionary mansion, and is a public museum.

As for Robert Morris' house, Lemon Hill, there is now nothing left of it, the present Lemon Hill having been built by Henry Pratt, son of Matthew Pratt, the artist, who purchased the estate at a sheriff's sale in 1799; Robert Morris, "financier of the Revolution", being at the moment in debtor's jail, where he remained for three years. It was by the merest chance that he didn't die there, but he was finally released, to die five years later.

There has been considerable bitterness, especially in Philadelphia, over the fate of Robert Morris, and his name is hardly ever mentioned without some reference to the "ingratitude of republics". The "ingratitude of republics" is true enough, but Morris was not ruined by the Revolution, as is generally supposed. He was a great patriot, no question of that, although a much more cautious and conservative one than Franklin, and he helped to finance the Revolution largely out of his own pocket or in notes at his own risk, but he came out of the Revolution a rich man. He was ruined, not by his patriotism, but by speculation in western lands. Despite his caution along certain lines, he was in other ways extremely extravagant. He was a great builder of fine houses, for instance, and lived extravagantly.

A much clearer case of the "ingratitude of republics" is that of Haym Solomon, Polish Jew and gallant American, who came to Philadelphia, a price on his head, after setting fire to a New York filled with Tories and occupied by the British army, following Washington's evacuation of Long Island, and who lent the Continental Congress $300,000, all he had. The debt, although acknowledged by the Federal Government, has never been paid. Haym Solomon died a bankrupt.

Without question, Captain John Macpherson of Clunie was one of the most extraordinary and fascinating persons who ever descended upon William Penn's "Holy Experiment" to make it his home. He must have been a wonder and delight to his friends, and at times a source of annoyance.

Captain Macpherson was a younger son of the head of the Macpherson clan, the Laird of Clunie, and at an early age he went to sea, becoming, at the age of thirty-one, captain of a privateer, the twenty-gun *Britannia*. In 1758 the *Britannia*, overtaken by a heavier French ship, gave battle and was defeated. Macpherson, who had lost his right arm during the battle, was taken aboard the Frenchman together with his officers, and was afterwards released, but as for the *Britannia*, she was set adrift with her crew, who, despite many hardships, managed to bring her finally to the port of Philadelphia, where Macpherson, two years later, in 1760, rejoined her as captain. Thereupon began a most profitable decade for Macpherson of Clunie; he took enough French prizes to make himself an extremely rich man. By the time of the Revolution he had become thoroughly American and was employed as a secret agent of the Continental Congress, although what he wanted to be was commander of the Continental Navy. Congress sent him to Cambridge with a plan to burn the British navy in Boston Harbour, but Washington rejected this, although later on, according to the hero of the tale, Macpherson entered the Hessian lines near Trenton as a spy and was responsible for the information that led to Washington's victory. However that may be, Captain Macpherson did serve his adopted country well, for he built with his own money five Continental men-of-war, which he presented to the Pennsylvania navy: the large vessel *Perseverance*, the sloop *Tyger*, the schooners *Cat* and *Jackal*, and the gunboat *Anti-Traitor*.

Meanwhile he had built Mount Pleasant on the first profits of his privateering.

An ardent patriot, one of his sons, John, was the first Philadelphian of distinction to be killed in the Revolution—he fell at the assault on Quebec—and another son, William,[1] organized and led the famous Macpherson Blues as a Continental major.

Rich, successful at everything to which he turned his hand, John Mac-

[1] William Macpherson, who rose to be a brigadier-general in the American army, arrived in this country in 1779, where his father had been for many years, and four years earlier his brother John had fallen at the siege of Quebec, as adjutant of the Sixteenth British Infantry. Almost at once he handed in his resignation to Sir Henry Clinton and was permitted to resign but was not allowed to sell his commission. The whole proceeding is typical of the strange and punctillious warfare of the eighteenth century—strange to our ruthless modern ideas—and of the confusion the American Revolution caused in so many English minds. It was indeed an ideological war. General Richard Montgomery himself, the American hero of Quebec, was an Irishman, who before settling in New York in 1772, where he married the daughter of Robert Livingston, had for many years served gallantly in the English army. In 1757 he had served in the attack upon Louisburg, and in 1759 in the Lake Champlain expedition. The night before young John Macpherson was killed, he wrote a letter to his father which contained this curiously fair-minded sentence. In case he should not survive the approaching battle, "I could wish", wrote young John Macpherson, "my brother did continue in the service of my country's enemies".

pherson of Clunie, once peace was declared, settled down to the happiest years of his life. In the sunshine of peace he blossomed like a rose. He lectured on astronomy and natural philosophy, accompanied, as the records state, by "vocal and instrumental Musick, and a boy who danced horn-pipes"; he published the first trade paper in the country, the *Price-Current*, 1783; and he undertook the first city directory in the United States. The latter was compiled in his own individual way and therefore contains, after certain street addresses, such notes as these:

"Mrs. No Name"; "Mr. I Won't Tell"; or even one entry as succinct as, "Cross Woman".

Macpherson of Clunie, or Mount Pleasant, was also an inventor, like Benjamin Franklin, if not as practical a one. Among his inventions was a machine which moved, from within, a house to any place where you might want it, and which he operated himself, and a folding cot which he advertised as bidding "defiance to everything but Omnipotence". He was equally busy with the arts and with pamphleteering, writing what he called "comic tragedies" for the stage, and indulging in such furious and insulting controversies with Dr. Cadwalader, John Dickinson, and other eminent men that at one time he was locked up for three months as being insane. Finally, in 1789, he published an autobiography entitled, *A History of the Life, Very Strange Adventures, and Works of Captain John Macpherson, Which Will, in Many Parts, Appear like an Eastern Tale.*

Despite all of which, he was an eminently successful man, founded a distinguished American family, and was an outstanding rifle-shot with one arm—the left.

It is easy to see why Philadelphia, with this increasingly urbane and prosperous life, was loath to go to war, and why, when it went to war, it was divided as much as New York, but for different reasons, and more than Boston, and considerably more than the South, where the planters led a self-contained and agrarian life and were not as intimately entangled with Europe as were the great northern seaports.

In addition to this, there was also in Philadelphia the Quaker influence and tradition, which was predominatingly and sternly pacifist. The German influence, which was equally pacific but in a milder way. And the Church of England influence, as in New York, closely connected with the mother country. It is a wonder, then, and a compliment, that Philadelphia as a whole behaved as gallantly and patriotically as it did, although there is nothing odd about the fact, as pointed out before, that many of the Church of England men were leading men in the war to follow. The same thing happened in Virginia and Maryland. Equally prominent were the Scottish and Scottish-Irish Presbyterians. But revolution is a dreadful and portentous word, even more dreadful than the word war, and it must again be remembered what these American men and women were called upon to do.

Time collapses as we look back upon it. The decades fold up against each other like a closed fan or accordion. And so it seems to us in survey as if Philadelphia, still less than a hundred years old at the time of the

Revolution, was as a young town almost a frontier town, with a frontier town's inevitable inclination toward rebellion and tumult. But if you place ninety-three years against the slow but active years of your own living, you achieve a different perspective. A lot can happen in ninety-three years; they mean at the least three full generations. Ninety-three years would take us back to 1851 and the presidency of Millard Fillmore. There have been nineteen presidents since then. Moreover, all these Americans had been brought up to regard themselves as loyal Englishmen and believers in monarchy. Americans, and even more, the rest of the world, forget that America has had eleven kings and queens, and one Lord Protector, Oliver Cromwell, beginning with Elizabeth and ending with George III. Kings and queens are no news to America.

So, considering everything, it was pardoxical that Philadelphia, the heart of Quakerdom, the richest and most pacific city in the colonies, should have become the very heart of the Revolution, its nerve centre. And yet it was inevitable. It was written in the stars. Geographically, commercially, and politically, Philadelphia was destined, as it has always been destined. It was a cross-roads, it sat at the middle point of the colonies, neither too far to the north to inconvenience or to make jealous the southern delegates, nor too far south to do the same to the men of New England and New York. Moreover, in an age without aeroplanes, its long harbour and river made its port safer than most. To these advantages were added its wealth, its ship-building, its intellectual leadership, and the men living there who were responsible for the last.

The history of Philadelphia between 1774 and 1783 is the history of the Revolution; the history of Philadelphia between 1789 and 1800 is the history of the young United States.

Fate and geography were again doing strange things to Penn's port of refuge, his wilderness plantation of peace, his carefully designed "Holy Experiment". But, as always, no man, not even the wise Franklin, was able to read the future accurately, and Penn's town was as unprepared for war and revolution as were the rest of the colonies, and as amazed when it came. As amazed as if war, most clearly, had not been on its way for ten years, or even since the stupid Stamp Act of 1765. War isn't a flash of lightning, it is a slow piling up of thunder clouds. There are always plenty of warnings, although as yet no government has ever heeded them. And in Philadelphia the War of the Revolution was to be as disrupting a war as all ideological wars are; as painful a war as the present war, as sad as was the Civil War in the Border States, of which Pennsylvania was one. Brother was against brother, father against son, even an occasional wife was against her husband, or a husband against a wife. William Peters of Belmont was a staunch loyalist; his son, Judge Richard Peters, was an equally ardent patriot.

Nonetheless Philadelphia, although it was not as rough or turbulent as Boston, or as oratorical as the South, was equally determined, in its own demure way.

In the early summer of 1773 letters from Philadelphia warned England not to send Philadelphia any tea ships, despite which the "tea fleet" sailed, one of its numbers, the *Polly*, "an old black ship, without a head or any ornaments", commanded by Captain Ayres, "a short, fat fellow, but obstainate withal", destined for Philadelphia. But Captain Ayres, despite his obstinacy, was also a cautious man. He cruised for a long while off the Delaware Capes before daring to enter the river. When he did, Boston had already dumped her tea in the harbour, Edenton, North Carolina, had done the same, and Charleston, South Carolina, had ordered her tea ship to leave in two days. Christmas morning the *Polly* furtively entered the Delaware; the night before, Christmas Eve, the news of Boston's "tea party" had reached Philadelphia, adding to the enjoyment of most, the fears of some, and the annual festivities of the early "Mummers".

Eight thousand of the citizens of Philadelphia met in mass meeting and adopted an uncompromsing declaration which was broadcast throughout the colonies. Captain Ayres was given twenty-four hours in which to provision and refill his water-butts before returning with his cargo to England. Continuing to be a cautious man, he did exactly what he was told. He had seen a couple of sinister handbills which were in possession of the river pilots who eventually met him.

You are sent out on a diabolical service, and if you are so foolish and obstinate as to complete your journey by bringing your Ship to Anchor in this Port, you may run such a Gauntlet as will induce you in your last moments most heartily to curse those who have made you the dupe of their avarice and ambitions. What think you, Captain, of a Halter round your Neck, ten gallons of liquid Tar decanted on your Pate, with the feathers of a dozen wild Geese laid over that to enliven your appearance?

That was one; here is another:

So much the worse for him [Captain Ayres]; for as sure as he rides rusty [this means the neglected POLLY] we shall heave him keel out and see that his bottom be well fired, scrubbed, and paid. His upper-works, too, will have an overhauling, and as it is said he has a good deal of quick work about him, we will take care that such part of him undergoes a thorough rummaging.

Captain Ayres was a canny fellow, so he sailed home, but Captain James Allen of the brig *Greyhound*, which came later and entered Cohansey Creek down the Delaware, wasn't so canny. The local farmers took the *Greyhound's* tea and made a bonfire out of it, and danced about it as it burned.

In May 1774 the port of Boston was closed, and Paul Revere brought word of it to Philadelphia. The indignation was intense. On the first of June, when Revere's message was given to the people, flags were lowered to half-mast, practically every shop was closed, the churches were opened, as if it were Sunday, and they were packed with grim congregations, listening to grim sermons. There was no service at Christ Church, but all day long the bells of Christ Church, muffled, tolled for calamity, and the people listened.

Christopher Marshall wrote: "Sorrow and anger seemed pictured in the countenances of the inhabitants, and the whole city wore the aspect of deep distress, it being a most melancholy occasion."

THE OLD CHESTNUT STREET THEATRE (Kennedy)

FOURTH OF JULY CELEBRATION, CENTRE SQUARE, 1818, by Kremmel

The city as a whole responded mightily; rich man, poor man, even a number of leading Quakers led by Thomas Mifflin, who, oddly enough for a Quaker, was nonetheless a man of fashion and in his youth had been a "macaroni". Many of Quaker descent and tradition, like the Cadwaladers, root and branch great patriots, forgot that descent and tradition utterly. Charles Thompson, whom John Adams called "the very life of the cause of liberty", and who, like William Penn, was known among the Indians as "the man who tells the truth", John Dickinson, Joseph Reed, Thomas Willing, Provost Smith, and others met at the City Tavern and adopted resolutions of sympathy and dispatched them to Boston.

A year later John Peter Gabriel Muhlenberg, Lutheran and Church of England parson, for he took orders in both, and Continental general, was to dramatize forever the American church in war.

John Peter Gabriel, great friend of Washington, and tall, impressive man, was of the Philadelphia and Pennsylvania Muhlenbergs; oldest son of that equally great patriot but by then venerable man, the Rev. Henry Melchior Muhlenberg, graduate of Göttingen and Halle, born at Einbeck in Hanover, who had come to America in 1742 as a Lutheran missionary, finally settling in Trappe, Montgomery County, just to the north of Philadelphia. John Peter Gabriel had charge of what were called the "Valley Churches" of the Blue Ridge in Virginia, and on that Sunday he ascended the pulpit in full canonicals. He preached quietly and simply as was his wont, and then said, "There is a time for all things, as is said in Holy Writ. There is a time to preach, and a time to pray, but those times have passed, and now there is a time to fight, and that time has come," and with that he let slip his dark robe from his shoulders and showed beneath it the gold-and-blue uniform of an American general.

Peter was a Philadelphian, although born at Trappe.

On December 5, 1774, the First Continental Congress assembled in Philadelphia, every colony except Georgia represented. It met in Carpenter's Hall and used for reference or relaxation "Mr. Franklin's Library", which at the time occupied rooms in that building. The fifty-five delegates included such men as Washington, John Adams, Samuel Adams, Benjamin Franklin, Roger Sherman, Richard Henry Lee, Patrick Henry, Peyton Randolph, Christopher Gadsden. Peyton Randolph, of Virginia, was elected president; Charles Thompson, of Pennsylvania, secretary; the Rev. Jacob Duché, "Tamoc Caspipina", with his curled wig, chaplain. The Rev. Jacob Duché was overcome with importance and delight, and appeared with his clerk and in his pontals, and offered eloquent prayers.

This was still—the First Continental Congress—a body of loyal Englishmen. Resolutions and a petition affirming loyalty and asking for relief and discussion were sent to England; at a great banquet given by Philadelphians to the delegates, many toasts were drunk, and the first was "To His Majesty King George III, our Royal Sovereign".

It was a time of much entertainment. John Adams, who noticed everything and always wrote about it to his wife, speaks of a society "happy, elegant, tranquil, and polite".

All would be settled peaceably.

H

The First Continental Congress sat for six weeks and went home.

The Second Continental Congress met on May 10, 1775. Down from New England on April 24, 1775, had come a tired and muddy rider. The British had fired on the farmers and New England militia at Lexington. Late in June came word of Bunker Hill; 1,054 British killed and wounded, including eighty-nine commissioned officers; 441 Americans killed and wounded, including General Joseph Warren.

"This, gentlemen, is war!"

But the Second Continental Congress, although now, unlike its predecessor, frankly rebellious, still hoped desperately for peace; in the beginning, that is. It sent another conciliatory petition to George III, not the obese, obstinate old man most Americans think him, but at the moment a gay, handsome, tall fellow of thirty-seven. At the same time, however, the Second Continental Congress rushed through bills for a militia and for appropriations, organized the troops around Boston into the "American Continental Army", appointed Washington commander-in-chief, dispatching him to New England, and prepared in every way for hostilities.

"Proclaim liberty throughout the Land, unto all the inhabitants thereof."

Once more it was a coincidence, wasn't it, that the great bell should have that as its motto? And it was a coincidence that in 1774 Benjamin Franklin, over in London, had dispatched to Philadelphia, to edit his friend Robert Aitken's *Pennsylvania Magazine*, that gaunt and fiery Englishman, Thomas Paine, born thirty-seven years before in Thetford, son of a Quaker stay- or corset-maker. But then Benjamin Franklin had a way of making coincidences, or else bending them to his will. Half of greatness is the ability to be around where coincidences happen, or else to so weave the threads of life that they occur.

In the lives of most great men, coincidences are more common than ordinary events.

CHAPTER XXI

The Hub of War

"They that can give up essential liberty to obtain a little temporary safety deserve neither liberty or safety."

BENJAMIN FRANKLIN.

RUFUS CHOATE, FAMOUS lawyer and ambassador to the Court of St. James, making an after-dinner speech in Philadelphia, began by congratulating the city on "those two great Philadelphians, William Penn and Benjamin Franklin—one an Englishman, and the other a Bostonian".

He could have gone further, and more or less straight down the line, and have congratulated Philadelphia on numerous other famous "sons", most of them also born elsewhere: James Logan, England; James Wilson, Scotland; Robert Morris, England; Provost Smith, England; Dr. John Morgan, England; Commodore John Barry, Ireland; Stephen Girard, France; Edgar Allan Poe, Boston; Walt Whitman, Huntington, Long Island; and so on endlessly; and Whitman did not live in Philadelphia, but in Camden, Philadelphia's Brooklyn, although he visited Philadelphia almost every day. Finally, there is that extraordinary "American" and "Philadelphian", Thomas Paine, an Englishman until he was thirty-seven.

Mr. Choate was being witty and so not necessarily accurate, but it is an interesting fact, and possibly significant, that Philadelphia has always attracted so many famous men—not so many now as formerly—and, outside of the professions, has produced so few. Perhaps the land is too fertile, the conditions too easy, the climate too well balanced between the rigours of the north and the sharp languors of the south. Gardeners know that "too much pot", too much earth, that is, too much richness, is as bad for a plant as too little. Pennsylvania is in every way a "middle state"; well called the Keystone State, for there abundance reaches an apex. Despite its great political power, the one president Pennsylvania has ever given the United States, James Buchanan, was certainly a middle-of-the-road failure if there ever was one, and yet he should have been very much of a fellow, since his ancestors were the fierce, long-rifle Scottish-Irishmen of the Pennsylvania frontier.

But take a Lancaster County farm in the middle of summer—in late July—with the small distant hills slumbering in the blue haze and the grain white-silver with the imperceptible breeze. Or take the markets of Philadelphia ripe with fruits and vegetables—it is difficult to realize the acrid sense of tragedy and final death that makes for greatness. Generation after generation Pennsylvania sleeps in the fullness of its summers and the rich quiet of its winters.

Thomas Paine did not stay long enough in Philadelphia to be affected either by the climate or the customs, and it is doubtful if he would have changed much even if he had spent his allotted seventy-two years there. He was too much a man of a single idea, a devotee, a fanatic, if you will, to be changed by anything. It is a question if half the time he knew whether it was snowing, hailing, or raining. And the idea that so preoccupied him was liberty: liberty and democracy. He was sort of a monk, a barefoot friar of liberty and democracy: the St. Francis of Assisi of the Revolution.

He was no speaker, no orator, nor demagogue; his words were hard and bitter and lucid; but when he wrote, he was a two-sworded angel. And his *Common Sense*, and his other pamphlets, did for the War of the Revolution what "The Battle Hymn of the Republic" did for the armies of the North in the great war that was to follow eighty-five years later. One moment there was doubt and irresolution, and the next there was a decision, and a winnowing out of the weak from the strong, and a great wind blew across the fields and through the forests and the towns of America.

"These are the times that try men's souls! The summer soldier and the sunshine patriot will, in this crisis, shrink from the service of his country;

but he that stands it now deserves the love and the thanks of man and woman. Tyranny, like hell, is not easily conquered. . . ."

That was it! That was what men wanted to hear.

Strange that all of us, knowing how powerful is the word, more powerful even than the sword, and knowing that the sword is of little avail without the word, so invariably belittle the word. Every crisis awaits the great word, and if the great word does not come, then the crisis has been of no value. The Civil War would have been fought in vain had it not been for the Gettysburg Address.

And it is equally strange and tragic that this great user of the word, this great—by deliberate choice—American and Philadelphian, Thomas Paine, should have been for a hundred and sixty-eight years treated with contempt and hatred and suspicion by the nation he helped to make. Only now is he barely coming into his own.

For a while after the Revolution he was so beloved that Congress granted him a large tract of land in New York State and three thousand dollars, and then, after thirteen years, in 1787, he went back to England to fight tyranny there, and, driven out of England, fled to France. In France, although speaking French badly, he got himself elected a deputy to the French Assembly and, although a revolutionist, was the only deputy brave enough to stand up to the cold wrath of Robespierre and vote against the execution of the king. He was flung into jail for that, and was nearly guillotined; instead of which, he found time to write his greatest work, *The Age of Reason*. By now his immense popularity was waning, and his foolish letter to Washington accusing Washington and the Government of Toryism and ingratitude, the latter because he thought Washington was not interested enough in getting him out of the clutches of Robespierre, gave his enemies just the handle they needed; also, it alienated Paine's friends. You cannot attack a nation's hero, its symbol, just at the moment of his greatest popularity and expect to go unscathed. *The Age of Reason* finished it; all the Tories and all but the wiser churchmen proceeded to destroy Paine, and now he had hardly anyone to defend him.

Released from prison in France, he came back to America an old and penniless man, and Congress added final insult—it rescinded his citizenship and refused to allow him to vote. He died obscure and despised. William Cobbett, no tactful man himself, finally had his bones brought to England and buried there. And so for a hundred and sixty-eight years this great American—in his own way, one of the greatest of the "Founding Fathers"— has been maligned and grossly misunderstood. He has not even been granted the dignity of his full name but has been called "Tom" Paine as if he were a street-corner rabble rouser. For a hundred years his books were printed inconspicuously and handed around secretly as if they were pornographic, and those who read them, and there have always been some, were looked upon as dangerous radicals and eccentrics. Theodore Roosevelt, a great American himself, but a man of action rather than deep thought, publicly called him "a filthy little atheist", which is amusing in more ways than one, as Paine was lean and well proportioned, and five feet ten, two inches taller than the late President. Only here and there has some wise, far-visioned

American, notably Thomas Edison, risen to defend Paine; but then Edison
was an inventor, and so a clairvoyant, a clairvoyant being a man who adds
the past to the present and, with that synthesis, assesses the future.   Paine,
interestingly enough, was an inventor, too; and a good one.   Even Paine's
admirers have as a whole misinterpreted him.   As a rule, radicals themselves,
they have delighted in magnifying his drunkenness, his rudeness, and his
unkempt dress.   Their enthusiasm has been misplaced.

Paine did drink too much; so did most of the men of the eighteenth
century; but is it likely that Benjamin Franklin, wisest of men, would have
sent a drunken ragamuffin, in such a parlous year as 1774, over to run the
Pennsylvania Magazine?[1]   Paine was rude and tactless when angry, but we
have the testimony of his contemporaries that he was delightful and persuasive
when he wished to be.   As to his appearance, there is the charming portrait
of him painted for his friend, Colonel Henry Laurens, president of the
Continental Congress, and Laurens was not the sort of man who would have
made a friend of a foul-mouthed uncouth blasphemer; and there is also the
equally charming portrait by Romney when Paine was somewhat older.
Finally, there is that magnificent bust of Paine as an old man, executed by
his friend and protector John Wesley Jarvis, nephew of the great Methodist,
John Wesley, with whom Paine lived for a while upon his return to this
country in 1802.   The bust now belongs to the New York Historical Society,
and any time you wish to go up and look at an eagle, there one is.   Nor was
Paine an atheist.   He was born a Quaker and became an eighteenth-century
Deist; in other words, a man who believed firmly in a God, but did not believe
in revealed religion of formal churches.   His religious position is exactly
that of any number of popular preachers of to-day, and what he believed is
stated unequivocally in *The Age of Reason.*   "All religions are in their nature
mild and benign" was his initial premise.

And yet it is not so difficult after all to see why Paine has been maligned
and suppressed; he too, of course, was a clairvoyant, a political one, and the
political clairvoyant is the deadly enemy of the *status quo* and the arrogant and
of all those who would try to stop with their selfish fingers the leaking dam
of the future.   Instinctively, or consciously, they know that it is not the
clairvoyant so much, but the future, which is their enemy.   Benjamin Franklin
said, "Where liberty is, there is my home".   Thomas Paine said, "Where
liberty is not, there is my home", and this far more subtle statement meant
that Paine had dedicated himself to seeking out tyranny and destroying it.

Of all the great men of the Revolution, he was the only one who saw
clearly the age-old and endless struggle between tyranny and liberty, and
who knew that sooner or later these two giants would—must—lock in final,
mortal combat.

Thomas Paine was the St. Francis of Assisi of the Revolution; or, to
make the metaphor modern he was its spark-plug.   But he was more than
that; he was also that rare thing, the political thinker with a scientific mind.
He was aware of the preventive-medicine side of politics just as the sanitation

[1] To the contrary, Franklin wrote to his son-in-law, "Mr. Thomas Paine . . . very well
recommended to me as an ingenious, worthy young man. . . . I request you to give him
your best advice and countenance. . . ."

expert is aware that if in a single corner of the world a plague lingers, then the whole world is still in danger from that plague. You do not kill rats by taming them; you kill them by preventing them.

Paine knew that liberty could not live in the same world with tyranny, and so he knew that tyranny must be extinguished.

No wonder he has been feared and hated.

Eighty per cent of revolutionists, once their especial revolution is accomplished, become reactionaries. If you wish proof of this, read most books by later-day Philadelphians on the Philadelphia of the War of Independence. They are almost apologetic. One does not see how the Revolution was won at all, considering the charm and good breeding of Howe's young officers, their grace at dancing. But one does understand the story of the distinguished Philadelphia lady who, for six weeks following Queen Victoria's death, wore Court mourning.

War, starting in New England and the north, came closer and closer to Philadelphia. First it shifted to Long Island and New York, then into New Jersey. Finally, it was at the very gates of the town itself, coming up from the south after Howe's fleet had entered the Chesapeake. Chadd's Ford, a small battle, little more than a skirmish, was the first defeat of this campaign. The battle of the Brandywine was the next American defeat. The "Paoli Massacre" followed, on the very outskirts of the city. Paoli had been the home of the Corsican patriot, Pasquale Paoli, who had lived there in exile in the middle of the eighteenth century, and near-by Paoli was the estate of "Mad" Anthony Wayne, that dashing and handsome American cavalryman whose troops had been surprised at "the Massacre". The small American army fell back upon the hills to the north of Philadelphia along the Schuylkill. The long, frozen agony of Valley Forge was soon to begin. The British entered the city. The Delaware forts held out for a while, but finally Howe captured them, and his fleet came up to the city itself.

For the Tories in Philadelphia all this was delightful and a vindication; for the Whigs, it was a sorry time, although some of the more complaisant managed to live through it comfortably, and some of the daughters of even the more thoroughgoing Whigs found the younger British officers not unattractive: Major André and such.

The winter of 1777–78 proved to be one of the darkest winters of the Revolution. And yet there were cheering signs for those who could read them, for Baron von Steuben had arrived and was drilling the American army into the resolute body it became, and Lafayette, the French boy of nineteen, had arrived, and the surprising victories of Trenton and Princeton had been written on the record, and what turned out to be the decisive battle of the war, Saratoga, had been won. Finally, on February 6, 1778, the treaty with France was signed. But on the surface it was a bleak winter for Americans. Across the snows of Valley Forge fell the huge indomitable shadow, dark by day, blue at dusk, of Washington. This, however, must not be forgotten: Howe knew very little of what Washington was thinking or doing; Washington, on the other hand, was in constant touch with Howe's plans.

Nowadays it is the fashion to describe Washington as a tall, gangling, not very bright man, with enormous hands and feet, unhappy in company and distinguished solely by an unconquerable will. As a matter of fact, Washington was one of the greatest spy masters of history and one of the first of military men to recognize the vital importance of military intelligence. Again and again he outwitted his enemies, although frequently they were not so difficult to outwit. Together with the long rifle and the various other factors that have been mentioned as winning the War of the Revolution, one must never forget the insouciant genius of the British generals for losing it.

Just a year earlier Howe had missed by a hair's-breadth capturing Washington and ending the Revolution then and there, when, after the disastrous Battle of Long Island and the equally disastrous fighting on Manhattan in the autumn of 1776, he was chasing Washington and his disorganized army out of what is now Harlem and the Bronx. Instead, Washington slipped away to New Jersey and to the victories of Trenton and Princeton. Howe, a charming fellow, if growing a trifle plump, on the most crucial day stopped with his staff for a leisurely and delightful luncheon with Mrs. Robert Murray at her country seat, Incleberg, on the hill about Kip's Bay. Attractive herself, Mrs. Murray had other attractive women present for the occasion. Howe, of course, thought his plans to trap Putnam were secure, but Putnam knew Howe's plans and had slipped round the trap. Mrs. Murray, incidentally, was half-Philadelphian.[1]

And during the winter of 1777–78, when Howe was so cosily quartered in Philadelphia, he could have obliterated, or at least scattered, the freezing Americans at Valley Forge, instead of which, the freezing Americans, after first nearly scattering Howe at the Battle of Germantown, which they would have done had it not been for the thick early morning fog and Musgrave, barricaded in Cliveden, seized the opportunity of what was practically an armistice to strengthen themselves in every way. The British, under Lord Howe, Lord Cornwallis along with him, had entered Philadelphia on September 26 some eighteen thousand strong, and on October 24 the Battle of Germantown was fought. After that, the Americans settled down to their Gethsemane, bloody tracks in the snow, and the English to habitual gaiety.

There were weekly balls at the City Tavern, stag dinners and punch parties at the Indian Queen or the Bunch of Grapes. Major André and Colonel Charley O'Hara and Captain De Lancey, the handsome young Tory from New York, were constantly busy with amateur theatricals and charades. There was much drinking of tea. And everywhere, making himself agreeable, was another young British officer, only twenty-one at the time, who was to leave on the pages of American history a bloody scrawl like the finger-prints of a murderer examining the papers of his victim. This

[1] Recently considerable doubt has been cast upon this story by historians. Maybe it is true, and maybe it isn't. At all events, Howe didn't catch Putnam. One becomes weary of meticulous historical investigation, the sole purpose of which is to spoil good and useful tradition and to reduce all events to a dreary level of uneventfulness. In any essential summation heroic folk fables are far truer and of more determining importance than quibbles over fact.

was Colonel Banastre Tarleton, "Butcher Tarleton", who was to die many years later as a British general and an English baronet. Young Colonel Tarleton interested himself mostly in horse-racing and cock-fighting.

How strange this must have seemed to anyone thoughtful enough to remember the summers and winters of 1774, 1775, and 1776, the First and Second Continental Congresses sitting, the narrow streets and open places of the city crowded with the planners: first, of the perturbed but still loyal colonies, and then with the statesmen and soldiers and officers of the angry and rebellious young "United States of America". And if stones and trees and houses have memories, they too must have been surprised by these new white-wigged, scarlet-clad visitors, so confident and so careless. Different people these from the men in buff and blue, or civilian small clothes, who had temporarily fled the city; different even from the equally dashing young officers like "Light Horse" Harry Lee, or Anthony Wayne, or Major Stoddard of Sally Wister's journal, only nineteen, but "justly celebrated for his powers of mind". The men who had fled were graver, all of them, because they knew that they were holding their heads to their shoulders only by the skill of their swords and the muskets or long rifles of their men. They were engaged in one of the gravest and most dangerous enterprises of history.

Particularly down around Fifth and Sixth streets between Spruce and Market, where they still cling like invisible ivy, these memories were thick. Around the State House and the open space to the south, set aside for it, and farther to the south, in and around what is now Washington Square, but which was then Potter's Field.

Washington Square is old and shabby, with the huge brick monolith of the Curtis Publishing Company looking down upon it from the north and, tucked away on its east side in an inconspicuous building, one of the most fascinating libraries, with its reading-rooms, in the country: the Athenæum. The Athenæum, a private library and chess club, still gently insists that, so far as it is concerned, literature and knowledge are inherited matters confined to certain distinguished families in which shares are handed down like jewels from generation to generation. In the Athenæum's backyard, a typical Philadelphia backyard—private places that can be made charming if the owners so desire, and often are—is one of the oldest and biggest wistaria vines in the city. In the spring, with the big back french windows open, you can raise your head from print to the violet beauty of the wistaria. And also in the backyard of the Athenæum are the remains of little houses that were once, it is said, slave quarters, though this is now doubted. The nearness of the Athenæum to the bustling *Saturday Evening Post* is typical of Philadelphia.

But Washington Square, old and shabby as it now is, is still beautiful with its ancient elms, and its sun, and its few remaining old brick houses facing it, and the soft noiselessness of its fat grey squirrels. And it is a place of many memories, for under the feet of the crowds that cross it are the bones of British prisoners of war, and near them, in the armistice of death, are the bones of even more Americans—many of whom died during 1776 when the American wounded were pouring into Philadelphia, and others, a couple of thousand of them, suffering dreadfully of gangrene, or jail fever, or neglect, during the gay winter of 1777–78 which followed, when, as military jailer, there was an especially brutal fellow named Cunningham.

It is satisfactory to relate that upon his return to England, Cunningham was court-martialled and hung; but it is odd why, in every war, so many brutal men are given charge of prisoners. Prisoners are the most helpless of men.

The hot summer of 1776 and the cold autumn that followed had contributed the greatest memories and also some of the most despairing ones. It was a glorious time for the struggling colonies, for they became the United States of America; but it was also a dark one, for the autumn marked Washington's withdrawal from New York and his slow, agonized retreat through New Jersey, his men falling away from him, the Pennsylvania and New York and some of the New England militia behaving particularly badly. Only the tall shadow of the huge man on horseback, his military cloak black against the frosted trees, held the dwindling Continental Army together; that tall shadow, and the handful of stalwart generals like Greene, the Quaker from Rhode Island, and the handful of troops who knew exactly what they were fighting for. Those months were the heyday for Thomas Paine's "summer patriots" both in Congress and in the Army. Termites thrive where the air is bad. And these were especially fattening months for that arrant rascal and double traitor, General Charles Lee, late of the English army. How General Charles Lee ever escaped being shot either by the English or by the Americans is one of the mysteries of American history.[1]

---

[1] It is a pity, and confusing, that Charles Lee, the renegade British soldier and American traitor, should have had the same last name as the magnificent Lees of Virginia: Richard Henry, the first man to move for independence in the Continental Congress; his brother Arthur; his four other brothers; and his cousin, "Light Horse" Harry, father of General Robert E. Lee. Charles Lee was no relation to these. Having served with some distinction in the British army, he had settled in America, and, owing to his military experience, when the Revolution broke out, was given an important command. Almost at once he showed his true character. He disobeyed and hampered Washington on the painful retreat from New York and, had it not been for the sensible and stalwart General Heath, who refused to obey Lee's orders, might have done worse. Captured on December 13 at White's Tavern, near Baskenridge, New Jersey, whither he had gone with only an aide and a few troopers, he was for a while a prisoner of his former countrymen until exchanged. Interestingly enough the troop of cavalry which captured him belonged to his old regiment, the Queen's Light Dragoons, and interestingly enough, instead of hanging him as a traitor, the English treated him well and finally exchanged him. Incidentally, he was captured in his night-shirt, and, incidentally, he had gone to White's Tavern because of an amour he was conducting with a serving-maid.

It is now fairly clear that while he was a prisoner of the British, he told them all he knew of Washington's plans and laid before them a plan of his own to defeat Washington. And it is obvious that the British exchanged him gladly, knowing how useful he might be to them once more in command of an American army. That the Americans received him back so innocently can be put down to amateur and provincial admiration and trust in the supposed capabilities of a professional soldier. Before he was finally detected and retired from the American army, Lee managed to betray Washington at the Battle of Monmouth Court House, and also, by means of the "Conway Cabal", came near to capturing for himself Washington's post as commander-in-chief.

It is an incredible story, but in every war, especially the wars of a democracy, there appears a "political general", debonair, glamorous on the surface, personally courageous and dashing, adroit and sinister.   Lee could be a very charming and convincing person for his own purposes. And, like all "political generals", he thought himself a "man of destiny".

H*

Unfortunately some fine men, including some fine Philadelphians, notably Dr. Benjamin Rush and General Thomas Mifflin, were drawn into the "Conway Cabal", the conspiracy led by General Conway, the Scottish adventurer who was Inspector-General of the Continental Army, and the object of which was to replace Washington by Lee. General Horatio Gates, although also involved, much to the damage of his reputation, was probably more of a victim than an actual conspirator. Later on in the war he proved himself a loyal and capable general. However, this black and mortal stupidity on the part of otherwise patriotic and intelligent men like Rush and Mifflin is not without its discernible basis. Benjamin Rush was in many ways a great man, and American medicine is deeply indebted to him, but he was also a vain and self-opinionated man; Thomas Mifflin in his youth had been a "macaroni", and any man who in his youth is a "macaroni", or its equivalent, is an exhibitionist.

In times of crisis the vain and the exhibitionistic—the terms are practically synonymous—invariably skirt the edges of sedition. Others are not doing what they think should be done, or else they themselves are not sufficiently appreciated. Vanity is the mother of treason, public or private. Vanity accounted largely for Benedict Arnold, also for Aaron Burr.[1]

Down from New England on January 15 had come riding Paul Revere to find out the secrets of powder-making from Oswell Eve, who owned Philadelphia's powder-mill. As a contemporary writes, "Whenever there is a particularly important message to go from the patriots of Massachusetts Bay to any point in the colonies, Paul Revere of Boston is more than likely to be the man delegated". Oswell Eve proved to be a selfish and short-sighted man. He refused to tell Paul Revere his trade secrets despite the angry urging of Robert Morris; but he did ask Paul Revere to walk through his mill, and Paul Revere, clever man, learned enough on that visit to go back to New England and start New England powder-mills at Andover and Canton.

On January 19 the first American navy was ready to take to the seas and was commissioned in the Delaware off Philadelphia.

There it lay, eight ships, flying the yellow silk of the first American flag, the Rattlesnake, with its motto, "Don't Tread on Me", and at nine o'clock, it being a brisk, clear morning, a barge put off from the flagship *Alfred* to meet Commander-in-Chief Esek Hopkins and bring him abroad from the Walnut Street Wharf. A long ruffle of drums from ship to ship, the squealing of boatswains' whistles, the admiral's pennant going up. There lay the *Alfred*, Captain Saltonstall; the *Columbus*, Captain Whittle; the *Andrew Doria*, Captain Biddle; the *Cabot*, Captain John B. Hopkins; the *Providence*, Captain Hazard; the *Hornet*, Captain Stone; the *Fly*, Captain Hacker; and the *Wasp*, Captain Alexander. With that first American fleet as a lieutenant was young John Paul Jones.

---

[1] For a long while there was a tradition about Benedict Arnold, given wide credence. The story ran that he was the son of a Hessian druggist who had settled in Connecticut, and that the name Arnold, sardonically enough, means "honour" in German. Of course there is not a word of truth in either of these statements. Benedict Arnold came of a most distinguished American family and was the great-grandson of Benedict Arnold (1615-78), thrice colonial governor of Rhode Island. The tradition is interesting, however, as an example of how, in all periods, the lie, repeated often enough, is finally believed even by some of the intelligent.

There were now fourteen colonial navies, large or small, including the American navy. Each colony had some ships of its own, and this, of course, was not counting the swarms of privateers. A great sailing nation had challenged another. Glover's Regiment of Marblehead fishermen was soon to make a reputation for itself in the fighting around New York.

So all that first half of 1776 was fairly encouraging and was leading up to the great apex of July, and that apex was the main question in Congress; nor was it a struggle between patriots and non-patriots: all the men in Congress were patriots. It was a struggle between those who wished a definite break with England and those who didn't. Excellent men were against a definite break. John Dickinson of Pennsylvania, for example; James Wilson and Robert Morris of the same delegation. All the South Carolina delegation, except Edward Rutledge. Georgia was doubtful; New Jersey. Several of the other colonies. Delaware was split. Thomas McKean was in favour of independence; George Reed advised caution.

All through those hot nights of late June and early July a light had burned steadily in the second-storey windows of a small brick house at the corner of Seventh and Market streets—a house now destroyed. Thomas Jefferson, the tall, red-haired, violin-playing Virginian, the handsome man of thirty-three, was writing the Declaration of Independence. On June 7 a committee of five had been appointed for this purpose: together with Jefferson, John Adams of Massachusetts, Benjamin Franklin of Pennsylvania, Roger Sherman of Connecticut, and Robert Livingston of New York. And now it was done—the Declaration—and now its fate depended on the four legs of a horse and the courage of a man with a cancer.

There have been many historic rides in America: Paul Revere's and William Dawes's rides out of Boston; Sheridan's at Winchester; "Portugee" Phillips' during a Wyoming blizzard, when he rode two hundred and twenty-five miles south to tell Fort Laramie of the Fetterman Massacre and the siege of Fort Kearney by Red Cloud and his Sioux. But in all American history there has been no more dramatic or crucial ride than that of Cæsar Rodney, delegate from Delaware. On that one vote, and that one horse, and that hard-riding man hung the immediate future. Suppose that horse had stumbled!

Not so long ago, by one vote hung, if you remember, Lend-Lease, as well.

Brigadier-General Cæsar Rodney was a slight man, and he was in the first stages of the illness that killed him. At the moment he was on leave from the Continental Congress, sent to put down a rising of Tories in lower Delaware. On June 7 Richard Henry Lee of Virginia had brought in the resolution for independence; by July the debate was touch and go. Of the nine Pennsylvania delegates only three, John Morton, Benjamin Franklin, and James Wilson, recently convinced, were sure to vote the right way. South Carolina was still doubtful. Maryland was undecided. So was New York. The majority of delegates were in favour of independence, but the fuse smouldered and might go out. It was ticklish. And it was hot. And Congress was tired. McKean had sent for Rodney to come post-haste, but he had had no word, and now it was late afternoon, and the vote could be held off no longer. All the while, up through Delaware, Cæsar Rodney was galloping. Twenty hours after McKean's express rider had left Philadelphia, Rodney slid from his saddle in front of the State House and, swaying with fatigue and pain and grey with dust, entered the hall of Congress.

McKean looked up. There was a deep silence. Rodney took his seat, and the calling of the roll began. D, for Delaware, is near the top of the alphabet. Rodney's name was called. He arose. Only McKean and a few others knew how he was going to vote.

"As I believe," he said, "the voice of my constituents and of all sensible and honest men, is in favour of independence, and my own judgment concurs with them, I vote for independence."

This was on July 2. On the eighth the Declaration was read from the steps of the State House, which was now to become Independence Hall, and as the words died away the bells began to ring. Such a ringing that even John Adams, staunch patriot from the beginning, said at the end of it that he had heard enough bell-ringing for the day. The militia paraded on the Common. Down from everywhere to make a bonfire came the coats of arms of George III and all other signs of English sovereignty, save on the steeple of the main building of Germantown Academy. Somehow or other, that was forgotten.

Deborah Norris, a girl of fifteen, climbed the wall surrounding the garden of her house to hear the Declaration read. She could not see the speaker, Captain John Nixon, because of an angle of the building, but the solemn words frightened her. Years later she wrote: "It was a time of fearful doubt and great anxiety with the people, many of whom were appalled by the boldness of the measure; and the first audience of the Declaration was neither very numerous, nor composed of the most respectable class of citizens."

Some of the Quaker diaries of Revolutionary Philadelphia convey a strange note of coldness and are not altogether fair to the city. Too many Quakers of the period seemed to have forgotten that the most crucial moments in the life of their original leader, the first Christian, are known as the Passion. A year later, on the first anniversary of the Declaration, a date set as July 4, Elizabeth Drinker, granddaughter of the "first white child of Coaquannock", and indefatigable diarist—she kept one for fifty-nine years—entered this wry and chilling note:

"*July 4th, 1777. The town illuminated and a great number of windows broken on ye Anniversary of Independence and Freedom.*"

Elizabeth, however, had her private grievance. Henry Drinker, her husband, was one of the Quakers forced to leave the city because of his equivocal views.

But nonetheless Philadelphia was singularly fortunate in the number of these diarists. By means of them it is possible to reconstruct, in a way not otherwise possible, the intimate life of the city. Moreover, each diarist represents a distinct personality and point of view, so that a well-rounded picture is available. For instance, there was Christopher Marshall, the thoughtful and worried and conservative Quaker. Elizabeth Drinker, the wry, succinct, and not-to-be-swept-off-her-feet young woman, and mature woman, and older woman. Sally Wister, the gay, flirtatious, and pretty girl —who being outside the city during the British occupation, at her family's country place at Gwynedd, near Germantown—gives us as charming a picture of the young American officers as Rebecca Franks, within the city, gives of the young British officers.

Sally Wisters was only sixteen at the time, but in the eighteenth century this was fairly mature, and the fact that she was a Quakeress did not in the least interfere with Miss Wister's love of dainty dresses, chintz or otherwise, or her intention of flirting with every American officer, young or old, she came across, even mature General William Smallwood of Maryland, whose headquarters at the time was the Wister house. But the especial victim of her charms was young Benjamin Stoddard, he of the outstanding intellect and extreme bashfulness, who later on was twice Secretary of the Navy.

"*I am going to my chamber to dream,*" she writes in her diary, "*of bayonets and swords, sashes, guns and epaulets.*" And later on—continuing in the pursuit of the bashful Major Stottard: "*But still, I won't despair. Who knows what mischief I yet may do?*"

Miss Franks, as charming a Tory as Sally Wister was a patriot, had an equally devastating time within the city. The voices of the two girls are contrapuntal. Miss Franks to her friend Mrs. Paca, of Maryland:

You have not the slightest idea of the life of continued amusement I live in. I can scarce have a moment to myself. I have stole this while everybody is retired to dress for dinner. I am just come from under Mr. J. Black's hands, and most elegantly am I dressed for a ball this evening at Smith's, where we have one every Thursday. . . . Oh? how I wish Mr. P. would let you come in for a week or two. I know you are as fond of a gay life as myself. You'd have an opportunity of rakeing as much as you chose, either at Plays, Balls, Concerts, or Assemblies. I've been but three evenings alone since we moved to town. I begin now to be almost tired.

Miss Franks remained in Philadelphia for a while when the Americans came back in the summer of 1778, and she describes the balls and routs given by General Arnold and the richer patriots in their turn, but she belittled them. Her heart was with the British, and presently, migrating to New York, she fell in love with and married a young British officer, Colonel Johnson of the 17th Regiment, with whom she eventually sailed to England, never to return. Colonel Johnson had a distinguished military career and was made a baronet. Absent from her country, Lady Johnson became more and more gently nostalgic. She forgot her youthful satire and scorn and delighted in entertaining her former compatriots. Years later she said to General Winfield Scott, who was visiting her in Bath:

"Would that I too had been a patriot." She sighed. "I have gloried in my rebel countrymen," she concluded softly.

A declaration of war and a Declaration of Independence are two things. Carrying them through is a third. Rebellion always means dire dislocation, and for a while confusion, from the new currency, up or down, reigned. The year following the Declaration was an increasing difficult one for Philadelphia, as it was for all places in American hands. Over and beyond fighting the war, food and materials of all kinds became scarce; money depreciated, the faint-hearted fell away; and neighbour began to look at neighbour askance. Every now and then mobs in all their ugliness formed and maltreated Tories and sometimes harmless Quakers or misunderstood patriots. Salt, the most necessary of all foods, almost disappeared, and when there was any of it, sold for twenty-five shillings a bushel.

In the winter of 1776, the Rev. Henry Muhlenberg, another diarist, notes:

"The people push and jostle each other wherever there is the smallest quantity of salt to be found. The country people complain bitterly because they suppose there are hidden stores in Philadelphia."

The hospitals overflowed and reeked with the American wounded and ill. Hundreds of the dead were buried in trenches dug in Washington Square. By December word reached the city that Howe, by now at New Brunswick, was marching on Philadelphia. Panic and an exodus followed. Congress departed for Baltimore, leaving that brave man, Robert Morris, as chairman of a Committee of Safety. Washington, up in New Jersey, sent down General Putman as military governor. Universal enlistment for all able-bodied men was decreed, runaway prices were pegged, and merchants were commanded to accept Continental currency at its face value. Black markets thrived. James Allen bitterly resented all this, as did numerous others. "The prevailing idea," he wrote, "is that no man has any right to property that the public has use for, and it is seldom they even ask the owner."

Sounds modern, doesn't it? In every war there are numerous intelligent people who seem unable to get through their heads what war means.

When Howe reached Trenton in the early spring of 1777 and issued a proclamation telling all loyalists to seek his protection, several prominent Philadelphia families took him at his word, including the Galloways and the Allens. The city became more tense. In July, forty well-to-do men were arrested for treason, including such personages as Jared Ingersoll, John Penn, Chief Justice Benjamin Chew, and Provost Smith, the last a staunch patriot, but one who had been unlucky enough to wish to delay complete independence. No harm came to these gentlemen, however.

And by now another portent had risen above the horizon; a new kind of Quaker: the "Free Quakers", as they call themselves, or the "Fighting Quakers", as they speedily came to be known. These were the Quakers who saw the issue clearly and who were willing to lay down their lives for it. Their leader was Samuel Wetherill, Jr., great-grandson of one of the original Quaker settlers of New Jersey, but who himself had become a resident of Philadelphia. Samuel Wetherill, Jr., almost at once found himself at the head of a powerful group of his faith, mostly young; all the men eager to fight, all the women eager to help them. Among the women were Lydia Darragh, long known as the "Quaker Heroine of Philadelphia", and Elizabeth Ross, "Betsy Ross", whose supposed making of the first Stars and Stripes is almost as vague as the story of the Liberty Bell.[1]

The more orthodox Quakers referred to these two-fisted co-religionists as "apostates", and they were promptly read out of Meeting. They were even refused burial in the Quaker burial ground, despite the Free Quakers' most reasonable statement, "For however the living may contend, surely the dead may lie peaceably together", and despite Samuel Wetherill's very fine statement of his side called, "Apology for the Religious Society Called Free Quakers, in the City of Philadelphia".

Undismayed, the Free Quakers met first in the various houses of the

[1] For a number of years Lydia Darragh, "Mistress Darragh", was the heroine of a story which, unfortunately, has no basis in fact, so far as can be discovered, and which, in 1910, Henry Leffmann, of the City History Society of Philadelphia, described as "a lie made out of whole cloth".

The story goes that while the British were occupying Philadelphia, in December 1777, a conference was held in Mrs. Darragh's house by General Howe and his staff to decide final plans for a surprise attack on Washington at Valley Forge, and that Mrs. Darragh, "Fighting Quakeress", listened at the keyholes, and the next day, under pretence of needing flour, obtained a pass from the British provost-marshal which would take her through the American lines, and started on foot, in the bitter cold and across the miles of intervening snow, to warn Washington. Falling in with an American scouting party when almost exhausted, Mrs. Darragh finally reached Washington, with the result that when the surprise attack came the American army easily repulsed it.

This story did not appear until long after the War of the Revolution, and there are no contemporary records of it. It was not mentioned in Washington's correspondence, although there was a "surprise attack" by the British in the vicinity of Chestnut Hill on the morning of December 5, and, as usual, Washington knew all about it before it came.

In answer to Henry Leffmann's paper, in 1916 Henry Darragh, a descendant of Lydia Darragh, prepared a paper in defence of the tradition, entitled, "Lydia Darragh, One of the Heroines of the Revolution". Whatever the truth of the legend may be, and all the facts seem to be against it, Lydia Darragh needs no embellishment. She was a singularly fine, courageous, and patriotic woman.

An almost equal confusion, if not quite as dark, surrounds the making of the first American flag; that is, the Stars and Stripes. Everyone knows the story of how General Washington, Robert Morris, and Betsy Ross's brother-in-law, George Ross, called upon the young widow and expert seamstress, born Betsy Griscom, in June 1776, and got her to make a flag based upon the Washington coat of arms, and of how she in return taught them to cut five-pointed stars with a single slash of the scissors. The fact that Washington was at the moment exceedingly busy with the British around New York, the fact that there is no record of payment to Betsy Ross, and the fact that the Ross family was at the moment indignant with her because they thought that she, a widow of only a year and a half, was too preoccupied with Captain Joseph Ashbrook, whom she subsequently married—these and numerous other contrary facts do not deter those who wish to believe in the legend, and to-day the demure and charming brick house of Betsy Ross is a national shrine, although there is considerable doubt whether that house, even, was her home. Many historians think she lived at 233 Arch Street and not at 239.

That Elizabeth Ross was an expert seamstress and made many flags for the Pennsylvania navy is a matter of record, but whether she made the first Stars and Stripes or not, no one will ever know. It is much more likely that Francis Hopkinson made the design. At all events, we know definitely when the American flag first flew in battle, replacing the Rattlesnake Flag, the Pine Tree and other emblems. The Stars and Stripes was officially adopted June 14, 1777, and within two months saw its first action in Delaware at Cooch's Bridge, when seven hundred Marylanders and Delaware "Blue Chickens", or "Game Cocks", and nine hundred Pennsylvania horse under General William Maxwell, "Scotch Willie" Maxwell, tried unsuccessfully to stop Howe's advance toward Philadelphia. Shortly afterward the Stars and Stripes flew again at the Battle of Brandywine.

It is always a pity when a worthy and inspiring legend has to be questioned, and, once more, the worth of so doing is doubtful. Strong folk legends represent the will and aspirations of a people, and so, fundamentally, in their factual untruth are often truer, imaginatively and spiritually, than the actual truth.

members, those who were not in the army or navy, and then built a meeting-house of their own at Fifth and Arch: a lovely small brick building, still standing. Opposite it, on the south-east corner, is Christ Church Burial Ground, where Franklin lies buried, and one block, or "square", farther east, at Fourth and Arch, is the Arch Street Friends' Meeting-House, quite splendid in its brick simplicity—in its burial ground James Logan, and the wife of Governor David Lloyd, first person buried there, and Lydia Darragh.

This latter meeting-house was not built until 1804, but the land was granted by William Penn, and William Penn spoke at Mrs. Lloyd's funeral.

The Free Quakers had a curious history. As the bitterness of the Revolution disappeared into the past, the members of the sect drifted away to return to the original fold or to join other denominations. Elizabeth Ross, who had become Elizabeth Claypoole, was the last of the original members. She lived until 1836, but was bedridden during her later years. Finally, John Price Wetherill, son of Samuel, by this time a very old man, was left alone to conduct services. One day he turned the key in the lock of the meeting-house and as a regular sect the Free Quakers were finished. But the difference in attitude is still visible, and during the Civil Way it was strongly in evidence. It was the Free Quakers who again marched off to war, at least in the beginning. As a result of Free Quakerism arose one of the quaintest of Philadelphia customs, the annual gathering of the Wetherill family in the old Free Quaker Meeting-House. Once a year the Wetherills, most of them no longer Quakers, meet for a long session, and they come from many parts of the country and decide to what charitable purposes they will put the moneys of the defunct society, now for a long while in their keeping.

Since they are all of one family, and that family once led those doughty people, the "Fighting Quakers", there are rumours of occasional argument.[1]

Fourteen months after the signing of the Declaration of Independence, the British had captured Philadelphia. A month earlier, August 27, 1777, Washington, on his way to try to stop Howe, had marched through the city with all he had—eleven thousand men; "ragged, lousy, naked regiments", a spectator called them. Howe had twenty thousand well-fed and well-drilled troops. But the American troops marched, nonetheless, with the long, almost loping stride that all through history has marked the American infantry, and if they were not well fed, they were at least well led.

In these days of endless taking and retaking of cities all over the world, it is interesting to see how it was done in the eighteenth century, when war, at least among the better classes, was conducted with a degree of etiquette. The War of the Revolution was a cruel war in many ways, but the greatest cruelties took place in the more remote sections among partisans, Tory or patriot. The British entered Philadelphia in great state and with no disorder.

[1] Dr. S. Weir Mitchell's novel, *Hugh Wynne, Fighting Quaker*, describes the Free Quaker movement and gives a splendid picture of Revolutionary Philadelphia. It is one of the best of American novels and should be revived. It is also a thrilling and colourful motion picture, waiting to be read and produced by some imaginative and patriotic producer.

Regiment after regiment they came: foot soldiers white-wigged, scarlet-clad, their accoutrements twinkling: the 42nd Highlanders, bagpipes squealing; the Hessians in their green uniforms, stiff and inhuman. Town's *Evening Post*, a Tory paper said: "The British entered Philadelphia under Lord Cornwallis, marching down Second Street, and encamped to the southward of the town. The fine appearance and strict discipline of the soldiers, and politeness of the officers, soon dispelled the fears of the inhabitants— kindled joy in the countenances of the well-affected."

"Plunder! Plunder! Plunder!" said another spectator, was the way the drums and deep brasses of the Hessian bands sounded.

Lord Cornwallis, being first billeted with a lady who most politely told him he and his staff would crowd her house unbearably, most politely said he was sorry, and withdrew, and found other quarters.

Lord Howe was equally considerate, but he did commandeer the coach and horses of Mrs. Mary Pemberton, and this worried very much some of his more sensitive junior officers.

Lord Howe, still Sir William, so long as his older brother the admiral survived, which was until 1799, was a fine figure of a man, six feet tall and well proportioned; graceful, dignified, and greatly beloved by his officers. Many Americans thought he resembled George Washington. He liked Americans. His eldest brother, now dead, had been one of the heroes of the last French-Indian War, and his memory was revered, especially by Bostonians.

Lord Cornwallis was short and thickset, his face well formed and agreeable, his hair somewhat grey, his manners remarkably easy and graceful. He also was much beloved by his men. And he also liked Americans.

General Sir Henry Clinton, who succeeded Lord Howe because he was thought to be more energetic, was quite a different man, short, fat, with a prominent nose and full face. He was by no means as popular as Howe.

Colonel Tarleton was below middle height, strong, extremely muscular, with very large, strong legs. He was dark, and his eyes were small, black, and noticeably piercing.

General Knyphausen, commander of the Hessians, was slender and straight and not very tall, but extremely martial in his appearance. On the streets he was constantly bowing to all respectable-looking citizens. The lady at whose house he was quartered said he spread butter on his bread with his thumb. She was shocked. Otherwise, he was such a polite man.

Some of the younger British officers became restless as the winter passed, despite the gaiety surrounding them. This advertisement appeared in one of the local papers:

Wanted to hire with two single gentlemen, a YOUNG WOMAN to act in capacity of housekeeper, and who can occasionally put her hand to ANYTHING. EXTRAVAGANT wages will be given, and NO CHARACTER required. Any young woman who chooses to offer, may be further informed at the bar of the City Tavern.

CHAPTER XXII

The Business of the World

"We have it in our power to begin the world all over again? A situation similar to the present has not happened since the days of Noah, till now. The birthday of a new world is at hand, and a race of men perhaps as numerous as all Europe contains are to receive their portion of freedom from the events of a few months. The reflection is awful and in this point of view how trifling, how ridiculous, do the little paltry cavillings of a few weak or interested men appear weighed against the business of the world?"

THOMAS PAINE.

THE MESCHIANZA WHICH, incidentally, means medley, and which was given on May 18, 1778, by the junior officers of the British army in occupation in Philadelphia, led by Major André, in honour of General Howe, who was relinquishing his command to Sir Henry Clinton and sailing back to England, was one of the most gorgeous parties ever given in the history of the world, and certainly the most gorgeous ever given in Philadelphia. In its extravagance it equalled the Field of the Cloth of Gold at which Henry VIII of England, Charles V of the Holy Roman Empire, and Francis I of France, wasted their own and their people's money. It is said that the silks alone of the *meschianza* cost £50,000, or $250,000, which you can at least triple according to the values of those days. The expenses were taken care of by the same junior officers, most of them rich young men.

The occasion failed of its purpose, as most extravagance does. Naturally it displeased Sir Henry Clinton, who had arrived a couple of weeks before, and back in England it did General Howe no good, for the English Government looked upon the fête as a rebuke for relieving the genial Howe, who, as a matter of fact, was only too delighted to be relieved. He had never liked the war against the Americans.

John André, prime mover, has left a detailed description of the gorgeous and absurd party. It took place, as has been said, at Walnut Grove, the fine country seat of the Wharton family, and if there were any Quaker ghosts about they must have been mightily surprised. The festivities lasted all of one day and until four o'clock the next morning. As the "queens" and other belles of the party—all Philadelphians save a Miss Auchmuty, who was British—were being escorted home by their scarlet-clothed beaux in the May dawn, they heard sounds of firing from the outskirts of the city. The young Englishmen assured the frightened girls the noise was merely concluding salutes in their honour; but to the contrary, it was Captain Allan McLane, devil-may-care, and rich young Philadelphian, and his hard-riding dragoons, who, like will-o'-the-wisps, and with an excellent sense of humour, had attacked the British outposts, strewing time-bombs made of iron pots filled with gunpowder along the breastworks as they galloped past.

Allan McLane, at the time just past thirty-two, is one of the most engaging and forgotten of Philadelphia heroes. A fox-hunter himself, he led the English fox-hunters many a chase, again and again fighting his way out of ambushes, or else laying them. One time, naked and badly wounded, he stood hidden in an ice-cold pool until his wounds were staunched. Left a fortune of £15,000 to begin with—and it was a fortune in those days—upon the outbreak of the Revolution he presented every cent of it to his government. It is nice to know that this young cavalryman lived to be eighty-three years old and led a distinguished and satisfactory life, leaving sons and grandsons and great-grandsons as distinguished as himself scattered all over the country, but principally around Baltimore. One of the grandsons was governor of Maryland.

As Allan McLane galloped in the grey of the dawn along the British lines, thrown into much confusion and panic, no doubt he was thinking of the dancing girls inside the city, with most of whom he had danced himself. Probably as he flung his time-bombs he was saying to himself, "That for you, Peggy Shippen! . . . And you, Jane Craig! . . . And you, Peggy Chew! And you, Becky Franks! . . ."

The *meschianza* began with a water pageant, all the generals—Admiral Lord Howe, General Sir William Howe, Sir Henry Clinton, Lord Rawdon, General Knyphausen, embarrassingly polite as usual—and their staffs, and their other officers, and the young women, and the older ladies, going up the river in decorated barges, with bands and flags, until they were opposite Walnut Grove, where they descended and walked up between rigid files of troops to the jousting field with its grandstands and marquees. The young ladies, those chosen by the fourteen knights who were to take part in the tournament, wore Turkish costumes, seven of them carrying on their turbans the ribbons—the favours—red and white, of the Knights of the Blended Rose; seven, the ribbons, yellow and black, of the Knights of the Burning Mountain.

All having seated themselves, there was a ruffle of drums and a flourish of trumpets, and out from one end of the jousting field galloped a herald and four trumpeters in the colours of the Knights of the Blended Rose, and reined their horses back on their haunches before the grandstand. Following these, one by one, gorgeous in silks and satins, came the Knights of the Blended Rose. First, Major Lord Cathcart, Chief of the Knights of the Blended Rose, superbly mounted on a *maneged* horse and attended by two black slaves dressed in sashes and drawers of blue-and-white silk, large silver claps around their necks and arms; the upper part of their bodies naked. The slaves held Lord Cathcart's stirrups, and on either side of the slaves, right and left, walked Lord Cathcart's esquires, Captain Hazard and Captain Brownlow, one bearing his lance, the other his shield. Major Cathcart's lady was Miss Auchmuty, and the device on his shield was a Cupid riding on a lion, with the motto, "Surmounted by Love".

Next came the Honourable Captain Cathcart, Lord Cathcart's brother; lady, Miss N. White; esquire, Captain Peters; device, a heart and sword; motto, "Love and Honour". And then Lieutenant Bygrove; lady, Miss Craig; esquire, Lieutenant Nichols; device, Cupid tracing a circle; motto, "Without End". Third knight, Captain André, not yet a major and to be hung two years later because of the treachery of the future husband of a girl, Peggy Shippen, sitting in the grandstand; lady, Miss P. Chew; esquire,

Lieutenant André; device, two gamecocks fighting; motto, "No Rival". Fourth knight, Captain Horneck; lady, Miss N. Redman; esquire, Lieutenant Talbot; device, a burning heart; motto, "Absence cannot Extinguish". Fifth knight, Captain Matthews; lady, Miss Bond, esquire, Lieutenant Hamilton; device, a winged heart; motto, "Each Fair by Turns". Sixth knight, Lieutenant Sloper; lady, Miss M. Shippen; esquire, Lieutenant Brown; device, a heart and sword; motto, "Honour and the Fair".[1]

Having encircled the tournament ground, saluting as they went the ladies of their choice, the Knights of the Blended Rose took their stand, each in a line with his lady, and the herald, stepping forward, made proclamation that in all the world there were no ladies so distinguished for "wit, beauty, and every other accomplishment" as the Ladies of the Blended Rose, and should anyone be so rash as to challenge this statement, the Knights of the Blended Rose would defend it with their lives. With this the trumpeters blew three blasts on their trumpets, and as the last notes died away, into the ring came galloping the herald of the Knights of the Burning Mountain with his four trumpeters. After him, one by one, led by their Chief of Knights, Captain Watson of the Guards, came the Knights of the Burning Mountain, each with his esquire and his device and his motto, and when they, too, had made the circle of the grandstands, their Chief threw down a gauntlet and the Chief of the Blended Rose picked it up.

The tournament was on. The knights fought with lances, harmlessly unseating each other; toward dusk, their two leaders engaged in a furious mock combat with swords, until finally the trumpets blew again, and the heralds stepped forward and proclaimed that honours were even and all were satisfied. With that the party went up in the blue dusk to the Wharton house, in whose windows candles were already beginning to shine like stars. And very magnificently had the stone house of Joseph Wharton been arranged, or disarranged, for the occasion: repainted, redecorated, a ballroom introduced into it. Everywhere were bars, upstairs and down, where one could get lemonade or tea, or harder liquids of all sorts. The "Holy Experiment" rocked and shivered in the silver mist from powdered wigs and was warm and sweet with the smell of rum. Joseph Wharton's house anticipated by a century and a quarter Philadelphia's famous Racquet Club which in the lush 1900's boasted that on every one of its numerous floors was an expert bartender with all the appurtenances. In one room of the Wharton house, called by Major André the "Pharaoh Room", were gaming devices of every description.

At ten the dancing stopped for the time being and on the lawn were fireworks: rockets and Roman candles and set pieces. And at midnight concealed double doors were flung open, and beyond was the dazzling supper room, two hundred and ten feet long by forty wide and twenty-two feet in height, candles, in crystal candelabra, reflected in fifty-six pier glasses extending from the ceiling to the floor. In addition to these and the ones in side brackets were three hundred wax tapers arranged on the supper table. Four hundred

---

[1] The Shippen family denied categorically that any of its members, including the beautiful Peggy, Arnold's future wife, attended the *meschianza*. Dr. Edward Shippen was a loyalist, but of such a mild and reasonable description that his attitude injured him very little either at the time, or later, in the estimation of his American friends.

and thirty covers were laid; twelve hundred dishes were served; twenty-four blackamoors in oriental costumes, and hung with silver chains, stood in double lines and bowed low as Admiral Howe and his brother, Sir William, led the procession—"all these forming together", as Major André writes, "the most brilliant assemblage of gay objects, and appearing at once as we entered by an easy descent, exhibited a *coup d'oeil* beyond description magnificent".

After supper the dancing was resumed and lasted until four o'clock.

Washington, a few miles north in the hills of Valley Forge, spring and warm weather come, his troops well disciplined by now and well fed, his army steadily growing, must have been very much amused. Already he knew, of course, every detail of the proposed *meschianza*, and there were plenty of guests, male and female, especially the young, who would speedily send him a further description of it.

Five weeks later General Sir Henry Clinton, realizing the untenability of his position in Philadelphia, abandoned it and set out, lock, stock, and barrel, for New York, three thousand loyalists, young and old, male and female, with all the baggage they dared take with them, along with him. They never saw Philadelphia again. At Monmouth Court House in New Jersey on June 28, Washington overtook Clinton, and would have defeated him had it not been for the dreadful heat and Charles Lee's treachery. Over a hundred men on both sides died from heat exhaustion. Lee disobeyed orders, and it was then that Washington showed his memorable command of profanity. He cursed Lee on the battlefield and broke him. But all that Congress did was to dismiss Lee from the American army for a year, although subsequently he was cashiered for good.

Back to Philadelphia came the Continentals, now the Americans, not so ragged as they had been. And back to Philadelphia came Congress from its game of hide-and-seek. And back came all the rest, including Christopher Marshall, who, the year before, had called Washington "a supine coward" and Howe "a savage monster".

For three more years the war dragged on, sweeping now into the Carolinas and the South. The Tories, the ones who hadn't left with Clinton, had an increasingly hard time of it in Philadelphia. Two, John Roberts and Abraham Carlisle, were hanged as traitors—which they were—upon the return of the American troops. Carlisle, a carpenter, had kept one of the city gates for the English; Roberts, a miller, had enlisted under Howe and had not had the good sense to leave with Clinton. The more orthodox Quakers, who seem to have been little troubled by the treatment of American prisoners during the British occupancy, were deeply shocked by this example of American brutality. The only shocking thing about it was that the two men selected were not prominent enough. Elizabeth Drinker, in her diary writes:

"*They have actually put to death, Hang'd on ye Commons, John Roberts and Abraham Carlisle, this morning. An awful day it has been.*"

Later on, but still in the middle of war, she complains of the servant problem. "Times are much changed," she says, "and Maids have become Mistresses."

But the interesting thing is that times do not change in many ways, nor people. The crop of those who put comfort, weighted, into the scales with flesh and blood and liberty is always perennial.

Philadelphia at the time produced as well its only Robin Hoods, the five Doan brothers, who, being Tory sympathizers, found themselves with their farms confiscated, and so took to the roads and pretty soon built up for themselves an undeserved romantic reputation. Like all Robin Hoods, they robbed only the rich and gave to the poor, and legend about them grew. They were very handsome, very bold, and very rollicking. Finally they were surrounded by troops led by a wearied sheriff, and two were shot, and one escaped, and the remaining two were hanged in Philadelphia. Many women wept, most of whom had never seen the Doans.

By now the town had settled down again, if you can call it settling down, to inflation, and the quarrelling of Congress, and to increasing war weariness. The Continental paper currency was worth practically nothing. A pair of boots cost $600; calico was worth $85 a yard; chintz, $150. Paid with this currency, the troops, too, were becoming sullen. Once more the Revolution was at a very low ebb. Washington was alarmed, and Rochambeau wrote to France, "Send us ships, troops, and money, but do not depend upon these people, nor their means."[1] Washington said that never had he seen the country in such a discontented state.

Moreover, at the very darkest period, Arnold had turned traitor, finally to flee to England. His wife begged the Executive Council to let her remain in Philadelphia with her father, but this privilege was denied her, and she was ordered to leave in two weeks. Later, in London, Banastre Tarleton, now a baronet, called her "the handsomest woman in England". But that was hardly a compensation, flattering as it was, for a girl who loved her home.

There were, however, increasingly encouraging signs, although only the far-visioned noticed them.

On August 25, 1780, the Chevalier de Luzerne gave a great banquet for the members of Congress and numerous prominent citizens in honour of the birthday of the French King.[2] D'Estaing and his fleet were in American waters. De Grasse and his fleet were sailing from Toulon. With 1781, the defeats in the South began to turn into American victories, and in September of that year the French army under Count Rochambeau, beautifully equipped, colourful, and gay, passed through Philadelphia headed for victory. Some of the most famous regiments of France paraded in Philadelphia that day, including the De Soissonnais—white and rose-coloured plumes, rose-coloured facings with white uniforms—the names of many of whose officers and men were within a few weeks to be subjects for future

[1] One hundred and forty years later an American Expeditionary Force was to know and say the same of the French, and as in the Revolution, help came just in time, but the other way about.

[2] The Chevalier de Luzerne, first French minister to the United States, not to be outdone by the British, on May 15, 1781, gave Philadelphia its second most gorgeous party; most gorgeous, at least, until the fabulous 1900's and the debutante balls, given by Philadelphia millionaires in honour of the coming-out of their daughters. Chevalier de Luzerne's entertainment was only slightly less sumptuous than the *Meschianza* and celebrated the birth of the Dauphin who, by an early date, missed the fate of his young brother, the martyr of the Temple. Fifteen hundred guests were asked; in the garden of the minister's house a pavilion was erected, and the garden was brilliantly illuminated. Within the house a ballroom had been constructed, and that in six weeks, and this, like the dining-room of the *Meschianza*, was lit by hundreds of tapers. In the ballroom four statues stood in niches: Flora, garlanded with roses; Diana, hurling her spear; Hebe, holding Jove's cup; and Mars, leaning on his shield, upon which was painted the cipher of General Washington.

memorial tablets at Williamsburg. Uniforms and munitions and food were also by now going forward to the American troops. It was a well-equipped American army to whom the British surrendered. Meanwhile the Bank of North America, organized upon the plans laid down by Washington, had been chartered and had begun to restore credit and commerce.

Cornwallis allowed himself to be trapped in Yorktown. De Grasse and his fleet came up Chesapeake Bay and cut him off from the sea. Washington and his armies closed in by land like a band of steel. The fox-hunter from Virginia knew a "kill" when he saw one. On October 19, 1781, Cornwallis gave up his sword. That night he and his staff dined with Washington and his staff.

In some ways the wars of the eighteenth century were fairly decent.

And here is one of the most ancient of Philadelphia stories, told to all Philadelphia children:

Five days later, in the middle of the night, an express rider galloped into Philadelphia with the news, and a "Pennsylvania Dutch" watchman, going his round, announced tranquilly:

"Dree o'clogk! All's vell. Und Cornvallis iss tagen!"

Some awakened; the majority slept; and the next day all were patriots, and all had predicted that in the long run America was unconquerable.

CHAPTER XXIII

Republican Court

"Sir: With a mixture of great surprise & astonishment I have read with attention the Sentiments you have submitted to my perusal. Be assured, Sir, no occurrence in the course of the War, has given me more painful sensations than your information of there being such ideas existing in the Army as you have expressed. . . . Let me conjure you then, if you have any regard for your Country—concern for yourself or posterity—or respect for me, to banish these thoughts from your mind & never communicate, as from yourself, or anyone else, a sentiment of the like nature.

With esteem, I am Sir, Yr. Most Obed. Ser.

G. Washington.

PART OF A LETTER WRITTEN BY GENERAL WASHINGTON IN 1782 TO COLONEL NICHOLA, WHO, AT THE HEAD OF A CABAL OF ARMY OFFICERS, HAD OFFERED WASHINGTON THE CROWN OF THE UNITED STATES.

THE EIGHT YEARS between the surrender at Yorktown—formal peace was not made until the Treaty of Paris in 1783—and the signing of the Constitution on the 17th of September, 1789, have been called by certain historians

the "Lost Decade"; lost because they were years of so much confusion and
doubt, and lost because most modern Americans have so little appreciation
of what they meant.   Most Americans, having a profound and unquestioning
respect for every act of the Founding Fathers, and, indeed, for most Americans
except their contemporaries take it for granted that a miracle was performed
by these supernatural men, and that the thirteen extremely various colonies,
each with a different history, a different settlement, and different traditions
a century and a half, or more, in the making, slipped automatically into a
workable Union.

America, that is, like the phœnix, arose full-winged and triumphant
from the ashes of the Revolution.

Nothing could have been further from the fact, and if Americans wish
to achieve both astonishment and infinite respect for their country they
should study well those eight years, more perhaps than any other period
of their nation's history, and then add to them the first years of Washington's
administration.   A miracle was accomplished, but it was no easy one.   Only
a handful of the Fathers—Hamilton, Washington, Adams, Franklin, and so
on—kept to the point, working unceasingly through thick and thin, and
often under the most discouraging circumstances.   Otherwise, you had
thirteen quarrelling and jealous sovereignties, the New Englanders hating
the southerners, the southerners despising the New Englanders, the Middle
States much more interested in recapturing commerce and sound currency
than anything else.   Every state had its own money and set up tariff walls
against the others.   Connecticut farmers coming into New York had to
pay customs.   Vermont and New York were close to a serious war.   The
Yankee-Pennamite disagreement was still vigorous.   It was calculated that
if a man left Georgia with fifty dollars in his pocket, by the time he reached
Boston it would be worth only ten, owing to the exchange.

The three most crucial periods in our history are (1) these eight years
following the Revolution—they were even more crucial than the Revolution
itself, for that would have happened again sooner or later, if at first defeated;
(2) the Civil War period; and (3) the present moment.   And in each you
witness a curious counter-tendency best explained by psychoanalysis.   In
each instance, when the test comes, certain Americans in too large minorities
show an inclination to slip back into the womb of European separatism,
suicidal local pride, and even tyranny if it promises a false security, and
yet all Americans came to America to find the gallant peril of liberty and
democracy.

One wonders again, as one must all through American history, that the
United States ever became a nation at all, and remained one, indivisible,
proud, tremendous, and common in speech.   And again one has a feeling
of fate, or predestination, that for a long while, at all events, has worked
well.   Only the will and the final conviction of the majority has saved the
unique experiment, and that the will of the majority in the long run has been
so wise is in itself a miracle.

But difficulties or not, the future trembling in the balance or not, the
"Lost Decade", as far as Philadelphia was concerned, and the years that
followed until 1800 were the most brilliant and important in the city's history.

All of America came to it at one time or another, and plenty of Europe. The main question troubling the minds of men, of course, was federal union, but along with this was a further question: the fact that America could not escape Europe, no matter how much it wished to do so, any more than any man, however remote, has ever been able to escape life and what happens to his fellow-men the wide world over. Should America look to England for permanent friendship or to France? The more conservative and, at the moment, more far-visioned, including Washington, and even, a good many years later, Jefferson, favoured the former attitude; the more radical, and the majority of the populace, especially after the French Revolution until its excesses sickened them, favoured the latter.

In 1789 Washington was unanimously elected President and was inaugurated in New York, and presently the Administration moved to Philadelphia, largely owing to the efforts of Robert Morris. Washington occupied the Morris mansion at Sixth and Market streets, of which he had written, "It is, I believe, the best single house in the city". And a very lovely place it must have been with its small-paned, white-shuttered windows, and its brick wall surrounding a garden and an orchard.[1] Here Washington and Mrs. Washington began their receptions and soirées which caused so much unfavourable comment from the more radical, but which were in reality so simple, so sensible, and such an excellent method of keeping in touch with the country. There have been many descriptions of these receptions.

The general held his audiences at three in the afternoon in the State dining-room, and his favourite costume was black satin smallclothes, a pearl-coloured waistcoat, and shoes with silver buckles. In his hand he carried gloves and a cocked hat, and at his side he wore a state sword with a white leather scabbard. The general, or rather, now, the President, stood at one end of the room and bowed gravely as each guest entered, and then, at a quarter-past three, the doors were closed to prevent lateness and straggling, and the President moved about the circle of gentlemen, conversing briefly with each one. This done, he returned to his original position, and the guests, bowing, took their departure.

The majority found these audiences slightly overpowering, and it is recorded that the President's State dinners were alarmingly solemn. Mrs.

[1] This Presidential Mansion, one of our earliest "White Houses", in fact the second, if you count as first the New York house Washington occupied when he was inaugurated, and surely one of the most historic buildings in America, was torn down in 1833 and replaced by stores. By that time it had fallen on evil ways and was first a cheap boarding-house and then a confectioner's shop with, above this, lodgings. The then owner of the property transferred numberous brass door-knobs, a fanlight, heavy locks, and various other furnishings to a house he was building for himself at the north-west corner of Twelfth and Walnut streets, and which, because it was then so far out from the residential quarter, and so far beyond where that quarter "would ever possibly go", was looked upon as a rich merchant's folly.

For over a hundred years this later house, with its brick-walled garden, one of the most beautiful examples of early-nineteenth-century Philadelphia architecture, stood untouched, despite the fact that business crept up to it, surrounded it, and passed it. Then it was torn down because of the mediæval tax laws of Philadelphia, one of the several causes of the depreciation of Philadelphia real estate, and the space it occupied is now Philadelphia's favourite "town residence", a parking lot.

Washington's brasses, etc., were removed by the owners to their present residence in Wissahickon, where they now are. It is interesting to touch door-knobs handled by Washington, Lafayette, Adams, Jefferson, Hamilton, and scores of others of the same kind.

Washington's receptions, given bi-weekly in an upstairs drawing-room, were much more amusing. Not only were all the pretty women of the town present, and not only were there food and drink, but the President, who usually came in late and informally without cocked hat or sword, moved among the guests not as head of the state but as an ordinary mortal.

The President also liked to stroll about his capital in his black velvet smallclothes, visiting the markets, and saluting the citizens, and chatting with them occasionally, and almost every noon he walked down to Front and Market streets to set his watch by a standard chronometer; but when he drove out in state, he drove in state, his vehicle a great cream-coloured French coach, globular in shape, ornamented with cupids and carven wreaths of flowers; his horses Viginia bays, his coachman, the converted Hessian, sitting up stiff as a ramrod. And all this is very interesting if you analyse it, and shows a definite intention on Washington's part. And it has to do with a particular stress and strain, a lesion, a misinterpretation on the part of less discerning democrats, which was to reach its apex with Andrew Jackson, and traces of which still survive, although it is becoming less noticeable as we become wiser and less provincial.

Too many ignorant democrats have taken the appearance for the fact, and have assumed that the essence of democracy was largely a matter of uncovered suspenders and bad manners; these, with a contempt for decorum and beauty in all their forms. And the demagogue, and those bent upon cold-blooded plunder, have played upon this theme throughout American history. Hence the most vicious of all phrases, "a regular fellow". To the contrary, Washington knew that democracy, or, to put it better, in his case, republicanism, was a far more severe self-discipline, and required a far more individual sense of fitness, than a formal aristocracy, or a monarchy, or a tyranny. Democracy, like Quakerism, is classic in its form, and the democrat who regards it as an excuse for ignorance and slipshod ways is like the Quaker who mistakes the disciplining of passion as an injunction aimed at its destruction, and not, as is actually intended, a channelling of passion toward great ends. Both democracy and Quakerism are sonnets.

Washington was not a gay man, and he was inclined to be a shy one, but we also know from plenty of testimony that, relaxed, he was a genial man, fond of laughter and informal entertainment; a warm man in many ways, and a kind one. Indeed, he was alarmed at his own delight in robust and earthy humour. He was at his best at Mount Vernon, and there are many charming stories about him down there. But he had a grave notion of the dignity of the office of president of what, all but fools knew, was to be a grave and great nation, and so it is obvious that with a good deal of thought and deliberation he set a standard and established a tradition.

Nations and men must to a certain extent live by symbols, and Washington was responsible for the two most important ones in American life: the American flag, and the dignity of the office of President of the United States as apart from the man occupying it. A few undignified men have been presidents, and that is serious enough, but if the office itself ever becomes undignified—and once or twice this has come perilously near to happening, and often in times of stress the unthinking try to make it happen—the results will be dire.

The beautiful and graceful Mrs. Bingham opened her salon in her town house modelled after Montagu House in London; the President and Mrs. Washington gave their receptions; many others followed Mrs. Bingham's lead, although in a lesser way. The fortunate habit of writing diaries and keeping letters continued, and so we have a clear picture of the Philadelphia of the last decades of the eighteenth century, both while the Washingtons were there and from 1797 on, when John Adams was the second president. The comments, naturally, vary; the majority of visitors found Philadelphia amusing, interesting, and gay; very much of a world capital. The majority of the Frenchmen in the city, young and mature, and they were the most numerous foreigners due to conditions in France, agreed with these favourable comments, although all did not, and even those who did showed the curious French tendency, existing even to-day, and beginning with the adoration of Franklin, to regard this country not only as a political experiment, but one also in which the Arcadian virtues are, or should be, practised. The results of this confusion are often amusing; the visiting Frenchman, while frequently trying personally to break down as much as possible whatever virtue he finds, and delighting in the luxury and gaiety he meets with, nonetheless deprecates, with a sad shake of his head, the absence of the "beautiful savagery" he traditionally anticipates.

Thus we find Brissot de Warville, to be guillotined with the other Girondins on October 31, 1793, despite his liking for Philadelphia, saddened by the love, even of the young Quaker maidens, for feminine finery. "These youthful creatures," he writes, "whom Nature has so well endowed, whose charms have so little need of art, wear the finest muslins and silks. Oriental luxury would not disdain the exquisite textures in which they take delight." And three gentlemen of greater fashion, the Comte de Rochambeau, the Duc le Lauzun, and the Marquis de Chastellux, although expressing equal admiration for Philadelphia girls and women, also feel it their duty to sigh over their fondness for Parisian fashions. The Abbé Robin, more blunt, says that in the absence of promenades and parks (what he means is the absence of the Latin custom of walking in them, for William Penn had provided for parks—five) the young Philadelphia women went to church more to display their finery than to pray.

Finally, the Duc de la Rochefoucauld-Liancourt says: "The young women of Philadelphia are accomplished in different degrees, but beauty is common to all. They lack the ease and grace of French women, but they are charming, and have singularly brilliant complexions. . . . Ribbons please the young Quakeresses as well as others, and are the great enemies of the sect."

Domestic comment was more understanding and naturally more enthusiastic. Miss Sally McKean, writing to a friend in New York, says of a Philadelphia party: "You never could have had such a drawing-room. It was brilliant beyond anything you can imagine. And though there was a great deal of extravagance, there was so much of Philadelphia taste in everything, that it must have been confessed the most delightful occasion of the kind ever known in this country."

Which must have pleased New York, smarting at the time from the loss of the national government.

Perhaps the most mature and intelligent critic was Mrs. John Adams. She found Philadelphia delightful and the women beautiful, "elegantly, if not superbly dressed", and remarked upon "the dazzling Mrs. Bingham, and her sisters, the Misses Allen, the Misses Chew, and a constellation of beauties", but she also says that she became a trifle tired of meeting everywhere the same people, a charge that can still be made. Her daughter writes that Boston women are better educated, but Philadelphia women more charming. Cities find their pattern early and do not change much.

The stricter Friends, of course, did not like this cosmopolitan atmosphere and proclaimed against it, and on one occasion a leader of the church even went so far as to refuse to enter the house of an acquaintance who had laid down a carpet in his hall.

Perhaps of all the residents of Philadelphia at the time, the most interesting in some ways were the French: first the emissaries, military or otherwise, of Louis XVI, such as the Chevalier de Luzerne; then the royalists, fleeing from the Terror; then a few of the republicans fleeing from the counter-revolution; and finally the Bonapartists. To these were added, around the turn of the century, the French colonials from Santo Domingo and the other West Indian islands, driven out by the slave insurrections. The last came with their servants and all the possessions they could save, and settled down definitely as Philadelphians, adding a further strand of colour to the texture of the city and also numerous new dishes to Philadelphia's bill of fare.

Several of the more famous Philadelphia caterers, until recently seen at most large Philadelphia entertainments, were descendants of these same West Indian cooks and major-domos, highly educated, delightful-looking light-skinned folk, with such names as Augustin or Baptiste, and so on, to whom are due the particular texture of Philadelphia chicken croquettes, the best in the world; the consistency, also individual, of such desserts as *meringue glacé*; the Philadelphia method of preparing terrapin, an altogether different method from the Baltimore one, and so the source of age-long controversy; and above all, unless most Philadelphians are mistaken, the discovery of ice-cream.

The last statement cannot be verified, and no proper research has ever been made, but it is fairly certain that cream was never added to the ices of the ancients until the West Indian cooks of Philadelphia thought up the novel enterprise. Water-ices, of course, are as old as history, but ice-cream, the American national dish, is fairly new, and paradoxically enough, since it is the national dessert, hardly anyone except Philadelphians know how to make it. The dreadful cotton-like substance sold throughout most of the country is an offence to the Philadelphia palate. It takes an American to make ice-cream, but it takes a Philadelphian to know whether it is good or not.

Talleyrand was in Philadelphia, Chateaubriand, the Viscount de Noailles, Lameth, Talon, Volney, Louis Philippe, in addition to their countrymen already mentioned, and many others less distinguished. Indeed, the section of the city down near the Delaware, around Third and Fourth and Walnut streets, became almost a French quarter, and it is not uninteresting that the Philadelphians, meeting and watching them, were astonished that these visitors, each fleeing from some deadly danger, could break up into so many different circles and quarrel so much amongst themselves. The French had their own clubs and cafés, and the more liberal used as their headquarters —Talleyrand and so on—Moreau de St. Mèry's bookshop at the corner of Front and Walnut. Here they frequently gathered for supper, often a frugal but dreadful one of rice, milk, and Madeira, which Talleyrand especially liked, and then would sit up into the small hours discussing France, until Madame de St. Mééry intervened.[1]

Most of the visitors were homesick, of course, as most *émigrés* are, especially Frenchmen. Some didn't like Philadelphia at all, and agreed with the Chevalier de Beaujour, who a few years earlier had found Philadelphia insufferably dull, "cut, like a chess-board, at right-angles." "All the streets and houses resemble each other," he wrote mournfully, "and nothing is so gloomy as this uniformity, unless it be the sadness of the inhabitants, the greater part of whom are of Quaker or Puritan descent."

So, as usual, you have your pick and can take your choice.

Upon one thing alone the Frenchmen seemed to agree, and that was the coldness of the Philadelphia girls and matrons despite their beauty. They resented this. The "beautiful savages" retained a virtue, at least where these visitors were concerned, true to their imagined Arcadian state, but nonetheless annoying.

Philadelphia retorted to this criticism angrily and did not altogether agree with the foreign summation concerning coldness. "These *coureurs des dames*," writes an observer bitterly, "ogling and sighing like a furnace, bowing *à la distance*, dangling in doorways by day, and chanting *dans votre lit* by night, under the windows of our fair ones, bewildered by the novel and delightful incense of flattery, so unusual and offered so romantically by young gentlemen elegant and debonair!"

The use of the adjective "unusual" after "flattery" indicated that the Philadelphia swains had something to learn.

Meanwhile, two events of infinite importance had happened, although none, not even the principals, realized their full import at the time. Poor John Fitch had begun his experiments with steam locomotion, and on July 27, 1786, Philadelphians along the Delaware water-front were astonished to see a boat, belching smoke, propelling itself by mechanical oars. In 1787 Fitch demonstrated this boat before the members of the Federal Constitutional Convention, and three years later, in 1790, with an improved model, a paddle-wheel steamer, began a regular service, advertised in the Philadelphia papers, between Arch Street Wharf and Bristol, Burlington, and Trenton, up the river.

As has been said, no one was deeply interested, and the majority thought Fitch a drunken crackpot, and the President didn't even go down to look.

[1] Talleyrand shocked Philadelphia by his volubility and dreadful table manners. Apparently he was able to accomplish a dexterous and almost impossible feat, the piling up of the back of a fork with food, the putting of it into his mouth, and then the slow withdrawal of it empty be tween partially closed teeth, this with a sucking noise. And all the while he talked. Try it!

After all, John Fitch's steamboats did have a disconcerting habit of blowing up at intervals.

But on the other hand everyone was deeply interested in the already proven fact that a bag filled with hydrogen gas could fly, and so on January 9, 1793, in the yard of the old Walnut Street Prison, on the south-east corner of Sixth and Walnut streets, a great assemblage, including the President, witnessed, from "America's first airfield", America's first balloon ascension and "America's first air mail". The balloon was piloted by Jean Pierre Blanchard, the famous French balloonist, and he carried a letter of introduction from President Washington to all whom he might come across or fall upon.

Blanchard ascended to an altitude of 5,813 feet and drifted fifteen miles across country, and accomplished all this in forty-six minutes.

Here then, within the space of seven years, and all taking place in Philadelphia, had occurred three determining events without which America, with its huge spaces, could never have gone forward; at least, in the shape we know: federal union, the application of steam to transportation, and experiment in flight.

Within four decades Philadelphia, challenged and surpassed by New York as a port, was to turn its eyes steadfastly toward the interior of the country; was to become more and more of an inland city and less and less of a coastal one. Almost with the turn of the century this interest in land transportation had begun to accelerate, abetted by Oliver Evans' declaration in 1773 that he could, and would, apply his steam engine "to propel carriages" overland and by the demonstration, in 1805, of his *Eruktor Amphibolis*, which proved him right. In 1809 the first railroad in America was built, a model one, and not a steam one, by Thomas Leiper in the Bull's Head Tavern yard, Third Street above Callowhill, in the Northern Liberties. This consisted of a track sixty-three feet in length. The rails were oaken scantlings laid four feet apart, and along these a carriage was drawn by a horse. A Scotch engineer, Somerville, built the track, modelled upon a similar one he had seen in England, and shortly afterwards a wooden railway was constructed at the Leiper quarries at Crum Creek to haul the rock a quarter of a mile to the landing at Ridley Creek, Delaware.

From this it was just another step to the steam railway, and in 1822 John Stevens, the great New Jersey engineer, after whom Stevens Point and its technicological school are named, presented a petition to the General Assembly of Pennsylvania, asking for a charter for himself and his associates to build, according to a new invention he had perfected, a railroad from Philadelphia to Columbia in Lancaster County. In 1823 an Act was passed incorporating this association as "The President, Directors, and Company of the Pennsylvania Railroad Company", and by 1833 the railroad was completed. The 1830's saw railroads being built in all directions, although for a while it was debated whether canals were not more efficient and less expensive.

Along with this began in 1830 what in some ways is Philadelphia's most famous business, the building of locomotives. For over a hundred years now Philadelphia locomotives have stuck their headlights into every quarter of the globe and have been discussed in practically every human tongue.

Matthias W. Baldwin, born in 1795 in Elizabethtown, New Jersey, jeweller, silversmith, inventor, and stationary engineer, had been building stationary engines in a little shop on Minor Street in Philadelphia, and in 1830 the Philadelphia, Germantown and Norristown Railroad, incorporated, but not in operation until June 6, 1832, commissioned Baldwin to build a locomotive more or less along the design of an English locomotive imported for the Camden and Amboy Railroad, which was put into use in 1833. Baldwin took this English model and adjusted it to what he thought were American needs, and the result was "Old Ironsides", ancestor of all American locomotives. Baldwin's little shop within thirty years grew into the immense Baldwin Locomotive Works, which for many years covered block after block on North Broad Street and which has now moved to even more spacious quarters at Essington, just down the Delaware.

Robert Wharton and others bewailed the dwindling traffic on the river, but Simon Snyder, who had been governor of the commonwealth in 1808, with the Philadelphia and Pennsylvania custom of accepting things without too much struggle, made a virtue of necessity and congratulated the state and city for abandoning the sea for the interior. "It is a cause of much satisfaction," he said, "that in proportion to the difficulty of access to foreign nations is the zeal and exertion to supply our own wants by home manufactures."

But the point is that Philadelphia could have had its railroads and also retained its outstanding harbour had it exerted itself.

Men invent and govern, and make laws and machines, and fight wars, and all the while, a fairly separate thing, their private lives go on, largely adventitious and filled with chance, good or bad. And it is a question if the world as a whole is not always much more interested in this than anything else. And this is paradoxical and fairly tragic, because personal relationships, especially between men and women, are about the only things which cannot be amended, experimented with, or to any great extent improved. They lie outside the realms of mathematics or logical procedure and are not subject to invention, although they fall into a myriad of patterns. All these myriad patterns, however, have been known for countless generations.

Philadelphia in the last decades of the eighteenth century, while it was still a teeming state and national capital, and in the first decades of the nineteenth century, when it had settled down, perhaps with a sigh of relief, to its present rôle of a great commercial and provincial city, although with a difference, as will be pointed out later, was the scene of four historic American romances. One wistful and restrained, aromatic and poignant, like pot-pourri. Two fairly sordid. And one, to say the least, violent and dramatic.

The first was the tragic love affair of lovely Mary Vining of Delaware; everyone agreed on that adjective, foreigners as well as Americans, and Anthony Wayne. The second—it was more of an escapade than anything else—was the love affair, if you can call it that, between a somewhat mysterious Mrs. Reynolds and Alexander Hamilton, first Secretary of the Treasury.

The third was an even more mysterious affair, if it happened at all, between Aaron Burr, Vice-President of the United States during Jefferson's first term, a man then in his forties, and one of the comely Misses Hassel, daughters of the proprietor of the Half Moon Tavern, opposite the State House in Philadelphia, a girl of sixteen or seventeen. While the fourth, which did not emerge into the public eye until 1816, and which included a murder and the hanging of a young lieutenant of the United States Army, was the celebrated case of the "beauteous", as she is always called, and well-born Mrs. Ann Carson.

The first is mentioned discreetly in every polite Philadelphia history. The second is hardly ever mentioned, although it almost ruined Hamilton politically and probably prevented him from running for the presidency, and came very near, as well, to damaging seriously the position of Secretary of the Treasury, and Hamilton's behaviour was certainly as dramatic and courageous as could be desired. The third is treated as if it never happened, which perhaps it didn't, although even if it didn't, what did happen is interesting enough. And the fourth is usually relegated to the proportions of a night-court case, which it was not at all. Ann Carson, born Ann Baker, although one with justice could call her wayward, was not a waterside trollop. She was a well-brought-up young woman, daughter of an officer in the United States Navy, and her case was a *cause célèbre*. In Paris she would have been a heroine; in Vienna, a secret toast. As for Philadelphia, it regretted her behaviour and was puzzled, as it has been again and again in its history, that any Philadelphia girl could behave in such a fashion.

Philadelphia has never yet admitted the obvious fact that a woman is a woman first and then a Philadelphian, and not the other way about.

CHAPTER XXIV

Yellow Visitor

"I ascribe my freedom from fatigue and my sleepless nights wholly to the stimulus of the contagion [of yellow fever] in my system, for I am so full of it that it has now become part of myself. It is not dangerous unless excited into action by heat, cold, fatigue, or high living."

DR. BENJAMIN RUSH.

MARY VINING, COUSIN of General Cæsar Rodney, vivacious, and speaking French so well that even the French admitted it, was in Philadelphia as much as in Wilmington; at Mrs. Bingham's balls and receptions, at the McKeans', at all the other festivities of the infant capital. Young Louis Philippe, later on to be Louis XVIII, who had fled from the Terror, to be

Residence of John K. Kane (Kennedy)

The Old London Coffee House, 1859 (Kennedy)

joined in Philadelphia in 1797 by his brothers the Duc de Montpensier and the Comte de Beaujolais, was one of the many foreigners and Americans attentive to her, and all agreed that of the numerous lovely women in the city she was the loveliest. The gayest, the wittiest, and the most beautiful.

Lafayette had adored her; the young British officers during the British occupation. Francisco Miranda, the great Venezuelan, then in exile, added a South American note to the circle of her admirers. But although she would flirt and dance and talk, she would go no further. For twenty years she had been in love with Anthony Wayne, and he with her. She had met him first when he was a man in his early thirties, shortly before the taking of Stony Point, where, leading his troops at midnight over the walls of the British fort, he had earned, because of his reckless gallantry, the nickname of "Mad". But Wayne, unfortunately, had an invalid wife, two children, and an aged mother whom he had to support, and in those days one did not get a divorce. So the hopeless love affair dragged on, known only to a few.

The Revolution ended, and in 1792 Wayne, raised to the rank of major-general, was sent by Washington to succeed General St. Clair in command of the army fighting the Indians in Ohio and Kentucky. There, in July of 1794, he won his great victory of Fallen Timbers which opened what was then the North-west to settlement. Meanwhile the bedridden Mrs. Wayne had died, and Wayne, forty-nine, and Mary Viving, thirty-seven, announced their engagement. Wayne in the spring of 1796 came back on leave, and it was arranged that at the following Christmas he and Mary Vining should be married. They were rapturously happy, as all their friends noted.

Wayne went back to the frontier. The year drew to its close, and Wayne started back to Philadelphia. But he never reached there. On December 15, 1796, he died *en route* at Erie, Pennsylvania, from what we now know was appendicitis, but what the attending surgeons thought was gout. Word of this came to Mary Vining just as she was sending out invitations for a welcoming dinner.

Mary Vining lived for twenty-five years longer, and in all that while only left her house at Wilmington three times. The tall, grey-haired, hardly ever seen woman became a tradition. On Good Friday, 1821, she died.

Mrs. Reynolds was a different sort of person, and she nearly got the United States Government into a lot of trouble. Whether, to begin with, she was a blackmailer or not is a question, but before she ended she was playing, in conspiracy with her husband, James W., a wretched person, what is now known as "the badger game", and her victim was our first Secretary of the Treasury. That small, handsome and brilliant man, however, was known to have very much of a roving eye, despite his affection for his wife Elizabeth, daughter of General Philip Schuyler of New York, so Mrs. Reynolds experienced little difficulty slipping into her rôle. Hamilton describes his first meeting with her as follows:

Some time in the summer of the year 1791 a woman called at my house in the city of Philadelphia and asked to speak with me in private. I attended her to

I

*a room apart from the family. With a seeming air of affliction she informed
that she was a daughter of a Mr. Lewis, a sister to a Mr. G. Livingston of the
State of New York, and a wife to a Mr. Reynolds whose father was in the Com-
missionary Department during the war with Great Britain, that her husband,
who for long had treated her very cruelly, had lately left her, to live with another
woman, and in so destitute a condition, that though desirous of returning to her
friends she had not the means—that knowing I was a citizen of New-York, she
had taken the liberty to apply to my humanity for assistance.*

*I replied, that her situation was a very interesting one—that I was disposed
to afford her assistance to convey her to her friends, but this at the moment not
being convenient to me (which was the fact) I must request the place of her residence,
to which I would bring or send a small supply of money. She told me the street
and the number of the house where she lodged. In the evening I put a bank-bill
in my pocket and went to the house. I inquired for Mrs. Reynolds and was
shewn up stairs, at the head of which she met me and conducted me into a bedroom.
I took the bill out of my pocket and gave it to her. Some conversation ensued
from which it was quickly apparent that other than pecuniary consolation would
be acceptable.*

*After this, I had frequent meetings with her, most of them at my own house;
Mrs. Hamilton with her children being absent on a visit to her father. . . .*

And so on, and very much so. And then James Reynolds reappeared.

James Reynolds, it seemed, to judge from a letter of his wife's and one
of his own, had had a reconciliation with his wife, and loved her dearly,
but to the exquisite agony of his mind, all of this expressed in the worst
possible spelling, he had learned of her liasion and she had confessed it.   What
was the Secretary of the Treasury going to do?   With that, the blackmailing,
mostly for small sums, but persistent, began, and Hamilton, alarmed about
his wife and his official position, foolishly submitted. He was wise enough,
however, to keep all the correspondence he received, although he bade Mrs.
Reynolds destroy his letters to her, which she did.   Because of her obedience
in this respect, if nothing else, it is possible to surmise that Mrs. Reynolds
was more a tool of her husband than, at least to start with, a deliberate
conspirator, and that for a while she had entertained what the eighteenth
century would call a "lively passion" for the victim. But before long it
began to be a cat-and-mouse business, with Hamilton striving desperately
to disentangle himself from the sordid affair and Mrs. Reynolds bringing
him back with pitiful protestations of love and, as Hamilton admitted,
although delicately, through his own desire for her charms. Meanwhile
James Reynolds' imagination grew by leaps and bounds. First he asked
Hamilton for a position with the Government, which was refused. Then,
having been flung into prison for debt, he demanded that Hamilton get
him out. And finally, together with a couple of other conspirators whom
he had picked up, after having asked Hamilton for a large sum to invest in
the bonds of the new Lancaster toll road, a request Hamilton naturally denied,
he began to threaten Hamilton, claiming that the moneys Hamilton had
given him, and of which Reynolds, careful as Hamilton in this respect, had
documentary proof, had been taken from the United States Treasury. Reynolds

also let it be known in various quarters that he had Hamilton entirely in his power and could ruin him if he so wished.

The charges, of course, were absurd, as Hamilton pointed out in his lucid and detailed defence, published six years later, in 1797, as one of his collected papers under the title, *Observations on Certain Documents, Contained in No. V & VI of "The History of the United States for the year* 1796*", in which the Charge of Speculation against Alexander Hamilton, late Secretary of the Treasury, is Fully Refuted. Written by himself. Philadelphia. Printed for John Fenno, by John Bioren.* 1797.

As Hamilton says, the charges need no further contradiction than the size of the sums involved. A Secretary of the Treasury, were he to go in for private peculation and speculation, would certainly not risk disgrace for ten dollars here and fifty there. But Hamilton had many political enemies, especially in the opposing Democratic, or as it was then called, Republican, party—"THE FACTION . . . the Jacobins . . . the Jacobin Scandal-Club" as he calls them, not too tactfully, because of their leaning toward France. And this party had many powerful men in its ranks, including Thomas Jefferson and one who turned out to be Hamilton's most mortal enemy, James Monroe. Nor does what happened redound much to Monroe's credit. He seems to have been inclined to use a pretty poor handle with which to assail a political enemy. The rumours grew, as rumours do, and pretty soon it was believed, by those who wished to do so, that Hamilton had taken large sums from the treasury for his own purposes. Hamilton decided to meet this gossip head on, and so he asked three members of Congress to confer with him, F. A. Muhlenberg, James Monroe, and A. Venable —also present was Oliver Wolcott —and laid the whole matter before them. These men agreed that Hamilton was entirely innocent. But Monroe and others were not willing, apparently, to let the matter drop, and the scandal kept cropping up, especially when there was a hint that Hamilton might run for president after Washington's retirement. Hamilton found himself confronted with a dilemma.

Either he could lay before the world, including his wife and family, the full details of his sordid romance, and so exonerate his party and his former office, or else he could save himself personally, but damage his party and cast suspicion upon the Treasury Department of the United States and the administration of his beloved leader, George Washington. He made a wise and courageous choice. He published every detail of his intimacy with Mrs. Reynolds and let the world make of it what it would. And incidentally, from this revelation, one discovers that he and Monroe came very close to fighting a duel which might have deprived the country of its fifth president. American duels have always been extremely mortal affairs, as Hamilton discovered himself a few years later.

Meanwhile the Reynoldses, husband and wife, had disappeared, and no *bona fide* reports of them have ever been found, although there were many rumours that they had been seen in various parts of the country.

This confession of Hamilton's is one of the most dramatic episodes in American history, and certainly one of the most dramatic in the history of Philadelphia, and it is extraordinary that it is so little mentioned. In all ways but one, and that a very human one, it redounds to Hamilton's credit. Several years ago George Arliss took the part of Hamilton in a motion picture that had the story as its theme.

It is impossible to proceed without quoting a letter of Mrs. Reynolds, Mary, although she signs it in several ways, including "Mari", and one from her husband, not only for their extraordinary spelling, but for the glimpses of character revealed. Mrs. Reynolds' letter, moreover, is an interesting example of the curious formality of most eighteenth-century love-letters.

Here is Mrs. Reynolds. Her entire lack of punctuation would please Bernard Shaw:

Dear Sir

I once take up the pen to solicit The Favor of seeing again oh Col hamilton what have I done that you should thus Neglect me Is it because I am unhappy But stop I will not say you have for perhaps you have caled and have found no opportunity to Come In at least I hope you have I am now A lone and shall be for a few days I believe till Wensday though I am not sartain and would wish to see you this Evening If poseble If not as soon as you can make It Convenient Oh my deer freend how shall I plede Enough what shal I say Let me beg of you to Come and If you never se me again oh if you think It best I will submit to It and take a long and last adieu

Mari

Col hamilton

For heaven sake keep me not In suspince Let me know your Intention Either by Line or Catline

And here is James Reynolds:

Sir

I am sorry I am in this disagreeable sutivation which Obliges me to trouble you So offen as I do, but I hope it wont be long before it will be in my power to discharge what I am indebted to you Nothing will give me greater pleasure I must Sir ask the loan of thirty dollars more from you, which I shall esteem as a particular favor. and you may Rest ashured that I will pay you with Strickest Justice. for the Reliefe you have aforded me, the Inclosed is the Receipt for the thirty dollars. I shall wate at your Office. Sir for an answer I am sir your very Humble Servant.

Miss Hassel is mysterious, and will remain mysterious. Discreet historians have abandoned her in despair on the principle that if you ignore something it won't bite you.[1]

[1] Before his duel with Hamilton, Aaron Burr wrote a long letter of instructions to his son-in-law in case he was killed. It contained this cryptic clause: "If you can pardon or indulge a folly, I would suggest that Madame . . . too well known under the name of Lenora, has claims on my recollection. She is now with her husband at St. Jago de Cuba."
This letter was written in 1804. Whether the woman referred to is Miss Hassel is not known, but it looks very much as if she was.

Undoubtedly there was a young lady of that name, the youngest of several beautiful sisters, and undoubtedly these sisters were the daughters of the proprietor of the well-known tavern on Chestnut Street, directly opposite Independence Hall, much frequented by members of the Government while Philadelphia was the national capital. Also it is true that Miss Hassel went to the West Indies—to Haiti—to visit her sister Clara, who had married a young French Creole planter named St. Louis, and was then caught in the siege of Cap Haitien by the black insurrectionists under Henri Christophe and Dessalines, Toussaint L'Ouverture having been kidnapped by Napoleon in the most dastardly fashion and taken to France, where he died. But whether Miss Hassel ever actually had an affair with Aaron Burr, soon to be Jefferson's Vice-President, and at the turn of the century a man of forty-four and she a girl of sixteen or seventeen, is not definitely known. Nor has it even been proven that she was the real author of the small volume, a collection of letters from Haiti, which appeared in 1807 and created a pleasant aroma of scandal for a while in Philadelphia and elsewhere. There is certain interior evidence which would prove that these letters were at least doctored, and amended, or deleted, by a professional hand, and by someone with a keen perception of possible gossip sale. The name of this slim volume, now fairly difficult to obtain, is: *Secret History; or, The Horrors of St. Domingo; in A Series of Letters, written by a Lady at Cape Francois to Colonel Burr, late Vice-President of the United States. Principally During the Command of General Rochambeau. Philadelphia. Published by Bradford & Inskeep. B. Carr. Printer.* 1808. And the preface, dated Philadelphia, November 30, 1807, reads, and nowhere does Miss Hassel's name appear: "Should a less partial public give them (these) a favourable reception, and allow them to possess some merit, it would encourage me to endeavour to obtain further approbation by a little work already planned and in some forwardness." This sequel was not forthcoming. In one of the volumes preserved in Philadelphia is the note on the fly-leaf in faded ink: "The Library Company of Philadelphia, purchased from James Cox, artist, of the City of Philadelphia. This book was written by Miss Hassel. Her father kept the Sign of Ye Half Moon opposite ye State House. She had a sister who married one of ye Indian's on a visit here in 1791. She went with them, but I believe was never heard from after." This would set Miss Hassel's visit to her sister at least ten years before it could have happened, and does not explain the date of the preface written in Philadelphia.

Valid or not, however, the little book is an amazing and valuable historical document if for no other reason than its disclosal of the persistent human inability, especially among the young and frivolous, or the old and obstinate, to realize the terror of gravity of any given situation. The French troops, twenty thousand of Napoleon's picked Rhenish veterans, together with half of his famous Polish Legion, were trapped in the tiny Haitian town with no escape except by sea. Yellow fever was rampant, and half the army died, including their leader, General Le Clere, Napoleon's brother-in-law, whom rumour said Napoleon had sent to Haiti hoping he would die or be killed because he was not considered of sufficient rank to remain the husband of Pauline Bonaparte. Every night young officers and soldiers were picked off in the tropic blackness on the outskirts of the town by lurking insurgents, yet the writer of the letters was interested solely in the miniature court the foolish and beautiful Pauline Bonaparte had set up (Pauline was the Bonaparte sister who loved to be painted in the nude); the dances and other gaieties; the various scandals, including General Rochambeau's attentions to the writer's sister which nearly resulted in a duel with her sister's husband, St. Louis. These, and in the smallest kind of small-talk. It did not seem to disturb Miss Hassel in the least that one night she would dance with a young officer only to discover that a few hours later he had been killed. The only thing that troubled her was the infrequency of Colonel Burr's letters, for which she upbraided him tenderly.

Both the Hamilton episode and the possible Burr episode express the difference between the attitudes of a hundred and fifty years ago and the present where it is a question of the private lives of public men. We are no better, but—less formal in outer manners—we are more discreet in private ones. Miss Hassel's letters if written to any recent Vice-President would certainly have caused considerable excitement.

The Victorian Period did not begin until the 1830's and the death of George IV in England. Thackeray said there were no ladies or gentlemen before that.

There is a nice Princeton story about Burr, and Princeton is near Philadelphia, and the university is almost a second Philadelphia institution. Burr, a Princeton graduate, lived to be an old man, eighty years old, and the last twenty of these, this gay and beautiful and brilliant creature lived in almost total seclusion in New York, discredited, penniless, broken. The story goes that on a cold, rainy day in early September 1836, an old, small gentleman descended from the New York coach at Princeton and walked to the Princeton graveyard, known as the Presidents' Graveyard because so many Princeton presidents are buried there. For a long while—a full couple of hours—he stood, the old gentleman, bareheaded and in his long black cloak, in the pouring rain, looking down at the grave of his father, the Rev. Aaron Burr, second president of the College of New Jersey. Then he went back to New York.

A few days later, word came that Aaron Burr was dead.

There is also a delightful, and not untypical, further story about Haiti and Philadelphia.

Henri Christophe, you remember, made himself emperor of northern Haiti, Dessalines being the president of the so-called republic to the south. Henri Christophe built the fantastic palace of Sans Souci in imitation of Versailles, and high above it, on the great crags overlooking miles of tropical forests and valleys, one of the wonders of the world, the extraordinary citadel, La Ferrière. As emperor, Henri Christophe wanted a couple of English-speaking governesses for his children, so he went to Philadelphia. Two sisters, mature ladies, arrived and stayed five years. Their only comment afterwards was that Henri Christophe and his court, the Duc de Limonade, the Duc de Appolonairis, and so on, were "very uninteresting compared to Philadelphia".

And now, finally, for the story of the "beauteous" Mrs. Carson, whose collateral relatives are today numerous and prominent. This is merely a straightforward story of a handsome two-fisted Philadelphia girl and of an Enoch Arden who didn't behave the way he should. Ann Carson, born Baker, was the daughter of a merchant-marine and, at times, naval officer, John Baker, who drank, although his erratic behaviour was put down, as it so often was in those days, to a sunstroke in tropical waters. Ann, a wilful girl, had an unhappy childhood. Prevented from marrying the young man of her first choice, a Quaker, she was more or less urged against her will into a marriage with Captain John Carson, also a merchant-marine and naval officer, and who also drank. Ann seems to have been surrounded by hard drinkers. Possibly she attracted them. At any rate, in 1813 Captain Carson sailed for India and was gone for three years, and everyone thought him dead, especially Ann, who was supporting herself by keeping a china shop near the Delaware water-front, and in her spare hours was living happily with a young army lieutenant named Smyth. Having waited three years, Ann and Lieutenant Smyth decided to get married, and did so at a gay party at the Jolly Post Boy at Frankford. Hardly had they recovered from this party, when Captain Carson reappeared, and behaving in no peaceable manner, was shot dead by Lieutenant Smyth. Both Smyth and Ann were tried for murder, and Ann was acquitted and Smyth was convicted and sentenced to be hung. But before this happened, Ann showed her true metal, and when you come to think about it, you find considerable to admire about her, and the story becomes all of a sudden tragic and Greek, and not without its high nobility.

While her lover was awaiting execution, Ann was not idle for a moment. First she collected some of her water-front friends and tried to rescue Smyth from the old Walnut Street Jail. This failing, she attempted to kidnap ex-Governor Snyder of Pennsylvania and force him to sign a pardon. Failing in this also, she decided to kidnap the son of a prominent politician, a close friend of the ex-governor's. By now even the "indolent" Pennsylvanians of the Rev. Jacob Duché's description felt that Ann was dangerous. So she and her companions were flung into the same jail from which her lover had recently been taken to be hanged, and there she stayed for eight years or so. In 1824, getting into a quarrel with another prisoner, she was badly beaten and succumbed to her injuries.

Her history is contained in a volume entitled, *The memoirs of the Celebrated and Beautiful Mrs. Ann Carson, Daughter of an Officer of the U.S. Navy, and wife of Another, whose life terminated in The Philadelphia Prison. By Mrs. M. Clarke; Authoress of The Fair American, Life of Thomas L. Hamblin, Edwin Forrest, etc. Philadelphia. 1838.*

With the exception of Miss Vining, the ladies mentioned can hardly be regarded as typical Philadelphians, and Mrs. Reynolds was a New Yorker, but an interesting treatise could be written on Philadelphia women past and present. They are a distinct breed, as women always tend to become, much more than men, wherever you put them. One could start by saying that, superficially, they stand halfway between the women of New York and the women of Baltimore, just as Philadelphia is the most northern of southern cities and the most southern of northern cities. And the fact that Philadelphia is the most masculine of all American cities except Boston, as masculine as London, has had even more to do with forming the character of its female population. Like everyone else, women bloom under handicaps, if not too severe. New York, as feminine a city as Paris, gives its women such authority that eventually they cease to be women at all and become no more than beautifully masked men. Philadelphia, less enslaved, produces women far more feminine and hence women that have far more actual influence. And they are very beautiful too, and with less adventitious aids.

They are inclined to be blonde, tall, and athletic. They dress simply and have simple manners. They are still as charming as Mr. Black found them, although not always too well educated. As a rule, they share the convictions of their men, and so are likely to be hampered by a number of unanalysed prejudices, but if they survive the vicissitudes of life, they also, naturally, become more open-minded, and this, on top of an excellent foundation, is likely to end in the most charming old ladies in the world.

To use a horticultural simile, if New York women are like brilliant greenhouse plants, Philadelphia women are like the white dogwood so noticeable about the Philadelphia suburbs in the spring. And old ladies in Philadelphia reach their perfection.

Franklin, returning from France in 1785, lived for five years longer, busy as usual, happy with his family, Sarah Bache and her husband and their children; exerting a great influence on the Constitutional Convention; and fairly happy in his public life, although well aware that he was no longer as universally beloved and honoured as formerly. The split between those more democratic and radical and the more conservative found a peg with the French Revolution and turned them into pro-French and pro-English parties. Franklin, although a strong Federalist, did not always agree by any means with Washington and Hamilton, and so was not as popular with some of his wealthier friends as he had been. Occasionally he sighed and said he had lived too long; and an incredible snob (the species lives under logs and appears in every period) actually put down on paper that "Mr. Franklin was no longer the fashion".

With the French Revolution, William Penn's fairly placid city went through one of its strangest periods, evidence that subterranean fires could occasionally crack the surface; nor was this entirely the work of the thoughtless. Many respectable citizens were involved. Jacobin clubs were formed, and their members, who called themselves "Genetines", paraded and danced in the streets, singing "Ça ira" or the "Marseillaise", and demanded war with England, red mobcaps on their heads. John Adams was worried. "Ten thousand men," he wrote, "were in the streets day after day, threatening to drag Washington out of his house, and effect a revolution in the government. . . ." That extraordinary, brash, and insolent ambassador, Citizen Genet—Edmond Charles Genet—had arrived in 1792 and had proceeded to act as if neither Congress nor the President existed. He instigated military operations against the Spanish possessions in Florida and Louisiana and against the English in Canada; fitted out privateers in American ports; and attacked Washington and Congress persistently and insultingly. Extraordinary as it may seem, such men as Thomas Jefferson, Charles Biddle, Alexander Dallas, David Rittenhouse, and General Thomas Mifflin, then governor, were for a while his friends and admirers, and painful as it is to relate as a matter of good taste and decency, a civic dinner was given to Citizen Genet in which a boar's head, severed from the body and labelled "Louis XVI", was passed around the table amid cheers and cries of "Down with Tyranny!"

And this was Philadelphia!

Washington treated Genet with dignity and for the most part with silent contempt. Finally he requested the Government of France to withdraw him. This came at a crucial moment for Genet, as Robespierre had fallen, and not only was the French Government willing to replace Genet, but was eager to have him back to stand trial, a request brought to America by the new minister, Citizen Fauchet. Washington showed his accustomed wisdom and mercy and refused to extradite Genet, and Genet, his head still on his shoulders, with the cool self-preservation of his race, immediately turned about and not only became an American citizen, but a most conservative one at that.

He went to New York and married Cornelia Tappen Clinton, daughter of Governor Clinton, and she dying in 1810, four years later he married Martha Osgood, daughter of the first Postmaster-General. In 1834 Citizen Genet died, a wealthy and respected New Yorker.

In this same year, 1794, the "Whisky Rebellion" burst into flames in western Pennsylvania and was the cause of one of the most significant and determining events in American history. This was the first use of the presidential executive power, as, in the final analysis, overriding all states' rights. Washington, by calling out the militia under the national command, set the final seal on rights Congress had recently defined, although the presidential power in times of crisis is still a matter of argument among those who do not know their American history.

The year before this there had occurred the most dreadful calamity in Philadelphia's history, the yellow-fever epidemic of 1793.

It had been a very hot and muggy summer, which, to those who know their Philadelphia, means something, for there are times when the "Holy Experiment" resembles no place so much as Bengal. Along the Delaware and Schuylkill the heat-mist hung, and then, on August 5, a stranger came to the city, a Mr. Moore, and died in his lodgings in Water Street. He had been ill three days and had at first ascribed his faintness and nausea to the smell of some rotting coffee on the Arch Street Wharf, sickening in the dreadful humidity. Afterwards the city, in the grip of the French influence, said that the name "Moore" in French means death.

The day after Mr. Moore's death, a Mrs. Parkinson, lodging in the same

1*

house, died with similar symptoms, and then Mr. Denny, owner of the house, and then his wife. People began to die all along Water Street. Suddenly the unseen visitor, instead of creeping and walking, ran all about the city, terror in its breath. Within a week Philadelphia was in its grip, devastated as never before or since.

The inadequate hospitals were crowded to overflowing; people began to die in the streets. Soon the gravediggers and their carts could not collect the dead, and the dead lay rotting where they fell. For a while the church bells tolled all day long for funerals, until the mayor had the sense to stop them. Sheer panic added its horrors, and unbearable stories survive. Stories of husbands deserting their dying wives, and the other way about; of bridegrooms leaving their brides of a night. Of brides fleeing their bridegrooms in the same way. Of friends refusing to help friends. Twenty thousand people left the city; the rich in carriages, the poor on foot. Hundreds of children were lost and orphaned. Huge bonfires burned, reddening the night, under the delusion that they purified the air. In the morning heaps of corpses, some of them naked, thieves having stripped them, were found where the gravediggers, dying themselves, had abandoned them. Housewives, opening their doors, saw dead men or women lying on their steps. Robbers broke into houses and murdered the dying and fell dead in the streets before they could carry their loot home. Some four thousand persons died, a large number for a city of Philadelphia's size, especially when over twenty thousand had fled.

As an apex to the horror, at the very height of the epidemic a ship arrived in the Delaware loaded with refugees from Santo Domingo fleeing from the same yellow visitor and slave insurrections. The passengers, short of food and water, were forbidden to land and were visited by the necessary officials only once a week. The ship lay in the river, in the poisonous haze of the heat.

The "Holy Experiment" had suffered one of the very evils—the other was fire—Penn, with his memory of the Great Plague of London, had planned to prevent.

But, as always, there was as much heroism as panic and cowardice. The Philadelphia doctors, completely in the dark as to what caused the illness and how to fight it, were incredibly brave. The clergy were the same. Ten physicians and clergymen died, including two Roman Catholic priests. The Quakers, invariably outstanding and noble, once something has happened, were conspicuous for their courage. Stephen Girard was magnificent. Dr. Rush, extraordinary man, not only did not die but even flourished, as he says, and experimented as far as his enormous imagination and energy would take him, which was far. He came to the conclusion that drastic bleeding, plus a compound composed of mercury and jalap, which is a drastic purge, was the cure instead of quinine, which his fellow medical men at least knew had some connection with the illness. So a war broke out between Dr. Rush and his confrères, adding its bitterness to the confusion. Dr. Rush was attending a hundred and twenty-five patients a day.

Dr. Rush is one of the most fascinating figures in the history of American medicine and certainly one of the most interesting. A man of great ability and knowledge, he had an almost totally unchecked inventiveness and enthusiasm. The great epidemic of 1793 ended with the coming of cold weather, but the unwanted visitor returned again in some of the summers that followed, although in a much milder way, and in 1797 William Cobbett, Paine admirer, the dour and caustic English reformer, and a friend of Moreau de St. Mèry's, attacked Rush fiercely in his *Peter Porcupine Gazette*. Not only did he call him a quack, but he labelled him "Dr. Sangredo". These attacks became so outrageous that Dr. Rush sued for libel and was awarded damages of five thousand dollars. Cobbett, who had some intention of settling in Philadelphia, was ruined by this. His property was seized, and he returned, still more embittered, to his native country, which, in the first place, he had left with bitterness.[1]

Dr. Rush was one of the most beloved men in Philadelphia; William Cobbett, never silent and never flattering, one of the most unpopular.

Amongst his voluminous writings, Dr. Rush leaves some enchanting explanations for the prevalence in Philadelphia of tuberculosis, or as it was then called, "consumption"; "our most common disease", he named it. Hot drinks, for one, had much to do with susceptibility to it, and staying in bed too long; eating too much meat; drinking too much spirituous liquor. But you could get it coming or going, for the quiet Quakers were in equal danger. "The habit of gravity and immobility," says Dr. Rush, "which they [the Quakers] contract early in life and which they preserve for hours in the silent meetings" was a principal cause of the disease among members of that church, especially the women; but then, women of other sects were equally liable, because of excessive dancing, the drinking of cold water afterwards, the eating of unripe fruits, and the drinking of boiling tea. Also because, in winter, women went lightly clad and paid no attention to changes in the weather. "Women," Dr. Rush concludes, should have "the gayety of a woman of fashion with the prejudices and precautions of a Quaker." But there was an even more fundamental reason than these for female predisposition toward the white plague. Dr. Rush is convinced that political equality would make women just as healthy as men. Nor is this as funny as it sounds. Dr. Rush was on the track of something. "A moral or political cause," he writes, "may likewise aid us in explaining why women are more subject to consumption than men. It is the want of a will or a civil existence. The submission to which women are habituated has the effect of chains."

When it came to Philadelphia's climate, Dr. Rush was on surer ground.

Brissot de Warville records that in a fine frenzy Dr. Rush said to him, "We have the humidity of Great Britain in the spring; the heat of Africa in the summer; the temperature of Italy in June; the sky of Egypt in autumn; the snows of Norway and the ice of Holland in winter; the tempests of the

[1] Cobbett went first to New York before returning to England, and attacked not only Dr. Rush but Philadelphia as a whole, and especially Chief Justice Thomas McKean, in a fierce pamphlet called *Rush Light*. He said Pennsylvanians were "the most malicious and cowardly race in existence", and ended with the pious hope that Dr. Rush would bleed them all to death.

West Indies in each season; the variable winds of Great Britain every month of the year."

Although exaggerated, this is not entirely inaccurate.

In short, as a witty Frenchman remarked, "America hasn't a climate —merely samples of weather". And yet, on the other hand, what has France in this respect, or any place else, for that matter?

Before the Revolution a spring had been discovered near the State House, its waters having a curious taste, and Dr. Rush, analysing it, decided, together with other members of the medical faculty, that it had excellent curative properties. He announced that the water "exceeded in strength any chalybeates yet known in the province". People came from everywhere to drink. And then it was discovered that the powerful taste of the water was due to near-by gutters and outhouses. For some strange reason, no one died.

The great yellow-fever epidemic of 1793 was responsible for Philadelphia's best ghost story. For a city of its size and age Philadelphia is singularly lacking in ghost stories, perhaps because of a certain underlying matter-of-factness. Philadelphia has never had any famous haunted house like the La Laurie house in New Orleans, or the Hyslop house and the Woodlawn Cemetery house, and others in New York. Or the haunted houses of Charleston or Natchez. Or those of numerous other American cities. There was, to be sure, a plumed hearse, drawn by four coal-black horses, nodding plumes on their heads, which drove up Walnut Street at midnight, some said, the devil driving. The corpse inside was reputed somewhat vaguely to be "one of our deceased rich citizens who was deemed to have died with unkind feelings to one dependent upon him", which would take in most of the rich. But no one saw the coach, and there was an equal lack of excitement about the Nagle house at Second and Noble streets, "where a man was to be seen hanging without a head", a difficult feat even for a ghost, and about the house near Centre Square, around which in the dark of the moon "the five Wheelbarrow men", who had been hanged for murder, walked, pushing their wheelbarrows. The most famous haunted house, although, like the others, this tale too found little credence, was one at the north-east corner of Fifth and Walnut streets, where a gentleman, whose name has not survived, murdered his wife and then, so the enemies of the Federalists said, presented Hamilton with his entire property, to obtain for him an acquittal.

To the contrary, the country-side around Philadelphia has many legends and superstitions, as have most of the older American country-sides. "Headless Hessians" ride a couple of lanes, and at least one of the old country houses is haunted by George Washington, indefatigable in that respect as in others. The "Pennsylvania Dutch", moreover, with their belief in witchcraft—hexing—and some of the Welsh and German Catholic farmers, with their belief that on Christmas Eve the kine kneel down and worship in their stalls, add extra colour. And every now and then a hexing trial takes place near Philadelphia, sometimes for murder. But the great yellow-fever epidemic of 1793 gave Philadelphia a real ghost story. A beauty. It can be told in a few sentences.

On the night of September 5, 1793, the epidemic raging, nonetheless a meeting of the directors of the Library Company, "Mr. Franklin's Library", was scheduled. No one attended but a Mr. Benjamin Poultney, a prominent merchant, and he entered this rebuking memorandum in the minute-book: "At a Meeting of the Directors, September the Fifth, 1793—present, Benjamin Poultney, who, after waiting till Eight o'clock, retired!" Evidently Mr. Poultney was angry, for the exclamation mark is large and deeply inked. But apparently the injustice of this anger weighed on Mr. Poultney's mind, for on October 3 there is another entry in the minute-book in the same unmistakable handwriting which says: "The Directors being generally out of Town by reason of the prevailing Sickness were not notified to attend."

But you see, Mr. Poultney—and this is a matter of record—had died on September 21, sixteen days after the first entry; twelve days before the second.

Twenty-five years before the turn of the century, in May of 1776, right in the middle of the Revolution, an interesting stranger had come to Philadelphia: a young French sea captain, whose father before him had been a sea captain out of Bordeaux, where this young stranger had been born. The stranger was twenty-six years old, slight, dark, taciturn, with chiselled features and only one eye. He had come up from the West Indies in his little ship *La Jeune Babé* and was headed for New York, but had first put into Philadelphia. Shortly after stepping ashore he came across a girl—a very beautiful one—drawing water from a pump near the river. He decided to marry her. This, and the war which made the seas dangerous, decided the young sea captain to sell his boat and remain in Philadelphia. The young sea captain was Stephen Girard.

And so America's first multi-millionaire, and Philadelphia's greatest shipowner and banker, came to the city that was to be his home for fifty-five years.

CHAPTER XXV

Cradle of Finance

"*Oct.* 29, 1802

"*Dear Papa:*

"*Will you be so good as to send orders to the milliner—Madame Peck, I believe her name is, through Mrs. Madison, who very obligingly offered to execute any little commission for us in Philadelphia, for two wigs of the colour of the hair enclosed, and of the most fashionable shapes, that they may be in Washington when we arrive? They are universally worn, and will relieve us as to the necessity of dressing our own hair, a business in which neither of us are adept.*

"*I believe Madame Peck is in the habit of doing these things, and they can be procured in a short time from Philadelphia, where she corresponds, much handsomer than elsewhere.*

"*Adieu, dearest father.*"

PART OF LETTER WRITTEN BY MARTHA JEFFERSON RANDOLPH TO HER FATHER, THOMAS JEFFERSON, JUST BEFORE HIS INAUGURATION AS THIRD PRESIDENT OF THE UNITED STATES.

PHILADELPHIA HAS HAD many nicknames: "the Quaker City", "William Penn's Town", "Birthplace of the Republic", "City of Brotherly Love", and so on. It was called "the Clydebank of America", "the Liverpool of America", when its port was pre-eminent. And "the Cradle of American Finance". And the last is correct, as are the former. Not only was Pennsylvania the first of the colonies to establish an adequate fiscal structure, but it was Philadelphia, with its Bank of Pennsylvania and, later on, its Bank of North America, established in 1781, that financed the War of the Revolution and restored the commerce and credit of the country. More than to any other man, this leadership was due to Robert Morris, who was as far-sighted in public affairs as he was extravagant in his personal life.

Morris, born in Liverpool, came to Philadelphia while still in his teens and entered the counting-house of Charles Willing in Willing's Alley. In 1754, when only twenty-one, he helped to establish Philadelphia's stock exchange; like all stock exchanges, an institution that had been going on for some time in the shape of informal gatherings of merchants, shipowners, and bankers at various coffee-houses, the favourite one being William Bradford's Coffee House, or, as it was alternately called, the Old London Coffee House, which stood at the south-west corner of Front and High, now Market, streets. Here on a spring afternoon in 1754 four men—Robert Morris, Tench Francis, Archibald McCall, and Thomas Willing—decided to formalize their gatherings.

Until the 1830's Philadelphia was the principal money centre of the country, and then that supremacy departed according to the well-established pattern. Nor in all the history of American finance, filled with its strange characters and consequent tragedies, can there be found a more tragic history than that of Robert Morris. He was such a great and far-visioned American; such a wise and imaginative financier; he had such an Achilles hell. Toward the end of his life he went in for an orgy of housebuilding. First there was the mansion at 526 Market Street, which became the Presidential Mansion. Then there was the fine and extravagant country estate, Lemon Hill. Finally, in 1794, there was the start of that urban palace, "Morris' Folly", on a lot on Chestnut Street between Seventh and Eighth. This was never completed, for three years later the owner became insolvent, and on February 16, 1798, was committed to jail. For the "palace" on Chestnut Street, Morris had employed Major Pierre Charles L'Enfant, the French engineer and architect who later laid out Washington.

But Morris already had a great coadjutor in finance and a more cautious one, the Frenchman, Stephen Girard, and Philadelphia's supremacy in this respect for a while continued.

In the long annals of Philadelphia, Girard in some ways was the most interesting citizen, the most curious, the most contradictory, the most misunderstood, and, in many quarters, the most hated. The tradition of a saturnine, dark, silent, one-eyed man, cold, ruthless, unsmiling; of an atheist who had founded a college for orphan boys upon whose grounds no minister of the gospel was ever to set foot; of a man who quarrelled bitterly all his long life with every member of his family—brother, sister, nieces, nephews —and who cut them off without a cent., was handed down from generation to generation. Nor were any ameliorating traits ever mentioned. No one said Girard in his private life was one of the great romantics of history, no one said that he was one of the most patriotic and unselfish of Americans, and one of the most daring. No one said that he was an equally unselfish and enthusiastic Philadelphian. And no one said that he was as much admired and beloved by those who worked for him as he was dreaded by his rivals and those against whom he had a grievance.

With his far-flung shipping and, later on, banking interests, he could follow, and did follow, all around the world, until he caught up with him, anyone he wished to punish; but no one worked loyally for Girard and regretted it. On one occasion Girard spent thousands of dollars in tracing down a slave who had escaped and fled to the West Indies. On another, he did the same with an apprentice who had run away to the west of the state and married an innkeeper's daughter. Girard had the boy flung into jail on a diet of one meal and one glass of water a day; but a sheriff, indignant at this brutality, released the apprentice secretly. In 1811, when Girard was sixty-one, he was the proposed victim of one of America's earliest kidnapping plots for the purpose of extortion. He foiled this plot largely by his own efforts, and so greatly enjoyed the intrigue and detective work involved that for a while he practically abandoned all other business.

And yet this was the man who named his first ship *La Jeune Babé*. Who, going ashore, saw a lovely girl, Mary Lunn, daughter of a Kensington shipbuilder, drawing water, and at once fell in love with her and married her. And who, coming to this country more or less by chance at its darkest period —*La Jeune Babé* had lost its reckonings, and Girard, hailing another ship, was told he had best seek a port, as British warships were on blockade— decided then and there to cast in his lot with the struggling colonies. And this is also the man who, living quietly in Mount Holly, New Jersey, during the British occupation of Philadelphia, and in typical French fashion contenting himself with running a small shop until times got better, resigned in a fury from the Mount Holly volunteer fire company because its members objected to his young bride keeping flowers in the leathern bucket he was supposed to have as a fireman on his front porch.

Nor has any wife ever had a more devoted husband. Girard's private life was a bitter tragedy. The beautiful girl he had seen in her father's yard went insane after fourteen years of marriage, and for twenty-five years, until her death in 1815, was in an institution. Girard, although he was only a man of fifty-five at the time, never remarried, nor did he show any real love for any other woman. There were some casual affairs in his life, but for the most part he settled down to a succession of comely serving-maids in the lonely house that few entered.

In no way more did Girard's bold and romantic imagination show itself than in his tall and beautiful ships, his lovely China traders, with their carved figureheads and their shining interior fittings and their names; each one named after a great liberal French philosopher. And his imagination, and his love of Philadelphia, showed itself in his will, one section of which shocked the respectable. He left the bulk of his fortune—vast for those days, to the city he had adopted—to be used in improving the police force, to be used for lessening taxation, and especially to found a college for orphan boys, Girard College, with the proviso, as has been said, that no minister of any religion should ever set foot on its grounds. This gave the disgruntled and disinherited heirs a chance, and they employed the great Daniel Webster, who made a roaring speech on Christianity, but the judge, Justice Joseph Story, was unimpressed and the will stood. Work on the classic white marble building of the college began in 1833, and the college was opened in 1848. The main building has been called "the most perfect Greek temple in existence".

But the poet in Girard did not stop there. He was one of the few rich Philadelphians, in fact the only one, who ever seems to have thought that perhaps it might be a good idea to beautify his town, and who decided, apparently, that William Penn was, after all, a fairly sensible man. Girard left £500,000, a very large sum in 1831, for the widening and beautification of the Delaware water-front according to William Penn's plan. The water-front was widened, but it is still waiting its beautification.

Girard must have brooded over his city as he walked about it during the long days of his life. His frustrated love for his wife seems to have turned, with this ruthless and bitter and often cruel man, into a love for his city. And cities, like everything else, do better if someone broods over them.

Girard's foresight and patriotism, which are usually the same thing, were visible in everything he did. When the War of 1812 loomed, with its inevitable effect upon shipping, Girard turned from shipping to banking, although he loved ships, and had been a sea captain and signed his will "Stephen Girard, Merchant and Mariner". When the War of 1812 actually came, he underwrote his country with practically his entire fortune. The small United States opposed the great and powerful England; and Stephen Girard threw his wealth into the balance! The rest of the country had subscribed $20,000 of the $16,000,000 War Loan; Stephen Girard, along with John Jacob Astor and David Parrish, took the remaining $15,980,000 and saved the credit of America. Girard's gallantry, however, had been tested long before this. In the great yellow-fever epidemic of 1793, and the milder one of 1798, not only had he opened his purse lavishly but had played a conspicuous part personally. The Bush Hill Hospital was a scandal. The nurses were mostly drunken women of the town who neglected the patients except when they stole from them. The place had become a charnel-house. Stephen Girard offered to take over the management, and coolly did so, and soon restored order.

And then in December of 1831, when he was eighty-one years old, he was run over by a dray while crossing one of the streets of his city. It is interesting that his great rival, Jacob Ridgway, was killed in the same fashion.

Now here, one would say, is the subject of a great American novel. Surely there is plenty of action, plenty of romance, plenty of colour, and even mystery. Six biographies have been written; among them a long and scholarly one by John Bach McMaster, and recently a shorter, warmer, and more sympathetic one by that other Philadelphia historian, Harry Emerson Wildes. But even with these two excellent books the full man has not yet come altogether to life. The cruel, ruthless, one-eyed, bitter, often vulgar, rude shipowner and banker and multi-millionaire, the first American "tycoon"; the delicate-minded builder of ships, the instant lover, the husband spiritually faithful, whatever his physical alleviations may have been. The brooding lover of his city and its beauty; the fearless American.

It has been over a hundred years since Philadelphia has been the financial centre of the country, or anything like, although in Civil War times it had another great and patriotic banker, Jay Cooke, who, coming to Philadelphia in 1839 from his birthplace in Ohio when he was eighteen years old, became a Philadelphian and twenty-two years later largely financed the Civil War for the North as Stephen Girard had financed the War of 1812. Caught in the great panic of 1873, Cooke achieved a reputation he did not deserve. The truth of the matter is that he turned over all his assets to his creditors and eventually paid every cent of his obligations. In addition to this, the banking firm for which Cooke first worked when he came to Philadelphia, E. W. Clark & Co., and of which, in 1842, he was made a partner at the age of twenty-one, had had an equally fine record in the Mexican

War and was largely responsible for its financing. For a long while Philadelphia money had a brilliant record so far as patriotism was concerned.

But the city's financial supremacy ended in the 1830's when Andrew Jackson crushed the Bank of the United States, largely a Philadelphia institution and largely owned by Stephen Girard, by that time dead, and to-day Philadelphia is not even in the first rank of banking cities. New York, of course, far surpasses it, just as London does, and even Chicago and Montreal. And what banking is left to Philadelphia is now entirely dominated by its huge neighbour on the Hudson. On the other hand, Philadelphia is still the home of the trust company, which it invented; and its trust deposits, a large proportion of which are private, are enormous, running far up into the billions. And these trust companies and the Philadelphia banks, with their trust departments, are interesting affairs.

The vast majority are officered by descendants of William Penn's original settlers, or, at the latest, the scions of Revolutionary families. Generation after generation various members of these families have, upon graduating from their universities, entered these institutions almost by right of inheritance just as the sons of English families enter the army, the navy, or the Church, and as the sons of other Philadelphia families enter law or medicine. As a result, if you happen to impinge upon or belong to the strong and powerful nucleus of older families which, with constant additions of new blood, still in many ways runs the city, financial transactions in Philadelphia have a curiously intimate and pleasant social atmosphere. Everyone knows everyone else, just as everyone's father has known everyone else's father, and so on back for a couple of hundred years, and in addition to this, the trust company officials have a great deal of contemporary knowledge that may, or may not, be embarrassing. The exact status, for instance, moral and monetary, and also psychological, of the drunken and spendthrift uncle; the vagaries of the rich and widowed aunt; how the sister, married to a Portuguese or a British nobleman, is getting on with her husband. Fortunately, like the little oriental monkeys, trust officials are trained to see nothing, hear nothing, and above all, repeat nothing.

Boston is still the richest city per-capita investment in the country; New York second; and Philadelphia third in this respect, astonishingly outclassing fabulous Chicago. And like Boston, Philadelphia's per-capita investment represents in many cases long-inherited wealth, which is another reason for Philadelphia's point of view. Long-inherited wealth tends to good and simple manners, and charm, and lack of pretentiousness, but it also tends to quiet arrogance and a belief in predestined property, allocated shortly after the Ark by a jealous God who devoted part of His time from then on to deciding who should be rich and who should not. There is very little in Philadelphia of the ordinary American knowledge that money is evanescent, and that if you have any, either you or one of your ancestors was bright along that line and also exceptionally lucky.

Philadelphians don't think their ancestors were lucky; they think they were selected. In which respect, as in many others, they resemble the British.

Nor have trust companies, with all their virtues, been any more of an unmitigated blessing to the city than has their big brother, the Pennsylvania Railroad. Owing to restrictive, if necessary laws, and to their own rather remote attitude, trust companies are now what could be called gallant investors. Their inclination is to cut down dividends and increase capital, so one has the curious spectacle of widows and orphans steadily growing richer and, at the same time, steadily having less to spend. One waggish statistician —if the combination is possible—has figured out that the ordinary estate left in charge of the ordinary trust company will, in three generations, unless the heirs take an active part, have increased so much in gilt-edged investments and decreased so much in dividends that the end result will resemble nothing so much as the gold fund of the country, buried and guarded by military police.

The former institution of "family lawyers", while having its dangers, was more personal. To some extent, therefore, the great trust companies of Philadelphia are another finger, perhaps the thumb, of the town's mortmain. Finally, as has been said, the great banking families of Philadelphia no longer live in the city, so in that respect also their attitude isn't very personal. They control the wealth of the city, but they neither live in it nor vote in it. Almost inevitably they are among the seven or eight hundred thousand Philadelphians who every afternoon shake the dust of the city from their feet under the delusion that they are "going out to the country".

With the turn of the century, Philadelphia was no longer either a national or state capital. The national capital had moved to muddy Washington and the state capital had moved west to Lancaster. Robert Morris had done his best to prevent the former, but without success. Pennsylvania was now a commonwealth, whatever that may mean. And as a matter of fact, it means nothing, although the term has a fine generous sound, if where Pennsylvania is concerned, a slightly sardonic one. But at least the title is exclusive, for there are only three other commonwealths in the country: Kentucky, Massachusetts, and Virginia.

Nor had loss of prestige hurt Philadelphia and Pennsylvania materially. Both the city and state were steadily growing in wealth and stature, despite the great depression of the late '30's and '40's. The mouth of the cornucopia was widening, the variety of its fruits increasing. Philadelphia became more and more the home of the merchant prince and banker prince, and no longer at all the home of the statesman or moulder of public opinion. During the War of 1812 it was fiercely patriotic—there was no longer any question of division here—and with almost the last of its magnificent historic gestures the city sent out the tall frigates of the United States. Better than most American cities, it survived the turbulent and ugly '30's, and the outbreak of the Know-Nothing party with its early Ku Klux Klanism. There were some bad anti-Irish riots, and a Roman Catholic church was burned, and there were demonstations against the increasing Negro population, but the militia was called out. Subsequently the Know-Nothing element, the particular name of which at any particular time is of no importance, and which is a continuing disease of ignorance whose only steady directive is the persecution of the weak and the strange, as the Irish grew stronger, and some of them joined it, sought other victims.

The city, too, suffered that strange rash of volunteer fire companies which afflicted the America of the early 1800's, during which volunteer fire-fighters were much more interested in fighting each other than fires. And it also had its numerous and dangerous—for their peers—"gangs": the "Schuylkill Wharf Rats", and so on, another symptom of the America of those days. But, except rarely, Philadelphia has never been an openly turbulent city; on the whole, its record has been good-natured and easygoing, too easygoing. Penn's spirit of tolerance is still strong. The city had by now definitely turned its eyes inland, but even as late as the 1840's it was still casting backward glances at its once beloved sea. The newspapers, such as William Fry's *National Gazette and Literary Register*, and so on, were still filled with such advertisements as this:

Arrived: Ship "John Sergeant", Van Dycke master, from Liverpool, Sept. 8, consigned to J. G. & D. B. Stacey, merchandize. Oct. 1st, ship "General Hamilton", of Providence, from Havre, bound to Providence, in lat 42, long 45. Also spoke off Cape Clear, Sept. 14, ship "Shaw", David, from Liverpool, for Portsmouth. The "Sergeant" brings files of London papers to the 4th Sept, Lloyd's Lists, Price Currents, &c.

Two years earlier, in April of 1838, the tiny 700-ton British paddle-wheel steamer *Sirius* had made its history-making voyage from London to New York. Sail, however, was still the usual method of propulsion, and it still took thirty-nine days as a rule to reach Philadelphia from England.[1]

Lafayette, by now an old man, had come and gone on his second triumphant tour of the country he had helped liberate. Victoria had recently ascended the English throne. Louis Philippe, one-time refugee in Philadelphia, was King of France. Perhaps he remembered the wise statement of William Bingham, the Philadelphia merchant, one of whose daughters he had tried to marry over forty years before.

"Young man," William Bingham had said, "if you ever ascend the throne

---

[1] One does not realize the hardships, the perils, the brutalities, and often the horrors that attended the great urge of Europeans, mostly northern Europeans, and principally Irish and Scottish, who in the 1820's, '30's, and '40's set their hearts upon becoming Americans, and the descendants of whom are now amongst our most solid citizens. One must believe, then, that this desire to become an American was for over two and a half centuries one of the deepest passions in the hearts of men and women, so deep that its results cannot be obliterated or altogether forgotten. Certainly it was one of the most startling and determining phenomenons of history. These immigrants of the 1800's often suffered no less than the original adventurers of Raleigh, Penn, and New England. And in these annals, mostly sordid and frequently dramatic, there is no story more dramatic and tragic than that of the sailing ship *William Brown*, home port Philadelphia, which in March 1841 set sail from Liverpool with sixty-five Scottish and Irish immigrants of both sexes bound for the Delaware.

There is no time for that story here, as it is a long one and not especially germane to a description of Philadelphia, but it can be easily found by any, who are interested, and is one of the great horror stories of the sea. It is especially recommended to any scenarist who is looking for a subject for a motion picture. It is a *Lifeboat* plus.

you will be too highly placed for my daughter; if you don't, you will not be highly placed enough."

Another French exile had used Philadelphia as a refuge for two years beginning with 1815, Joseph Bonaparte, and his house, a charming one, is still standing on Ninth Street, south of Locust, on its dining-room walls the murals Joseph brought with him from France. Just around the corner from it, on Locust Street, is an equally historical building, but now in a sad state of repair: Musical Fund Hall, the oldest music-hall in the United States. Here Thackeray lectured, Jenny Lind sang, and here, in 1856, was held the first Republican national convention.

Philadelphia continued to be as much the home of exiles as ever. Achille and Napoleon Murat, sons of the King of Naples, Maréchal Murat, joined the list, and in 1825, the first and last native Mexican empress, the heart-broken Señora de Iturbide, came to Philadelphia with her two young sons after the execution of her husband, the Emperor Augustin. This Mexican empress is buried in Philadelphia. Not too far away from her grave is another memorable one.

Few Philadelphians remember any longer that Rebecca, of Scott's *Ivanhoe*, was a Philadelphian, Rebecca Gratz, and that her grave is in the little cemetery of the Mikveh Israel Congregation, the ancient Spanish and Portuguese Jewish cemetery, whose wrought-iron gate is opposite the grounds and buildings of the Pennsylvania Hospital on Spruce near Eighth Street.

Rebecca Gratz, one of the great beauties of Philadelphia, was an intimate friend of Matilda Hoffman, Washington Irving's fiancée, and Irving, meeting Scott in England, described Rebecca Gratz to him. After the publication of *Ivanhoe* in 1819, Scott wrote to Irving: "How do you like your Rebecca? Does the Rebecca I have pictured compare well with the pattern given?"

And then, in 1832, there appeared another refugee, a refugee from the Orient—cholera—and all that hot summer it stalked the streets of the city, although not as disastrously as the yellow visitor of 1793.

Philadelphia began to settle down, just as the country as a whole embarked upon one of its periodic upheavals, perhaps its greatest: the "Winning of the West". Many younger Philadelphians left Philadelphia, never to return, just as their ancestors had left Europe a hundred and fifty years before. Down in Washington, Daniel Webster, with orotund genius for being wrong, was asking contemptuously why anyone wanted anything to do with the vast desert wilderness beyond the Mississippi, inhabited by savage tribes; and up in Philadelphia, the newspapers, with an equal genius for near-sightedness, were printing editorials like this:

The question of the precise duration of the Presidential Term for a longer or shorter period is, of all others connected with national politics, the one most demanding the attention of the public mind, so that a fair and earnest consideration of the subject may lead to such a definite understanding and practice in relation to it as that past errors and evils may be avoided, and the fullest amount of future good be secured. The American people are indebted to General Jackson for the first officially promulgated theory of the Single Presidential Term. They will

*be indebted to General Harrison for the first voluntary official practice of the
same. The public sense has been expressed clearly in favour of a single presidential
term. The duplicate term may now be considered exploded.*

General Jackson had served two terms with the greatest of personal
satisfaction. General Harrison promptly put his theory into effect, but
not voluntarily. He died one month after taking office, and his vice-president,
Tyler, succeeded him.

CHAPTER XXVI

Sweet-Smelling Names

"To appoint unto them that mourn Zion; to give them beauty instead of ashes."
                                                                    ISAIAH.

JOHN FANNING WATSON, indefatigable and irascible chronicler of early Philadelphia, became alarmed over the increasing wealth and luxury of the mid-
century city. He decided that everything was going to the dogs, as men,
especially elderly ones, have been deciding every ten years since Jeremiah.
The women, of course, were especially going to the dogs. Wrote Mr.
Watson:

> *We, however, think of sundry prevalent and modish actions of society, such
> as did not, and could not, formerly, find toleration. They are just so special
> and striking as to form a proper and closing chapter to these Annals. Not for
> the sake of censorship, or objection, but as marking an era in "the progress of
> enlightened civilization" to be remembered.*
> *The generation of elderly ladies have not yet passed away who made a part
> of that society which could not behold such things as opera-dances and waltzes
> with complacency. They felt, as females, an instinctive, inherent modesty, pre-
> cluding them from such publicity. The encroachments upon female modesty have
> been progressive, and may continue.*

These encroachments Mr. Watson then proceeds to catalogue: "Man-
midwifery". Once again, opera dancing, that is to say, the ballet; and waltzing.
Circus riding, "wherein performers in the display of limbs and individual
symmetry have the countenance of society". And yet, as Mr. Watson points
out, "we have among us still, many who can well remember their first emotions
of confusion and blushes". Coloratura singing, which Mr. Watson admits
is more a disagreeable affectation than a vice. And "the exhibition of
figure, grace, &c.", that is to say, "living pictures", male and female, in

flesh-coloured tights. This due to an increasingly decadent point of view about classical statuary. All of it complicated by the difficulty of obtaining "genteel occupation" for growing sons, which apparently resulted in the turning of the thoughts of these frustrated and idle boys toward the ballet, waltzing, the circus, living pictures, and "man-midwifery". Young men, according to Mr. Watson, had no "genteel" opportunities left because of the overcrowding of the legal and medical professions and the decline of businesses, large or small.

Parents had changed as well as children. Philadelphians, the annalist complains—

from being once a domestic, quiet people, content to rest in their fire-side comforts, and indoor society [have become] all drawn abroad to seek for spectacles and public wonders. Now there are puffing advertisements to draw them abroad every night and day in the week—and this is not all—the whole must be indulged in at so much expense;—One sees that it is working a serious evil;—but who knows how to stay it! It is changing and corrupting society here, and is alluring from abroad all sorts of foreign artists—to batten on, and impose themselves upon our credulity, prodigality, and habits of display. . . . The aged among us deplore these things,—but the young, who never saw our former golden age of moderation and virtue, feel that we are in the way. . . .

To this, add the rivalship of grandeur in houses—expensive furniture— immense and luxurious hotels—elegance and cost of Passenger vessels—and Passenger cars—costly carriages—costly dresses and jewellery. . . .

Most of which "rivalship of grandeur" came from foreign influence; the "addictedness to imitate what is foreign and modish". The big cities on the coast set the example; the little inland towns followed.

Take, for instance, the practice of New York as "The Empire City and State" —and consider how appalling the act that the late City census there gives nearly the half of the whole City population, as foreigners! How can such a state of Society claim to be an American City! Say 237,000 foreigners—against 278,000 Americans!

No wonder the streets were so filled you could no longer walk in comfort or safety. No wonder the tall buildings overshadowed you. No wonder the noise and confusion bewildered everyone. "'Tis terrible now," concludes Mr. Watson, "to sicken and die at crowded streets, where the rattle of omnibuses is unceasing".

But even the sternest of us have our weaknesses, and in his description of "stage, or ballet dancing" there are certain indications that Mr. Watson, despite his years and convictions, was not altogether unsusceptible himself. Like so many reformers, it was necessary for him to witness a performance, and enjoy it, in order to appreciate fully the depraved thoughts of others. This is his description of the dancing of Taglioni, a popular figurante of the '50's. "Look!" he says, "there she comes from the back of the stage, turning round and round with the speed of a teetotum, in indescribable and fascinating grace—she pirouettes—she springs and vaults, her scanty drapery flying upwards, discloses to her enraptured admirers, among the young men, the beauty of her limbs."

Pin-up girls are not a modern invention. The only thing new about them is their name.

And let it be remembered again that this was Philadelphia of the 1850's, Victorian Philadelphia to which so many look back with pious nostalgia.

In 1850 the Consolidation Act was passed and the central city, like an octopus, stretched its tentacles across the Northern Liberties and all the surrounding separate little communities to the west and south. In one day the population jumped from a little over one hundred thousand to nearly half a million, and endless difficulties were ended, especially criminal ones. Heretofore, all a thief had to do was to cross a street from one jurisdiction to another to be temporarily safe. From now on, Philadelphia began its career as the huge city of to-day, so far as territory is concerned; a city that stretches thirty-eight miles or so north and south along the Delaware; almost as far in the direction of Germantown and Chestnut Hill; and many miles to the west, through West Philadelphia and its environs, until you come to Overbrook. Philadelphia County, which is the city, covers 129,744 square miles, and Philadelphia is the largest metropolis in the world laid out upon two perfect Cartesian co-ordinates: Broad Street, which bisects the entire city north and south, being one co-ordinate; Market Street, which runs from the Delaware to the Schuylkill and then angles off into the Lancaster Pike, being the other.

Like London and New York and most big cities, Philadelphia is a joining, an amalgamation, and each of the dozen or more towns which compose it has its own history and traditions, its own main street and shopping district, its own restaurants and motion-picture theatres, even its own customs and traditions. Numerous Philadelphians, many of the mill hands of Kensington and Frankford, the Italians and Negroes of South Philadelphia, for instance, are born, and die, and hardly ever, if at all, see the "main street", and the main business and hotel and theatre district; to wit, the centre of the original city, Penn's "green countrie towne", with its gigantic City Hall and Chestnut Street, one of the most crowded and richest shopping streets in existence, and one of the narrowest outside of the Near Orient.

A street so narrow and crowded that one can hardly move along it, and where at every step one is embarrassingly intimate with furs and women's underclothes, and jewels, smouldering in their velvet cases. Nowhere in such a narrow compass is there so much luxury for sale.

As for the separate communities, even their accents vary a little, although they are all overlaid by the general Philadelphia accent, which has in it a trace of the South, a foundation of Quaker matter-of-factness, and a great deal of the local sinus trouble.

But even before the Consolidation, the city was steadily expanding. It was reaching towards the west, toward the Schuylkill, and the woods and he wild-fowl ponds and the marshes where young people skated in winter were being gradually filled up and built upon. The architecture was changing, too, although the fundamental design remained the mellow Philadelphia brick house, simple but beautiful, with its wide, small-paned, white-trimmed windows, its white carved doors, fanlights above, and its white marble steps guarded by wrought-iron ascending railings, the designs of which for the most part were acanthus leaves or bunches of grapes. Back of these typical façades were the peculiar Philadelphia "back-buildings", extending to alleys which were sometimes mews for stables, or sometimes rows of small brick dwellings, or sometimes merely the similar "back buildings" and yards of houses on the parallel street beyond.

These "back buildings" consist of a long ell at a lower level than the front of the house, and are totally different from anything in New York. The ell reaches toward the alley in the rear, and along it runs a paved yard, separated from the neighbouring side yard by a high wall usually of boards, which ends in a square backyard with a door that opens on the alley. The difference in elevation of the two parts of the house means a house not of three stories, but of one full floor, the ground floor, and then of two stories and two three-quarter stories, and because of the side yards and backyards the possibilities for planting are endless. Usually trees, hidden, and many of them large and old, grow in these backyards and side yards, and almost always there are wistaria vines, and frequently porches with wrought-iron supports up which vines grow. And usually the dining-room, which is in the "back building" on the ground floor, and the library, which is on the second, are filled with sunlight and are quiet and remote. You can hardly hear the sound of traffic. Altogether it is a sensible and lovely and gracious arrangement, and in all the world there are no lovelier houses than the old houses of Philadelphia.

But most of these are gone now, and those that are left are for the most part given over to other uses. They are doctors' offices, or shops, or have been turned into apartments. In the central part of the city, Penn's old town, which was once, and still is, the wealthier and the fashionable section, only a couple of residential streets are left, and these are short. The result is curious. It is as if you were confronted with a huge body, one of its essential organs gone, its heart or both its kidneys. It is as if you took away from New York its entire East Side.

By the 1850's another type of architecture, due to Mr. Watson's hated foreign influence, was beginning to make its appearance, and this was a very gracious style, too. Some of the richer families were beginning to build houses in the Italian style: square and of yellow stucco, with columned porticoes, and with large surrounding gardens protected from the street by spiked iron fences. All this lasted until well into the 1900's. Until then, physically, Philadelphia—this part of it—was an exceptionally comely city. A beautiful city. Big trees lined the streets, and the air was fragrant, and the summers bearable. And people used their gardens and attended to them. And song-birds still haunted the city and nested in the trees. The city was not given over entirely to English sparrows and those other hideous aliens—the starlings.

Philadelphia is still a curious city where trees are concerned, as has been said, despite the present desert-like appearance of its streets. It is still the largest urban forest reserve in the world, if you count Fairmount Park. In this respect it outranks even Paris or London. But to realize this you have to climb to a high place, or rather, take an elevator, and in the summer. Then, surprisingly, you will see the greenness of all the hidden trees. Penn's wish is partially fulfilled, but in a backyarded sort of way.

Philadelphia at the same time was developing a third school of architecture: its "slum architecture". The city was beginning to build its "bandbox" houses, as distinct from the "railway tenements" of New York, but even more terrible. Even more terrible physically, and terrible, too, because they mock one of man's deepest instincts and take advantage of it; an instinct which, because of the Quaker tradition, has always been singularly evident in Philadelphia, so much so that the place has been called—another of its nicknames—the "City of Homes".

The "bandbox" houses, small, narrow, sunless, jerry-built brick hovels, three stories high and without back buildings or any conveniences except a central spigot, are indeed homes in the sense that they are not apartments or tenements, but they are homes no human being should live in. Every now and then they fall down, killing some of their inhabitants.

Nowhere are there worse slums than those of the "City of Brotherly Love".

The Real Property Survey, made in 1934, reported that, of 506,420 family dwellings in Philadelphia, 19,035 were unfit for occupancy, 20,768 were in need of major repairs. Philadelphia has about nineteen thousand houses without bathing facilities of any kind and whose most modern convenience is a privy. Until comparatively recently, pigs were kept well within the limits of the central city, especially under the régime of the Vare brothers who were garbage contractors, and on warm nights, the breeze right, everyone could smell them—the pigs. Over three hundred thousand Philadelphians are improperly housed. During the WPA and rehousing period, Philadelphia, led by its politicians and some of its political millionaires, proudly resisted government loans—the only large city in the country to do so—and when the Government moved in to attempt some work of its own, it threw up its hands in despair and went out into the suburbs to build its housing projects. Surveys have shown that these slums—"ribbon slums" they are called, because of Philadelphia's peculiar rectangular design—are Philadelphia's principal source of crime, vice, and disease; not a very profitable investment, looking at it just from the lowest level.

As the city grew in wealth and size, so did the slums grow south and north, pooling out for swampy miles, practically unheeded and untouched. And as with London, because of the characteristic alleys or mews, thin trickles of the slums, like stagnant little rivulets of crime and vice and disease, had a way of running through even the most respectable districts; had a way of flowing past the backyards of the wealthiest houses. Were a coloured map to be made, the white areas of the rich would show everywhere the black veins of the dangerously poor. Often from their quiet, sunny, book-lined libraries, Philadelphians could look down upon houses where for generations most of the occupants had died of tuberculosis; or upon other houses, better kept and more discreet, where, after dark, their sons, merely by turning a corner, could find for sale none too expensive women.

Philadelphia has lovely street names, fresh and fragrant, and some of them, aromatic. No city has lovelier street names. Pine, and Spruce, and Locust, and Walnut, and Chestnut. Vine and Cherry. Poplar. Sassadras, now Race. Spring Garden. Fairmount. Water. Nectarine. Mulberry, now Arch. Cypress, Buttonwood. . . . Philadelphia also has a local custom—an early morning rite—wherever the fine old houses with their marble front steps still stand; a rite often remarked upon by strangers to the city.

Every morning these steps must be scrubbed, no matter how dirty are the quiet streets beyond. On each one of these steps is a housemaid, or a houseman—or, in the old days, a footman, for Philadelphia once had plenty of the last—down on her knees, or his, busy with buckets and holystone. For a while the streets in the early morning look like congregations at prayer. No matter what else is done, the front steps must be scrubbed.

There is something strangely Freudian about this local passion. Lady Macbeth washed her hands, so did Pontius Pilate.

CHAPTER XXVII

Society Hill

"I hope my Richard will not marry out of Meeting."

REMARK OF MRS. ROBERTS VAUX WHEN, IN 1858, SHE HEARD THAT HER SON RICHARD, THE FUTURE "LION OF THE PHILADELPHIA BAR", AT THE MOMENT SECRETARY OF THE AMERICAN LEGATION IN LONDON, AND A VERY FASHIONABLE YOUNG MAN DESPITE HIS QUAKER UPBRINGING, HAD DANCED WITH QUEEN VICTORIA, THEN A WOMAN OF THIRTY-NINE AND MOST HAPPILY MARRIED.

SEVERAL DECADES AGO a distinguished English cleric, visiting Philadelphia, and preaching to a most fashionable congregation, began his sermon with the words, "I take it I am addressing members of the middle class".

Middle class in England, of course, means something different from what it does in America. In England it merely means someone who hasn't a title and therefore is not formally an "aristocrat", even if he is the younger son of a baron. But although the majority of the visiting cleric's congregation probably knew this, a noticeable coldness nonetheless swept across the pews, and from then on the visiting cleric had what he would have described in his own language as "a thin time".

Another visiting English cleric, a bishop, somewhat later remarked that Philadelphia was "one of the few Tory cities left in the world; Birmingham being the other".

Englishmen, however, like Philadelphia; as a rule they like it better than any other American city. They like it because the tempo is slower. They like it because the climate is damp and the city smells of soft coal. They like it because Philadelphians at night go back to their homes and not to restaurants or night clubs. They like it because Philadelphians entertain in their homes. They like it because Philadelphia women, both in their looks and their manner, are more like Englishwomen than most American women. They like it because the streets, with the exception of Market and Broad, are narrow. They like it because Philadelphia men wear tweeds, and because they are so quietly self-assured that, like the English, they are given to amused understatement and to enjoying jokes about themselves. They like it because Philadelphia homes and clubs and offices are not too shiny and new, and their owners do not care in the least if things are a little shabby and worn if they were once good. They like it because rich Philadelphians take their riches for granted and not as something to get excited about. And they like the sense of family and tradition that practically all Philadelphians of every class, except the newest-comers, tacitly maintain. And very much they like the quiet, kindly, and slightly melancholy contempt Philadelphians have for outer barbarians. The last attitude makes them feel especially at home.

They like, too, the way in which country life, and the almost universal playing of games, is interwoven with the life of the city, and when it comes to professional sport, the way in which Philadelphians, bruised but placid, continue doggedly to patronize the very worst big-league teams in the country. They like the fact that Philadelphia is a centre of those two essentially English games, soccer and cricket. And they like the way Philadelphians continue to call sidewalks "pavements" as they themselves do, and not "sidewalks" as is the custom of aliens such as New Yorkers or Chicagoans.

All this makes the English feel that they and the Philadelphians have one up on the Americans.

Philadelphians even enjoy immensely such ancient jokes as the one where a stranger asks a Philadelphian if Philadelphians like to eat snails, and the Philadelphian answers, "Yes, we're very fond of them, whenever we can catch them".

For a long while New Yorkers—that is, New York critics, authors, newspapermen, and other articulate New Yorkers, hardly any of whom are New Yorkers to begin with—did not believe in Philadelphia. They thought someone was pulling their leg, and when anyone tried to tell them about Philadelphia, they behaved like the countryman who, upon seeing a giraffe for the first time, remarked, "There's no such thing!" For years there was a superstition in New York publishing houses that the one American city that could not be written about successfully was Penn's "Holy Experiment", an idea that has been knocked into a cocked hat during the past decade by the spate of Philadelphia novels and plays.   Meanwhile, the great sprawling city was there, with a ponderous heart-beat of its own, and a lot of people, including its inhabitants, knew it existed.

As a matter of fact, nowhere else in the country is there a better fictional background, simply because there is this weight of tradition, these vestiges of a code, although the latter are getting to be pretty ragged; these prejudices, rational or otherwise.   And above all because there is some stability.   All these mean atmosphere and conflict; and if there's no conflict, there's no story.   One of the most difficult problems the modern novelist has to face is the modern lack of barriers.   As the old lady, taken to see Niagara Falls by her family, who expected enthusiasm, remarked to their chagrin, "What's to hinder?"

If there's no renunciation, what becomes of a love story?   If there's no virtue at all, where's the heroine?

At all events, you can't understand Philadelphia by denying it.   It is true that you cannot describe accurately an immense, solidly rich, steadily growing metropolis of now, since the war, over two million people; a huge manufacturing and commercial and shipping and railway centre, with Italian quarters and German quarters, and Russian and Chinese, and every other kind of quarter, thirteen per cent of whose population is Negro, and 250,000 of whose citizens are factory hands, and 300,000 of whose inhabitants have an income of less than $1,500 a year—you cannot describe such a city solely in terms of three hundred or so families, no matter how powerful these may be.   On the other hand, you cannot describe Philadelphia at all unless you emphasize the fact that, in contradistinction to most other American cities, these same families, many of whom have been in the city since the time of William Penn, still exercise, and show every sympton of continuing to exercise, a power far in excess of their numbers.   They control Philadelphia's wealth, and their power and traditions are understood by all other Philadelphians and either looked up to or resented.   But there is more to it than that; for these powerful folk have not relinquished their political control as in other American cities.   The people who ran William Penn's "Holy Experiment" are still running it.   As a rule they disdain actual participation in politics, but what they say goes.

There is a definite resemblance here to the early Quaker Assembly, which retained its power not by the popular will but by controlling appropriations and gerrymandering the vote.

Philadelphia still retains definitely a ruling class, an "aristocracy", if you wish to call it that, and these people, intimate and interrelated, have their own ways of life, and their rules and taboos, and their own ways of enforcing the latter.   They are not café society, they are an upper class, and furthermore, in certain ways, a very intelligent and self-preservative upper class.   They are vigorous and handsome physically, they fox-hunt and live much out of doors.   They work hard but not too hard, and believe in thrift and prudence.   They invest their money wisely, and, above all, just as the same class does in England, they have always, despite their conservatism, had the wise habit of incorporating worth-while new blood after, that is, a proper period of trial and inspection.   Pretty soon the new blood is likely to be more conservative than the conservatives themselves.

There are certain rewards and privileges, not as formal as being made a peer, but definite and desirable; certain desirable clubs, country and city, numerous houses, certain ancient organizations, including dancing parties. But the last—for this is Philadelphia—also include scientific, artistic, and professional organizations. Philadelphia takes these things seriously, and invariably with a social and personal coloration, and if you wish to belong to the first and last—and they are worth belonging to for material reasons, over and beyond the fact that they are exceptionally pleasant—and if you wish to enter the second, you must behave in a certain way, and even think in a certain way, unless entry and the right to think as you please is a matter of well-established inheritance.

Just as in Georgian England, with its great Whig families and its great Tory families, there has always been in Philadelphia a strong and brilliant nucleus of bold-thinking liberal clans, and by its own rules Philadelphia has to accept these families and put up with them as best it can. But woe betide the new-comer who takes this as a sign that anyone can be radical or aberrational. You do not become, for example, a political or social experimenter by experience and trial and error as happens elsewhere: you are one by inheritance; and so frequently you witness the curious spectacle of a liberal, caught in the web of family tradition, who is at heart a conservative, and a conservative, caught in the web of family tradition, who is at heart a liberal. If this is the case, both are very timid about it.

Finally, to tie everything down securely, there is no political cleavage between city and state as in New York, and, as has been pointed out, no cleavage between those with a college education and the rough-and-ready boys who go directly into politics. There are occasional personal quarrels and jockeying for power, such as the bitter feud of the early 1900's between the gigantic senator, Boies Penrose, who controlled the State, and the extraordinary Vare brothers, who controlled Philadelphia; but as a whole the machine is beautifully interlocked and co-ordinated, the State intermeshing perfectly with the city. Only Pittsburgh, to the extreme west, is recalcitrant. The Scottish-Irish as always, now aided by the South Europeans of the steel mills, have opinions of their own. But on the whole everything is beautifully smooth on the surface. It becomes rude and abusive only when some rash reformer runs for office.

There are no ugly recriminations as in New York against Tammany, or as in Chicago against the Kelly-Nash machine, or as there are all over the country against the Hague machine of Jersey City. Why should there be? If the overwhelming majority of the best people in Philadelphia are allies of the Philadelphia machine, then it must be all right. Aren't these allies very honest people personally? Certainly. Meanwhile, Philadelphia is ruled by the most quietly, and yet crudely wasteful city government in the United States—yes, far more wasteful than most—has the worst water system in the country, the dirtiest streets, a traffic control that still permits policemen to stand at intersections and move little hand signals, a huge public debt, an absurd and crushing tax system, an immense amount of absentee landlordism, and real estate, the basis of all wealth and stability, so mishandled and badly taxed that it is worth almost nothing. These, and unbelievable slums, are some of the costs of collaboration.

During the depression large estate after estate—those unfortunate enough to hold parcels of Philadelphia land—had to pay annual tribute in order to hold their properties. Federal tax, state tax, city tax, and then, down into your own pockets to hold your own! A curious situation for a city of business men, and a sign, perhaps, that collaboration is often worse than active dishonest participation.

Some of the oddest things have happened in Philadelphia, resembling nothing so much as Alice's adventures in Wonderland.

Philadelphia is the only city in the world that built a subway, four blocks long, at a cost of $6,000,000, keeping one of the best shopping and residential streets, and a main artery of travel, Locust Street, torn up and in turmoil for five years or so, and then, the subway completed save for tracks, signals, and station equipment, abandoned it as abruptly as begun. There it is, the subway, a wonderful air-raid shelter if necessary, but otherwise a home for rats. Archæologists a thousand years from now will think it the catacombs of some persecuted sect.

Philadelphia, having conducted a most successful world's fair in 1876, the Centennial Exposition, tried another in 1926, the unfortunate Sesqui-Centennial, located in the swamps of extreme South Philadelphia, and lost $50,000,000. Even Philadelphians were depressed about that for six months or so.

On July 4, a sardonic date, 1874, Philadelphia began the erection of one of the largest, most expensive, and ugliest city halls ever conceived by the mind of man; a monstrosity of bad taste, inconvenience, and graft. It took almost a quarter of a century to complete, and its tower is 510 feet, and the total cost was $26,000,000. On the top of the tower is a 37-foot metal statue of William Penn, hand outstretched, blessing his city. It is a final ignominy that the Founder's outstretched hand points directly at what was once, and may still be, Philadelphia's "red-light" district.

These are only a few of the bewildering things that have happened in Philadelphia.

When it became necessary to install electric lights and a modern water system in the City Hall, it took months and hundreds of thousands of dollars to drill through the miles of solid marble. And this sort of thing, with occasional rare interregnums of reform, which have left little trace, has been going on ever since the Civil War. One of the quickest and surest roads to success in Philadelphia has been to plunder the city, and this has often led eventually to social success as well, as witness what happened to many of the descendants of the McManus "Gas House Ring" and "the Rapid Transit Boys".

But do the worst you can, it is impossible to break, or even hinder for long, a city that has a metropolitan area of 129,714 square miles, with a population of 1,931,334, and which is the hub of an outlying district with a further population of 2,898,644 and an area of a thousand square miles. That's a total population exceeding by more than half a million the population respectively of the state of New Jersey or Massachusetts. Philadelphia and towns and cities in New Jersey and Delaware centring upon it at the present moment produced about one-third of the total war output, and in bewildering variety, for that is another thing about Philadelphia which makes for economic stability and wealth. Philadelphia went through the last depression, save for a real-estate crash, better than any other large American city, for Philadelphia is also the home of small and solid industries and businesses, many of them family-owned. It has everything, and at both ends of the scale. You can't break a city that has one hundred and sixty businesses and firms over a hundred years old, and most of these manufacturing or handling specialities; a city that specializes in ships and locomotives, and also false teeth and the best sombreros the western cowboy or the Argentine gaucho can wear, Stetsons.

This variety and frequent solid smallness, this specialization, made Philadelphia, until the depression, the paradise of employers. Resistance to unionization came from labour itself. Now that is different, but the majority of otherwise intelligent Philadelphians still think labour is a commodity that should be purchased in the open market, and continue to speak about labour as mediæval nurses spoke to their charges about dragons.

A perfect example of the immemorial political set-up of Philadelphia, and hence of most of the state, is the present "boss" of Philadelphia, Mr. Joseph Newton Pew, Jr., although one hates to use such a term as "boss" about anyone of Mr. Pew's calibre. Together with his brother, John Howard Pew, but even more so, Mr. Joseph Pew runs Philadelphia and most of Pennsylvania. But neither Mr. Joseph Pew, Jr., nor his brother is a politician, nor are they originally Philadelphians. They came from the north-west section of the state and are owners and officers of the Sun Oil Company, a family company, whose net annual profits even as far back as 1935 were $7,000,000, and whose gross for the same year was $88,000,000. In addition to this they own the Sun Shipbuilding Company. Both the Messrs. Pew are handsome, extremely charming, and deeply religious men. They are active Presbyterians. They are not in politics because of any desire for power or fame. In fact, they do not like politics and remain as inconspicuous and invisible as possible. They have for politics the proper well-bred contempt. They are in politics solely because of a sense of duty. They are idealists and imaginative. Their only trouble is that politically and socially and economically their imaginations stopped somewhere around the time of Louis XIV, and so, in common with numerous other charming Philadelphians of the same kind, they have never heard very distinctly what happened in the city in 1776.

They are suffering from the delusion that the first verse of the first chapter of Genesis begins with the words, "In the beginning was the *Status Quo.*"

It is exactly as if Mr. J. Pierpont Morgan, Jr., had run, with an iron hand, New York.

This state of affairs has existed in Philadelphia, with but few intervals, since the Civil War, and at the heart of it sits the Union League, with its huge Victorian edifice on South Broad Street, its huge membership, its magnificent restaurant, and its collection of somewhat embarrassing and, certainly, lifelike nudes. You cannot belong to the Union League Club if ever, even once, you have voted the Democratic ticket; not even if afterwards you have repented in sackcloth and ashes and made the pilgrimage to Canossa. You cannot belong if ever, even in your youth, you have so much as toyed with the idea of voting any other ticket but the Republican. Unlike the Union League clubs of other cities, the Union League Club of Philadelphia remains a potent and determining force.

The gigantic figure, both physically and intellectually, of the late Senator Boies Penrose, who for three decades or more dominated the city and state, is a complete symbol of the strange and unholy alliance which distinguishes Philadelphia and Pennsylvania; the alliance of what should be the best of the country and with what, frankly and stolidly, is the worst. Senator Penrose represented the heart of the Philadelphia tradition. In fact he was the Philadelphia tradition. He came from one of the most distinguished of Philadelphia families: a family that belonged to that select group of idealists who in the beginning had helped Penn found the "Holy Experiment", and Senator Penrose had all that a man could want. He was distinguished, he had a brilliant and cultivated mind, in his youth he was extraordinarily handsome. He was an outstanding undergraduate at Harvard. He had wealth. He began as a reformer. He ended as one of the most cynically corrupt of United States senators in an era of fantastic corruption. Yet he never lost his membership in any exclusive Philadelphia organization, nor did anyone think of applying to political corruption—few Americans do—the automatic punishments applied to open financial corruption.

Vast, sardonic, witty, arrogant, totally disillusioned, he went down to his death assured that what he represented was the best the "Holy Experiment", the Declaration of Independence, and its sister document, the Bill of Rights, could do. Only a few had ever taken the trouble to tell him otherwise. But his ruthless and brusque reign was not altogether unmarked by fissures in the usually smooth surface and the rumblings of internal disturbance. Three quaint figures arose to challenge him locally: the Vare brothers, George A., Edwin H., and William S.; and for a long while Philadelphians didn't know to whom they belonged, Senator Penrose or the Vare brothers, although the quarrel, strictly in character, was as much a social one as one for political power.

Senator Penrose, who had in addition to his other gifts a tongue like a scimitar, always referred to the Vare brothers, affectionately known as "the Vare boys", which shows their popularity, as "the Pig Men" or "the Slop-Cart Statesmen", which was unkind, and like most sarcasm, acted in reverse. The Vare boys used these words to their own advantage. Especially in America, an aristocrat, no matter how powerful, should be careful how he sneers at an opponent's origin or the means by which he arose from nothing to riches. Even if the means consists of the collecting of garbage and the foresighted allied business of feeding it to pigs, the results, if successful, make

J

you an Horatio Alger hero. Besides, the Vare boys were everything that Senator Penrose wasn't. They were circumspect, they were quiet in their behaviour, they were devout Methodists, they adored and were ordered about by an ancient and strict Methodist mother, they gave large sums to the church and to charity, they had no open personal vices, and they never took a cent of graft over and beyond their lifework, which was, first, the collecting of Philadelphia's garbage, and then, a lucrative contracting business. Philadelphia's garbage is exceptionally rich and good garbage; it would be, except that of the slum districts. The feeding of it to thousands of pigs, which the Vare boys kept in South Philadelphia within the city limits, when the wind was right, permeated the city.

Any graft you could make out of pigs and garbage, and, later on, contracting, was "legitimate"—was business; otherwise, the Vare boys were incorruptible. They even refused the city salaries due them for the various public offices they occupied, and made a habit of turning these salaries— no mean ones: $10,000, for instance, as city recorder—over to the Catholic, Jewish, and Protestant hospitals, or other worthy institutions, of their home district. Of course they didn't need the salaries; they made millions out of pigs and garbage. But it was a nice gesture, and, besides, no one could point to the slightest alliance between them and the vice of the city. Their mother would not have approved of that. Laxness in one direction, however, leads to laxness in another, and so, during the benign rule of the Vare boys, brothels multiplied, gambling houses were well protected, and street-walking, never very common to Philadelphia's sober streets, showed everywhere its tragic and painted face.

A demure old lady of eminent position lived in a splendid old house opposite another which, with the advance of trade into residential quarters, had become, on its first floor, a fashionable men's tailoring shop, patronized by her grandsons. Sitting at her second-storey window, she remarked the number of men who, during the afternoons, seemed to enter the tailor shop; and they came in even greater numbers at night.

"It is astonishing," she said, "how So-and-So's trade has gone up. I'm so glad because he is almost part of the family—he's made clothes for us for so long. But he must be overworked, poor fellow. Why, do you know, customers keep coming until eleven o'clock at night!"

All the rest of the house, except the first floor, had become one of the city's leading gambling resorts.

There is something fairly disarming about the Vare boys. They are not like people who know better. There is always something disarming about those who have worked their way up and are not ashamed. The voters of Philadelphia appreciated this. When in 1926 William Vare ran for the United States Senate against George Wharton Pepper, eminent lawyer and charming aristocrat, if not a very forcible one—he was known in the Senate as the Great Conciliator—he chose as his slogan:

I milked the cow,
And followed the plough.

On the whole, however, the attitude of the Vare boys worked perfectly, perhaps because within their limits they were candid, courageous, and honest, and, as William said, had learned to meet a lot of people simply and pleasantly, and become intimate with them, by collecting their garbage.

During a bitter political campaign, Ed Vare, stung more to sorrow than anger by Senator Penrose's tongue at its most outrageous, took a reporter to a small street, Ionic Street, south of Chestnut and east of Seventh, which might have been called "Ironic Street", and pointed to an alley upon which certain saloons and small restaurants backed. "We Vares," he said proudly, "are not ashamed of our parents, our friends, or the work we did, or the way we made our way up in the world. Many a cold morning as a boy I came out of that alley at dawn carrying a half-barrel of frozen swill on my shoulder. If Penrose and his high-toned crowd find anything to laugh or sneer about in that, let them laugh."

The Vares even had the distinction of an exceptional heritage, especially in Philadelphia. They were Channel Islanders, hence, originally French, as their name would imply. Their father, Augustus Vare, came from the Island of Jersey, and emigrated to New Jersey, where he married Abigail Stites, whose ancestors had been Puritans in Massachusetts, and Augustus and Abigail had ten children. Augustus and Abigail ran a pig and produce farm, so pigs came naturally to their sons, only the sons improved upon their parents' methods. They played the middle against both ends. Instead of labouring to raise food for the pigs, they carted it away from the back doors of Philadelphia and got paid for doing so. Out of garbage collecting came eventually the immense and powerful Vare Construction Company, among whose clients were the Pennsylvania Railroad and the Bell Telephone Company, and naturally, of course, the city of Philadelphia and the state of Pennsylvania as well.

To the Vares is due the noble and stirring theme and marching song of the Philadelphia Republican machine:

> *Hail, hail, the gang's all here!*
> *What the hell do we care! What the hell do we care!*
> *Hail, hail, the gang's all here!*
> *What the hell do we care now!*

This was first sung by the First Ward delegation of the Matthew Stanley Quay Club, Senator Matthew Stanley Quay being another famous and typical political "boss" and Pennsylvania United States senator of the vintage of Senator Penrose. Since then the song has been taken up by lesser breeds.

The First Ward delegation of the Matthew Stanley Quay Club had boarded a bus, charted to take them to a county convention at old Industrial Hall at Broad and Vine streets. But one of their number, Charlie Fowler, was missing, so the First Ward delegation was worried. Every vote counted. And then Charlie Fowler appeared, and an unknown bard shouted with

J*

joy the first extemporized line, and as the omnibus drove up Broad Street the song was completed, and the delegation entered Industrial Hall singing at the top of their voices.

So great folk music is born, although it is a sad commentary on fame, also virtue, and also fate, that Charlie Fowler is remembered because he was late, while the minstrel who acclaimed his coming is forgotten.

William Vare began his business career as a cashboy in John Wanamaker's store at one dollar-fifty a week; then he was promoted to the soda fountain, and finally to the auditor's office. When he resigned after two-and-a-half years' service he was making two-fifty a week. Wages like these give young men big ideas and lead to scrupulous financial integrity.

When in 1903 Lincoln Steffens wrote for *McClure's Magazine* his series of sensational articles, published a year later under the title *The Shame of the Cities*, the section devoted to Philadelphia was headed, "Corrupt and Contented". The label stuck and is still current coinage. Philadelphia is not as blatantly corrupt as it was then; nothing is as blatantly corrupt. Shamelessness in such matters is no longer so much the fashion. Nor is the city as manifestly corrupt. Nowadays political corruption is more demure and better-mannered. As a matter of fact, it is the only thing that is more demure and better-mannered. But in everything that counts, the "Holy Experiment" is just as corrupt and contented as ever.

"Age cannot wither, nor custom stale" in this respect the city's infinite lack of variety. It is no longer possible perhaps to refer to the "voting list of the Founding Fathers of the country; residence, Independence Hall", solid machine men every one of them, even one by the name of Thomas Jefferson, as was done by amused politicians in the days of Lincoln Steffens, nor is "macing" any longer popular, or the other ruder forms of blackmail, coercion, or theft; but it is still possible for a successful candidate for the office of mayor to meet his defeated rival in a club frequented by both the day after the election, as happened not so long ago, and say to him genially, "Oh, by the way, you didn't know that you really won yesterday, did you?"

Philadelphia has voting machines, but if you are adroit enough you can do queer things even with voting machines, and there are equally queer things you can do with registration, pro and con. And Philadelphians, even more than other Americans, are pretty careless about voting. In a recent election 696,192 registered Philadelphia voters stayed at home and only 237,000 voted. In army terms this means that at the moment Philadelphia had approximately twenty army corps of voters, of which thirteen full army corps were deserters.

You can't fight much of a campaign on that.

But there is another side to this picture, and one of much beauty and mellowness; of a patina like well-used, well-polished, well-made, completely dependable furniture. A picture of a security and assurance like a well-built, four-square old house. A picture that has the colour of tawny port. Or Philadelphia's own favourite and hereditary wine, Madeira. Philadelphians, high or low, do have a code, and, high or low, some sense of their own and their country's past. They couldn't help having something of the latter; it is in the streets and the bricks and the air. They have, at all events, what is so often lacking elsewhere, a vague sense of what might be called the "American stream of consciousness". They know that both their country and their city have had a history; they do not think that they began in 1900, or even 1776, as so many New Yorkers do, if they think about such things at all. They have a sense of being heirs to something, however much they may misinterpret what that thing is.

One has a feeling, even at one's most despairing, that at any moment the city can do exactly what it wants, if it only wants to do so; that at any time it may decide once more to be great. It is large, sprawling, careless, prejudiced and unaware, but there is not a trace of decadence or fatigue. Penn's "Holy Experiment" has immense reserves of vigour. After all, a code, however mistaken in parts or however hampering, and a sense of history and of tradition are better than nothing, for they have a form, a shape, and are therefore a vessel into which new wine may be poured with a hope, perhaps, that it will not be wasted. Otherwise, too often new wine is merely poured out upon the sand where it soon dries up.

When a Philadelphian learns something, he remembers it. The difficulty lies in getting him to learn.

Meanwhile in all the country, and for that matter in all the world, there are no finer men and women than Philadelphia's best; none more charming, more simple, more dignified, more interesting, more good-looking, more cultivated, and more intelligently liberal. And they are dependable in a way a great many otherwise fine people are not. In all the world there are no houses where you can find better talk, or better thought, than in certain Philadelphia houses, and fundamentally it is reassuring talk and thought, because these people have form, as has been said, both mental and moral, and so you are aware that when it comes to the point, the issue, the dilemma, small or large, intellectual or actual, you know where you will find them, where they will be. A matter of immense importance in these amorphous times. But which does not mean, of course, that in the ordinary and conventional definition of morals, these same people may not be almost anything they may privately want. One way in which the former is shown is the manner in which the city eventually meets any national crisis.

By tradition and instinct most Philadelphians are bitterly conservative; by tradition and instinct when their country needs them, despite preliminary talk, without hesitation they respond magnificently, whatever privately they may think.

Before Peal Harbour, Philadelphia with its great Italian and German elements, its Quaker inheritance of pacifism, and its Tory upper class, was looked upon as a potential "danger point". The die cast, its young men volunteered by thousands before they were drafted, and back at home the city went instantly to work, and the pulse of production has been as steady as a great heart.

It is interesting and much more important than it seems, to mention a few of these institutions, these customs, these survivals that tie Philadelphia to its past, for outside of their individual flavour they mean a great deal. And the especial point is that they are known to the city as a whole, and are respected and understood by it. Finally, there is every intention of preserving them.

The city as a whole does not regard them as absurd, or anachronistic, or confined merely to a small element. They are looked upon as an integral part of the city.

CHAPTER XXVIII

Patina

"We are omnibuses in which our ancestors ride."
OLIVER WENDELL HOLMES.

The story is so old and has so often been repeated that one hesitates to mention it, but possibly no Philadelphia chronicle is complete without it. . . . Already you know what the story is: the remark of Edward VII of England, while Prince of Wales, after visiting Philadelphia.

"I met," he said, "a very large and interesting family named Scrapple, and I discovered a rather delicious native food they call biddle."

NO OTHER AMERICAN city, not even Charleston, not even Boston, has so many ancient and honourable and still vigorous institutions and customs, most of them endearing and worth-while, as has Philadelphia. Here are a few of them.

We can begin with the First Troop Philadelphia City Cavalry. Or the First City Troop, to give it its older and traditional name. Or the Philadelphia Troop of Light Horse, to give it the name it bore during the Revolution, when it was first organized.

Here is a military organization, continuous in its history, with a record and morale as proud as any in existence, professional or otherwise, a military organization older than any regiment of the regular United States Army; indeed, the oldest military organization in the country, on whose battle flag are the engagements of every war fought since we began as a nation. A militia organization which throughout its history has earned the complete respect of all professional soldiers, and which furnishes a beautiful answer —one of many—to those historians who would have us believe that Washington's army, rank and file, was a rabble, and that all educated and well-to-do colonials were inevitably Tories.

The Troop, organized November 17, 1774, was composed of "young bloods", sons of the best families of the city, fox-hunters and sportsmen, with a goodly sprinkling of similar young "Fighting Quakers", and from the beginning had a magnificent record. At the Battle of Princeton, in a famous charge, it routed the British cavalry and captured twice its number of British dragoons. Subsequently it served as Washington's bodyguard and, until recently, was the presidential bodyguard at all inaugurations. Washington cited it as follows:

"Though composed of gentlemen of fortune, they [the Troop] have shown a noble example of discipline and subordination, and in several actions have shown a spirit and bravery which will ever do honour to them and will ever be gratefully remembered by me."

In the last war the Troop served as a machine-gun company; in this war, according to the present custom, it has been submerged in a bigger unit, and many of its members have been drafted off to, or have volunteered for, various other organizations. Its percentage of officer material is high. But peace will reconstitute it as it has been for a hundred and seventy years; and for generations, father to son, certain Philadelphia families have served in it. In its full-dress uniform, worn for state occasions—massive light-dragoon helmet, with clipped horsehair plume, short body-fitting tunic of black broadcloth, faced with gold braid and gold buttons, tight breeches of white buckskin, and immense patent leather jack-boots, the Troop is a colourful and impressive organization. The captain and the two lieutenants, or as they are still called, "cornets", wear the same uniform except that their tunics are scarlet.

When the Troop rides through the crowded streets of the city, or marches on foot, sabres at side, as it does, for instance, to its annual service at Christ Church, the city is respectful and admiring. It does not think the Troop or its dress uniforms anachronistic; it knows all about both and is proud of both.

Philadelphia also has the oldest and most distinguished dancing parties in the United States, even older and more distinguished than the St. Cecilia in Charleston; two of them a year in the middle of the winter, the First and the Second Assembly. And the city knows all about them too, and if not their exact history, at least has an idea of their antiquity and prestige. They do not function in a cultural vacuum as do similar parties in most cities. And very dignified, yet gay and beautiful balls they are, where the ladies, upon entering the foyer, curtsy low to the long line of receiving patronesses, young and old, of the year, and their escorts, back of them, bow from the waist. The Assemblies have many rules, and these have not changed very much from the founding of the parties in 1748—just four years short of two hundred years ago. Also, as has been stated, it is astonishing how many of the families—the great majority—of those on the original list are still subscribers. Those who belong to the Assemblies often affect to laugh at them as being stiff and old-fashioned, although they are not really, as those who belong to anything can always afford to laugh, and the younger generation has been in the habit of shrugging its shoulders at these formal occasions, generation after generation, since they were first started; but the younger generation ceases to laugh as it too becomes mothers and fathers, or grand-mothers and grandfathers. And meanwhile, try to take the privilege away from any family which has inherited it! Or try to prevent new-comers of any prominence to the city, or new-comers by way of recently acquired fortune, from using every known means to get the names of their children on the subscription list!

The Assemblies exercise an altogether extraordinary power, both social and material, in the city, and to say you belong, which mustn't be said at all unless absolutely necessary, and then in the most casual manner, is exactly like announcing your rank in a country of hereditary titles.

One of the most spectacular of the Assembly rules in these days of divorce and remarriage is that if you do this—get a divorce and remarry, that is —you are automatically dropped. Your children by the previous marriage may still belong, but not you. It used to be that your name disappeared from the list if you got a divorce, but the Assemblies have been liberalized, and now it is possible to be divorced so long as you remain in that state, suspended, as it were, between hell and heaven. This rule, like most moral rules, has had at times unexpected results, at least in the past. Sort of reverse-English results. Several of Philadelphia's most famous extra-marital romances were of such length and abiding faithfulness that their status can only be explained by the fear that change and legalization would lose the principals their right to go to the Assemblies.

Philadelphia also possesses the oldest men's city club in the country, and one of the oldest in existence, the Philadelphia Club. This was founded in 1834, seventy years after the founding of Brooks's in London. At first it was called the Adelphia, and then for a while, out of respect to the Quaker dislike of the word "club", the Philadelphia Association and Reading Room.

Somewhere at the back, or forefront, of almost every Philadelphia custom, or organization, or meeting of any kind, annual or otherwise, you will find an excellent supper or superb dinner, frequently featuring especial Philadelphia dishes and usually accompanied, whatever else there is to drink, and as a rule there is plenty, by Philadelphia's historic wine, Madeira. Public eating in Philadelphia is unbelievably bad; private eating still maintains a high, historic standard. All during colonial times, when Philadelphia was a capital and a cross-roads, and until comparatively recently, Philadelphia had a fine tradition of food, as fine as New Orleans, and this tradition persisted until about four decades ago, when American food everywhere began to break down under the infiltration of bastard Franco-Italian cooking. At one time Philadelphia had dozens of excellent restaurants, large and small, some of which, like the old Bellevue, Green's, the old Continental, were world famous. To-day in all the city there is not a single first-class restaurant, although there is one excellent and historic sea-food place, and one excellent chop-house. Outside of these, the majority of Philadelphians, when not at home, eat in strange frowzy teashops or, if they are rich, in restaurants where the marvellous products of the native cornucopia are disguised or ruined by Mediterranean self-conviction. In many of Philadelphia's private houses, however, in the city or in the suburbs, you can still find what William

Penn talked about, and the generations that followed him. It should be so, for the city is a middle city, exactly placed to receive the benefits of both the North and South, and at its back door is the richest farm land in the United States.

Philadelphia, then, has, or could have, superb mutton and beef, and so it still has if you want them, and know how to cook them, for, whatever may have happened to the city's restaurants, traditional and matchless markets remain. As for vegetables of every kind, fruits, dairy products, the town is golden and green with them. "Philadelphia butter" is everywhere spoken of with reverence, and so are "Philadelphia capons". Philadelphia cream cheese is a local invention and, incidentally, the best thing in the world for your teeth: it is filled with calcium. Sooner or later one always gets back to teeth in Philadelphia. The American love of cottage cheese, *Schmierkase*, is due to Philadelphia, or rather, the neighbouring "Pennsylvania Dutch". Philadelphia ice-cream and ice-cream meringues, and Philadelphia's especial soup, pepper-pot, invented in colonial days, are things to be talked about. Philadelphia terrapin is a delight, and its cousin, Philadelphia stewed snapper, is equally good. And with these can now be listed Philadelphia's éclairs, unlike any other éclairs in existence, and Philadelphia lady-fingers, lady-locks, white-mountain cake, and above all, Philadelphia cinnamon buns. In just one place in New York can you get real cinnamon buns, and there the Philadelphia recipe is followed.

Philadelphia has presented many dishes to the rest of the country, and in almost every instance the rest of the country ruins them. Few Americans, for instance, know what cinnamon bun is—not the glacéed, brown celestial kind. Nor do they know coffee cakes, which, in Philadelphia, owing again to the "Pennsylvania Dutch" influence, are flaky *croissants*, iced with sugar, and raisins inside to make your mouth water. Philadelphia is one of the few places where you can get real doughnuts; those without a hole in them, and which are as light as thistledown. The list is endless.

Philadelphia not only has a perfect gastronomical latitude, but two ancient strains of cooking: Quaker cooking, the Quakers being the only English who ever understood cooking, and "Pennsylvania Dutch" cooking. The pretzel is a "Pennsylvania Dutch" invention; although, even if you are a Philadelphian, unless you know one or two hidden-away shops, you have to go to Reading to discover what a pretzel is.

In Reading they are large, but thin and crisp. Golden brown from butter; and with just the right sprinkling of salt. Not common salt, but salt crystals. And in Reading they still fold their arms symbolically across their breasts, seraphim in adoration, as the Moravian monks, who first made them, meant them to do.

Nor does anyone north of Philadelphia know what an oyster is; a statement that will cause unbelief in the minds of New Yorkers and rage in the breasts of Bostonians. But Philadelphians, except in restaurants ruined by alien influence, do not eat the white, unhealthy, broken-spirited creatures found in New York, first cousins of liver-fed mountain trout, whose only taste is supplied by the horse-radish or tomato catsup furnished on the side. Nor

do Philadelphians like the huge white bedspreads favoured by New England
—"naked babies", Charles Dickens called them.   To the real Philadelphian
an oyster cocktail, unless one is forced to eat the debased sea creatures described,
is an abomination.   Why disguise the taste of an oyster?

A touch of lemon; a touch of horse-radish—that is all.

Philadelphians eat slim and lovely grey oysters, caught far from the
wicked ways of cities.   When you swallow them, you taste the native salt,
and if you close your eyes, you hear the tide on the shingles of lonely
islands.

Scrapple, or *pon-haus*, which is not a "Pennsylvania Dutch" discovery,
as is so generally supposed, but dates from the even earlier real Dutch and
Swedish settlers, need not be gone into too deeply because it is a bitter nation-
wide controversy: Philadelphians on one side, all the rest of the United
States on the other.   But Philadelphians who have married maidens from
the barbarous outer forests speedily show them what a delectable dish scrapple
is when properly cooked.   It is not slimy, it should not be greasy, it should
not be thick; it should be thin, piping hot, crisp as an October day, and as
golden brown as a Reading pretzel.   It should crunch.   Correctly cooked
and served, it will woo even the most reluctant breakfast appetite.

On that statement, like all others reared in Philadelphia, I will take my
stand.   Let the forest dwellers rave!

Even more formal than the dinners of Mr. Franklin's Pennsylvania
Company for Insurance on Lives and Granting Annuities—the Hand-and-
Hand—with their S-shaped ginger cookies and oysters—are the monthly
dinners of the Green Tree, the rival and more liberal company, which tried
to save the trees of Philadelphia rather than destroy them.   The Green
Tree begins invariably with terrapin, goes on to real Virginia ham, and for
a hundred and sixty-eight years two formal toasts have been drunk, one
in Madeira, one in sherry: the first to General Washington, the second to
the continued welfare of the Green Tree.   Presiding at the Green Tree dinners
is always some distinguished Philadelphian, noted not for business, but for
science or the arts, for Philadelphia, as has been pointed out, is by no means
a materialistic city.   To the contrary, it is an extremely intellectual one
if you do not make the error in taste of expecting Philadelphians to do the
work themselves.

Such dinners as those of the Green Tree, annual or monthly, are duplicated
by dozens of other societies, scientific, cultural, or business, and such dinners,
after all, are extremely important, for they remind an American of the long
and colourful and dignified history of his country.   Men cannot live by
bread alone, nor can they live well if they think the world began with them.
Such dinners also confirm the statement that Philadelphia is the most masculine
city in the country; as masculine as London.   Muliebrity has so far made
little impression on Penn's "Holy Experiment".   In this respect the attitude
of the average Philadelphian, even that of the younger generation, is still
clear-cut, and hearty, and tinged with the eighteenth century.   Philadelphia

is one of the few places left in the world where you still occasionally hear, when reference is made to the life of some self-indulgent friend, "so-and-so's woman". Not "girl friend"; not "mistress"—"Woman".

It is fitting then, taking all things together—this traditional interest and pride in food, this local supply of it, this delight in excellent and purely masculine conversation, and this belief in form, and a pleasant shining formality—that Philadelphia should be the home of the most famous and historic social organization in the country, by far the oldest social organization in the United States, and that this should be a cooking club, in the beginning also a fishing club—rockfish and perch—although this excuse has long since been abandoned, due to the polluted waters of Philadelphia's two rivers. This is The Fish House, or the State in Schuylkill. And the more you look into The Fish House the more interested you become.

The Fish House, or State in Schuylkill, or as it was originally called The Schuylkill Fishing Company of the State in Schuylkill, or, more briefly, The Colony in Schuylkill, was founded in 1732 in the reign of George II, and many of its members also belonged to the Gloucester Fox Hunting Club, the oldest organized hunt in the country. The Fish House is now two hundred and twelve years old, and the name "State in Schuylkill" is no idle boast or assumption, for the State in Schuylkill was originally and actually a separate state within a state, granted complete extra-territorial rights by colonial governors. Within its mansion, Eaglesfield, or Ecclesfield, situated first on a hill above the Schuylkill, and on the few sloping acres pertaining to it, the law and officers of the province of Pennsylvania did not function, and that is why the officers of The Fish House are known as the Governor, The Counsellors—three in number—the Sheriff, the Coroner, and the Secretary of State. In its earliest days The Fish House maintained a pleasant little jail, something like a summer-house, for the benefit of obstreperous members, where they could recover in the cool of the afternoons.

The land at Ecclesfield, the original site of The Fish House, was rented from William Warner, Esq., a member, and the annual rental was three fresh sun-perch, presented on a pewter platter.

During the Revolution, the State in Schuylkill, in an outburst of patriotism, deeded its rights back to the United States, an act greatly regretted when, a hundred and forty years later, Prohibition went into effect. There has been much speculation as to what would have happened had The Fish House kept its foreign status. In 1822 The Fish House moved from its original mansion, or "Castle" as it was called, on the Schuylkill, above the present Fairmount Dam, and went downriver to Rambo's Rock, opposite Bartram's Garden, where another "Castle", the present one, was built. Several decades later, the lower Schuylkill threatening to become the malodorous ditch it is to-day, The Fish House made another migration, this time up the Delaware to Andalusia, twenty miles or so north of the city. This time the "Castle", lock, stock and barrel, was taken along, transported on the decks of flatboats, a journey of fifty or more miles. Only a year ago The Fish House, with its "Castle", moved again, this time only a few miles away from its former site.

The Fish House meets twice a month during the summer, thirteen

J**

"Company Days" in all, from May first to October first, and the members come from miles away. You do not miss the meetings if you can help it. And these meetings begin before lunch and last well into the night following the superb dinner, cooked by various members appointed, in rotation, under the supervision of "a caterer", likewise appointed, each course cooked by a different appointee for that night, and his crew of assistants. The meal is served by the "Apprentices"—young aspirants to the honourable society. The Fish House is especially proud of its beefsteak, and it should be, for to obtain a properly cut and properly cooked beefsteak anywhere in the world nowadays is as rare as finding a Koh-i-noor diamond. Here is a note for housewives. And here is a note especially for Franco-Italian chefs. One of the rules of The Fish House is never to cleanse a steak of its exuding juices; never to puncture it with a fork, but always to use a pair of tongs in turning; never to butter the fat beef; and never to sprinkle with too high seasoning.

General Washington was a frequent guest of The Fish House; so, on one occasion, was Lafayette. Inlaid on the dinner table are little silver plates marking where they sat.

But beefsteak is only one of the many culinary specialities of the State in Schuylkill, and each one of the members has a particular speciality, besides being a *cordon bleu* in all other directions. It is interesting to see eminent surgeons and doctors, eminent lawyers—eminent everything—bending over great ranges preparing, with delicate knowledge, everything from capon with white wine to string-beans, and the latter, believe it or not, are worth eating when properly prepared. Two stated toasts are always drunk by The Fish House; the first to "The Memory of Washington", the second to "The Memory of our Late Worthy Governor Morris"; Captain Samuel Morris, Governor of The Fish House from 1766 to 1812, and first captain of the City Troop. The most famous product of The Fish House, however, is its historic drink, Fish House Punch, which, delectable and deceptive, stems straight down from colonial days, and at first taste seems to the ignorant or unwary rather like glorified Moselle cup. This punch is always served in a Chinese bowl presented to the State in Schuylkill a hundred and forty-three years ago by Captain Charles Ross, and brought by him from the Orient. It has, as a matter of fact, the "strength of ten", or even more, "because its heart is pure".

For generations the secrets of Fish House Punch were kept inviolate, and then, somewhere around the turn of the century, the members, in another outburst of generosity, gave them to the world. The drink made its first public appearance at an afternoon reception given for a young lady. The tradition is that all that evening, until late, the quieter streets of the city roared with mature and ancient female friends of the girl's mother, or grandmother, waving from their carriages or being escorted home by stronger members of their family.

A few years ago the First City Troop repaid a debt—double debt—a hundred and twenty-three years old. In 1815 The Fish House entertained the Troop at its "Castle". In 1915 The Fish House did the same. In 1938 the Troop invited The Fish House to a formal dinner at its armoury. On the appointed day, Washington's Birthday, the Troop in full uniform, sabres and jack-boots clanking, marched down Walnut Street nine blocks from its armoury to the Philadelphia Club, where The Fish House, in its uniform, straw "boaters" on head, ribbons with the colours of The Fish House around them, was waiting. Together, in formation, the two organizations marched back to the armoury for cocktails and then dinner.

Since there are no more than thirty "Citizens" at any one time in the State of Schuylkill—the "Apprentices" not counting as "Citizens"—there have been to date only a few over three hundred members of The Fish House in the two hundred and twelve years of its existence.

Similar to The Fish House, but a winter club and a younger one, is the Rabbit, which has a lovely old yellow stucco colonial house on the outskirts of Philadelphia. As you enter the door on a winter's noon, your coat is taken away from you, and a cook's apron is tied on, which you wear until you leave, any time between ten-thirty and the small hours of the following Sunday morning; for the Rabbit holds its meetings on alternate Saturdays. Lunch, a very simple but delicious one, consisting of one meat dish, a vegetable, a dessert, and cheese, is prepared by the club servants. Afterwards, through the winter afternoon, you talk, or play cards, or—the most popular pursuit —play that almost extinct but very exciting game, shuffleboard, on *de luxe* courts in a building built for that purpose. Sometimes the stakes are high; usually, moderate and friendly. At five a warning bell is rung and all those appointed cooks for the day, followed by their helpers, gather in the low-ceilinged colonial kitchen, where there is a battery of great shining ranges. The kitchen walls twinkle beautifully with serried copper pots, soon to be put to use. If you are a guest, you are always accorded the honour of being one of the cooking crews, but your task is an humble one such as chopping spinach or peeling onions.

At eight, dinner is served in the long, low-ceilinged dining-room, its walls decorated only by a couple of historic portraits, but the mahogany furniture is magnificent, and the endless table shines beneath the light of silver candelabra and shimmers with its linen, its glass, and other silver presented through the generations. The seating is strictly according to protocol, and the dinner is served by the youngest members. The cooks and their crews, their duties over, relax. At ten the cloth is drawn, and coffee and liqueurs and brandy are brought, and the lovely dark mahogany table shimmers even more than before, and the lights from the candelabra form in wine-coloured pools on its surface. Two formal toasts are drunk: to "Mr. Washington" and to "The President of the United States"; then other necessary toasts, and then, perhaps, a few speeches, short and usually witty. But here is perhaps the most interesting thing of all: until the brandy is brought, no strong liquor has been drunk at all during the day. With dinner there has been sherry to begin with, and appropriate white and red wines, but no strong liquor until the brandy is brought.

Before the great hearth in another room, all day long, brewing in great leather jerkins, there has stood a bubbling hot punch, as secret as Fish House Punch once was, that has been mulling for twenty-four hours. As a result, almost all evil has disappeared and only smoothness and warmth are left.

You are at liberty to drink as much of this punch during the day as you want—the supply seems endless—and it cannot hurt you; it merely makes you feel sociable and pleasant. With the brandy, however, at ten o'clock, bang! . . . all rules are off, and you are at liberty to do what you want, although Heaven help you if it's unpleasant. When you leave the dining-room and go back to the other rooms to play cards or talk, in each one is a sideboard bearing whiskies and bottles of soda and other after-dinner drinks. Nor is there any feeling of age, up or down, to either of these organizations. The membership ranges from men well up in the 'eighties to boys just out of college, and all are equally enthusiastic, and no one thinks in terms of generations.

Dr. Caspar Wistar, he of the wistaria, started considerably over a hundred years ago as pleasant and worth-while men's parties as can be found any-where. They are known as "Wistar Parties" and are famous in Philadelphia and with anyone lucky enough ever to have been asked to one. There are twenty-four members, and each member brings a guest—the more distinguished, the better—and these stand-up buffet suppers are held during the winter in rotation in the various houses of the members. No one does anything but eat and talk, and the conversation is only matched by the food. Whoever of interest happens to be in the city—statesman, soldier, actor, artist, writer, scientist—is likely to be there, meeting the best minds of a large and elderly city. As for the food and drink—it is suprising how many members of the Wistar Parties seem to have inherited cellars featured by Madeira.

American advertising, like the "little girl with the curl", when good, is very good indeed, and when bad, which is most of the time, "is horrid". Recently there has been appearing in the magazines some excellent and dignified advertising, extolling the merits of a popular brand of whisky which bears the name of Penn's "Holy Experiment". Two men, one young, one mature, are bending over a table in a handsome room, studying lovingly a small brass saluting cannon. On the wall back of them is a portrait of a Revolutionary commodore in buff and blue; possibly John Barry. The men, good-looking, sunburned men, look like Philadelphians. The room looks like a Philadelphia room. Whoever did the illustration knew what he was doing.

Now all this, of course—the texture and the traditions, the paradoxes, the adherence to custom, or the opposition to it—makes Philadelphia, as has been said, a marvellous, if difficult place, to write about. There's plenty to set your teeth into. But by the same token it is a dangerous place for a writer to be born. Philadelphia writers take longer to mature than most American writers. They are likely to go through a period of arrested develop-ment. The weight of the city bows them down. Either they have to find their way out of the webbed taboos of two hundred and fifty years, or else they revolt without understanding and mistake small cobwebs for big. Literary movements in Philadelphia, when there are any at all, are usually ten years behind those of the rest of the country.

At the end of the twenties young Philadelphia writers still thought sex was something men and women over forty had not yet discovered.

The city is as difficult for aspiring writers as its leisurely tempo, its slow damp skies and silvery mists make it a good place for painters and musicians. Painters and musicians live, to a large extent, apart and talk a special language and exercise esoteric crafts. All they need is appreciation and patronization, ignorant or otherwise, and this they get in Philadelphia. Writers alone of all artists must mingle with their fellows and live in the market-place. Moreover language, at least at first glance, is not esoteric. Everyone more or less talks it, and everyone, more or less—that is, unless they know better—thinks he or she can write it, and there have been a surprising number of fairly good books, single novels and so on, written by Philadelphians of all kinds in what the French call "the play of the spirit", or even, "for to pass the time", as the French would also say. None of this makes for the knowledge in Philadelphia of the blood and sweat involved in actual authorship, or the vast training in technique required. And then authors use ideas—that is, some of them do—and ideas by their very nature are likely to be revolutionary.

If an author is satisfied with the world as he finds it, what he has to say will not be very interesting.

Above the heads of young Philadelphians, male or female, who wish to write, tradition and opinion brood like a December sky. So the first thing young Philadelphia writers do is to go somewhere else. But like so much else in the city, this was not always so. There was a time during the first decades of the last century when Philadelphia was vigorously literary, and when a "Philadelphia school of literature" flourished. At the same time the city was the centre of the magazine world and the centre of publishing. During that period over a hundred magazines and journals of all kinds, literary, scientific, artistic, and trade, were being published, among them such famous ones as *Godey's Lady's Book*, *Graham's*, the *Gentlemen's Magazine*, and, until comparatively recently, *Lippincott's*. There was one that bore the delightful name of the *Dental Cosmos*. Philadelphia even has a claim upon that immortal series, *McGuffey's Readers*. Their originator, Mr. Winthrop Smith, was a New Englander, but after he had made his fortune by illumining the Middle West and then the rest of the country, he retired to Philadelphia, where his descendants became gentleman farmers and famous fox-hunters.

Philadelphia is still an important text-book and technical publishing centre, with such famous firms, a century or a century and a half old, as Blakiston and Lea & Febiger, and such distinguished but younger firms as W. B. Saunders and the John C. Winston Company; but its pre-eminence in general publishing has passed to New York and Boston. Two important general firms are left: Lippincott, venerable and famous; Macrae Smith, young and vigorous. As for magazines, Philadelphia no longer publishes many except technical and trade journals, but the few general magazines it continues to publish, all owned by the same company, have, to say the least, considerable weight—the *Saturday Evening Post*, the *Ladies' Home Journal*, and the *Country Gentleman*. The *Ladies' Home Journal* has the largest circulation of any magazine in the world, and interestingly enough is much read by men.

Philadelphia's own, especial "literary school" came at a curious time, and flourished oddly and rankly, like the strange, almost tropical growth —johnny-jump-ups and skunk cabbage, and other orchid-like things—that appear with spring in the dark gorges of the Wissahickon. The Romantic Movement was sweeping the world, and before it the matter-of-fact realism of the eighteenth century was in full flight. Philadelphia, strangely enough, fell heavily. But then it is not so strange; the Quaker, beneath his sober outer behaviour, has always been a more romantic fellow than the hard-headed New Englander. In every way Philadelphia is a softer city than Boston.

Mr. Austin Gray has called this one and only "school of Philadelphia literature" the "underground school", because, as he sees it, it flourished so rankly apart from, and almost unnoticed by, the growing city, become now more soberly business-minded than ever, since state and national capitals had been removed, and given to reading Hawthorne and Washington Irving more than native products. But the "Philadelphia school" couldn't have been so "underground", for some of the authors had immense, world-wide circulation. George Lippard, for instance, the wildest and most Gothic of the lot, was as popular in England as America. He was the Marie Corelli of his time. His novels sold by the thousands.

Lippard was an extraordinary young man, and has become a collector's item. Nowadays no one remembers him but historians and antiquarians. His speciality was huge novels setting forth the sins of Philadelphia, and if one were to take his descriptions at their face value, Philadelphia in the 1830's and '40's was only a shade better than Gomorrah. All rich young men were villains, seducing the innocent females of the poor, and Chestnut and Walnut streets and various other thoroughfares were seething after dark with young "bucks" in expensive great-coats and pearl-grey top-hats, inflamed with brandy or Madeira. Like so many authors of the Romantic Period, and not a few of to-day, Lippard surrounded himself with mystery. He dressed in a poverty-stricken fashion, but with a black cape, and lived in a disused warehouse. Born in 1822, he died when he was only thirty-two, in 1854.

His novels are really priceless gems of flamboyant writing, and an interesting comment on what our near ancestors must have taken for reality.

Here, for instance, is the introduction to one of Lippard's best-known novels, *The Quaker City, or the Monks of Monk Hall*, the sub-title of which is "A Romance of Philadelphia Life, Mystery and Crime", and the motto of which is "Woe to Sodom!":

The motive which impelled me to write this work may be stated in a few words. I was the only Protector of an Orphan Sister. I was fearful that I might be taken away by death, leaving her alone in the world. I know too well the law of society which makes a virtue of the dishonour of a poor girl, while it justly holds the seduction of a rich man's child as an infamous crime. These thoughts impressed me deeply. I determined to write a book founded upon the following idea.

That the seduction of a poor and innocent girl is a deed altogether as criminal as deliberate murder. It is worse than the murder of the body, for it is the assassination of the soul. If the murderer deserves death by the gallows, then the assassin of chastity and maidenhood is worthy of death by the hands of any man, and in any place. . . . Would God that the evils recorded in these pages were not based upon facts. Would God that the experience of my life had not impressed me so vividly with the colossal vice and the terrible deformities presented in the social system of the large city, and in the nineteenth century.

How's that for the quiet and supposedly moral manners of our mid-Victorian grandparents?

Lippard's other books bore such titles as *Paul Ardenheim, the Monk of the Wissahickon* and *Blanche of Brandywine*.

Like so many other ill-balanced people, Lippard wanted to start a secret society, slightly fascist in character, although the term had not been invented at the time, so he started "The Brotherhood of the Union", of which he was the self-appointed "Supreme Washington". Lippard did not confine himself entirely to romantic novels. Some of his work is historical, such as *Washington, and his Generals.*

Contemporary with Lippard was Henry Hirst, who wrote some fairly good poetry and died insane, thinking that he had written Poe's *The Raven.*

There were many lesser writers whose fame was even more ephemeral.

The "school" in reality had been begun by Charles Brockden Brown, who, born in 1771, began as a writer in the classical style—and no mean one—but who also wrote novels which had such titles as *Edgar Huntley; or, The Memoirs of a Sleep-Walker*, published in 1801, and *Ormond; or, The Secret Witness*, published in 1799. Brown died in 1810.

Out of the "Philadelphia school", soon gone and soon forgotten, emerged a few really excellent writers, although they had no connection with the "school" either in their methods or ideas. George Henry Boker has already been mentioned, and Princeton-trained Charles Godfrey Leland, editor and traveller and author of *Hans Breitmann's Ballads*, is also, and deservedly, remembered. Living outside of Philadelphia, at West Chester and Kenneth Square, but a part of the city, was another writer, Bayard Taylor, of almost, if not quite, major importance. Now about the only thing of his remembered is the "Bedouin Song"—"Till the sun grows cold. And the stars are old, And the leaves of the Judgment Book unfold!"—and not many who hear the song recall who wrote it.

In the '90's two really first-class novelists appeared on the Philadelphia scene, Dr. S. Weir Mitchell and Owen Wister, and, unlike most Philadelphia writers, they stayed where they were, intimately indentified with their city. Frank Stockton, born in 1864, had left, like the majority, his city, and so had, much later, young "Dickie" Davis, Richard Harding Davis, son of the managing editor of the Philadelphia *Press*. But "Dickie" Davis, a glamorous figure, tall, extremely good-looking, and dressed in the latest fashion, came over frequently to see his family, and, a white carnation in his buttonhole, cane in hand, almost stopped with excitement the Sunday "church parades" on Walnut Street. Philadelphia is extremely proud of its sons, once they have been approved by New York.

Meanwhile, the one in the 1830's, the other, years after, two great Americans, neither of them Philadelphians, had known Philadelphia well. The first was Edgar Allan Poe, who arrived with his child-wife, Virginia, in 1838. Poe came to Philadelphia because it was then the magazine centre of the country, but he didn't have much luck. Friendless, proud, shabby, he quarrelled and drank, and was not allowed to use the Members' Room of "Mr. Franklin's Library", still on Fifth Street, but was made to use the outer, vulgar, public room. The officials of the Library Company who disbarred this shabby stranger would have been surprised had they known what would happen to the poem and stories he was then writing—*The Raven*, *The Gold Bug*, and *The Tales of the Grotesque and Arabesque*. One of the houses Poe occupied while in Philadelphia, a small brick house at 530 North Seventh Street, is now preserved as a shrine.

The other great American was Walt Whitman, who arrived, not in Philadelphia, but in Camden, just across the Delaware, in 1873 and who lived there all the rest of his life.

For years Whitman was a familiar figure on the streets of Philadelphia. Sometimes he walked up Chestnut Street, looking neither to left nor right, his magnificent snowy-white beard covering the front of his great black cloak, on his head a black sombrero. At other times he crossed the ferry and got on the front platform of a waiting horse-car and rode out to West Philadelphia and then back again. He was very fond of the latter diversion. In the late afternoons and evenings he sat on the stoop of his small frame-house in Camden, talking to anyone who came to visit him.

Once a young man, an admirer of *Leaves of Grass*, made a pilgrimage to Camden to see Whitman. He had never seen Whitman before. The "Good Gray Poet" did not look up from his position on the stoop as the young man paused beside him.

"Sit down," he said. "Sit down. It has been a long time, boy, since you have been to see me."

Finally there came the really top artist and novelist, Joseph Hergesheimer, although, like Bayard Taylor, he was not actually a Philadelphian, and although, like many first-class writers, he had little gift of self-criticism. Someday, however, Philadelphia will awaken to the fact that it entertained —occasionally—"an angel, unaware".

Mr. Watson, in his jeremiad against the slackness, luxury, and lack of morals of Philadelphia of the 1850's, had, like so many other Jeremiahs in history, wished for war. Like other Jeremiahs, Mr. Watson mistakenly thought war a cleansing and strengthening process. Ten years later his wish was fulfilled, and Philadelphia, after some initial hesitancy and some fairly mild draft riots, made its mind up firmly and marched out to war, thousands upon thousands strong. It also produced two famous northern generals: George B. McClellan, great military organizer and drill-master of the Army of the Potomac, but also one of the inevitable political generals who turn up in every war—he was a thorn in Lincoln's side; and George Gordon Meade, victor of Gettysburg. The Civil War did many strange things to Philadelphia, and set what seems to have been the final seal on Penn's "Holy Experiment". Lucan says, "Civil wars leave their scars".

The War Between the States found Philadelphia a half-southern city, and a half-northern city, and left it definitely—at least, spiritually—a northern city, its eyes turned for ever to the industrial North.

One is apt to forget that Philadelphia is, of all the great eastern cities, the one nearest to the Mason and Dixon Line, and its climate, its tempo, are still southern. And Philadelphia has always been closely connected with the South. That was true from the beginning. There has been always a great deal of inter-marriage with South Carolina, especially Charleston, and Virginia, and the lower counties of Maryland; a great deal of business connection as well. At the start of the Civil War there was much southern sentiment in Philadelphia. There were many prominent "Copperhead" families. Lincoln was not popular. When the Union League was organized, its members carried stout clubs to defend themselves. It was rumoured that their club-house was to be attacked. But as the war went on, and the troops poured through, and regiment after regiment left for the front, and especially when the great river of wounded came pouring back, all this changed, and the "Copperhead" families kept their mouths shut.

Gettysburg was the climax.

The greatest battle of the Civil War was fought on Pennsylvania soil. Pennsylvania had been actually invaded; some of its towns had been burned.

The guns of Gettysburg were as formative, where Philadelphia is concerned, as the Quakers of the *Welcome*.

Until recently there were many elderly people in Philadelphia who had convinced themselves that as children they had "heard the guns of Gettysburg".

Gettysburg is a long way from Philadelphia, but in war one's imagination is vivid.

Until the Civil War, Philadelphia and the state were inclined to be Democratic; after the Civil War, Philadelphia and all but the western part of the state became rock-bound Republican. The Civil War had frightened Philadelphia; the slopes of Gettysburg. Little Philadelphia boys were brought up to believe that Democrats and Southerners had horns and cloven feet. To be a Democrat in Philadelphia carried with it the same social stigma as to be a Republican in the South. Only recently has Philadelphia at times shown signs of getting away from this attitude.

So there it is, the great sprawling, obstinate, tenacious, slow-moving, but steadily moving, city, lying between its two rivers. And all around it is its lovely, luxurious countryside. And in it are a hundred things that stir the heart of an American, and a hundred things that make him angry. And what will happen to it, no one knows. But this at least is certain:

Run away if they may have to; stay away as long as they will; upbraid the city often, as is the habit of Philadelphians; let the native son, or daughter, come back for a visit, or for good, and they find themselves suddenly and strangely happy and content. As they step once more into the narrow crowded streets, and smell the soft, sooty air, and see the faces of the people who pass, they are suddenly happy.

There must be some sort of magic, mustn't there?

INDEX

A

Abbey, Edwin, 181
Aberdeen University, 165
Academy of Music, 146, 149, 151, 154
Acrelius, Rev. Israel, 31n., 39, 94
Adams, John, 135, 175, 196, 201, 211, 212, 213, 227, 240
Adams, Mrs. John, 228
Adams, Samuel, 71, 201
Addison, Joseph, his *Cato* performed, 123, 142, 143
Adelphi Hotel, 151
Adolphus, Gustavus, 27, 29, 33
Age of Reason, The, 204, 205
Agnew, Dr. Hayes, 182
Agnew, Gen. James, 194
"Agnew Clinic," painting, 182
Aitken, Robert, 183, 202
Alexander, Capt. Charles, 210
Alfred, 210
Allen, Capt. James, 200, 214
Allen, Misses, 228
Allen William, 175, 194n.
Alleys in Philadelphia, 55, 57
Almquist, Karl, 163
America, 52, 54
American Company (light opera), 151
"American Idea," 14, 17
American Line, 100
American Monthly Magazine, 103
American Ornithology, 180
American Philosophical Society, 123, 183, 193
American Weekly Mercury, 143, 183
Amish, their characteristics, 52
Amity, 40, 96
Anderson, Marian, 151
André, Major John, 145, 159–60, 163, 194, 206, 207, 218
Andrew Doria, 210
Anne Boleyn, 148
Anne, Queen, 63–64, 74, 135
Anthracite deposits, 14, 137, 140–41
Anti-Irish riots, 95, 251
Anti-Roman Catholic riots, 95
Anti-Traitor, 197
Apology (Robert Barclay), 10
Arch Street Theatre, 146
Archer, Samuel, 93
Argall, Sir Samuel, 24, 33
Argo, 89
Aristophanes' *Lysistrata* produced, 154
Arliss, George, 236
Arnold, Benedict, 196, 210, 222
Arthur, Timothy Shay, 103
Ashbrook, Capt. Joseph, 215n.

Asla, 93
"Assemblies, The," 144, 271–72
Astor, John Jacob, 249
Athenæum, the, 208
Auchmuty, Miss, 218, 219
Austrian Succession, war of the, 72
Ayllon, Vasquez d', 23
Ayres, Capt., 199–200

B

Bach Festivals in Bethlehem, Pa., 151
Bache, Richard and Sarah, 135, 240
Bachelor Father, The, 148
Bagatelles, 121
Bainbridge, Commodore William, 98
Baker, John, father of Mrs. Carson (*q.v.*), 239
Baker (Boulanger), Joseph, hanged, 69
Baldwin, Matthias, and the Baldwin Locomotive Works, 231
Balloon ascension, 230
"Bal Masque," 68
Baltimore (George Calvert), Lord, 13
Bancroft, George, 147
Bank of North America chartered, 223, 246
Bank of Pennsylvania, 246
Bank of the United States, 250
Barbary pirates, 89, 98
Barclay, Robert, his *Apology*, 10
Barde, Capt. John Louis, daughter marries Matthew Brooke III, 191
Barnum, Phineas Taylor, 146
Baron Renfrew, ship-raft, 96
Barrett, Lawrence, 148
Barron, Capt. James, 67–8
Barry, Commodore John, 89, 93, 203, 278
Barrymore, Ethel, John, and Lionel, 146
Barrymore, Maurice (Herbert Blythe), 146
Bartram, John, 158, 175, 177
"Battle Hymn of the Republic, The," 203
Baylor, Col. George, 135n.
Beaujolais, Louis-Charles, Comte de, 233
Beaujour, Louis-Félix de, 229
Beaux, Cecilia, 181
Becky Sharpe, 148
Bedford, Gunning, 67
"Bedouin Song," 281
Beerbohm, Max, 62
Bell Telephone Co., 267
Belton's submarine, 90
Bemelmans, Ludwig, 155
Benezet, Anthony, 175

285

D

E

F

Lewis, William, 196
Liberty Bell, 82, 126, 135, 215
Library Company of Philadelphia, 115,
  155, 157–63, 237, 245, 282
Life of Bulstrode Whitelocke, by Penn, 74
Lighthouses and lightships, 108–9
Lincoln, President Abraham, 159, 195, 283
Lind, Jenny, 146, 253
Linnaeus, Carolus, 175
Lippard, George, 280–81
Lippincott, publisher, 279
Lippincott's, 279
Livingston, Robert, 139, 197n., 211
Lloyd, David, 216
Lloyd, Dr. Thomas, 166, 168
Lloyd, Thomas, 64, 78
Locke, John, 35
Lodovico of Aragon, 156
Log of the Mayflower, 161
Logan, James, 37 *passim;* his importance
  to Philadelphia, 44; appointed colonial
  secretary, 73; his language studies, 113
Logan, William, 177
Loganian Library, 155–56
London Company, 24
London Magazine, quoted on Catholics, 134
Long, John Luther, 148
Long Island, Battle of, 207
Lorimer, George Horace, 176
"Lost Decade," 224, 225
Louis XIV, 45, 264
Louis XVI, 154, 155, 228, 241
Louis XVIII, 310
Louis Philippe, 228, 232–33, 252
Lovelace, Sir Francis, 31n.
"Lovely Nancy," 183
Lubin, Sigmund, 154
Lucas, Nicholas, 37
Lukens, Rebecca, ironmaster, 190, 191
Lukens Steel Co., 190
Luks, George, 181
Lum, Mary, marries Stephen Giraud, 245,
  247–48; dies, 248
Lutherland, Thomas, 65
Lützen, Battle of, 28, 33
Luzerne, Anne-César, Chevalier de la, 222,
  228
Lysistrata, 154

M

MacDonald, Jeannette, 147
Mackenzie, William, 156
Macpherson, Capt. John, 183, 196–98;
  his sons, John and William, 197
Macpherson Blues, 197
Macready, William, 147
Madam Butterfly, 148
Madison, President James, 175, 193
Maennerchor Society, 151
Malin, Joshua, 140–41

Markham, Capt. William, 39, 55, 78
Marlborough, privateer, 123
Marmie, Peter, 192n.
Marquette, Jacques, 72
Marshall, Christopher, 200, 213, 221
Martin, David, 121–22
Masonic lodge, first in America, organized,
  92
Matisse, Henri, 179n.
Mattson, Margaret, accused of witch-
  craft, 70
Maximilian I of Austria, 62
Maxwell, Gen. William, 215n.
May Day celebration prohibited, 63
McCall, Archibald, 246
McCall, Virginia, 181
McCarter, Henry, 181
McClellan, Gen. George Brinton, 283
McClure's Magazine, 268
McDermott, William, 86
McGuffey's Readers, 279
McHugh, H. Bart, 153
McKay, Donald, 93
McKean, Sally, 227
McKean, Thomas, 175, 211–12, 243n.
McLane, Capt. Allan, 218–19
McManus, "Gas House Ring," 263
McMaster, John Bach, 249
Meade, Gen. George Gordon, 283
Mecklenburg Declaration, of North Caro-
  lina, 131
Meng, John, 178
Mercer, Gen. Hugh, 135
Meredith, Hugh, 156, 183
Merion, 100
Meschianza, the, 68, 160, 194, 218, 222n.;
  story of the pageant, 219–21
Metamora, 148
Metropolitan opera season, 150
Mexican War, 98, 249–50
Mey, Capt. Cornelius Jacobsen, 25–6, 33
Michielse, Rev. Jonas Jansen, 42, 43
Mifflin, Gen. Thomas, 179n., 201, 210, 241
Mikveh Israel Congregation, its cemetery,
  253
Minuit, Peter, 30, 33
Miranda, Francisco, 233
Mississippi, 99
Mitchell, Langdon, 147
Mitchell, Dr. Silas Weir, 147, 163, 171,
  216n., 281
"Monks of the Wissahickon," 150
Monmouth, Battle of, 180, 209n.
Monmouth Rebellion (English), 35, 95
Monroe, President James, 235
Montesquieu, 93
Montezuma, 98
Montgomery, Gen. Richard, 197n.
Montour, Esther, 140
Montpensier, Antoine-Philippe, Duc de,
  233
Moon, John, 65
Mooney, William, 43
Moore, Mr., dies of yellow fever, 241
Moran, Thomas, 181
More, Nicholas, Chief Justice, 64

Date Due